Very best wishes
Pau 1.

Harry I

CW00422428

Many memories

A Life of
Motor Cycling

Kenneth J. Chandler

Baughan

Published by Walls Quarry Press
2 Roseleigh, Walls Quarry,
Brimscombe, Stroud, Glos.
England.
GL5 2PD

ISBN 978-0-9562533-0-9

Printed by
Anthony Rowe Ltd Bumpers Farm Chippingham Wiltshire SN14 6LH England.

Henry Percy Baughan

12. 5. 1895.   13. 11. 1968.

In Memory of

Harry Baughan

Chris Stagg and Bill Hayward B.E.M.

along with
Marjorie, Auriol, Grant Heelas. Auriol, Marjorie, Grant Heelas.
and
Geoff Fisher O.B.E.
who helped make it all possible.

Introduction

The British motor cycle industry has all but disappeared, the once famous names have fallen by the wayside, bad management, poor labour relations, lack of vision, investment in new technology, and, more importantly, understanding what the motor cyclist really wanted.

Two manufacturers who have a great pedigree, Norton and Triumph are all that remains of a once great industry which had perhaps the largest diversification of models in the history of motor cycle production. Norton it seems has just been refinanced. Triumph on the other hand are selling machines that appeal to many discerning riders, not only in this country, but overseas. Seventy years ago things were very different. Rudge, Matchless, Ariel, BSA, AJS, Scott, New Imperial to mention just a few, they were all household names and provided affordable and reliable transport after the great war. While the large manufactures won the day many other companies were also producing machines on a limited basis. Montgomery, Dunlet, Baughan . . . Baughan?

To many enthusiasts who have a feeling for motor cycle history this name is not entirely unknown, certainly not in the same category as Sunbeam or even Cotton who were just fifteen miles away. The name Baughan still remains something of a mystery, reference books tend to be vague and inaccurate only mentioning that they built machines some time between 1925 to 1939, not one even made a guess as to how many were actually made, and there the story ends. Today the latest books on the history of motor cycles have dropped the Baughan marque entirely. What this company achieved is poorly documented along with its competition history. Back in the early 1930s Harry Baughan was vilified when he introduced a sidecar-wheel drive motor cycle combination, soon after it was supposedly 'Banned' and this was how it was remembered.

This book will give a greater insight of a tiny company that consisted of just one man at its outset, Harry Baughan. To many people involved in competition he was the enthusiast's, enthusiast. His whole working life which ran parallel to his business was devoted to trials motor cycling, both competing, and in later years organization. This led to the very pinnacle of off-road riding, the International Six Days Trial. His skill in the Western Centre was renowned and respected, raising the standards of national trials to a height that few people and organizations could aspire to, let alone equal. For many years the 'British Experts' trial was entrusted to him along with his many faithful helpers. These volunteers produced first class trial after first class trial, which continued for many years. Although Harry Baughan remained a bachelor throughout his life his early trials career was helped by two very attractive identical twin sisters, who, later became the very cornerstone of the organization he built–up in the Western Centre of the Auto Cycle Union. They also mastered skills at the drawing board in his factory where they became vary competent draftswomen under the skilled eye of Bill Hayward. Right up until the second world war Baughan

Motors was a very small concern, their work consisted mainly of motor cycle and car repairs along with agricultural and commercial vehicles. This combined with general and precision engineering stood them in good stead when it came to sub-contract work in the second world war. When Harry Baughan started to design and build motor cycles in the early 1920s he was soon assisted by Chris Stagg and later Bill Hayward who knew exactly what was required for the riders of the day.

Gradually, Harry Baughan involved himself ever deeper in trials related matters. He pushed the motor cycle industry incessantly in an effort to increase the quality of their products, ever mindful that motor cycle competition should be at the forefront of development. His letters to competition managers of many high profile factories and accessory manufacturers were always met with respect and understanding. As the years passed trials competition by some manufacturers diminished, cost being sighted as the reason why support was not forthcoming. One company that did give Harry Baughan great backing was Royal Enfield, especially when it came to the ISDT. Jack Booker as competition manager provided machines for route surveys and extended testing, certainly when it involved combinations and the company generously bore all the costs.

Eventually Harry Baughan perhaps outlived his usefulness in the modern era of trials organization when 'Mickey Mouse' sections became the norm. Time had moved on, the age that had prevailed between the wars when premier trials took in seventy or eighty road miles was drawing to a close. Ralph Venables MBE once said to me, "The ACU were fortunate indeed in having Harry Baughan to run the ISDT in Wales, he was an absolute master when it came to organization." Decades have passed since the name Baughan last figured in the result sheets, their achievements and sportsmanship are but a distant memory, they were pioneers in motor cycle trials and showed foresight and innovation in their machines. If there is a motor cyclists Valhalla they will surely be up there with the best of them as they were over three quarters of a century ago.

K.J.C.

The author is the Vintage Motorcycle Club Ltd marque specialist for Baughan Motor Cycles.

Acknowledgements

Researching for any book takes a great deal of time and effort. Frustration is commonplace, events, places; all have to be cross referenced, along with numerous letters, telephone calls which often led to more disappointment when one tries to close a certain aspect which happened in the dim and distant past. I was lucky that the major players were still alive when I started to gather the facts surrounding this little known concern deep in Gloucestershire. Sadly, I missed Harry Baughan for his input. I did speak with him on a few occasions, at the time I was not fully aware of his achievements. Only when Pat Mather brought the Red Car to South Woodchester did I start to make further enquiries. Harry died in 1968 which left a gap; however, things were not entirely lost. Chris Stagg, Bill Hayward, Geoff Fisher and the remaining Grant Heelas sister were still around and provided the most invaluable information that I could possibly hoped for. Their knowledge and recall of all matters concerning both the company and the trials that they entered, was inspirational.

Perhaps the person who gave me the greatest insight to the company was Chris Stagg. He was taken on as an apprentice and eventually retired when the Gaffer sold up. Chris was a joy to interview, nothing was too much trouble and he had a ready recall of the working practices and the many competition events that he took part in. Working for an employer who had a passion for motor cycle competition was heaven sent to a fifteen year old back in the mid 1920s. It was not long before he was as keen as Harry Baughan and started to ride motor cycles at any opportunity. Every interview with Chris unearthed many fascinating things that had almost been forgotten. A week would pass and in that time something new would be remembered. Chris had an enthusiasm for motor cycles that was so infectious that his son's also caught the bug and have been riding motor cycles competitively since they obtained their licences.

I was fortunate to interview Bill Hayward just before he died. Bill perhaps had more exposure than Chris in the motor cycle press when he rode the very controversial Baughan sidecar-wheel drive. His early solo career took in long distance pioneering rides such as the London-Edinburgh, London-Lands End, just as Harry Baughan with his close association with the Motor Cycling Club. Bill's son, Edwin also made photographs available from his father's early records at Lower Street.

Delving into the history of Baughan Motors started a number of years ago. Gradually I acquired material and made many valuable connections, I now have the chance to thank them for their cooperation. Sadly, as the way of all flesh many have passed on, those that remain who I have overlooked will recognize their contribution.

With the Yorkshire connection being so strong through Ted Morris buying two Baughan swds it was essential to check out this part of Baughan Motors history. Steve Taylor B.Sc., a fellow motor sport enthusiast who originated from Yorkshire kindly offered his parents hospitality for a week in Harrogate in order to find anyone connected with Ted Morris and his threewheeler trials competition. Mrs. Morris was closely involved with her husbands exploits and was very forthcoming with details and photographs. Just before I left Yorkshire Eric Oddy made contact through Mrs. Morris and he gave me quite a few stories when he and Ted tried to come to terms with the Baughan swd. As Bill Bradley was perhaps the foremost pioneer of swd coming from Addingham, his connection with the Ilkley and District Motor Club was very close. Janet Kitchin, the archivist for the Ilkley and District MC gave me valuable assistance in obtaining from the club archives several photos of Bill Bradley and his famous swd Scott, 'Felix'. Janet also solved a few result problems regarding Ted Morris and furnished me with photo copies. Geoff Hill comes in for special mention and supplied me with photos and background information about his father, Alec. Alec was indeed a great all-rounder when it came to motor cycle competition. While still in Yorkshire, Maurice Rispin who was a close associate of Bill Bradley paved the way in checking out 'Felix' at the Bradford Industrial Museum before I was able to pay them a visit. The staff there were more than helpful and gave me every opportunity to have access to Felix. While on organizations thanks must go to The National Archive, The National Patent Office, Lutterworth Folk Museum and the Auto Cycle Union. The Beatrix Potter Society who solved the mystery about the Grant Heelas connection that everyone in the Stroud district thought existed. Their Heelis has a different spelling, especially as Archibald Hay Grant Heelas was also a solicitor and came from Yorkshire just as Beatrix Potter's husband. Even so this supposed connection lasted for decades.

Bob Currie and Ralph Venables MBE were very forthcoming with facts and enthusiasm. The former for giving me many leads concerning the Midlands motor cycle factories and his introduction to Bill Mewis, long time trials passenger to Dennis Mansell. Mewis also had a ready recall when it came to the Baughan/Norton swd conversion and their own swd after they abandoned the Baughan device. Ralph Venables knew all about Harry Baughan and his wonderful organizational ability from 1933 onwards. He knew him even better when they sat on the same ACU sub-committee for the 1951/53 International Six Days Trial. Also from a journalistic background with a great involvement is Bob Light. Bob has been instrumental in unearthing information and photographs from bygone years. Nothing was ever too much trouble for Bob. Jim Whiting was also a close associate of Harry Baughan when he was involved with him whilst running the Welsh Two Day Trial, and latterly the ISDT at Llandridod Wells. Jim was quite amazed with Harry Baughan's close connections with not only the riders, but the trade as well. The man who had a great insight to Baughan Motors was Geoff Fisher. He was a great source of information despite his independence from the factory. Geoff was a meticulous keeper of notes which proved to be a gold mine in terms of dates and places, certainly concerning trials. Whatever question I asked the note books would be consulted and an answer readily given.

Ted Baughan, the son of John Kilminster Baughan (who sadly passed away in July 2009) has been most supportive providing family history and photos. In my research at the National Motor Museum I came into contact with Annice Collett, their research librarian. Annice over the years has passed all manner of things in connection with Harry Baughan, now she has a new post with the Vintage Motor Cycle Club, again in the library. Also involved with the National Motor Museum is fellow enthusiast, Mike Budd. Mike has been closely involved with cataloguing and archive research in the museum library for years, he has supplied me with countless items to do with motor cycles and cyclecars that would have taken me a considerable time to find.

I am grateful to Bill Boddy MBE for his wisdom on Booklands. Along with Bill Mewis who gave me background information about Joe Craig was Stan Dibben who also worked in the competition dept at Norton when he was passenger to Eric Oliver when they won the sidecar world championship in 1953. John Hayden was the person responsible for the collection of Bill Hayward's famous sidecar wheel-drive at the same time as Pat Mather retrieved the Red Car. The swd was a project too far for Hayden and it was left to Graham Stagg to complete it. Thanks also to Bob Gordon Champ who solved the ambiguity surrounding the swd Sunbeam that Peter Bradley rode in the 1930s. I am grateful to the late Olga Kevelos who gave me background on Harry Baughan's involvement with the ISDT when she was a works supported rider for the CZ factory in the early 1950s. Unice Guy gave me a great insight to Bill Peters and his connection with Baughan Motors along with his competition riding. Fred Halliday with his close connection with Baughan Motors gave me a better understanding as to Harry Baughan's thinking on all manner of things to do with trials competition.

Tommy Barker, a long time supporter of the Stroud Club provided inside information on the Cotswold Scramble, post war. Also, two riders who were regular winners at this premier event are the Dave's, Curtis and Bickers who gave me their thoughts on both the event and Harry Baughan. Two more people who gave their input on the Cotswold Scramble were Richard Halliday and Jack Durn. One person who was well acquainted with the inner workings of Lower Street was Guy Babbage when he was a youngster. He like many other riders found the atmosphere at the works very convivial. In later years he was the proud owner of a Baughan special.

Cliff Searle, the last owner of the Baughan Engineering works at Lansdown gave me the opportunity to search through the many tea chests that occupied the top floor at the factory. However, the person who was far more successful than I was in searching through these was Jan Seymore who was employed there in the 1980s. It was Jan who uncovered all the works drawings that Bill Hayward and the Heelas sisters had penned in the 1930s. The most that I discovered in the attic was Harry Baughan's correspondence relating to the ISDT from 1948 to 1953 which amounted to many hundreds of letters, all undamaged. The one great disappointment was Harry's comprehensive note books on the ISDT, sadly beyond salvage. The accounts that are contained in the ISDT letters are worth a book on their own. As the Baughan motor cycles were mainly sold locally they often went to brothers. Austin Gardiner and Trevor were just two of them. They both used their's for years. Austin told me many stories about the Lower Street days and the friendship they enjoyed with Chris Stagg. Peter Falconer the Stroud architect gave me a close insight to Chris Stagg when they shared his Triumph speed twin when scrambling and grass track racing. Adrian Moss has in his possession a remarkable engine from Lansdown which is surrounded by mystery and has defied an explanation. The one other item that he discovered was the clock that was used by Marjorie Grant Heelas in the sidecar of Bill's outfit. Quite a find, and it still works! One very special mention must go to Graham Stagg who unstintingly gave me access to the famous swd that his father built, truly a family steeped in motor cycle culture. Paul Faulkner whose knowledge of PCs and related software programmes is encyclopedic and without his considerable help, I would be still struggling, thanks Paul. If there is anyone who I have missed I can only apologize.

Finaly, to my long suffering and patient wife Janet who never thought the book would be finished.

Errors and omissions are entirely mine. KJC..

Contents

Foreword

On one of my many visits to Llandrindod Wells was in March 1952. To my surprise I met Mr. Baughan and Chris Stagg who were on a reconnaisance trip to find new tracks for the Welsh Three–Day Trial and also the 1954 International Six Days Trial. Later in 1952 I met Mr. Baughan again, this time he was the time keeper for the team and Chris was the rider who recced the course and reported to the teams the more difficult parts of the route.

As time passed I was picked for the Vase B Team in 1953 which was to be held in Czechoslovakia, but there was a problem for me, I was called–up and serving my time as a national serviceman. At the time Army personel would not be allowed behind the Iron Curtain. Mr. Baughan stepped in to see if he could arrange leave for me and contacted the War Office. To my surprise they wrote to me saying they would 'Demob' me for fourteen days and the missed days would be added to my two years service–of course I was over the moon to be allowed to compete.

There is no doubt Mr. Baughan managed to pull many strings which enabled me to compete with the British Team where I went on to win eleven Gold Medals and three Silver ones. This gives an indication just how Mr. Baughan was held in such high esteem within the motor cycling sphere and was such a wonderful person who could be relied on to do his very best, not just for me but every rider he was responsible for.

As my many contacts with Mr. Baughan were mostly to do with the ISDT, I knew very little of his background as a motor cycle manufacturer. Hardly anything is known about his tiny factory in Stroud. He is proably better known for his famous, or rather infamous, sidecar-wheel drive combination that was supposedly 'Banned' from trials competition. Ken Chandler gives the complete story to this little known company and explores in detail just what Mr. Baughan achieved. He will always be remembered as a superb trials organizer in the Western Centre and his culmination came with the International Six Days Trial when he was Chairman of the Auto Cycle Union sub-committee that ran the event in Wales. Yes, Mr. Baughan knew everyone connected with the sport and was really instrumental in pushing the British factories to produce better and better machines, and the men to ride them.

Will we ever see his like again? Possibly not, he really was a 'One-Off' and will go down in trials history as, 'The Grand Old Man of Motor Cycling'.

John Giles
Penbury
Kent

If any reader has any knowledge or information, such as photographs, sketches, references etc on sidecar wheel drives concerning the following machines. Richard Wood swd of 1922. Bill Bradley and 'Felix.' The Williams drive used by Harold Taylor on his 490cc Norton, Peter Bradley's Sunbeam. Dennis Mansell's Norton (constant mesh) which was built by Bill Mewis. Stuart Waycott also had a hand in swd, he remains something of a mystery as to his machines, at one time he experimented with a Rudge then finished with a Sunbeam swd. The Brough Superior SS80 built by Freddie Stevenson. Howard Uzzell's BSA 998cc swd, the forerunner of the Williams device. Also the Matchless that was a late comer (1947) that used a V twin engine swd outfit that was used for experimental trials, and came to nothing.

Somebody, somewhere must have information on these fascinating machines, I would be delighted to hear from them.

KJC.

Early involvement with motor cycles. First World War military
service. Military transport. Family involvement with motoring.

Harry Baughan, came into this world in 1895, the youngest of three brothers
born to a father who was in the employ of the Great Western Railway and was to
remain with the company until he retired. As the close of the century was only
a few years away, Harry Baughan's birth almost coincided with the invention
of petrol-driven mechanical transport. Ten years previously Gottlieb Daimler
built his first motor cycle in Croustall, Germany, and as Harry grew up so the
development of the internal combustion engine and transport on two, three and
four wheels evolved. The Baughan household were no strangers to transport
and travel with Harry's father working as a signal inspector, this allowed him
to negotiate generous concessionary travel on an extensive railway system that
had almost reached its zenith by the turn of the century. These railway journeys brought to Harry Baughan an appreciation of things mechanical and along
with his eldest brother, John Kilminster, a closer understanding of all things
technical. Miniature scale stationary steam engines they were given as children
allowed them both to appreciate motive power and increased their desire for
more knowledge. Although Harry and John were kindred spirits when it came
to the technical, Charlie, the middle brother, did not share their enthusiasm and
was content to plough his own furrow and seeming to be fairly content with his
lot. Like many youngsters who were keen on mechanical things they had ample
opportunity with a father employed by a railway company which in many people's eyes was the most prestigious one in the country. Their many visits to the
railway workshops and engine sheds made them the envy of their school pals.

Even though Harry was eight years younger than John, they were thinking
along similar lines when it came to transport and all the new things that were
beginning to appear on the roads. One thing that really interested them was
motor cycles and in Harry's case was to hold his attention and influence him for
the rest of his life. Before John was old enough to gain a motor cycle licence
he used a pedal cycle and Harry, not to be outdone, managed to keep up on his
smaller model. It was not long before they both tired of the exertion and as soon
as John was old enough he bought a motor cycle and things changed for them
both. With Harry, once he rode his brother's bike, there was no turning back.
Harry Baughan relates as such in the many notes he kept at the time. "As I suppose was inevitable considering the physical energy expended in propelling a
push cycle, my eldest brother and I became interested in anything on two wheels
that had a means of mechanical labour saving. We read *The Motor Cycle, Motor
Cycling, Motor Cycles and How to Manage Them*. And after learning how an
engine worked, we, like so many others thought we knew all there was to know
about them. In some mysterious way – how I never discovered because he at

JM Baughan collection.

Twenty year old Private 216296 Harry Baughan shortly after enlisting in the King's Own Shropshire Light Infantry in 1915.

Samuel Baughan, Harry's father, who was a permanent way and signal inspector with the Great Western Railway, gave great encouragement to his son's many projects.

any rate was more or less honest — my brother acquired a 1911, 2.5 hp belt drive Triumph in 1912. And, such is brotherly love, allowed me to tinker with it almost as much as he did himself. We took it to pieces, repeatedly polished the already polished parts and put them together again on innumerable occasions. It says much for that machine that it still appeared to function as well as it did before." John quickly mastered his new acquisition, and was soon out on the open road with Harry accompanying him seated on a very precarious pillion seat. Once they were well away from home and in little danger of being found out, Harry seized the opportunity to try his hand at motor cycle riding. "Now came the big difficulty, my brother was old enough to have a driving licence, and was willing for me to try and ride his beloved machine. Well I ask you, could a little thing like a licence stand in the way of that, there are always ways and means. The ways in this case was for me to act as pillion passenger until we got as far enough away from home that people did not know JK from HP, then stop; transfer the precious driving licence from his pocket to mine, sit on the saddle and be pushed until the engine fired. Then, Aye for the open road."

So started Harry Baughan's tentative introduction to motor cycling. Trouble came at the outset. Harry, determined to emulate his brother after studying his starting technique with the belt drive machine. Pushing vigorously and attempting to mount, but was not quite quick enough and the motor cycle sped away from him with just a little too much throttle. Unable to keep up he let the machine go and fell in a heap. The gravel rash suffered by youngsters in those days was a common occurrence but the torn clothes would take a good deal of explaining, but with a sympathetic brother this was soon overcome. After this initial disaster Harry rode his brother's bike at every opportunity and soon became proficient. "The only way to start that bike was to run and jump, this was a bit much for my arm and leg reach, I had to keep on going until I came to a reasonable hill, then I could stop at the top, turn the machine round get on board and coast down until the engine started again. Returning to my long suffering brother, change places – and pocket said licence – and back home. Fortunately for me I soon grew tired of all this chopping and changing and at last decided that at any rate

I looked old enough to possess a licence of my own. So boldly filling in the form, and forgetting that year of birth, I made the application, sending it by post so that no one could ask awkward questions and become the holder of a licence to drive.

"By this time my brother had gone to London, taking the bike with him, but he rode it home–154 miles–and left it there for me to get used to it and take it back to London for him . . . that's what I call a trusting brother! I was glad that he was away when I first tried that carefree run and jump start. I pushed and the engine fired, then it was a competition between the length of my stride and the revs of the engine. The engine won. After picking up, first myself and then the bike, and endeavouring to hide a number of rather difficult to explain rents and tears in my clothes, then getting my breath back; the bike and I had a few more arguments until at last I was on it and it was going. I don't remember that there were any more troubles in mounting after that day and I don't remember how I accounted for the torn clothes and gravel rash (again) on hands and knees without admitting the facts. Early in 1914 my brother decided he would like a sidecar attached to the Triumph. He would get a three-speed hub gear and clutch fitted, would I get the sidecar? He rode the bike to Shrewsbury and left it there for me to attach the sidecar. Oh yes, I did that alright and then took it out on trial. I think most people remember their first efforts at driving a sidecar after riding solo. I tried to balance it round the corner at the end of our road, the men made quite a good job of repairing the fence of the corner house the next day! Experience is a good tutor, I soon learned that one just sat tight and pulled the outfit round bends and everything was lovely, except the hub gear which required major adjustment about every hundred miles and a strip down overhaul after every long trip. Next time

Harry Baughan later became a noted engineer, his army papers reveal that he started his working life as an ironmongers assistant.

I rode the bike solo I of course remembered that I must lean the machine over on corners. I did so effectively that I remember my face hitting the curb, after that introduction I had some good times on that Triumph."

With all this motor cycle activity Harry Baughan soon became fully immersed in things mechanical, but strange to say, he never in the early stages of his life pursued a career in pure engineering terms with a conventional apprenticeship, but instead went into blacksmithing, and of all things, ironmongery, as indicated in his army records. This held little fascination for him and there were other serious events that were taking place in Europe, enough to stall both motor cycle and car development for a four year period. This was to be little handicap as later years proved he developed a great understanding and feeling for designing, developing and problem solving things

PARTICULARS OF SERVICE.

Date of Enlistment *1 December 1915*

Proceeded on Furlough pending transfer to the Army Reserve, or Discharge on _____

Passed medically fit for the Army Reserve on _____

Due for Transfer to the Army Reserve on _____

Due for final Discharge on *27 march 1918*

Cause of Transfer or Discharge *DISCHARGED NO LONGER PHYSICALLY FIT FOR WAR SERVICE*

Campaigns, Medals and Decorations _____

Educational and other Certificates, and dates _____

Mather collection.

After 27 months of army service Harry Baughan is discharged on medical grounds, unfit for service.

of a mechanical nature. August 1914 saw the outbreak of what was to become, The Great War. Harry like many young men of his age joined the colours. December 1st, 1915, saw twenty year old Harry Baughan enlisted in the King's Own Shropshire Light Infantry to become private 216296.

In his letters and personal recollections HPB makes the direct comparison between service life and the civilian one he had just left. He found the issuing of army kit with its air of unflappability and absolute regimentation in direct contrast to when he went to a civilian tailor to be measured for a suit just before he joined up. (Anyone who was called up for National Service will fully understand, those who did not will have missed one of life's great experiences). After this initial period HPB found himself seconded into the catering side of army life and it was here that he started seriously to study mechanical transport. He

A newly 'Kitted out' Private Baughan, top right, with fellow soldiers of the KOSLI. Harry Baughan soon found army life far removed from his civilian one but soon started to study its transport methods.

witnessed large amounts of produce delivered to the messes from all parts of the country, and in all manner of vehicles, many totally unsuited to the conditions encountered.

At the start of the first world war the internal combustion engine was gradually developing and many old cavalry types referred to it as the 'infernal combustion engine,' needless to say they were soon surpassed and serious transportation began to take hold. The army was being spread far and wide over the country, often establishing itself in outlandish places without any permanent roads that would be recognized today. Fields were the common thing and in wet weather many vehicles just bogged down unable to cope with the difficult conditions. Fields soon became churned up with mechanical transport and mud became a nightmare. This coupled with lorries with solid tyres that were smooth just compounded the problem. This lack of grip was not lost on HPB and in later years made an attempt to address it when he designed a differential for a vehicle to tackle such difficult terrain and was to demonstrate it to the army on their tank

The Character here given is based on continuous records of the holder's conduct and employment throughout his military career.

This is to Certify that No. 216296 Rank *Lance Cpl* Name *Henry Percy BAUGHAN*

has served with the Colours in the *King's Own Shropshire L I* for 1 143/365 years.
Manchester Reg. (Army Res. 334/365 yrs.
Labour Corps)

He is a man of Very Good Character Honest & Sober

Disability aggravated by Ordinary Military Service

Signature *W-E Boullon dl*
Commanding

Date *27 March 1918*

If further particulars as to his character and record of service are required within three years of above date, apply to
where he is registered for civil employment,
afterwards to the Officer in Charge of Records, *Nottingham.*

* This space is intended to be filled in by any organization which has registered the man's name and is prepared to supply further information.

Mather collection.

Harry Baughan's character refers to his sober disposition. A lifelong teetotaller, but a weakness for Cherryade. He only broke with tradition when formal occasions required it.

ranges. In Harry Baughan's capacity for catering in the army he was well placed to study methods of transportation of food stuffs. Not only that, he took a keen interest in the vehicles that were involved. Lorries were many and varied and did not particularly take his interest, but the motor cycles and light cars certainly did. The despatch riders who were always involved with signal movements certainly took his attention along with the different makes of machines and their suitability. Three wheelers did not escape his attention either. In these he took a greater interest for many were equipped with all manner of things. Lewis and Vickers machine guns, large amounts of ammunition, provisions, and to cap it all, a crew of three. Driven in adverse weather conditions these combinations were in very much the same predicament as the four wheel machines, no

JM Baughan collection

Now a Lance Corporal, Harry Baughan finds himself in charge of messing provision, complete with seven loaves and a mascot.

JM Baughan collection.

Back row L to R. Harry, John and Charlie. Front. Mrs. Baughan and husband, Sam with John's son Ted on his lap. Ted in 1999 kindly provided these early photos of the family.

grip, and very under powered, and performance extremely restricted with all the excess weight. History has a habit of repeating itself and in the army's case this was entirely true. Twenty years on they insisted upon the same things when Nortons built their sidecar wheel-drive for the army when all manner of items were heaped upon the long suffering combination. The poor and difficult conditions that the army riders and drivers found themselves in was also noted by HPB, for there seemed no training available on which to call for expert advice. The army had a long history of horse drawn vehicles and they had centuries of expertise on which to fall back on, but mechanical transport was an entirely different thing and they had to learn as they progressed with this new method of transport. The learning curve was difficult enough without the bigoted attitude of the officer corps who saw their traditional horses being reduced to a permanent, ceremonial role with the rapid advancement of mechanization. All this took place through necessity. The Great War had changed many things. What it did was to bring

Sam Baughan was an early buyer of light cars and cyclecars. Harry, perhaps with thoughts already on cyclecars poses with the family transport. Sitting on his grandmother's lap is nine month old Ted. **Below**: Pa Baughan with his smart, disc wheeled AV Mono Car of the period, sans lighting system which was an extra. The Pratts petrol can was an essential accessory.

JM Baughan collection

The complete Baughan family. Sitting in front of Harry is John's wife while their son Ted sits on his grandmother's lap. Ted followed his father into photography. The photos of Harry's cups are his work.

to the fore people with vision who were devoid of preconceptions, who saw mechanical transportation as a means to an end which would soon become the norm as the years passed. Harry Baughan made due note of it all. HPB was eventually discharged as medically unfit for further service duty. By this time his parents had moved to Middlesex and were considering their future. Harry's brother John had found employment at AIRCO in the design department which included a photographic section. With this position he was able to put in a good word for his younger brother and from this introduction Harry moved into things that had a far greater interest to occupy his active mind.

Army discharge. Working for AIRCO. New motoring and introduction to cyclecars. Experimental work at de Havilland. Alan Cobham.
Aerial photography with elder brother. First venture into building a
cyclecar. The cyclecar movement gathers pace.

After Harry Baughan left the army through ill health he moved south to London and found employment at AIRCO.* Civilian life must have been a great change for him, away finally from the responsibility of feeding troops. Perhaps this was a forerunner to what was to come in the following years when he excelled in organization. With this ability and his charm he was able to get help in all his many undertakings. In 1918 he was lodging with his parents at 'Ivydell' in Pinner, Middlesex. It was from here that he started to make plans for building a cyclecar which quite captured his imagination at the time and had also reached great popularity with the public. Cyclecars covered a period from 1903 to approximately 1922 in which time all manner of vehicles were built, some covering the very basic needs of four-wheeled transport to others that were bordering on the light cars of the time. The cyclecars certainly caught the feeling of the public for this brought to a great many people a method of transport that started a revolution, the horseless carriage had truly arrived. When the cyclecars appeared this 'movement' as it was called, started just after the turn of the century followed a few basic principles, a chassis, four wheels, powered by an engine that was to be found more at home in a motor cycle frame, and that was about it. As to how sparse these machines were Harry Baughan's creation is a typical example.

These cyclecars gave the public their first taste of motoring, unusual in concept, and in turn extremely practical. The visionaries at the time saw a huge potential market to be exploited and within ten years they were to be proved right, but it was not carried out by the lure of cyclecars. The eventual development of the light car saw to that. Up until 1900 the British public had been adequately served by a railway system that was in most part, comprehensive. The Victorians had perfected this method of transport and a close study of Bradshaw's would enable anyone with a sense of adventure to travel the length and breadth of the country without too much difficulty, and on time! Nevertheless, the railways despite their coverage were inflexible and with the coming of mechanical transport on public roads offered a freedom previously unheard of. Motor cycles, also in their infancy were really catering for the solo rider and not a great deal of thought had been given to the family. When the cyclecars came on the scene these offered an opportunity, and an affordable one that would enable a husband and wife and a small child the means of individual transportation and flexibility that the railways could not offer. For Harry Baughan to undertake the building of a cyclecar in 1919 was a bold move and with his limited resources a risky one.

* Aircraft Manufacturing Co Ltd.

JM Baughan collection.

The left hand side of the pair of semi-detached houses in the centre of the photograph is 'Ivydell' where Harry Baughan lodged with his parents until they decided to move to Stroud. It was from this house that HPB decided to string a banner proclaiming his new cyclecar. John supplied the screen printed banner by his newly formed company ARTCO. This advertising was more than a little ambitious on Harry's part. He and Slater were not overwhelmed with orders, the sign subsequently came down. It eventually found its way to Lower Street and can be seen on page 60 in the lower photograph.

The demand for a small ultra-light car costing between £100 and £150 existed, the market for a cyclecar had been created. As soon as it became known that a new journal was in preparation to support cyclecars this was advertised to the public and it soon became obvious that a governing body of some sort would be needed to oversee and possibly control its development.

The Auto Cycle Union being an off-shoot of the Royal Automobile Club decided to take it under its wing, ever mindful of the new money that could be generated for their coffers rather than let the RAC have a total monopoly where mechanical transport was concerned. A number of people were responsible for its inception. Col. CL Holden and Col. Lindsay Lloyd were the prime movers, the former having a deep involvement in motoring, especially competition for he oversaw the plans for the Brooklands race circuit before its construction began. A further ACU committee member joined them. These three then came up with the term 'Cyclecar.' Before, these new creations had been called a 'Duo Car' or 'Mono Car' (see page 19), now a formal name defined their place with the other four wheeled brigade. With the Cyclecar name now established a definition was required for their separation from their near neighbours the light cars. This was drawn up and they were placed in two categories.

Group **1**. Large class.
Maximum weight 772 lbs (under 7 cwt).
Maximum engine capacity, 1,100cc (International class G).
Group **2**. Small class.
Maximum weight, 660 lbs, minimum 330 lbs (under 6 cwt).
Maximum engine capacity, 750cc, (International class H).
With this firm definition it was submitted to the ruling body of motor cycle sport, the Federation Internationale des Clubs Motorcyclistes in Paris and received International recognition.

The following cars listed is indicative of the pre-war period for the cyclecar and how well it was received by the public. However, by the mid 1920s many of these models had disappeared.

CYCLECARS IN PRODUCTION 1912-1913

AC Sociable*	Crouch
ALC	Day-Leeds
Alldays	Duo
Arden	Eric
Autocrat	GN
Automobilette (French)	Geha* (German)
Autotrix	Girling
Averies	Globe
Baby (French)	Gordon
Bedelia (French)	GWK
BEF* (German)	Humberette
Brough	Jackson
Chater-Lea	JBS
Crescent	Kendall
Lagonda	Rudge
La Ponette (French)	Sabella
LEC	Sherwin
Leo	Siemens-Schuckert (German)
LM	Singer
Lurquin-Coudert (French)	Sizaire (French)
Matchless	Sterling
Mead and Dakin	Super
Media	Surridge

Morgan*	Swift
New Hudson	Tiny
Orient Buckboard	Tourist* (German)
P and C	Tyseley
Parnacott	Violette (French)
PDA	Wall*
Perry	Walycar
PMC Motorette*	Warne
Portland	Welham
Premier	Wilkinson
Riley	Wilton
Rolo Monocar	Woodrow

* indicates a threewheeler

Just prior to the start of the first world war the cyclecar movement was flourishing and wherever enthusiasts met and talked the common theme was that there should be a club that would look after their needs and interests. Ernest Perman who was one of the founder members of the Motor Cycling Club made the suggestion to like minded souls that an exploratory discussion should take place. Present at this meeting were such luminaries as Frank Thomas, Osmond Hill, HR Godfrey, Glynn Rowden, WG McMinnies, with AC Armstrong chairing the meeting. This eventually lead to a public meeting in London.

All interested parties were given the chance to air their views and an open meeting was called in London at the Holborn Restaurant on the 30th of October, 1912. This eventually led to a committee being formed comprising of the following. HP White, W Cooper, FA McNab, E Hapgood, D Capadia, Rev. EP Greenhill, Dr. AM Low, EMP Boileau, EH Taylor, RM Stallybrass, AE Panacott, AW Ayden, RW George, R Cleave, Glynn Rowdwen, A Percy Bradley, GN Higgs, AC Armstrong, FS Whitworth, EC Paskell, R Surridge, RF Messervy, A Selwyn, Osmand Hill, Capt. Archie Frazer-Nash, WG McMinnies, Major. Lindsay Lloyd, Laurie Cade, Gambier Weeks, JN Barrett, CS Burney, and FL Goodacre. Famous names abound here for they were the leading lights of the day in the fledgeling cyclecar field. From this meeting the Cyclecar Club was born and with a membership fee of one guinea (country members paid only half) the movement was set fair to prosper. The motor cycle industry had the foundation and materials that gave the cyclecar manufacturers the ability to build these machines: for instance, wheels and engines were a prime source. Individuals all over the country started to chance their arms at building a cyclecar. Many had very little desire to produce more than one or two machines. In many cases they had very little expertise on which to call if it ever came to produce in quantity.

JM Baughan collection.

Some of the AIRCO design and drawing office staff. Captain Geoffery de Havilland in the centre front row. John Baughan first from the right in the second row and Freddie Slater first from the left in the third row. At the time there were 57 men and 3 women employed in this department.

More than three years passed and in this period the 'new motoring' had certainly caught the imagination of the public. That the Cyclecar did not fall into the category of either a motor cycle combination or a car that would be instantly recognized, for the journals of the day catered for one or the other. *Motor Cycling* and *The Motor* covered in depth their each respective subjects; neither ventured into the cyclecar scene.

All this was about to change for on November 12th 1912 when a new journal appeared on the bookstalls. *The Cyclecar* had arrived. With a cover price of one penny and 64 pages on the cars and the movement along with a further 84 pages devoted to advertising. It was an overnight success, with 100,000 copies being bought by a public who wanted to know more about this new form of motoring. With a journal dedicated to their needs, respectability had arrived. As the 1920s progressed the trend by the buying public was to the light car with its greater refinements and ability to carry up to four people in reasonable comfort. With clear guide lines that defined the cyclecar a whole new industry sprang up and produced for the public machines that were of a unique nature, almost a halfway house so to speak. Not quite a car, it catered more for two people than four. A cyclecar was described at the time as a combination of the worst characteristics of a motor cycle and the more depressing features of a motor cycle and sidecar. The light car and cyclecar development progressed and the competition was fierce between them.

By 1922 there were well over one hundred manufacturers producing either a light car or a cyclecar and the buyer was almost spoilt for choice such was the variety. By this time *The Cyclecar* had changed its title to reflect the changing mood of the buying public and now appeared as *The Light Car and Cyclecar* of October 1922 noted that there were 120 vehicles listed, but of these only 74 actually exhibited at Olympia. These were mostly the established manufacturers of the day such as Austin, Morris, ABC, Amilcar, Aston Martin, Bugatti, Citroen, Clement-Talbot, FIAT, Hampton, Humber, Jowett, Lagonda, Morgan, Renault, Riley, Rover, Standard, Talbot-Darracq and Wolseley. The above mentioned could hardly be classified as cyclecars. The following names have long since disappeared and if the truth was known many were no more than just a 'one-off.' Amazon, Bowser, Bow-V-Car, Cluley, Dandy, Diatto, Emms, Lecoy, Jewel, and of course Baughan. All the manufacturers listed above produced machines that varied in price. By far the most expensive of these was the Bugatti at £800, so there was plenty of choice for the prospective buyer. In the case of the Baughan which was placed in the £150 – £200 category there were no less than seventeen other builders all equally eager to sell their wares. Harry Baughan's venture into cyclecar manufacture was perhaps triggered by the prices that was being asked of fourth and fifth hand machines. Some were costing more than when they

Tyburn Lane. It was here that the first Baughan cyclecar was built, (MD264). Harry Baughan and Freddie Slater brought their meagre machinery to make a start with cyclecar manufacture. Before they found these lock-up garages they were forced to produce many items at AIRCO. Initially chalk marks on the floor served as an outline, later John Baughan drew up the final more accurate plans on wall paper.

Mather collection.

The prototype Baughan cyclecar outside of 'Ivydell' where Harry lodged with his parents. While many other cyclecars used acetylene lighting HPB went for less troublesome electric. The majority of cyclecars relied on the motor cycle industry for parts, Baughan was no different. The nearside rear wheel still has the belt drive rim clearly visible. A full description is in the next chapter. Compare this to the AV.

were first sold, giving rise to thinking that there was a potential market worth chasing and this spurred on many to chance their arm with the buying public. In reality only the strong manufacturers were going to survive. The likes of Morris and Herbert Austin who employed a production line system were in a position to build volume products at low unit cost. People like Montgomery, Phelan and Moore, Carden and certainly Baughan who made do with almost 'one-off' machines that lacked almost any method of pre-production and planning which would enable them to 'gear-up' for producing a machine every other day and certainly Harry Baughan was in no position to undertake such a venture.

As the 1920s progressed it became all too obvious that the mass producers were going to win the day. Their well structured assembly methods were not only designed to reduce costs but there would be sufficient money available to purchase the raw materials, or buy in manufactured items from a support industry. The latter was available to Baughan, the former was certainly out of his reach . . . and it soon told. The Baughan method of production, if it could be called that, was very labour intensive and was based on readily available parts manufactured by the motor cycle industry, rather than the automobile one. Cyclecars certainly gave the family man the opportunity to get away from the railway restrictions and brought a freedom that was to revolutionize the individuals travel movements. With this increased independence came the need for

How much was Harry Baughan influenced by the AV Monocar that his father bought? The price was very competitive for the time. When the Baughan cyclecar first appeared the price was almost £200, later this was reduced to under two hundred pounds . . . there were few takers.

greater creature comfort. The cyclecar was certainly lacking in this respect. The engine was invariably an air-cooled V twin that was more at home in a solo motor cycle. It was noisy and prone to vibration, that combined with rudimentary springing and very light motor cycle wheels, made every journey lively and over any great distance, very tiring. Weather protection was minimal with a thin hood (if supplied) that was ill-fitting, draughty and hardly waterproof. Windscreen wipers were often hand operated and minuscule, if they were even fitted. Lights in some cases were still acetylene and were difficult to keep alight even after they had been coaxed into life. As to see your way then they certainly lacked brightness, more really a sop to the Road Traffic Act to be legal. Brakes again came from motor cycle practice and deemed sufficient for only modest retardation. In certain vehicles (as with the Baughan) only on the rear wheels, front ones were considered a luxury. With very little traffic on the roads in the 1920s not much thought had been given to emergency braking. However, the serious motorist placed all these short comings behind him and the transport

Authors collection.

When Sam Baughan bought his Humberette did Harry have any influence in it? Manufacturers in those days placed great importance in competition to help sell their products, especially when a gold medal was the result. HPB was no different and achieved such on the London-Edinburgh, even so it proved little incentive for buyers, great satisfaction for the driver though.

owning public gathered momentum. Harry Baughan fresh from his war experiences saw as did many other people the need for individual transport that offered unlimited freedom, and in a somewhat 'loose' partnership with a friend decided to venture into cyclecar manufacture. Just as to why Harry Baughan decided to build cyclecars perhaps lies in a letter in which he relates to cyclecars that were selling at the time on the second hand market, these machines changed hands several times for more than when they were first purchased as was the case of his Carden Mono Car. (Harry Baughan's thoughts that he committed to paper give a fair insight to this new motoring, and at the time was clearly taken with the concept; later he became disillusioned with it all.) "Here I soon became friendly with a chap (Freddie Slater) who was just as mad on motor cycles as I was, and between us we had quite a number of different makes.*

"Then came the cyclecar craze. Anything on three or four wheels with an engine was the fashion and in spare leisure moments–and in quite a lot of time that I fear really belonged to Captain de Havilland–drew ideas for a vehicle of this type. Eight horse power JAP engine, three speed Sturmey Archer gearbox, chain final drive, and a body just wide enough for the driver only. My friend and I rented a shed at Harrow and started work on our machine. He had an old five horse power single cylinder Rudge–and before we had finished I decided to enter the Motor Cycling Club, London-Edinburgh trial. By working night and day we were nearly finished in time for the start. I knew there was no time to put mudguards on the car and painting was left until later. We did a bit of homework on it right up until it was time to start and then I got the word go in my first trial.

"Everything went well for about sixty miles then the rear sprocket decided that it was easier to turn round on the axle than to turn the axle as well. That was the end of my first trial." Despite these early frustrations he persevered and relates further problems . . . "Brake shoes flying to pieces at the top of a steep hill near Harrow. I believe the long scores in the wall where the hub cap was made to act as a brake are still a source of wonder to the inhabitants. However, with much work and optimism we decided that we would really attack the MCC organization the following year and once again turned up at the starting line, and somehow by extreme good luck arrived at Edinburgh and duly collected a second class award. Following this with an entry for the London-Lands End and arrived at that point to gain a Gold. I think the MCC got the wind up as they promptly cancelled the next trial. Meanwhile I had started a small engineering business at Harrow and I was getting fed up with living near London. I wanted to get away to some more rural area and consultation with my father disclosed the fact that he thought he would like to live in the Stroud area when he retired; good enough. That suited me and by moving my business there I should be

* HPBs letters and notes are from the Pat Mather collection.

A1

1919

No.
VICTORIA 4490.

Any further communication
on the subject of this letter
must be addressed to the
CLERK OF THE COUNTY
COUNCIL, and the following
number quoted:—

M. D. 264.

Office of the Clerk of the County Council,

Guildhall, Westminster,

S.W. 1.

22nd April, 1920.

Dear Sir,

        The Motor Car Acts, 1896 and 1903.
    The Motor Car (Registration and Licensing) Order, 1903.

        I beg to enclose a copy of the entry in the Register
relating to your Motor car , together with a formal receipt
for £1.

        The number   assigned to the car   is 264.
and the identification mark   will be M. D. 264.

        The positions in which you propose to place your
plates are approved subject to the requirements of the above
Act and Order being strictly complied with.

        The County Council will not supply plates ; they must,
however, be so lettered and coloured as to comply with the Act
and Order.

        The index mark M. D. 264   must not be used on any
vehicle other than {that / these} to which {it is / they are} assigned.

        If the ownership of the car   is changed, or if any
circumstance occurs which affects the accuracy of the
particulars entered respecting the car   in the Register of
motor cars and motor cycles, the County Council should be
notified thereof as soon as possible.

        Copies of the Motor Car (Registration and Licensing)
Order, 1903, may be obtained either directly or through a
Bookseller, from Messrs. Wyman & Sons, Ltd., Fetter Lane, E.C.

                        Yours faithfully, .
                        ERNEST S. W. HART,
                            Clerk of the County Council. .

H. P. Baughan Esq

Harry Baughan's official application for his cyclecar, dispelling the myth that it was built in Stroud. MD is clearly a Middlesex registration. Later this cyclecar became better known as the 'Red Car' when it had some fabric panels and covered completely in red aircraft dope.

No. N6607

County Council of Middlesex.

THE MOTOR CAR ACT, 1903.

2 1 APR 1920   192

RECEIVED OF Mr 49 Baughan

the sum of _____ pounds _____ shillings and

_____ pence, in payment of the following Fees.

	£	s.	d
Fee on Registration of Manufacturer or Dealer's Mark			
Fee on Registration of a Motor Car...	1		
Fee on Registration of a Motor Cycle			
Fee for Alteration in Register of Motor Cars on Change of Ownership of _____			
Fee for Copy of Register			
Fee for Driver's Licence			
Fee for Duplicate Licence			
Fee for Renewal of Driver's Licence			
	1	£	

Ernest W. Bad

Clerk of the County Council.

The sum of one pound changed hands and Harry Baughan and Freddy Slater had made their mark.

able to live at home once again when my parents came. When the war ended I was at the Aircraft Manufacturing Company (AIRCO, soon to become de Havilland) experimental dept. But at that time there did not appear to be much to experiment on. True, some one had a brain wave to illuminate a plane and fly it over London, just to contribute to the gaiety of the moment and incidentals it expected to gain a fit of cheap advertising. Come to think of it that stunt might have been developed to carry flashing signs. Think of the joy of waking up in the middle of the night and seeing 'Carters little Liver Pills' floating around the sky. Any way to get back to this idea. I spent several days at the Hendon drome, screwing little lamp holders on the fuselage and the underside of the wings. Batteries were in the observers cockpit–with a masterswitch for the pilot. Some how that job was not a success and most of the trouble was the pilot. The first day he discovered that the engine was not running properly so he could not go that night. The next day he managed to find that the accumulators were flat and no more could be found. The following evening he decided it was too rough. Other days it was too foggy for the lights to show, or he had a long standing engagement which he could not postpone. I rather think he did not want to fly the plane at night. We also had another job. We fetched a DH9 from the erection shops, removed the dual controls, machine guns and ammunition and a few other war like accessories.

"The sides of the two cockpits were padded with cotton wool and covered with American cloth on a domed lid. Something like half a double cheese box split lengthways was hinged to close over the cockpit. This was fitted with numerous windows and the painters got busy for a few days with pots of white enamel. Actually this was somewhat of a joke to us but it did justify itself in the end and was the forerunner of the London-Paris air route. It carried quite a number of government officials to the peace conference. Shortly afterwards there was a swarm of Royal Flying Corps pilots making the rounds of the aircraft factories looking for jobs as test pilots. Unfortunately for them there were

Seal of approval. The official registration document of MD264 with an 8 hp engine. HPB later replaced it with a V twin, air-cooled Blackburne after finding the JAP underpowered for serious road work.

not a large number of aircraft firms and one test pilot could go quite a long way, so the market for their business was not a brisk one.

"Just about this time my brother (John) was undertaking the uphill job of publicity for the firm and one of his brain waves was to write to firms all over the country and suggest that they had aerial views taken of their factory, a genuine birds eye view in fact. The mail answers did not cause the postman much extra work so the principle of Mohammed was evoked. He decided to send the aircraft and take the photos then offer these to the firms. This worked much better. I am inclined to the idea that the fact of careful selection of angles other surrounding buildings could easily be mistaken for part of the factory had quite a bit to do with the success of this plan. Just as this was in full swing and my brother having one of his heated arguments with the firms pilots who took the photos until another RFC pilot came on the chance of a job and in a few minutes was engaged on the spot, to start flying immediately. This was Alan Cobham. Soon to be better known for his 'Flying Circus' and pioneer of inflight refuelling. Alan soon made himself at home and proved to be a jolly good pilot with an eye for a decent photograph. He had good fun over this job, some photos were taken of large buildings and no one had the slightest notion of what they were. The procedure was then to plot the route of the flight on a map and from this he would know that building was somewhere on that line. Then the conference began. Alan would sit with his feet on the table, sucking a pipe, eyes shut, his face screwed up in an expression of profound thought whilst the rest of us would keep picking up one permit after another. Everyone who had been within miles of any part of that route would be quite certain that they had seen that building. But as they could not say exactly where or what it was, it did not materially assist in filing those photographs. Somehow most of these snaps got names put to them and large numbers of orders were taken.

"One I do remember, it was a view of a fine picturesque building with a square tower and battlements all around the parapets. No one succeeded in identifying it and it was sent to several photographic firms and editors of papers involved in large estates and the homes of the 'Landed Gentry,' all drew a blank. So it was filed with the pack of unidentified county residents. About fifteen years later I saw that confounded building. Its windows were dirty, there was mud in the courtyard, and round the side (hidden in the photograph) was a huge heap of discoloured hops. It was a brewery in Worcestershire. Meanwhile the old firm was not doing too well. We had a large order for frying pans and found that every frying pan had to line up to a certain standard of excellence. If you worked at AIRCO at that time you could have a well stocked shop with frying pans for a few shillings. Frying pans that the good people who ordered them refused to acknowledge them as respectable pans and had returned them without thanks. They also secured quite a sizeable order for car brakes for Buick cars, but this soon came to an end, assisted by the fact that one of the zealous upholsterers was so busy that he forgot to remove his needles from inside the padding of the seat he had made. Of course it would be one of the contractors manager who found that car. About this time there was a craze to own a car. Petrol had come off ration, and there were more prospective motorists than cars. The few that were available changed hands frequently. What ever price you paid you could be sure to find a bigger fool than yourself willing to hand over an even larger amount, until a tenth-hand wreck commanded about twice what it was worth when brand new in a manufacturers showroom."

As Harry Baughan became more serious about building his cyclecar there were many other companies starting up, it was indeed a futuristic step. As he had sampled the dubious delights of the Carden Mono car, many parts such as springs were breaking with greater frequency than he would have liked, how-

Mather collection.

IN THE COUNTY OF MIDDLESEX. — PETTY SESSIONAL DIVISION OF GORE.

Henry Baughan

To
of *"Ivy Dell" Southfields Bank Pinner*

Information has been laid this day by *C. Cosgrove*
Inspector of Police of *X* Division, for that you, on the *22* day of
September, 1920, at the Parish of *Pinner*
in the County aforesaid, did *unlawfully aid and abet Percy*
Hayes, in the commission of an offence namely driving
a motor car without same being registered at
1.55pm at Station Road

contrary to the Statute.

You are therefore hereby summoned to appear before the Court of Summary
Jurisdiction sitting at the Court House, Wealdstone, in the said County, on Tuesday,
the *16* day of *November* 1920, at the hour of 10.30 in the
Forenoon, to answer to the said Information.

Dated the *4* day of *November* 1920

J. M. Walton

Summons.   Justice of the Peace for the County aforesaid.

A criminal record? Harry Baughan caught driving an unregistered motor car, just what the fine was is
not recorded. No doubt many young men in those days got away with these misdemeanours.

ever, he made the move into what was the unknown. The cyclecars of the day
were uncomplicated machines. There was no hard and fast rules as to how they
should be built as long they were for groups **1** and **2** or what engines and transmissions should be employed. There was a variety of engines on the market that
would prove suitable and these could be mated to various gear boxes obtained
mostly from the motor cycle manufactures. Transmission offered three options,
belt drive that was variable friction, chain and propeller shaft; of the three the
latter was the most reliable and gave long life compared to the other two. In the
case of the Morgan threewheeler (Baughan was to use a similar system) it was
a compromise.

The primary drive from the engine to the clutch/gearbox was propeller shaft
and the final drive was by chain. In essence cyclecars were simple, being a
rudimentary chassis made invariably of wood and all the ancillaries bolted on.
Although Harry Baughan was still employed at de Havilland's he and Freddie

Slater were determined that they should build at least one car as a prototype, it was Harry who was the driving force and Slater who helped in some way to finance it. But first premises needed to be found, something that was not too big and outlandish but with enough room for their limited equipment and tools. Eventually they came across a small lock-up garage in Tyburn Lane that would allow them to make a start. Their methods of building were primitive in the extreme. Initially chalk marks were drawn on the workshop floor to get an idea of the overall dimensions, then plans were drawn by Harry and John on wallpaper which it seems was the only thing available in sufficient size at the time, paper post war being very scarce.

Many scraps of paper and backs of envelopes (yes they do exist, one example that survived is the engine reproduced on page 36), carried the measurements and an outline indication of the overall plan. The chassis was made of ash, seven inches deep, half inch in thickness and twelve feet long. The original front axle failed and was replaced with a second hand Chater Lea type. The rear axle was solid and has remained to this day. The original engine was a V twin JAP, side-valve with a capacity of 998cc, soon replaced by a 998cc V twin sv Blackburne which was more flexible. The gear box was a motor cycle Sturmey Archer being driven through a bevel box via the clutch. At the outset there was no provision for reverse gear, a case of getting out and pushing it when the time came. He soon found the limitations of no reverse gear a little too restricting. He promptly visited SA with the idea of having a reverse gear fitted but was staggered by the price quoted. Undaunted, he designed and manufactured one, but it proved temperamental. In the end this motor cycle gear box was replaced by a more robust Morris Oxford unit thus solving the reverse problem.

When the build was started Harry Baughan was greatly influenced by aircraft practice, longerons and stringers passing through lightweight bulkheads fore and aft of the cockpit. In actual fact it was of very simple construction and built without the need for expensive or complicated machinery. As Harry relates in his letters a great deal of the time officially belonged to Captain de Havilland as he and Freddie made up various parts for the car; 'foreigners' it seems have a long tradition no matter what the profession. These small parts consisted of fish plates, angle brackets, threaded rods and levers, as and when time allowed. All this activity took up their spare time in the evenings and week ends. Eventually the car took shape. The original featured a sloping back to the tail mirrored by the underside just behind the axle line. Later this was to change and the tail was extended and came to a vertical stem, a major alteration from the original shape. This later design was to become the basis for the remainder of the cyclecars built. Very little is known of the early car, but it went through a period of metamorphosis. The photos on page 32 taken at the time gives a good indication as to its original compact shape. It was in this form that Harry Baughan entered it in long distance trials and was moderately successful. In the letters that were exchanged between he and Freddie there seems to be a recurring problem with carburation and ignition, especially the former. Freddie went to great lengths to solve this, calling on various technical people and companies within the aircraft industry in an effort to find a solution. As there was so much trouble with the carburation on the prototype, Harry Baughan decided to design and build his own carburettor and the specification for the model advertised in 1922 states as much (see pages 68,69,70). Another factor that did not help was that Freddie Slater was being pursued by the Inland Revenue for unpaid tax. In actual fact Freddie made several changes of address around this time, one of them was from 'Claremont,' Whitchurch Lane, Edgware, Middlesex to 21, Roe Lane, Roe Green, Kingsbury, NW9. No doubt to ward off the intentions of HM Inspectorate, all this in less than five weeks. Harry was lodging with his parents at 'Ivydell' in Pinner which proved convenient. John by this time was married and moved away.

Harry it seems was the main financial backer to this whole enterprise for Freddie was no doubt feeling the hot breath of the Revenue men on his neck and money might be required for things other than building cars. John, being the ever faithful brother helped in the long term with the odd injection of cash, his real benefit was to make sketches and drawings that Harry could work from. For John, his ambition was a career in commercial art, and this proved to be a blessing in disguise. This flare for drawing was translated into dimensions for the car and after the prototype was finished and duly registered MD 264 they set about building a second one for him (see page 31). This machine was to be the first entry in the sales ledger that charts the progress of all the subsequent machines, both cyclecars and motor cycles that were built; starting at Middlesex and ending sixteen years later in Gloucestershire.

John, perhaps tiring of all these long hours that were not terribly productive and more importantly, financially draining, found it was not for him and decided that he should move and put his talent to good use and he soon set up a company called ARTCO. With his new company he continued to work through de Havilland with aerial photography, photographing numerous factories and then selling the prints to the respective companies. With all this work in the evenings and weekends Harry found it almost impossible to carry on his day job at de Havilland. He decided to chance his arm at building cars on a more serious basis, if not a sound financial one. With very little money he made a decision to advertise in the enthusiasts journal of the day, *The Light Car and Cyclecar* of October 1920 (see page 50) describing it as a Mono car. Like many budding entrepreneurs of the time they were all taking a big gamble; there were many tiny companies around who were in the same position. None of them had cars on the stocks to sell. Most had just the demonstration model that they hawked around with the hope of encouraging people to buy. If an order had been placed for ten to fifteen machines they would have been acutely embarrassed to fulfill it. The advert that was placed in the cyclecar journal must have been read by countless people and would have given rise for further orders. The sales ledger, however, tells a different story. Only one more car was built at Tyburn Lane and this, surprisingly, went overseas to Stockholm via the Anglo Scandinavian Agencies Ltd; this in the last month of 1920. One enquiry that was unusual came from a Mrs. Pelly who wanted to be the first woman to cross France and Spain in a cyclecar with her eventual destination, Gibraltar. If the lady in question had been given consideration, and the journey undertaken successfully then the resulting publicity should have been overwhelming. The letter is interesting enough and I'm sure Harry Baughan must have been highly encouraged, if not flattered. Realistically, it was a non-starter. To run a cyclecar across two countries in 1920 was a considerable undertaking. In that year the Baughan cyclecar was an unknown quantity and reliability was questionable. This reliability was severely tested on the 1920 London-Edinburgh Trial and was found lacking. On this basis a trip to Gibraltar would have required a trailer full of spares and endless amounts of time. Just what became of Mrs. Pelly and her proposed long distance journey remains a mystery. If she had been successful, the motoring press would have given it a lot of column inches; I wonder how many other aspiring young men like Harry Baughan received a similar letter that year from Mrs. T Pelly, of 16, Richmond Road, Surrey?

Dear Sir. 20/10/1920.

I am now negotiating with the Press to drive a small car through France and Spain down to Gibraltar and back in Nov and I am wondering whether your 2 seater Monocar could accomplish the feat, if so, you might care to enter into my scheme. I understand that no woman has yet succeeded in accomplishing this 'run' and therefore, the publicity of my tour would mean a very big acclaim for the car. My intention is to drive via Bordeaux, San Sebastian, Vitoria, Miranda, Burgos, Aiaisda to Madrid. Up to this point the roads are fairly good, especially the secondary roads; but south of Madrid, generally speaking, they are none too good, and in order to reach Gib I should have to take a circuitous course to avoid the worse passage. Still, from my experience of some Russian 'tracks,' you cannot call them roads. I don't think there would be great difficulty in negotiating these in Spain. It is not my intention to break a record with regards to speed, but to drive at a reasonable pace and nurse my car in order to make my trip a success. I might add that I am not a millionaire out for a 'Jazz' tour but one of

(Letter) Mather collection.

TELEPHONE	WORKS
GERRARD 4676	STROUD, GLOS

BAUGHAN MOTORS

Manufacturers of Baughan Cars and Motor Cycles

Victory House — Leicester Sq.
LONDON, W.C. 2.

The first official address of Baughan Motors. This was shared with Harry's brother John whose newly formed business, ARTCO, which specialized in photographic and commercial art operated from. It was only Freddie Slater who used this office chasing almost non-existent orders for their cyclecar. HPB had by this time realized there was little future in building cyclecars after a change to the vehicle taxation law. At the top right indicates HPB had already established his business at Stroud.

the 'New poor' sports women, who, having done her bit for her country does not think she need apologize for wishing to do a bit for herself. I am a good all-round journalist and descriptive writer and you would find that I would study your interests in every way, and do my best to get you orders. If you feel disposed to enter into my scheme I would be pleased to hear your views. Any suggestions will be appreciated, yours faithfully, (Mrs) T Pelly.

About this time the brothers decided to go their separate ways, John to pursue a career as artist/photographer setting up his business in London. Harry uprooted and moved to the West Country along with his parents who retired to Stroud, Gloucestershire. Harry's father having served with the Great Western Railway for many years thought this was the place to spend the rest of his years, and this time Charlie accompanied them as well, soon to find work with the GWR as a booking clerk in Stroud. Charlie married in 1933 and he and his wife Dorothy opened a small grocers shop at the north end of Walls Quarry and by mutual agreement Harry moved in with Charlie and Dol. When Charlie died in February 1966, both Harry and Dol moved down to Brimscombe and finished their years there. John found premises at the back of Selfridges in the West End of London where he established his business and undertook work for companies such as Lever Brothers. In later years the name ARTCO surfaces again when Harry called on his brother to produce competition number plates for riders in the International Six Days Trial when the Headquarters were based at Llandrindod Wells when Harry was Clerk of the Course and Competition Chairman.

Disappointing sales for cyclecars. Harry Baughan leaves de Havilland experimental department. Detail of HPB cyclecar. MCC London-Edinburgh Trial, disappointment, then success. HPB moves to Stroud, Gloucestershire. Freddie Slater left to struggle with sales in London.

The venture that Harry Baughan and Freddie Slater entered into was not terribly productive in terms of cyclecar output. Their method of construction could not be described as outstanding. The long laborious layout of the chassis would hardly be offset against the fairly quick assembly of the running gear and ancillaries. The bodywork on the prototype used aluminium and in the immediate postwar years was of such poor quality and suffered greatly from adverse weather conditions if left untreated. Once Baughan and Slater were away from de Havilland their access to manufacturing 'Foreigners.' finished and were required to make their own from materials they purchased. 1920 saw ever more cyclecars coming on to the market with varying specifications, to say nothing of the light cars that were becoming more popular with the public. It was these prospective buyers who dictated what they wanted and the likes of Morris and Austin were only too willing to accommodate them. After the prototype cyclecar had been built Baughan and Slater turned their attention to producing more. Cyclecars were still very popular with the public and there was no reason to think that their appeal would diminish, certainly not in the foreseeable future. Although the prototype was registered to Harry Baughan in April 1920 the sales ledger reveals brother John Kilminster as the next purchaser and became the first official entry in the sales ledger as (No.1) No.71. The build was started in mid 1920 and was finally completed in September of that year.

The sales ledger records this as completed in September 1920. There is some ambiguity concerning this cyclecar. Harry Baughan's MD264 is not in question as to its authenticity, but the John Baughan one has a question mark over it and will forever remain a mystery. According to Ted Baughan (John's son) he has no recollection of it at all. No photo exists and the family cannot recall it. HPBs Red Car was registered on April 22nd 1920, several months before the completion of John's machine. All Baughan cyclecars were equipped with electric lights and these proved to be very popular; the acetylene lamps had not been a great selling feature on motor cycles either and anyone moving on to four wheels were more than happy to get away from their idiosyncratic behaviour. Lessons had been learnt from the first build. From now on things would be a little more ordered and scientific, drawings were produced, chalk marks on the floor would just not do. Wooden jigs were made up and these enabled them to keep the chassis in the correct position and allow the fish plates and angle brackets to be attached without fear of movement taking place. The controls for the most essential functions were mounted on the steering wheel boss. The two most prominent ones were

Mather collection.

Mather collection.

Two views of the prototype Baughan cyclecar. The brake lever visible here was moved to the off-side when a change of gear box was made from the motor cycle SA to a Morris Oxford. The left hand was then used to change gear. The passenger in the 'Dickey' seat is seated higher than the driver and in poor weather would not be at all comfortable, this was abandoned a few years later.

the throttle and the advance/retard. These were two long levers with oval ends were mounted at the eleven o'clock position and fell easily for operation by the left thumb, the longest of the two was the throttle. The mixture lever was much shorter, also oval ended but this time its position was at twelve o'clock. A close examination of the original photographs with a watchmaker's eyepiece reveals the throttle lever was perhaps two inches longer than the advance and retard. These two essential controls were left mounted for the right hand was needed for gear changing. When MD264 was re-built new ones were fitted of the motor cycle Bowden type, this time mounted on the spokes and not the centre boss. With these controls on the steering wheel they kept position when the wheel was turned. One had to remember the position of the throttle in relation to the wheel when turning corners. One advantage in the driver's favour was that the steering was fairly high geared. Armfuls of lock was not necessary when negotiating tight radius bends. Parking, which involved plenty of arm movements was a different matter altogether. No good pushing the mixture control instead of the throttle in these circumstances. If the hands were fully occupied with steering one was also required for the braking department just to confuse the issue. Two pedals were in their usual position in the foot well, clutch as normal practice on the left and the brake on the right. Initially the original external brake lever was on the driver's near side. This was for convenience only. When the Morris Oxford gearbox was fitted the seating arrangement was changed and the passenger sat in the cockpit. This brake lever migrated to the offside and can be seen clearly on pages 99 and 235, when pulled backwards applied the offside rear brake (internal expanding) and the foot brake actuated the nearside rear (there are no front brakes). For smooth braking the driver needed to balance the foot brake pressure against his right hand while pulling on the lever; with a live axle just one brake would be sufficient, far better to even things out with two. Ambidextrous qualities on the driver's part spring to mind, get any combination wrong then serious consequences would surely follow. If this was not enough to keep the driver fully occupied then there was more employment for the right hand; changing gear was pretty essential at times.

The Sturmey Archer gearbox sported three forward speeds and gear changing was undertaken as it would be on a motor cycle of the period (a longitudinal gate), the change lever was under the scuttle and to the right. The most important consideration was to keep a close watch on the sight glass that fed the Best and Lloyd oil pump. The feed for this could be adjusted from several drips a minute to a small continuous flow (total loss system). Frequent attention to this essential function was of paramount importance, failure on the driver's part would lead to a very expensive seizure. When the seating arrangement was changed and the passenger sat to the left but slightly behind the driver instead of the previous arrangement where he/she occupied a 'Dickey' seat in the tail. This pumping could be delegated to the passenger and the driver could be better engaged keeping his eyes on the road. Looking at the photos of MD264 (page 32) it appears as a true 'Mono' car even though the dickey seat is hidden; this was only used when Harry Baughan became serious about trials competition. The dickey position for the passenger was not a very sensible arrangement as it isolated him or her from the driver and this turned out to be a very impractical place to be, plus

Mather collection.

Initially the Baughan used a tandem seat arrangement, shown here with buttoned leather upholstery. Later the passenger sat along side the driver and slightly to the rear. Compare this 1920 photo to the one on the opposite page taken in 1933 which defines a radical change in rear body shape.

the fact that they were sitting as they were over a very substantial final drive chain that was unguarded.* In the early trials that Harry Baughan took part in within the Stroud area a passenger was carried in the dickey seat, the prime function of this being to place greater weight over the rear wheels in an effort to increase grip. Creature comforts for the passenger were minimal, no aero screen, a rudimentary seat and a bar for the passenger to hang on to accompanied by an upholstered back rest.

When HPB really became serious about trials with what was eventually termed the 'Red Car' (MD264) the cockpit was changed and the seating arrangement became a far more practical side–by–side affair. This allowed the passenger to indulge in essential map reading as well as keeping an eye on the oil sight glass. To be a passenger today in MD264 is an experience not granted to many, it's lively, noisy, harsh and with plenty of vibration. However, in those far off days sitting in the dickey going up the Nailsworth Ladder must have been a great experience. Harry Baughan was noted for his forceful press–on style and gave many a spectator a thrill at close quarters, to say nothing of his intrepid passenger. The position now vacated in the tail was useful for carrying numerous tools etc. Later when the Red Car was employed for route marking it was used to store the red, blue and yellow dyes that indicated the turns on corners. For the cyclecarist of the day many had their controls scattered in the most outlandish positions and it speaks volumes for their drivers who were obviously far more adaptable than their counterparts today who have been brought up on a diet of

* Pat Mather made due note of this chain when he rebuilt MD264 and as his nether regions were perilously close to it he wisely decided that a guard was essential for piece of mind.

Hayward collection.

This photo taken at Lower Street clearly shows the changes. The lights have moved, the running boards have gone and the wings are more in keeping with a cyclecar. The spare wheel once mounted on the tail is now on the near side. The space in the dickey seat has made way for dye storage when route marking along with sundry spares. The aluminum over the scuttle has been replaced with fabric and the whole car painted red, which was really aircraft dope to tighten the fabric. Oil and petrol tanks remain as the original, in front of the windscreen.

self-cancelling indicators, electric windows and audio warnings when they leave the car with the lights on. As Harry Baughan revealed in the previous chapter he was drawn towards competition and his first taste of this was through the Motor Cycling Club and their wonderful classic trial, the London to Edinburgh.

This first attempt was to end in failure. Just over an hour into the run the Woodruff key failed in the live rear axle and there was precious little Harry Baughan could do to restore the drive at the side of the road. Such was the haste to get the car finished that their preparation was not as good as he would have liked. It taught him one valuable lesson . . . 'finish if you can.' That was his watchword, later instilling in his riders whether they were on two or three wheels, that was his parting shot as they left the start. Thus was Harry Baughan's philosophy. Attention to detail was always uppermost in his mind and in later years both his two employees, Chris Stagg and Bill Hayward were ever mindful that the 'Gaffers' bikes should finish. His second attempt was in 1922 when he once more ventured to Scotland and this time carrying competition number 342. On this occasion he was rewarded with a gold medal for a trouble free run within the strict time limits. The success of this prompted Freddie to write to Harry and congratulate him and he said, "I was of course very bucked to hear about the trial, I am anxiously awaiting *The Light Car and Cyclecar* to see what they

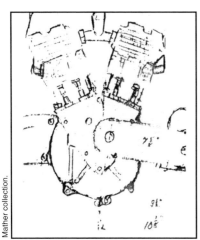

Sketches on the back of envelopes do exist. HPB used one to outline this V twin Blackburne which replaced the JAP.

have to say. Good old Mono! And good old Blackie eh? To say nothing of the poor old chain, etc!" Freddie was greatly impressed by this performance, no doubt thinking of the publicity to be gained, having expressed his feelings concerning the mechanicals. However, nothing is mentioned about the poor old Sturmey Archer gearbox that took the brunt of the transmission loadings. It coped remarkably well considering that it had to keep nearly five hundredweights of cyclecar on the move for over four hundred miles; its natural habitat was in the frame of either a 350 or 500cc motor cycle which weighed perhaps a quarter of the car. This type of long distance reliability trial greatly impressed Harry Baughan, with these seeds firmly implanted in Baughan's fertile brain and within a decade he was using the same concise methods when he was either Secretary of the Meeting or Clerk of the Course when he ran many trials in the Western Centre of the Auto Cycle Union.

It must be said that this classic trial relied more on reliability than pure competition for it was a straight run with time and distance being the criteria, with some difficult terrain thrown in for good measure. The schedules were fairly tight and they did not allow time for extensive repairs on the side of the road even punctures could be costly in terms of time. The emphasis was on mechanical integrity and it said much for the vehicles that were entered to travel the full four hundred plus miles to reach their destination. The sub-standard roads of the day more often than not defeated many a gallant effort as puncture after puncture became almost common place. However, the spirit of adventure would always win through and the London to Edinburgh was perhaps the trial that many were judged against. Others were equally taxing. The London to Lands End was looked on equally as tough and demanding. In order to gain a gold medal on the London-Edinburgh, competitors must not have been more than fifteen minutes early or ten minutes late at any one point of the time checks. A silver medal required a competitor to be not more than fifteen minutes early or twenty minutes late at any one of the passage controls, and to qualify for a bronze medal, it was again no more than fifteen minutes early and the whole journey to be completed within 25 hours. With many competitors on four wheels there was at the very least a crew of two, often as many as four. In Harry Baughan's case it was

A NEAT TANDEM-SEATED CYCLECAR.

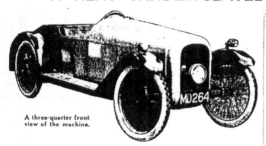

A three-quarter front view of the machine.

The Baughan, Embodying J. A. P. Engine, Shaft Drive — Sturmey - Archer Gearbox and Final Chain Drive.

To Sell at Approximately £200.

ALTHOUGH it experienced bad luck in the London to Edinburgh run, the Baughan tandem-seater, which will be made by Baughan Motors, Tyburn Lane, Harrow (temporary address) is a soundly constructed and well-thought-out cyclecar designed on the most approved cyclecar lines.

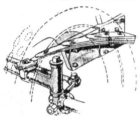

The front springing, showing how the spring is inclined.

A J.A.P. engine in conjunction with a Sturmey-Archer gearbox opens up illimitable possibilities, and in this particular case a departure has been made by placing the engine at the front and the gearbox at the rear. It is probable that a Blackburne engine will be fitted to future machines, but in any case the drive is taken from the engine by means of a propeller shaft and two universal joints to an aluminium bevel box mounted just behind the driver's seat. At one end of the short countershaft which passes through this bevel box there is a spider engaging with the sprocket of the gearbox itself, which is also rigidly mounted on a cross-member of the frame. The final drive is by a short chain to the differential-less back axle.

Absorbing Transmission Shocks.

An ingenious feature of the final drive is the cushioning device enabling a sweet drive to be maintained to the back axle. This is effected by mounting the axle sprocket so that it is actually rotatable on the shaft, the drive from it, however, being communicated to the axle through the medium of a number of helical springs coupled at one end to a driving plate keyed to the shaft and at the other end to the driving sprocket.

A30

The back axle runs on Skefko ball bearings, whilst means by which the chain may be tightened are provided at the ends of the radius rods. The springing on the Baughan is another interesting feature of its design, for although quarter-elliptic springing is adopted throughout, those at the front are canted so that the diagonal thrusts set up by inequalities in the road surface are absorbed by the springs and not by tie rods or other means.

Ingenious Springing Arrangements.

The springs at the rear are quarter elliptic inverted, the ends being free to slide in special pads provided for the purpose. The frame is constructed of ash, and upon it is mounted the neat sporting looking body which at first appearance looks like a single seater. Something more comfortable than a dickey, however,

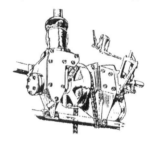

The aluminium bevel box on the left transmits the drive by means of a spider to the Sturmey-Archer gearbox, the final drive being by chain. The gears are operated through rods and lever shown on the extreme right.

is provided at the rear—in fact, when this is exposed the car has all the appearance of a proper tandem-seater. We understand that the present model is purely experimental, and that owing to manufacturing difficulties production will be delayed, but at the moment we are informed that the approximate price of the Baughan will be £200.

The full page write-up in *The Light Car and Cyclecar*, May 29th 1920, of the newly announced Baughan cyclecar. Enlarged drawings are on pages 39 and 40.

a solo effort. Not only was navigation and timing down to him, but an average speed was required between time checks and any error or fault was of his own making. For a solo effort by Harry Baughan was no light undertaking, reliability and good time keeping was the essence of the London-Edinburgh. This long distance type event finally manifested itself years later on a far greater scale when he was chairman and secretary of the Auto Cycle Union, sub-committee that was responsible for the International Six Days Trial when it was run in Wales in the late 1940s. In these latter years his ability was unsurpassed for route marking, planning and timing. This ability extended to spotting not only existing, but emerging talent that would warrant a place in the Trophy and Vase Teams.

The start for the London-Edinburgh in 1922 was from the London Country Club at Hendon where the first competitor of the 392 entered left at 7pm on the Friday. Grantham was reached at 2.30am where a one hour halt for early breakfast was taken. Then the next stop was Ilkley, 8.40am for a second breakfast, on to Carlisle for late lunch at 3.10pm, one hour allowed. Final stop was Moffat for late tea at 6.14pm, one half hour this time; then the final run in to Edinburgh. But to complete this alone was the mark of the man. Meticulous preparation and planning that was bordering on perfection was his style and in later years his praises were lauded in the motor cycle journals of the day, not only from the reporters, but the competitors themselves.

The London-Exeter was run on less strenuous lines than the London-Edinburgh by the Motor Cycling Club and also the London-Gloucester, admirably run by the North West London MCC. Many a manufacturer delighted in advertising their machines performance if it won a gold, silver or bronze on one of these classic trials for it spoke volumes as to their product's mechanical reliability and sound engineering practice. What it failed to mention on the London-Edinburgh was the state of the crews when they made the final mile down Princes Street. Once the Baughan was adorned with wings and running boards it certainly looked a trim machine and gave a fair turn of speed when required. Speed in the 1920s was as much a selling feature as it is today. Fuel economy was a strong consideration as well. The former it seems always carried more weight than just how economical the vehicle was. Advertising your product was always an important factor and from time to time the Baughan featured a half–page in the *The Light Car and Cyclecar* to bring it to the public's notice. Three months after the first Baughan was finished another order was placed, surprisingly from Europe. This passed through the Anglo Scandinavian Agencies and finished up in Stockholm. The sales ledger records this as (No.2) No.72, which was priced at £229. and left the country in 1921. For a company as small as Baughans this must have been something of a coup and greatly encouraged them to see this machine depart for foreign shores was perhaps a dream come true and was a portent of

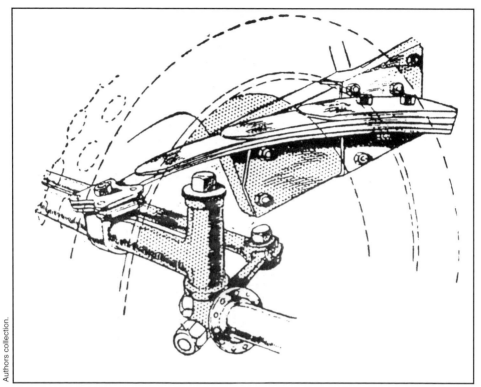

The original front axle, this was later replaced by a Chater Lea when the Baughan suffered damage on a trial. In all the trials that HPB used the Red Car the springs never suffered any damage.

things to come; or more realistically a false dawn! The letters that passed from Freddie Slater to HPB cast a different light on things. Slater, after making contacts with prospective buyers urged HPB to make the effort to use his monocar as a demonstrator so clients could assess its potential. At the time HPB was still living at 'Ivydell' and would have little difficulty getting to the various locations in and around London. One such request was to show a possible buyer in Potters Bar and use the Great North Road as a venue for showing the speed capability of the Baughan. As MD264 was the sole cyclecar it was used as a demonstrator, by this time development had taken place and the machine had quite a turn of speed for the carburation and ignition problems would seem to have been resolved. In the end it all came to nothing. Before Harry Baughan moved to the West Country there was a flurry of activity regarding his cyclecars. Many attempts were made by Slater to close sales with various people, but these proved inconclusive and many hours were spent fruitlessly chasing prospective buyers. When Harry Baughan finally moved to Stroud, Freddie Slater and he eventually went their

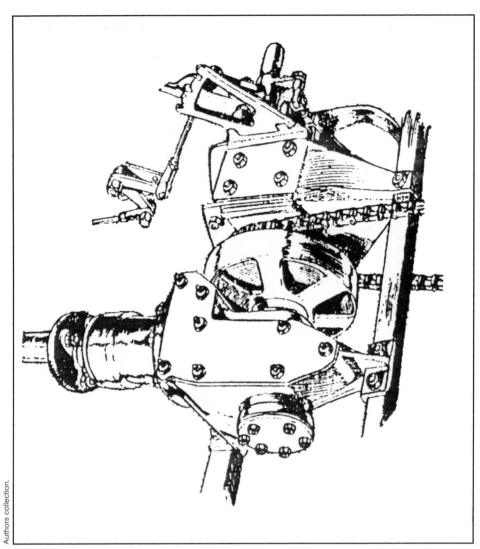

The transmission used both shaft and chain. The bevel box and clutch remain today, the major change is the gear box from the SA seen here, to a Morris Oxford. HPB modified the SA box to incorporate a reverse gear, but proved fragile. The SA box was the motor cycle pattern with a gate which was operated by the right hand. The Morris type allowed the use of the left hand which resulted in the hand brake moving from the left to the right side of the cockpit.

separate ways. The letters that passed between both parties referred to a London sales office (page 30) that was the domain of Freddie himself. Just how well this worked remains unclear for a reference in one of his letters he remarks on

Mather collection.

HPB at Old Wall on the 1922, MCC London-Edinburgh Trial. This resulted in a gold medal, the
cyclecar ran trouble-free for the whole journey. In
all his long distance trials he drove solo.

the precarious nature of employment at de Havilland's so one can
only assume he was still working
there. All manner of things were
discussed in correspondence and
there seems a genuine belief on
Slater's part that there was still
a strong market for cyclecars.
Despite his enthusiasm Harry
was not entirely convinced and
reading between the lines one
gets the impression that in his
mind the cyclecar period was
rapidly coming to a close. After
Harry's move to Stroud he started
to compete in local trials with
some small measure of success.
Freddie was keen to use this publicity to promote further sales.
Although Slater was still making
the contacts in London the other
half of the tenuous partnership was over a hundred miles away setting up an
engineering business with the only example of their efforts. With this considerable geographical difference it was little wonder that things came to a swift end
for communication was essentially by letter, anything that was urgent required a
telegram. Even so this was not a very satisfactory arrangement.

Eventually it all came to nothing, Harry Baughan by this time realizing that
the cyclecars were going to be overwhelmed by the light car manufacturers who
had so much more clout than any tiny firm trying to break into what was fast
becoming an established market place for mass produced motor cars. Away
from London Harry Baughan could indulge in his new found passion of trials
and enjoy the competition that was on offer in the Auto Cycle Union's Western
Centre. This Centre over the next few decades was to undergo great developments in motor cycle trials and saw Harry Baughan bring its organization and
competition to such a peak, effectively becoming the jewel in the ACU crown.
When Harry Baughan left London for the West Country he was to sever his connection with Freddie Slater. Before his final move there were various attempts to
sell more cyclecars and Slater was instrumental in making the necessary contacts
after his full day at de Havilland. Despite all the energy that Slater put into chasing sales the orders were not forthcoming. Even motor clubs* were approached

*See page 47

in an attempt to generate interest, but it was something of a lost cause. The true nature of motoring was changing and the public could see the progress Austin and Morris had made with their products. Comfort was one aspect that the family required and an enclosed one offered as much. Freddie Slater may not have had his vision clouded by these cars. Harry Baughan certainly did and he could see that cyclecars with their many shortcomings was not the future. From a sporting side of things cyclecars had their devotees and he was certainly one of them, from a commercial point of view it was not the route to go. As this chapter in Baughans life drew to a close all thoughts of serious manufacture was dropped. Certainly, when Harry Baughan moved to Stroud that was the deciding factor; engineering then took over. The move from Pinner finally came in March 1921. John had now left de Havilland and decided to stay in the London area moving into commercial art starting his business, ARTCO. Harry, on the other hand, started to look at various buildings that offered him enough space in which he could seriously pursue his engineering activity.

Just a short distance from Stroud Hospital he found what he was looking for a three storey building that offered room for sufficient expansion if things went according to plan. This red bricked building went by the name of Piccadilly Mill, Lower Street in Whitehall, which was to be the home of Baughan Motors for the next fourteen years. This move to the West country was duly noted by *The Light Car and Cyclecar*. The premises were not outstanding, mains water and gas were the only services available. There was overhead shafting and various belts that could be used to drive machinery but no source of power existed for them to be of any use . . . this was about to be resolved. Before serious consideration was given to building the proposed motor cycles some method was needed to drive the shafting in order to make a start. What was required was some type of engine to drive all this machinery for prior to that there had been a small gas engine that did the job but had disappeared before Harry Baughan took over the premises. Gas engines were costly and despite an adequate local manufacturer, Dudbridge Ironworks Company, they were an expensive investment for an under financed firm such as Baughans. It was not long before Harry came up with a solution, or at least his father did, he managed to obtain a 1000cc, single cylinder engine that had been once used in a Star Car, circa 1900. This for a period proved adequate as it was equipped with a substantial flywheel thus helping in its struggle to drive all the shafting. It had a somewhat temperamental nature first thing in the mornings. After a liberal diet of 'dope' it was persuaded into life, but proved a trifle unreliable at times. With the power to drive the shafting more investment was made in lathes and drilling machines that would enable him to undertake a greater variety of work. At first HPB occupied himself with all manner of jobs, mostly repairing cars and motor cycles. From this humble beginning Baughan

Mather collection.

HPB on the London-Lands End Trial of 1923 which produced another gold medal. Carburation and ignition problems had now been solved and the new Blackburne engine gave a fair turn of speed.

Motors slowly established itself. Motor cyclists in the district soon found out that there was a person with a similar interest as themselves and before long the fledgling company became an established feature with the two wheel brigade. Its reputation grew and HPB found himself fully occupied running the business and he started seriously to look for a suitable apprentice who would help to ease his increasing load. Up to this time Baughan had used subcontract labour in an effort to keep the business functioning, this, as it turned out was not a very satisfactory solution. Business started to increase. At first there were various casual helpers who, though willing were lacking in the necessary engineering experience. As the months passed and the business gradually expanded Harry Baughan found it neces-

sary to increase his staff on a more permanent basis, he looked for a suitable youngster who could be taken on as an indentured engineer. Eventually the word got around the grape vine and he received an enquiry from a person he thought might just be what he was looking for. Roland Stagg heard through his engineering contacts that Baughan Motors were looking for a young lad to be taken on with a view to an apprenticeship, so he took along his son Chris for an interview with Mr. Baughan. HPB was very considerate. He gave both parties ample time to consider the terms and left it to them. Chris took up the offer and started work in December 1924 and was to stay with the company for the whole of his working life. Chris found in Harry Baughan quite a kind, though often serious at times, but above all a quiet man, not one given to outbursts and flamboyant gestures, here was someone who had a great deal of sympathy and understanding. This was a trait that he carried throughout his life both socially and professionally. Bill Hayward started as soon as he finishing his apprentice-

Mather collection.

Harry Baughan was bitten by the competition bug early on in his life. He was also very much a hands on motorist before he started building motor cycles. Here, pictured on a touring spree at Teesdale in 1922. The nearside rear wheel no longer sports the original motor cycle one.

ship at Waller's which was a few months after Chris began. Even before this he spent many hours there after work on an unpaid basis and was instrumental in the build of the first nine machines. This close liaison is reflected in the fact he was the first purchaser of a Baughan motor cycle. In the sales ledger this appears as (No.5) August 1923, No.MC24/196. It would seem that it was ready on October 26th 1923, but has a prefix of 1924. This was not unusual for Baughan Motors and throughout their years of building motor cycles as a close study of the sales ledger will reveal. (See pages 325 to 336 for the full inventory.) Bill Hayward had a thorough grounding in engineering with TW Waller at Phoenix Mill, Thrupp. The one valuable asset that he did possess was his ability as a fully qualified draughtsman, to produce detailed working drawings. Harry Baughan knew Bill's background and quickly employed him when he finished at Waller's. Bill Hayward first made contact with Harry Baughan just after he moved into the district in 1922, at the time he was riding a 1921 two-stroke Enfield which suffered from out of true flywheels. Hearing that Baughan Motors were more than a little sympathetic to motor cyclists he went down to see for himself. Both men soon had the engine apart and both big end and main bearings were in need of replacement. Once the parts had been acquired, it was rebuilt. Bill, delighted at the outcome, struck up a firm association with Harry and was soon working at the factory. This was to be the start of a friendship that was to last all their working lives. Over the years there were many disagreements as there are in any company, but nothing that was insurmountable. Here was a man who could give him the necessary plans that he and John had struggled with in the past, now things could be drawn in a more concise manner. He could now leave this important function to Bill and get on with running the business. Perhaps the clinching factor was that they were both enthusiastic motor cyclists and these two kindred spirits formed a friendship that was to last until Harry sold the business when he retired. These formative years saw Baughan Motors in a very much hand to mouth existence and work was not too plentiful, taking on Bill was fortunate indeed for his father was commercial vehicle manager for the Stroud Co-operative Society and this position allowed him to send in the vehicles to Baughans for servicing and major repair. This proved a steady income for the fledgling company and they coped with varying and diverse work. Motor cyclists were soon arriving at their door when they found that both men had more than a sympathetic leaning towards two wheeled transport. This general repair work was often slow for the early 1920s did not exactly have a vast amount of traffic that required constant attention at a little backwater in Stroud. While this steady progress took place at Lower Street nothing was done on the cyclecar front for there was precious little call for such machines in the surrounding district, but within a year and a half there was another one on the stocks. Having built two previous machines (No.1 and 2) No.71 and 72 with plans drawn on wall paper Harry Baughan had one last attempt when it came to cyclecars. (No.3) No.73C673 for J Newton in Manchester, the last throw of the dice came when (No.4) No.D674 was completed for W Tuck.

The simplicity of the cyclecar was being surpassed by more robust vehicles, machines that had better creature comforts, brakes that were more efficient and reliable, steering that was more precise and accurate, lights that gave illumination for the driver to actually see his way and not something that was a throw back to a pedal cycle. Weather protection, that indeed protected, no longer was there a need to wear waterproofs whilst driving. In 1925 the cyclecar was gradually being ousted by the light car and the need for transport that belonged to the immediate post war period was being somewhat dated. This halfway-house between a motor cycle combination and a light car was slowly losing interest with the public and only the stalwarts continued with them. The public demanded something better than that and when the Austin seven appeared they finally found it. Harry Baughan knew that the cyclecar era was all but over, and if he raised any doubts about its future then Bill Hayward was under no illusions as to the ultimate fate of them. His logic was based on the progress of what the larger, well financed manufacturers were doing. There was no point in a three-

ON ADMIRALTY, AIR BOARD AND WAR OFFICE LISTS.

TELEGRAMS, CARBURETTO, ECCLES
TELEPHONE

TWO GOLD
MEDALS
AWARDED.

MEMO FROM

C. BINKS, LIMITED,

PHOENIX WORKS,

CHURCH STREET, ECCLES,

MANCHESTER.

MANUFACTURERS OF ENGINES, CARBURETTORS, OIL
INDICATORS, SILENCERS AND GENERAL MOTOR FITTINGS.

SPECIAL ENGINES AND OTHER WORK REQUIRING ACCURACY
QUOTED FOR. CONTRACTORS TO HIS MAJESTYS GOVERNMENT

H.P. Baughan Esq.,
Pitmer.

20/2/19.

Dear Sir,

RE MOTOR CYCLE CARBURETTORS.

I thank you for your valued enquiry and have pleasure in
enclosing the particulars you require. Few have had the experience
I have had in the design, construction and riding of motor cycles and
the original four cylinder motor cycle was introduced by me.   The
unique experience gained, I place at your disposal with the object of
improving the machine you are now riding.

My three-jet carburettors have done more to improve the
running of the modern car than any other invention and my latest
three-jet carburettor for motor cycles are doing the same for this
class of machine.   I know why ordinary carburettors fail and if you
read the circulars you will see why too.

I offer you a new and perfected instrument and it is with
confidence that I ask you to send me your order, I offer to send you
one so that you can examine it at home and if you do not like it you
can return it at once on the terms stated in my list.

They are very easy to fit, but if you experience any
difficulty, and will send your machine to me, I will fit it for you,
or if you will send me particulars of your engine, I will supply you
with an extension branch or elbow to fit on the end of your induction
branch, both at a reasonable charge so that the carburettor will go right
on without any difficulty.

In order to get my motor cycle sparkling plugs more widely
known, I am open to send you one or two for 2/6d. each plus 50%.
The regular price is 4/-.

Awaiting your esteemed commands, and always at your service.
Yours faithfully,

O. BINKS, LIMITED

Encl:- Motor Cycle list.

MANAGING DIRECTOR

P.T.O.

Initially HPB suffered trouble with carburation and ignition with the JAP engine, Binks were unable to
help him, in the end he designed his own carburettor. This became a standard item. Slater did his best
in the ignition department, eventually a cure was effected.

8/ KM.

21st November   1.

London Manager,
    Mr. F.P. Slater,
        21, Roe Lane,
            Roe Green, KINGSBURY, N.W.9

The Secretary,
    North-West London M.C.C.

Dear Sir,

        May we bring before your notice the "Baughan" 2-3
seater Cyclecar. We would particularly mention, firstly, the
sound "car practice" transmission and, secondly, the degree to
which accessibility has been obtained.

        We shall have a demonstration car in London during
the Motor-Cycle Show week and should be very pleased if you would
allow us to be present at any meeting of the North-West London
M.C.C. and demonstrate to its members the car's comfort, ease of
control, speed and climbing powers against any cycle-car you care
to put against it.

        In the meantime fuller particulars, complete speci-
fication etc. will be gladly sent to you.

                    We are, Sir,
                        Faithfully Yours,
                    for BAUGHAN MOTORS.

                    London Manager.

This was just one of the prospective leads that Freddy Slater made in an attempt to sell the cyclecar. Other correspondence indicates there were many fruitless efforts on his part to chase what was already a diminishing market. With Harry Baughan in Stroud, Slater gave up on a lost cause.

man concern trying to build machines on a purely speculative basis that might appeal to the public, for with the best will in the world they were never going to be in any position to fulfil an order over two machines, and deliver within less than a week. The enquiry that came from Wanganui in New Zealand (page 48) may have given a glimmer of hope, but it was no more than that. So ended a small part of pioneering in motoring history that was perhaps, not a really serious attempt to try and convince the general public that their machine was

LEVIN & CO., LIMITED

MERCHANTS, WOOL BROKERS
AND HEMP BUYERS
SHIPPING, INSURANCE, STOCK
AND STATION AGENTS

TELEGRAPHIC ADDRESS: "LEVINS"

HEAD OFFICE: WELLINGTON.
BRANCHES: BLENHEIM, BULLS, FEILDING
FOXTON, HAWERA, MASTERTON, NELSON,
PICTON AND WANGANUI

AGENCIES:
MARTON, STRATFORD, TAIHAPE

AGENCIES.

SHIPPING—

SHAW SAVILL & ALBION COY., LTD.
ORIENT COMPANY (VIA SUEZ)
CANADIAN AUSTRALASIAN
MESSAGERIES MARITIMES CO.
AUSTRALIAN MAIL LINE

INSURANCE—

VICTORIA INSURANCE COY. LTD,
FIRE, MARINE, FIDELITY AND ACCI-
DENT UNDER THE EMPLOYERS' LIA-
BILITY, WORKERS' COMPENSATION
ACTS
AND PERSONAL ACCIDENT RISKS

MACHINERY—

LISTER ENGINES
LISTER SHEARING MACHINES
LISTER CREAM SEPARATORS
REID & GRAY FARM IMPLEMENTS
DONALD'S WOOLPRESS
SANDOW WOOLPRESS
TREALOAR MILKING MACHINES
FENCING MATERIALS

GENERAL—

HIGHLAND SHEEP DIP
COOPER'S SHEEP DIP
LITTLE'S SHEEP DIP
SUTTON'S SEEDS
FERTILISERS
GRASS AND CLOVER SEEDS
WOOL PACKS
CORN SACKS
FARMERS' REQUIREMENTS

WOOL STORE—

WOOL SALES HELD REGULARLY
THROUGHOUT THE SEASON
HIDE, SKIN AND TALLOW, SALES
HELD MONTHLY

P.O. Box 69

WANGANUI
NEW ZEALAND

19th May, 1924.

Messrs. Baughan Motors Ltd.,

Stroud,

ENGLAND.

Dear Sirs,

It has long been my intention to import to New Zealand a fast cheap sports car, and I am much interested in the description of the car you manufacture, given in the "Light Car and Cycle Car"

I have already written to the A.B.C. Motors Ltd., who offer me a 20% export discount to mitigate the exorbitant duty payable out here. (The duty on a £200 two seater car works out at approximately £45.) I much prefer your car (Stream-line Brooklands Shape), however, and in the event of your seeing your way to quoting me a reasonable export discount I will undoubtedly buy.

The car should be worth the discount to you as an advertisement out here, there being a big undeveloped market for such a car. Of course, I shall do all in my power to popularise it.

Yours sincerely,

Morgan Dun.an Esq.,

c/o Levin & Co. Ltd.,

WANGANUI.   New Zealand.

This letter gives an insight to the difficulties any manufacturer wishing to export to the southern hemisphere. Levin and Co were the agents for Lister equipment in New Zealand and would have been acquainted with the engineering products from Gloucestershire. This correspondence may have given a glimmer of hope for further sales, alas, nothing came of it.

Mather collection.

Many tests were undertaken on the Great North Road when the carburation was suspect. Once cured prospective buyers were taken for a high-speed run. If the present day ride is anything to go by they quickly changed their minds. Comfort was never its strong point, and the roads of the day . . . well!

reliable and would give years of faithful service, backed up by a comprehensive spares service. So Harry Baughan abandoned any more thoughts of building further examples and then set his sights on his original love, that of two and three wheels. This new direction was to be a much more successful venture and saw it continue for the best part of fourteen years.

The following January saw the last cyclecar built (No.4) No.D674. This for all practical purposes was not a true cyclecar, more in name only. This was for W Tuck the baker and confectioner located in King Street, Stroud. This machine was described as a special five seater goods carrier. The chassis was no different to all the previous models and used the same type 10hp, 60° sv V twin, air-cooled Blackburne engine. The body work only extended to behind the driver's position. From there to the tail it was just a flat bed. This was ideally suited for carrying hundredweight sacks of flour from the LMS station in Stroud the short journey to their premises. This machine proved a good workhorse for Tucks. The late Lionel Tuck, son of the owner did not have any recollection of it for his father was using it six years before he was born and it was never mentioned in family conversation. After the model was delivered to Tucks all thoughts of building cyclecars as a commercial venture were shelved and the serious business of making a day to day living became more important. The engineering expanded and Baughans gained a reputation for carrying out just about anything large or small. Soon local farmers brought their agricultural machinery in for repair, and if necessary make new parts. With all these many diverse activities

2-3 SEATER

WITH HOOD TO EXTEND OVER ALL 3 SEATS, SCREEN, ELECTRIC LAMPS, HORN, TOOLS.

£255 - 0 - 0

Baughan

MONOCAR 2 - SEATER

HOOD, SCREEN, HORN and TOOLS.

£222-10-0

BAUGHAN MOTORS, Tyburn Lane, HARROW.

The advert that appeared in the *Light Car and Cyclecar* of 1922. The price compared to other cyclecars of the period was on the high side. Eventually it was reduced to under £200, even then it was over-priced. Later HPB was forced to reduce it to £165.

that their engineering skill brought them the 'Gaffer' still retained his enthusiasm for sporting trials and in the years to come Harry Baughan, Chris Stagg and Bill Hayward became fully immersed in it. Harry Baughan's interest in sporting trials really captured his imagination when he read about one of the first cyclecar trials that was run in March of 1913, the most significant thing was the route, or at least a part of it. After leaving Oxford it headed due west to Winchcombe in Gloucestershire, this was the turning point, and from here it was to pass through countryside that made a lasting impression on him and in the years to come would be earmarked 'Baughan Country.' Birdlip followed after the lunch halt at Cheltenham and then south to take in the famous Nailsworth 'Ladder' one of the more notable climbs in the district. In those days the Ladder was used in its entire length and passed through a small farm at the very top of the section, then exited at the final bend of the equally famous 'W'. The Nailsworth Ladder was to become well known to HPB in the coming years as it did with any trials rider worth his or her salt.

Harry Baughan moves to Whitehall, Stroud. HPB working in almost
isolation. Employment of Chris Stagg and Bill Hayward. Difficult working conditions. Limited space for engineering. First motor cycles leave
Piccadilly Mill. Three machines built in 1923.

With the break from London final, Harry Baughan moved in with his parents
at Spring House, Slad, while he set up his business at Lower Street. He moved
twice more. When Charlie married he left the GWR and with his wife started a
business in general grocery at the northern end of Walls Quarry. Harry moved in
with them. When Charlie died Mrs. Baughan moved a few hundred yards down
into Brimscombe and there spent the remainder of her years with her brother-in-
law as companion. With the acquisition of his new premises and two employees
it was his responsibility to find the necessary work to keep everything solvent.
However, he was fortunate in one respect for Bill Hayward's father was the
transport manager for the Stroud Co-operative Society and was responsible for
the running of the vehicles.

Times have changed very little, even in those distant days it was still a question of not what you know, but who you know. With these commercials requiring regular service and maintenance this proved to be bread and butter for the
budding Baughan Motors and lasted for many years. In general terms Baughan
Motors could turn their hand to most things and in due course they expanded
into agriculture machinery, much to the delight of the local farming community
who found an outlet that could repair the most outdated of machinery, and even
manufacture a new part if required. All manner of vehicles were serviced and
often rebuilt. At times there was hardly any room to move on the ground floor
with its confined space. In order to allow his two employees to carry on their
work Harry Baughan often employed various people on a very casual basis to
come in and tidy up, also to help push the cars around. One person was Les
Hosier, who at a later date was proprietor of Chalford Motors. On one such
occasion he came in to help with the moving of the cars from inside the factory
to allow much needed working space.

In the process of all this pushing and shoving one of the cars ran over his foot
resulting in an injury that dogged him for the rest of his life; the outcome was
litigation and he received industrial compensation for his injury. Eventually he
teamed up with Jack Lewis and formed a partnership that went by the name of H
and L Motors at Cainscross. Soon it became a famous dealership in the west country for the leading motor cycle makes of the day. At one time they were reputed
to have built their own motor cycle with a Grigg engine but it seems this was
just a 'one-off.' Despite the day–to–day problems of running a business Harry
Baughan's enthusiasm for motor sport was still as keen as ever and his cyclecar
was often seen in local events run by the Stroud and District Motor Cycle Club.
This club was founded on June 1st, 1910, at the Royal George Hotel, Stroud.

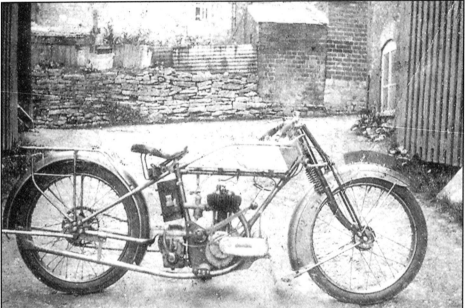

Top: Very early 500cc model with Blackburne engine. This featured a top tube which curved over the petrol tank. At the outset all Baughan machines featured front and rear drop stands, quite a rarity in those days. **Bottom**: This was the very first Baughan built, Bill Hayward being the customer. Straight through exhaust pipe was standard practice. The wall in the background remains hardly changed today. Piccadilly Mill is now divided into several small industrial units.

One of the early machines equipped with electric lighting, this may have been a photo of the first one as HPB usually made a point of photographing major changes to his motor cycles. Acetylene lighting was replaced after the eleventh machine was built. Photography was later undertaken by Edwin C Peckham FRPS at the County Studio, Stroud.

Present were Messrs, Browning, Burton, Derret, Eustace, Gardner, Ratcliffe, G Pavey Smith, F Smith, Dr. H Robertson (who incidentally delivered the author into this world at Stroud General Hospital), and finally Mr. Weaving. The annual fee was fixed at five shillings. Within less than a week the club was affiliated to the Auto Cycle Union and was duly inducted into the Western Centre. Like many new clubs of the day they were soon into competition, whether it was reliability runs, trials, or speed hill climbs. For others who lacked a sporting inclination there were social runs that helped bond the club together, so the members had quite a choice. This state of affairs lasted up until the first world war when hostilities broke out all activity ceased. In the four years that the club had been in existence the membership fee had increased to seven shillings and six pence. On February 23rd, 1920 the Annual General Meeting effectively saw it resurrected and continued on pre-war lines with reliability trials, social runs and speed events. Harry Baughan soon became their greatest stalwart, especially when it came to competition. The club ran two prime events, the Triumph Cup and the Marklove Cup Trials, the former was run on similar lines to that classic MCC event, the London to Edinburgh and was based on time and distance. The latter was a straight forward trial that catered for the more adventuresome motor cyclist who was sport minded and prepared to run his machine up many of the hills that surround Stroud. This gave a good grounding to the more strenuous events in the years that followed.

Both these events proved to be very popular with the club members, reliability trials invariably gave the clubman a run approaching the 120 mile mark and proved to be a very enjoyable event. The Triumph Cup ran at an average speed of 20 mph and the route was scattered with secret checks and passage controls both on the outward and return journeys. Baughan Motors went from strength to strength when Bill Hayward joined the company, certainly when Hayward's father brought the business from the Co-op which ensured steady, if not an over demanding work schedule as was the case in the 1920s. This contract covered the fleet of Morris vans and other associated vehicles. The Co-op also had a CWS–built Federation combination and Baughans were given the job of building a commercial box type sidecar for it. The initial thoughts on the proposed bikes was for normal utility machines that would give reliability, along with good handling based on sound engineering practice. The average working man was in a better position to buy a motor cycle than he ever was with a cyclecar, and as time passed he was more than vindicated in his judgement. Within less than a year Harry Baughan had established his name with motor cycles, progress may have been slow but his credentials were established.

With this decision taken Harry Baughan made the necessary contacts with the firms that could supply him with the parts he needed, the British Hub Company, both Sturmey Archer and Blackburne for the engines and possible gear boxes in the case of Sturmey Archer. Steel tube was required for the frame and Eccles and Pollock were the people with the best reputation at the time. This all took time and potential suppliers needed to satisfy themselves that they were dealing with a reputable company that from time to time might require extended credit. Once all these necessary formalities had been completed the serious business of designing motor cycles needed to be tackled, one thing, however, there was to be a sporting nature attached to the design once the factory had become established and its mark had been made. With the added security of the Co-op contract there were other sidecar related jobs that took up Baughan Motors time.

Hayward collection.

While researching in the Gloucestershire County Archive for the registrations of all the Baughan motor cycles various discrepancies came to light. According to the sales ledger (pages 325 to 336) many of the names do not tally with the proposed owners. On some occasions Baughan Motor Co, registered the machine for the new owner and is recorded as such. The ledger dates are questionable as are the years. Assuming chronological order the dates and years have been added by the author. (Some of the date entries in the ledger have been omitted.) The machine illustrated above was registered to Bill Hayward on Feburary 14th, 1927, but the sales ledger gives the month as January. Chris Stagg remarked that the new owners quite often went weeks, even months before they officially registered their new machine.

Bert Winstone who had not long started his ice cream business at Rodborough Common decided to have a float body built for his Matchless outfit. Not only was this type of work a steady income but also good advertising. A few builders at the time followed this principle of a float sidecar and proved to be far cheaper than any van at the time. So diverse was Baughans clientele they even serviced the James combination that belonged to Stroud's workhouse master and the local vicars Bugatti. Baughan Motors by 1926 had become a company that could turn its hand to most things. Motor cycle production was also well under way and some fourteen machines had left Lower Street by this time. All these were hand built by the combined efforts of Harry Baughan, Bill Hayward and Chris Stagg. Around this time the bulk of the motor cycle building was left to Chris and in the following years he was responsible for nearly 60% of all the machines that left the factory. Initially his job centred around the wheel building side of things and at first he found it a nightmare of a job.

"I learnt most of the skills from the Gaffer for he devised a jig that we could use for accurate building up of a wheel. In those days all the spokes had to be bent into shape so that they fitted into the hub and this proved to be the most troublesome of all. At first I found it the most difficult of all the jobs when it came to building the bikes, I went home at night with my fingers and thumbs bleeding only to come back the next day and start all over again." It took a while for Chris to master this technique and in the end the bloody fingers gave way to callouses and he finished up with true 'engineers hands' as he liked to call them. "At first I had the most terrible trouble but the Gaffer soon developed a method of cutting the spokes to a specific length and tapping on the threads that helped to cut down the wheel building time and in the end what had become such a chore soon developed into a fairly quick and accurate build."

The only things that Baughan Motors manufactured themselves were the engine and gear box plates along with the petrol and oil tanks. Sheet steel was bought in, mostly from a supplier in Gloucester, and on the odd occasions from Yate, just outside Bristol. The engines were either Sturmey Archer or Blackburne. With this standardization of motive power it took very little time to drill the necessary holes for the mountings. When building the machines all manner of short cuts were tried. Most were not as successful as they would have liked one that did prove to be very useful was a pattern that HPB designed for the drilling holes in the engine and gear box plates. From the engine and gearbox blue prints HPB made same size cut-out patterns in cardboard to allow easy positioning of the frame lugs.* This saved a lot of tedious measuring and marking out and it turned out to be quite a time saver. Mudguards, saddles, lighting equipment, magnetos, carburettors etc, were all supplied from the many subsidiary companies that made up the motor cycle industry. Like many other motor

* These are in the possession of Jan Seymore as are the original drawings.

Piccadilly Mill: circa 1925. The top floor was Bill Hayward's domain where he enamelled all the frames, dust was always a problem at Lower Street. Great trials riders passed through these doors. Anstice, Mansell, Williams, Foster, Povey, Brittain, and numerous ACU officials.

cycle factories Baughans followed the established practice of buying in parts from a booming support industry. The most difficult and time consuming part of building the motor cycles was that of the frame. Bill Hayward was responsible for most of the patterns that allowed the tubes to be bent into shape. The method used was to heat them up either from the coal fired hearth with a set of large bellows and build the fire bricks up accordingly to radiate the best possible heat. Once away from the hearth gas torches were used supplemented by very large capacity blow lamps that were bought in specifically for the purpose. (Incidentally, these lamps were still under the stairs at the Lansdown factory in the mid 1980s.) Chris remembers the problems. "The bending process was undertaken with the greatest care and every one involved found it to be a tedious and very time consuming process. The Gaffer was always insisting that nothing should be rushed. Time was not as important as it is today for all the bikes that were built it was always a leisurely affair. As far as Baughan Motors were concerned, product quality and reliability was uppermost in everyones mind. On some occasions it might take a month to finish one completely and this was the basis and understanding on which the customer placed an order. Sometimes I might build the wheels over two or three days and not touch anything for a week, then I moved onto drilling the engine plates or bending a few tubes and then brazing them up in the jig in preparation for the final de-greasing process before Bill took them for enamelling on the top floor." This slow, and at times painful process was the hall mark of Baughan Motors. The customer was always encouraged to pop in to the works to see the progress that was being made (or lack of it at times). One such purchaser was Austin Gardiner from Oakridge, who knew Chris Stagg and having been a motor cyclist for a number of years was invited by Chris to see what Baughans could offer. He was introduced to Harry and was duly impressed

Stagg collection.

Bill Peters on the left with his characteristic pipe at work on the hearth. The large capacity blow lamps supplemented the gas torch on many occasions. Peters was the man who discovered and named the famous hill, BB 1 and 2, eventually 3 was added but only featured once in the 1931 British Experts Trial.

with both him, the works, and just how much attention was given to the building of them. Over the years Austin rode all manner of machines and found them all fairly reliable. Austin relates the story of his purchase.

"At the time I was engaged in sub-contract building work and one of the jobs that was in the offing was the new Barclays Bank at Stow-on-the-Wold. For this I needed a reliable machine to get me from Oakridge to my place of work. So after my meeting with Mr. Baughan I was convinced that this was the machine for me." A week before he was due to start work at Stow he visited the works to see how the bike was going on. Much to his surprise it was still not finished for he wanted a day or two just to get used to it. "I was a little worried that I would have to ride my old machine for a week before I could collect the Baughan and with such an important job to be started I did not want to be late." Harry Baughan assured him it would be ready in time for him to start his new job, and so it proved. "I collected two days before the job at Stow started and I put a few miles on the clock. It really was a lovely machine, and I was delighted for it was the first one that I bought from new." But things turned out differently on the first journey to Stow. "I had just got to the other side of Cirencester when I picked up a puncture in the front tyre, by the time I had repaired it I was well over an hour late. After this hiccup I travelled every day for five months to the job and strange to relate coming home on the last day I picked up another front wheel puncture and that really was the only trouble I ever had with that Baughan." Austin Gardiner continued to use his machine (No.24) No.27/216 for a further ten years without any mechanical problems whatsoever. Finally, the frame cracked at the steering head lug, so back down to Baughans it went and within a couple of days Chris Stagg had repaired it. Gardiner ran it for a few more months and finally sold it on. "After that I lost touch with it, but it really was a lovely bike and was trouble free. It steered beau-

The 'Signal Box' which doubled as the office. Here many a trials route was planned on a Friday night. Enthusiastic games of shove-half-penny were also played after the plotting. In the foreground is a side-car with a down-turned nose which differs from the Hayward and Morris trials version. Chris Stagg built Hayward's, sub-contract labour often built others when needed such as builders 'Floats.'

Conditions were often very crowded on the ground floor. The cyclecar sitting on the beer crates might give today's Health and Safety inspector some cause for concern.

The famous steps leading from the ground floor to the upper workshop. It was on these that Chris Stagg bent nearly all the exhaust pipes for the early motor cycles. Eventually HPB designed a former to allow easier bending of the pipes and less chance of setting fire to the long suffering stairs.

The upper workshop floor where all the light assembly took place. All the body work for repairing cars and sidecars passed through here. A cyclecar is in the centre, sans wheels and with the engine in situ. In the right hand background a different chassis/body under construction. With such a large amount of space on the upper floors, many motor cycle frames were stored along with sundry items awaiting attention. Far different to the ground floor where available space was at a premium. The Red Car has a Baughan banner draped over the nose, sans engine. The one in the middle is another cyclecar, this time it has a full width windscreen and is powered by a V twin, sv, air-cooled, Blackburne. This is possibly the one that Tuck the confectioner bought to move flour from Stroud LMS railway station.

tifully and always gathered a number of people who were interested whenever I stopped outside the district. Harry Baughan and the lads certainly knew how to make bikes!" Two more of Austin Gardiner's brothers bought Baughan motor cycles (No.25 and 30) No.27/218 and No.28/223. One thing that Baughans did make was the petrol and oil tanks. Bill Hayward took on this task along with Harry Baughan. The various parts of the tank were soldered together after they had been formed on the fly press. This took considerable time and skill, eventually Chris was brought in to help with this very delicate task. Harry Baughan's philosophy was that everyone should be capable of doing every other persons job and at every opportunity he made sure this was carried out; if called upon all three of them could build up a machine from scratch, and complete it within a fortnight, and frequently did.

There was one area, however, that neither Chris nor Bill touched, and this was the painting of the petrol tanks. The standard colour scheme of all the Baughan motor cycles was black. The only colour that graced the machines was gold and this was applied to the outline of the fuel tank along with the Baughan logo (which appears inside the title page) was also in gold. Harry Baughan had such a steady hand and a complete flair for painting these gold outlines that every tank passed through Harry's hands (shades of his artistic brother). When Bill Hayward bought a pram for his first child (Edwin) the Gaffer thought that it needed a touch of colour to liven it up, so he set to and outlined it in silver. Chris remembers it well. "The Gaffer could outline a tank in one complete movement and he had a good eye for detail that the job was completed in just a few minutes and when it came to Bill's pram he was delighted with the result, and when he was on petrol tanks the Gaffer had them done in an instant he was that clever." All the small materials that Baughan Motors required were delivered to Lower Street. Engines from Sturmey Archer and latterly Blackburne along with gearboxes from Burman, were delivered by rail to the LMS goods siding at Wallbridge and were held there for collection.

With such a splendid railway network in the 1920s and 1930s it was only a matter of a few days before parts arrived and with the leisurely build rate at Baughans they were never waiting for bits like magnetos or hubs to arrive. On many occasions when parts were to be collected, Chris Stagg would pop down on his bike and bring back the necessary items. The LMS siding had a variety of other companies such as British Petroleum and Shell Mex. All these small support firms gave good service to local companies in the motor trade and nothing was too unreasonable to ask for, or order. Both BP and Shell supplied racing versions of their oils as did Castrol with their famous 'R.' If required a gallon of racing oil ordered on say a Monday morning, by late afternoon on the Tuesday it was at the depot awaiting collection. The one thing in Baughans favour was the

JM Baughan collection.

The ground floor where the majority of the engineering took place. At times it was so crowded that many vehicles had to be shunted around to find enough working space, some had to be pushed outside. It was on occasions like this when accidents occurred, Hosier was one unfortunate person.

JM Baughan collection.

The upper floor. From the ceiling joists hang numerous frames along with chain cases, crankcases and sundry chains. The body on the left remains unidentified, the shape is not in keeping for a cyclecar. Many of the frames hung up came from other machines in for repair.

Austin Gardiner astride his brand new 350cc sv, Blackburne Baughan. His niece sits on the special carrier that was designed to carry his building tools. Gardiner had many years of faithful service from it, his two other brothers were also Baughan riders and were delighted with their machines.

slow build rate of their machines, it was never a production based system in the true sense of the word, when a customer ordered a bike it was on the understanding 'oh give us a month and we will see how we are.' That was the nice part of Baughan Motors, plenty of time to give the customer the best possible machine for his money. With this very relaxed attitude towards them Harry Baughan built up a reputation for honesty and fair dealing, the potential buyer was given every opportunity to make his mind up as to just what he wanted on his motor cycle.

For a general work–a–day machine the customer was encouraged to visit the works to see the progress that they were making on his bike and many additional features were incorporated at the last minute to satisfy him. The Stroud Boot Company was one such buyer and the specification they required was for foot boards instead of the usual foot rests. Baughans had them cast-up in aluminium and this one feature displayed on this model (No.12) No.25/203 was that they were highly polished and as the outfit slowly showed signs of general wear

Authors collection.

Stagg collection.

Gladys Cottle, later to become Chris Stagg's wife astride her 250cc fore and aft Douglas. A keen motor cyclist all her life, their sons were imbued with the same enthusiasm.

and tear, the foot boards remained totally immaculate having being polished to perfection by the rider. This machine was the first combination that Baughans built and was of conventional design with a sidecar chassis bolted on to a solo frame as was their practice at the time. This featured a rectangular float sidecar completely finished in the usual Baughan black with the outlining completed in the usual gold by the Gaffer. This combination pre-dates their famous sidecar-wheel drive by five years.

Around the middle of the 1920s Baughan Motors saw the appearance of identical twin sisters. This came about through Geoff Fisher as the sisters were members of Amberley and Minchinhampton Church choir. As Fisher attended both churches and was a keen motor cyclist they asked where they could get their Enfield combination looked at. Fisher reccommended Mr. Baughan. He diagnosed out of true flywheels. Within days they were motoring again. Both were very taken by all the activity at Lower St, especially trials. Parental approval was sought for further interest. Geoff Fisher was contacted and his standing in the community was enough for the matriarch and approval was given. So the Grant Heelas sisters, Marjorie Ouriol and Auriol Marjorie later became a very important part of the Baughan Motors Company.

Authors collection.

This second picture of Austin Gardiner shows a very happy owner on his brand new motor cycle. Austin said he was so delighted that he had to put on his best suit in which to be photographed. The registration log in the Gloucestershire County Archive gives a date of July 23rd, 1926. The Baughan sales ledger is at variance stating May 17th, 1927. Some years are missing in the ledger, I leave the reader to draw their own conclusions.

Manufacturer: BAUGHAN MOTORS, Lower Street, Stroud, Glos.
Telegraphic Address: "Baughan, Stroud."

B3 BAUGHAN BRITISH

Suggested Additions and Improvements are Welcomed —Editor

1925 Specification.	Model, Super Sports	Model, Standard.
First Chassis No. 1925	25—300. On Bevel box	25—300. On Bevel box.
Makers' H.P. and T.R.	10 H.P. Tr. Rat 8.7 I.P.S. Rat. 8.88	8 H.P. Tr. Rat. 8.7 I.P.S. Rat. 6.24
Tax—Inland Revenue	£9 p.a. or £2 9s. 6d. per qtr.	£9 p.a. or £2 9s. 6d. per qtr.
Bore and Stroke	85 × 97mm. 1100.8cc.	85 × 88mm. 998cc.
Make of Engine	Blackburne. Overhead valves	Blackburne. Side valves
Cylinders & Cooling System	Overhead valves	Air
Lubrication System	2. Separate. Det. bds. Thermo Syphon	2. Separate. Det. bds. Air
Induction Manifold	Splash. Oil. Price's "A".	Splash. Oil, Price's "A"
Ignition	Own. Vert. Grav. Tank 4 gls.	Own. Vert. Grav. Tank, 4 gls.
Lighting and Starting	Between cylinders. Int. diam., 1-1/8"	Between cylinders. Inter. diam. 1-1/8"
Clutch	B.T.H. Mag. 45mm. Clock. Base	B.T.H. Mag. 45mm. Clock. Base
Make of Gear Box	Ltg. B.T.H. 6v. 60a.h. 3 S.P. lamps	Ltg. B.T.H. 6v. 60a.h. 3 S.P. lamps
Gear Ratios	Dry Plate (Stg. Mechanical	Dry Plate (Stg., Mechanical
Position of Gear & Brk. Lvn.	Sturmey Archer. 3 & R. Sep. unit	Sturmey Archer. 3 & R. Sep. unit
Type of Steering Gear	4.5; 8.17; 14.0; Rev. 20.0 to 1	4.5; 8.17; 14.0; Rev. 20.0 to 1
Type of Rear Wheel Brakes	Right hand side	Right hand side
Diameter & Width of Drums	Geared or direct	Geared or direct
Lining Sizes & No. per Drum	Expanding shoes	Expanding Shoes
Rear Wheel Brakes opr. by	8 × 1¼"	8 × 1¼"
Type of Transmission Brakes	16 × 1 × 1/8". Ferodo. 4 per drum	16 × 1 × 1/8". Ferodo. 4 per drum
Diameter & Width of Drum	1 pair by Hand. 1 pair by Foot	1 pair by Hand. 1 pair by Foot
Lining Sizes & No. per Drum	None fitted	None fitted
Transmission Brake opr. by		
Type of Front Wheel Brakes	None fitted	None fitted
Diameter & Width of Drum		
Lining Sizes & No. per Drum		
Front Wheel Brakes opr. by		
Type of Rear Axle & Drive	Own. Semi-floating. Shaft & Chain	Own. Semi-floating. Shaft & Chain
Drive & Torque taken by	Drive, Rad. Rods. Torque, Springs	Drive, Rad. Rods. Torque, Springs
Overall Length & Width	11' 0" and 4' 0".	10' 9" and 4' 0".
Wheelbase & Track	7' 8"; 3' 6"; Clearance 7"	7' 8"; 3' 6"; Clearance 7"
Rear Dash to End of Frame	6' 2"	6' 2"
Rear Dash to C.L. Rear Axle	4' 2"	4' 2"
Width of Frame	At Dash 2' 4"; Widest part 2' 4"	At Dash 2' 4"; Widest part 2' 4"
Dash to Rear of Rr. Wheel	11"	11"
Frame to under Str. Wheel	11"	11"
Diameter of Steering Wheel	16"	16"
Make, Type & Size of Whls.	Own. Det. Wire. 700 × 80mm.	Own. Det. Wire. 700 × 80mm.
Type of Springs	Front, ¼ Ellip. Rear, ¼ Ellip.	Front, ¼ Ellip. Rear, ¼ Ellip.
Std. Colours & Upholstery	Col. Aluminium. Uphol., Lthr. Cloth	Col. To choice. Uphol., Lthr. cloth
Prices and Weights	Chassis not sold. 2-Str. £190, 6 cwt.	2-Str. £130, 6 cwt.

Range of motor cycles. Problems with manufacture. Selection of original plans. Hayward introduces the Heelas twins to technical drawing. Machine and engine prices. Customer satisfaction.

With the increasing work that was finding its way to Lower Street in general engineering terms, Harry needed to concentrate on this rather than the more spasmodic building of motor cycles. One thing that HPB did change was the motor cycle frame jigs. Now that Bill was drawing accurate plans, things needed to change. He and Harry spent many hours together planning this important aspect. In the past when it came to building the cyclecars plans were not such a high priority. In actual fact none was thought to exist until unearthed by Jan Seymore in the late 1980s when he worked for Baughan Engineers (Stroud) Ltd. The original jigs for the motor cycle were made of wood which were not entirely satisfactory. Between them they designed metal ones which could be adjusted and ensured a more accurate build . . . and quicker. Despite Harry Baughan's incisive mind, this alone would give little comfort when it came to building future motor cycles, so Bill set about the task and with support from HPB working drawings were produced that would allow a degree of repeatability if future sales warranted. According to Chris the Gaffer had made enquiries to the various manufacturers of the support industry that would be able to supply Baughan Motors, for in essence they would account for almost 95% of the completed machines. Without this vital link the whole undertaking would be doomed to failure. Nevertheless, both men were keen motor cyclists, and whenever there was a slack period serious discussions took place as to the viability of expanding the motor cycle range.

Harry Baughan had the previous experience with the cyclecars to call on, perhaps not with the sales and marketing side for he had left this with Freddie Slater to cope with. Bill Hayward with his pure engineering background was quite aware of the commitment that would be required in engineering terms if they were to become seriously involved with the building of motor cycles. Harry Baughan had already made enquiries as to the availability of the various parts that would be required from the many and varied suppliers. They all knew they would not be in the same league as Norton or Triumph, nor did they wish to be. First they would build a prototype and then be in a better position to understand the costs involved and the many problems that they were sure to encounter. Despite their enthusiasm they had precious little knowledge of the time scale involved for a complete build. Harry Baughan certainly had his work cut out with the first few machines for he was virtually working alone, Alroyd Lees gave him a hand but he seems a somewhat shadowy figure who put in an appearance when he felt the need. Both Chris and Bill later said that even they were unsure if he had any engineering background. However, they were quite prepared to make the odd

The first Baughan 350cc ohv, Blackburne with outside flywheel and tapered push rods, a feature that identified their engines for years. The straight through exhaust pipe caused a few problems with the local constabulary at the time. Silencers were fitted later.

The early models featured a combined petrol and oil tank which was placed within the frame which was looped over it. Petrol and oil tanks for all models produced were made by Baughan Motors.

mistake along the way and they were never under any commitment to build to a time scale for by mutual agreement the first motor cycle to be produced would be purchased by Bill and if this was successful HPB agreed to proceed further. The hubs came from the British Hub Company, with engines from Sturmey Archer and latterly Blackburne with Burman supplying the gear boxes. Lighting was the same. This came from Miller when they changed over from Powell and Hanmer Ltd. Acetylene equipped the first eleven machines. Rims, were also

Chris Stagg started his involvement with building motor cycles with this type 1923/4 350 sv Blackburne with outside flywheel. The expansion box/silencer was positioned in front of the crankcases. This photo may have been the first serious production model that left Lower St. These photos are from the original letter press printing plates that belonged to Chris Stagg.

A 1924 2.75hp sv Blackburne engine Baughan. This model was one of the first with the gear change mounted on the petrol tank, a far better arrangement than the one above. Acetylene lighting in use with the carbide canister carried under the seat. The new frame does not run over the petrol tank.

bought in as were chains along with a selection of nuts, bolts and washers and long wire for the spokes; mudguards were also out sourced. Spokes were not as today's, all pre-bent and with the required threads and nipples attached. Later spokes were bought in which were complete for assembly. Chris had to apply all these extras to the straight wire and the lengthy process began on bending each one, then tapping the thread on where it passed through the rim. The early rims were beaded edge, later to be replaced with the well base type. What Baughans

Mather collection.

Little has changed since this photo was taken. If Allan Jefferies was still around he would recognize it immediately.

did manufacture were the petrol and oil tanks in aluminum, plus the engine plates in quarter inch sheet steel. Chris remembered the problems he encountered when building up a wheel. "The rim and hub was placed in a jig and then I cut the spokes to approximately the right length, then threaded through the eyes in the hub after being bent at 90° then passed through the rim. Once I had found the first one to be right I went on to cut the remainder. My thumbs and fingers were often bleeding at the end of the day and this was a very tiresome and time consuming job." HPB designed a wheel building rig that allowed a complete wheel to be threaded up. This proved to be a great boon and allowed Chris to lace up a wheel with great accuracy.

Wheel building for Chris was always a chore and the time involved was considerable, not only for new bikes that they built but for repairs that were always waiting to be completed, having been brought in by riders who seemed to find every pot hole in the district. If the time spent on fiddly wheel building was not enough then bending exhaust pipes proved to be even harder, these were always difficult; most of the Baughan models featured two. This was certainly true of the sports and trials machines so the job was doubly difficult for although there existed jigs for the frames nothing was available for these pipes in the early days, so they improvised. "The first thing that I did was to fill the pipe with sand then it was heated up in the forge" said Chris. "Then taking the pipe to the short stairs that led to a raised floor, I used this as a primitive jig and bent the pipe into shape and all the while trying to keep the sand inside to help with the bending process." Eventually HPB made up a former to assist in this bending process and a lot of the difficulties were overcome. This also reduced the fire risk to the long suffering stairs. One essential item was a well thought out jig which was something that had been lacking when HPB made his first attempt with the cyclecar and to make any serious progress with machine building this was soon undertaken. This first one was of wooden construction (later replaced by a metal one) with metal inserts that

A 1929 model with a 500cc Blackburne with parallel push rods. The engine was part stressed member as the frame finished at the lower front crankcase, then continued behind the rear engine plates. This particular engine was canted back a few degrees. Electric lighting now replaced the acetylene.

Webb forks had replaced the Druids. Eventually all their models used Webb, they proved excellent when it came to competition, especially when used on Hayward's swd. This engine used the less common parallel push rods. Fully enclosed primary chain case is fitted. This was a standard feature on all models. The only ones that differed were the swd for Hayward and Morris and were covered by a guard.

allowed a degree of adjustment when necessary. Bill made the patterns from his drawings that would allow any person to check the accuracy of alignment at any stage of construction. Both men knew that to make motor cycles successfully, and at a reasonably competitive cost, would involve some serious thinking and planning at the outset. These first attempts gave them a valuable insight to not only the difficulties involved, but also their own shortcomings. There was never

These are the original drawings from the factory. Bill Hayward was the originator for the majority of them. Eventually he taught the Heelas sisters the art of technical drawing and many of the later ones were theirs. Auriol showed the greatest flair for this work, many were just signed 'Heelas' so as to avoid any confusion. This also applied to trials when they were joint secretaries of the event.

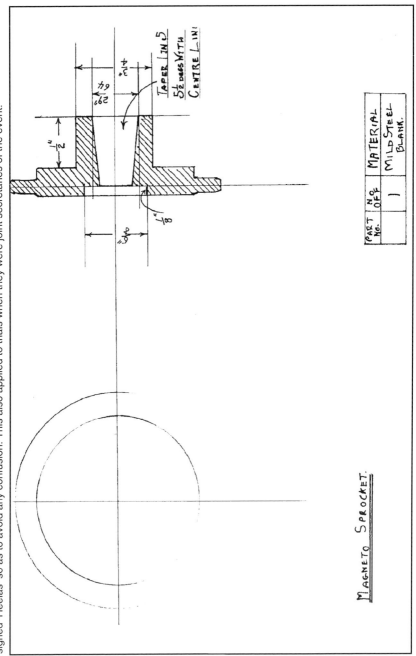

MAGNETO SPROCKET.

PART NO.	NO. OFF	MATERIAL
	1	MILD STEEL BLANK.

Yan Seymore collection.

any attempt at promoting this side of the business at such an early stage for even if they were successful the same old problem of building sufficient bikes in a short time span with very limited resources would always be there, so the first machine was kept very quiet. As Bill Hayward was the first purchaser in the true sense of the word, it was duly entered in the sales ledger and this practice continued right through until the last machine was built in 1936. Chris Stagg thought he had this last machine.* The sales ledger tells a different story placing it third from last. The final purchase of a Baughan motor cycle went to Mr. Cartwright, the number being (No.64) 36/257, three weeks after Chris took charge of his.

Although the sales ledger is accurate for recording the machines that were sold it does not take into account those that came back to the factory and were subsequently recycled in some shape or form. For example, one machine was brought back to the factory and was left for quite a while and Chris remembers there was some damage to the front forks. But he was not clear who the original owner was, or more importantly did it still belong to him? Eventually the Gaffer sanctioned its release and Chris set about modifying it for grass track racing. Some of these Baughan bikes had been returned and were taken in as part-exchange for other machines that Baughan Motors had acquired from time to time and very often they were stored at the factory for several months while they awaited new owners. Some changed totally from road going to competition. Sidecars were often fitted when required by a customer who was looking for a second-hand machine. Others were just in for repair. At one time there were several machines at Lower Street that were sold on with the consent of their owners. The one endearing feature of Baughan Motors was this very laid back attitude to the building of their motor cycles.

There was never any attempt at building a production batch, after discussing what specification he wanted, the customer placed an order and the build started almost immediately. For every machine that left Lower Street it was carefully hand crafted and hardly any consideration was given as to its cost effectiveness over the amount of time this construction took, a policy that was to last until the final machine was built. At times the building of motor cycles during this early period was almost bordering on a hobby from Harry Baughan's point of view. The frequency of building at Lower Street in the early years was hardly startling. Wise in some ways for the spectre of trying to build a batch of motor cycles in a very short period of time if the need arose was always in the back of HPBs mind, and admitted as much to his employees. Some machines that had been ordered were never picked up by their prospective owners, whether this was due to circumstances at the time (possibly financial) or simply a change of heart by the customer. Certainly a number of purchases were often a little ambitious on behalf of the customer when placed with Baughan Motors for they may

*This was before the sales ledger was discovered by Graham Stagg. This valuable document was in a very poor state suffering badly from dry rot, but readable nevertheless. For the full inventory of motor cycles built see pages 325 to 336.

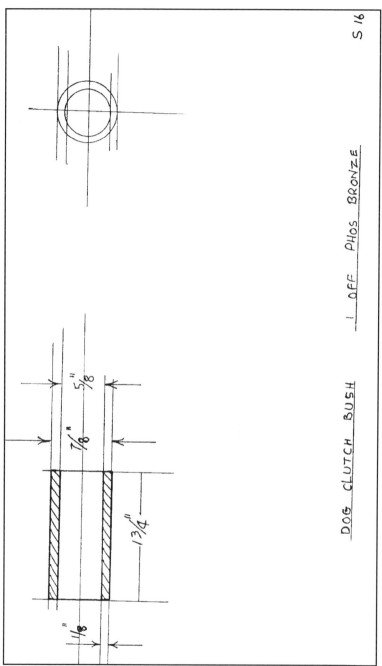

S 16

1 OFF PHOS BRONZE

DOG CLUTCH BUSH

$5/8''$

$7/8''$

$1 3/4''$

$1/8''$

Yan Seymore collection.

not have been fully prepared for the finances involved. I will leave the reader to draw their own conclusions on machines (No.14) 25/205 and (No.16) 25/207 on pages 327 and 328. At times deposits were not paid and a few potential customers backed out. Baughans at the time were like most manufacturers and offered a number of flexible hire purchase terms to their customers. The period from 1924 to 1925 was the busiest for bike building when eight machines were produced which saw the enhancement of Baughan Motors reputation through the competition riding of both Bill Hayward and Harry Baughan, followed later by Chris Stagg. There is very little known about these early machines. The very first model was officially ordered in August of 1923 and was not completed until the latter part of October. It was rather fitting that Bill should be the first purchaser of a Baughan motor cycle for within a few years his name would be inextricably linked with the marque when competing with the combination. So (No.5) MC24/196 emerged from Lower Street, with a two and three quarter horse power Blackburne sv with an engine number DC1115 and frame number 24196. From this first effort Harry Baughan had fulfilled an ambition and a new name in motor cycles had been established. The beginning may not have been very auspicious but was to lead to greater coverage through competition as the years passed. Chris Stagg came on the scene just when the tenth machine was being built. As a young apprentice he was guided completely by the Gaffer, even so, HPB had just the experience of the previous machines to call on and some of the shortcomings and bad practices were passed on to Chris and eventually as his experience grew he found his own method of building and this he gradually perfected.

These practices were perhaps not as bad as they were made out for initially there were some mistakes made and when Chris offered suggestions as to how, in his opinion things could be improved they were readily accepted by both Harry, and latterly Bill. Conditions were primitive at Lower Street in the mid 1920s and the working conditions left much to be desired and building motor cycles in these circumstances became more of a chore than perhaps related to good engineering practice. Gradually things improved, the bad habits were eliminated with a little bit of applied lateral thinking on Harry Baughan's part and as he was primarily responsible for the end product, he was keen to see the machines built to as high a standard as possible. Chris Stagg recalls that HPB was never overbearing in his attitude towards himself, Bill, or anybody else for that matter. He was always a good listener and amenable to suggestions that might improve the product no matter how trivial it would seem. To many outsiders Harry Baughan's countenance was somewhat dour and perhaps discouraged people from making conversation with him, if the talk was about motor cycles his attitude brightened considerably. Local people viewed him as slightly eccentric;

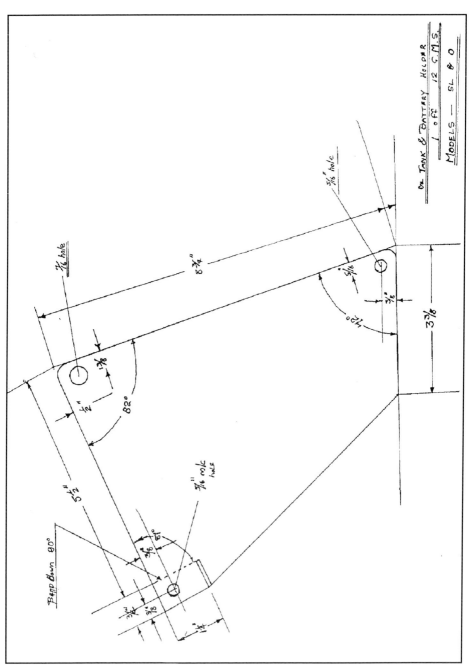

Yan Seymore collection.

keen motor cyclists knew him differently. The factory at Lower Street was not conducive to good building practices and with the very crowded ground floor made it difficult at times to even contemplate building a motor cycle. All the engineering machinery was sited on this level, when a complete frame had been finished it was taken outside and hauled up to the top floor on a pulley arrangement that had existed from the previous occupiers, Lewis and Godfrey. They used this when they wanted to store their furniture. Here Bill Hayward got on with the enamelling. This top floor was kept exclusively for Bill's use and great efforts were made to keep it dust free as conditions would allow. This he managed with some success and produced a finished frame to the best of his ability under the circumstances. Chris again: "With most of the bending and heating process taking place on the ground floor things had to be carefully planned to allow enough space just to walk around with the frame tubes and then start all the cutting and bending. The light machining was being undertaken in a quiet part of the ground floor and this required very little space to move about in but when it came to bending the frame tubes we usually had to clear some space in which to work. All the lugs were shaped by the Gaffer who did most of the brazing and Bill helped out when required. When the tubes came in they were cut and mitred and then rounded out to fit the end of the lug. One thing, you could never cut the tubes off square, you always made it fit the lug to avoid any possible breakages, the Gaffer always insisted on this.

"If the tube was left square there was always a chance that it would break in that corner and they were all mitred to stop that. Then some of the top tubes were bent. These were on the early bikes because the frame was one inch diameter tube (later to increase to 1.5 inches) and the engine was part of the frame. It did not have a full cradle frame like a lot of them did at the time. Ours had edging plates, later models had this left out. Then there was the saddle tank over the top, that was when you had the tank running in between the frame. We made our own tanks, the early models were soldered, the later saddle tanks were brazed. Bill at the outset did all the brazing on the tanks and later on took over the enamelling as well. But as I progressed I took on a few more jobs like that. I took over the wheel building completely. Brazing up the frames, that was the main frame then the seat stays that came down from the saddle, also the chain stays that carried the gear box and were all bolted up together. We could all do each others jobs eventually and that's how the firm continued throughout its life really, no one would specialize in any one job. You had to do any job. In the end I finished up the brazer and eventually the welder." The ground floor comprised of concrete but there was also a second floor level some four feet above this, several wooden steps bridging the gap. These steps proved to be highly convenient when it came to bending these exhaust pipes. Local heat was applied and Chris wrapped the

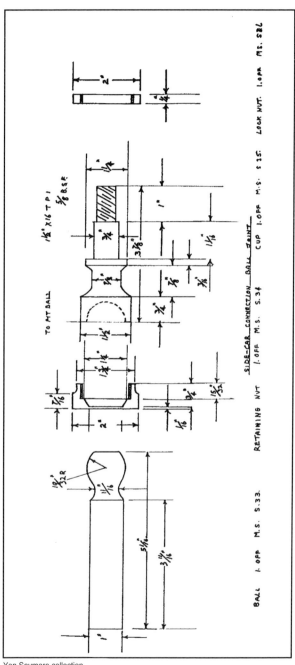

Yan Seymore collection.

pipe in damp rags and then used these steps to bend the pipes into the required shape. He found this to be one of the most difficult of all the jobs connected with the bike building and he never found an easy way around it nearly every pipe that was fitted to a Baughan was bent in this fashion. Chris explains further. "Building the wheels at first was difficult enough and until the Gaffer gave it some thought and came up with an easier solution, this compared to pipe bending, was less taxing.

"When I did those exhaust pipes you really had a job on your hands, The combination of ramming the sand down and then heating the areas you wanted to bend was a thankless job. I had a gas torch but the Gaffer had several large blow lamps that could be used to give extra heat and this helped a lot. In the end we made up a former and this made the bending more accurate. The heating took quite a while and then you had to juggle this hot pipe in between the stairs and then start bending it. Quite often the wooden stairs started to smoke but they never actually caught fire; this was a job I always tried to put off until the last moment."

This part of the building was never easy and as every customer had his own ideas as to just what type of bend he wanted on his pipe, nearly everyone was different so they could not make up a batch that would be suitable for several machines. Of all the jobs connected with building the bikes, this was the most detested and Chris remembers that Bill would avoid getting involved at all costs, as did the Gaffer, they soon cottoned on how difficult it was. By contrast the tubing supplied by Eccles and Pollock was not quite so difficult to work and the amount of bending involved was limited. The lugs were designed and manufactured by Baughans initially, then bought in from Brompton. The tubes that fitted into them all had a fine degree of mitre, followed by drilling through both lug and tube allowing a pin to be inserted and hence allowing a more secure fitting. Brazing used just ordinary borax as a flux and this proved to be quite satisfactory and hardly ever gave a moments trouble. After all the brazing was finished all the joints were given a thorough cleaning with petrol after being wire brushed and rubbed down with fine emery cloth.

The forks were bought in from Druid and came fully finished ready for assembly. Baughans favoured this make and found them sufficient for their purposes, only later did they use the product from Webbs. The customer was never influenced in their choice of front forks but were always aware of just what Bill and Chris used on their machines. It was pointed out to the customer in later years that in competition both men preferred the Webb type and invariably the customer followed suit. Chris felt they had greater rigidity; certainly Bill found them ideal for sidecar work when he moved on to three wheels. Magnetos were a headache in the early days. HPB built a test rig to check them for many were

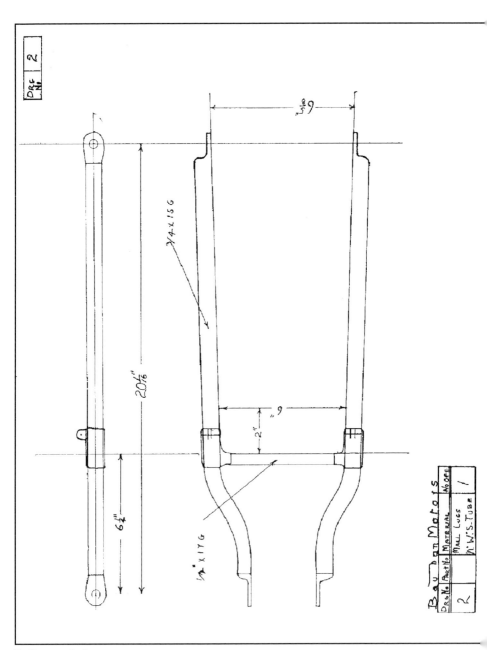

delivered faulty. This saved time and possible embarrassment for it was not unknown for a new customer to travel half a mile only for the mag to die. Fred Halliday recalls that the Gaffer ran the rig from the overhead belting and the test would be spread over several days. The early machines favoured a more conventional touring design and only later did Baughans opt for a more sporting version of their machines. Most customers when making their choice of engines nearly always insisted that sporting cams should be fitted, when ordered either from Blackburne or Sturmey Archer. Initially Baughans fitted Sturmey Archer engines and were slightly cheaper than Blackburne, the former lacked a little in performance and when tuned to any degree became a little less reliable than those produced at Bookham. Blackburnes offered various combinations of piston and cylinder heads at a small increase in price, HPB felt that SA did not have the depth of knowledge that Blackburnes had acquired through their engine development, both at the Isle-of-Man TT races, and much more closer to home at Brooklands where a great deal of testing was undertaken by selected riders. (One such contracted racer was Wal Handley.) On all the Baughan bikes was Harry's trade mark, that of lining the gold on the petrol tanks. He had a very steady hand and a flair for it and everyone was done by HPB. Four coats of paint plus the primer was the norm for the fittings. There was a different type of enamel for the wheels as there was a chance of distortion if they were subjected to too much heat in their treatment.* Up until 1925/6 the beaded edge was used and soon after the well based fitting became the standard. Working at Baughans was not without incident in these formative years and Chris clearly remembers one of these occurrences.

"A regular visitor to Lower Street, in those days was a certain 'Speedy' Jones who was employed at Moor Court Hotel, Rodborough Common. He was quite a character and one day he brought his 1927 AJS in for repair. While the bike was being tested a worn spark plug shot out of the cylinder head and punched a hole in the petrol tank which promptly burst into flames and finished up in many pieces on the floor when all the soldered joints melted. Though the fire was not too serious poor old Speedy was very upset and in the end I had to make a new tank for him."

Dudbridges, the Stroud accountants, also used a Baughan for its dispatch work and was regularly serviced at Lower Street. Baughans offered various options on their machines, leg shields, pillion seat, centre stand and a carrier on the back and was one of the first manufacturers to include front and rear drop stands. The most popular machine was the 350cc ohv fitted with a Blackburne. Baughan Motors policy was the customer should have just what he wanted and they went to great lengths to satisfy him. This care and consideration extended long after the bike was bought and customer relations at Lower Street was al-

*Wheel rims were eventually sub-contracted for this process.

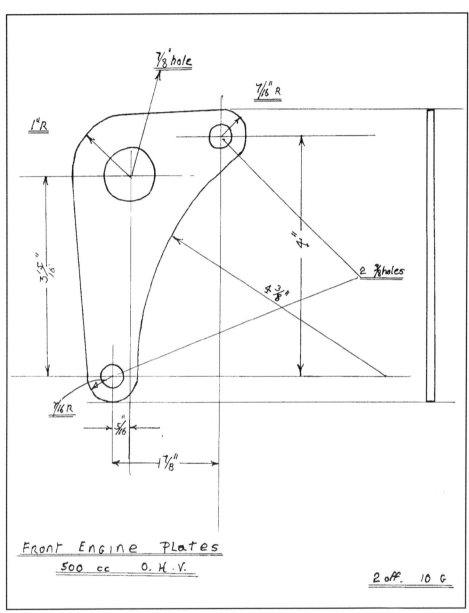

Front Engine Plates
500 cc O.H.V.

2 off. 10 G

Yan Seymore collection.

ways paramount. All the work on the machines was undertaken by hand. Lugs were cleaned out, brazing also. Frames were all polished up before the priming process was started. Drilling and pinning was all undertaken whilst in the jig. Chris says that only about two other people were helping out on a part time basis. The working hours varied and it was common practice to work until eight or nine o'clock in the evening before he left for home. This happened when a machine was required for a customer, and also very early mornings was a regular practice. All these extra hours was expected of not only him but Bill as well and these additional hours went largely unpaid. In fact he said he enjoyed working that late especially if he was building up a bike. Very occasionally parts were not delivered on time due to a delay by the suppliers leading to inevitable delays. On other occasions problems within the factory caused them to stop work. At that time Baughan Motors serviced all types of vehicles including commercials and this took priority over the bikes on rare occasions. If a bike was urgently required for a customer then Chris worked late into the night, or even all night if things were really desperate. If everything was to hand then a complete bike could be built up in 24 hours. (This was assuming that everything was completed, frame finished along with wheels and mudguards etc, and a straightforward assembly job could indeed be completed within less than a day.) AMAC controls also proved to be quite a time consuming task when making up the cables for the throttle, mixture, advance and retard. All the controls were bought in but the fitting took a big part of the building time. A week would often see the machine finished.

The frame tubes took the best part of a day to cut, mitre, bend and drill so that everything fitted and later serious efforts were made to cut down the build time. The drilling of the tubes took a large proportion of this. There were no electric drills in those days and these operations were carried out using either a hand drill or a brace. Eccles and Pollock supplied the tubes and the early machines used 1 inch diameter, later increased to 1 and 1/8th inch. Chris placed a liner in the down tube that was tapered and was careful to avoid sharp edges. On occasions the quality of the steel was a little suspect and in their early days a number of frames suffered breakages as a result, so they inserted this liner to help strengthen the joint. The one and a half inch outside diameter tube received this tapered insert and was brazed into position before the lugs were attached. When the frame was in the jig it was almost a day's work to carry out the brazing as time was required for the joints to cool naturally. This method was by far the best in the long term and gave added life to the machine. With the new metal jigs with their fine adjustments, it was a far simpler job to line-up the various lugs before brazing was started. This was a big advancement from the earlier wooden types. Baughans took great care to ensure that everything was positioned correctly

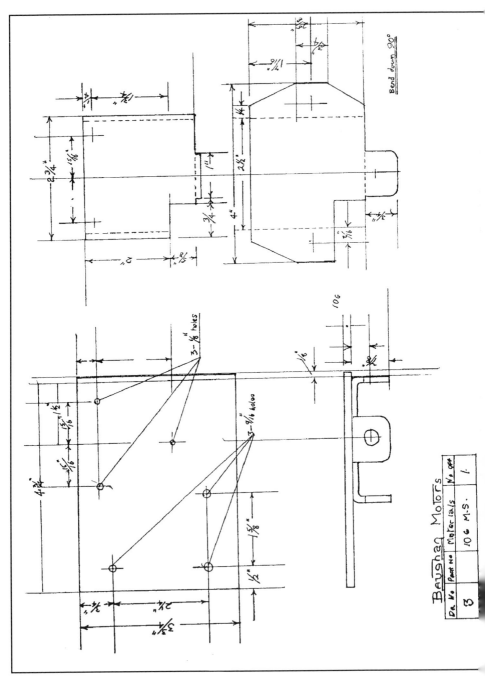

Yan Seymore collection.

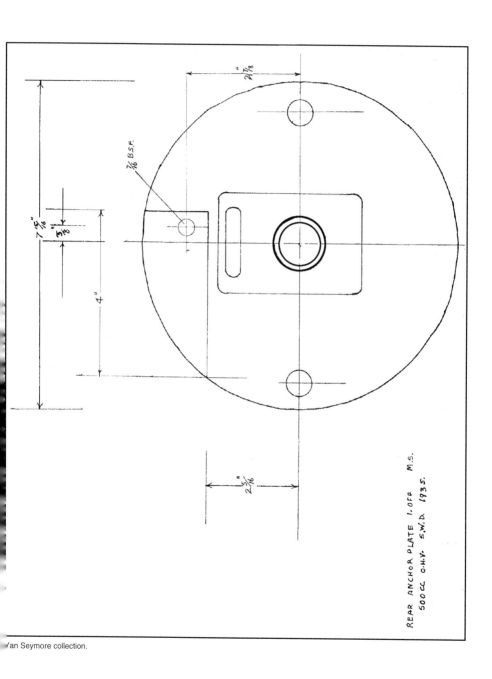

REAR ANCHOR PLATE 1. OFF   M.S.
500 cc O.H.V. S.W.D. 1935.

2⅞"

⅜ B.S.F.

7 ⅝"

3⅝"

4"

2 5/16"

Authors collection.

The enamel Shell badge opposite now adorns the dash on HPBs Red Car. Several of these were produced to be attatched to Baughan Motors tool boxes. The connection with Shell came from Jimmy Simpson when he was their competition representative persuaded Bill Hayward to change to their oil.* This association was brief as Hayward was a long time user of Castrol 'R' for all types of competition. The Gaffer and Chris Stagg also used this famous brand. Baughan Motors recommended Castrol to all who bought their machines. Fred Halliday tried to convert them to BP without success when he was manager of the BP depot at the LMS siding in Stroud.

and many times the frame was placed in the jig to double check. Equally, so did the engine and gearbox go in and out of the frame to make absolutely sure that everything was in the correct position; for the Gaffer was always very conscious of the company's reputation that would result from a machine that gave rise to customer dissatisfaction. Then the wire brush was used to clean everything up before being cleaned with petrol, then enamelled. The mudguards were bought in, the engines were delivered from Blackburnes to Stroud Station where they were transported to Lower Street, by horse and cart, if they were lucky. Chris Stagg kept a few sheets of paper with various figures relating to the cost of the items that went to make up a bike covering carbs, plugs, hubs and control levers and these were taken from the invoices that were placed in a ledger for payment at the end of the month. A typical example for a Sturmey Archer engine was £11.10/- (£418) and a gearbox was £6. (£228, at 1993 prices.) Frames and tanks were painted black and gold as was Baughans policy, the transfers were all gold. On occasions there would be a break from tradition and Chris at one time rode in competition a Baughan that displayed an ivory tank inlay (page 247) and on other machines there was the pale apple green or red inlay to the petrol tank. Transfers were identical on all the machines. Originally the oil tank was incorporated within the petrol tank and Chris made all these items from scratch. Best and Lloyd were the first oil pumps to be used but by 1929 Baughans changed over to Pilgrim. After 1930 they used separate oil tanks which were sited below the saddle. This change gave a far better appearance to the bikes. There was an attempt to outline these tanks in gold, but it was eventually dropped.

* This proved to be a disaster. Jimmy Simpson supplied several gallons of Aero Shell (Bill Hayward did use this oil when he was the winner of the Cotswold Cup 1932) and Bill duly changed from Castrol. One evening after work he decided to try his outfit on his favourite Ashmeads section. Halfway up the engine dropped a valve and the piston disintegrated, ruining the engine. Bill then had to change the engine for an ex-works TT Blackburne obtained from the Atlas works at Bookham. The next time Jimmy saw Bill he remarked on how well the Shell smelt. Bill replied: "I never had the heart to tell him it was Castrol R." Bill remarked it was nothing to do with the oil, just that a valve collet had broken. "I never did tell Jimmy the true story, we still used all the free oil though."

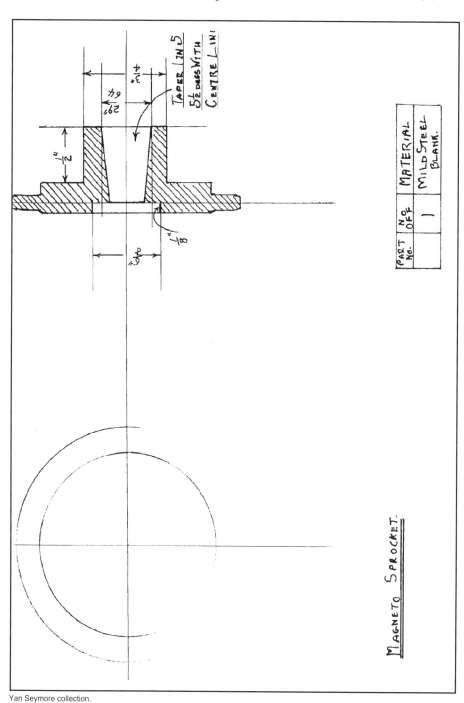

MAGNETO SPROCKET.

Authors collection.

Authors collection.

It is not our intention in this catalogue to make a lot of high sounding claims but rather to tell you just a few reasons why you should carefully consider our machines when purchasing a high class motor cycle.

Firstly they are designed and the manufacture supervised by actual riders, consequently you find that the various parts are where you as a rider, wish them to be, that everything is really accessible and that such items as handlebars, footrests, saddle and brake pedal are easily adjustable to suit YOU.

We take a great interest in the most important public motor cycle trials as we believe they provide an excellent test of a machine's performance in such things as steering, weight distribution, comfort, manoeuvreability etc. Should anything give trouble in a trial, it very seriously jeopardises the riders chance of success and, in our own interests the cause of the trouble is carefully investigated. If necessary the part is redesigned and any alterations made are immediately incorporated in every machine manufactured.

The exceptionally high proportion of successes gained by Baughan motor cycles in competitions are proof of their reliability, stamina and ease of control, all points of the utmost importance to the utility rider, whose chief requirement is a machine which can be depended upon to give the maximum amount of service with the least possible trouble and attention.

We have not attempted to build a cheap machine, every component and every piece of material used in the construction is that which we believe to be the very best that is available for the duty it has to perform the price being a secondary consideration.

Even so, if you will compare Baughan prices with those of other makes you will find that they are very competitive, if you will then compare Baughan machines with other makes we think that you will decide on one of our models.

FRAME, (with fork ends for SWD model)showing steel bridge to top tube, saddle fixing brackets, etc.

Baughan
MOTOR CYCLES

BAUGHAN MOTORS
LOWER STREET,
STROUD,
Glos.

Telegrams. Baughan, Stroud
Telephone Stroud, 373

The Baughan catalogue was originally printed in black on cream art paper and a number still survive to this day. Walter Collins was the printer and subsequently responsible for many of the trials programmes for the Stroud club and the Western Centre.

Sidecar-wheel-drive Model.

In nearly every case it is lack of wheel grip that brings a modern Motor Cycle Combination to a standstill on greasy hilly tracks. To overcome this defect we designed the Baughan Sidecar – wheel – drive outfit.

With this machine you can drive through deep mud or sand, cross ploughed fields, travel up or down hills on snow and ice, in fact almost anywhere on any kind of surface.

Its phenomenal success in Public Motor Trials leaves nothing for us to say as to its efficiency, suffice to say that it is being barred from a number of important events on the ground that it is not possible for other machines to win.

It is very noticeable that immediately the drive is engaged, the steering is much steadier over rough uneven surfaces. It gives twice the power for breaking, and we guarantee that tyres have longer life.

The Baughan combination has a direct shaft drive straight from the rear wheel of the motor cycle to the sidecar wheel. Both wheel spindles are mounted in journal bearings and revolve with the wheels. The connecting shaft is equipped with two universal joints – to allow for distortion and chain adjustment – and a dog clutch. The clutch is operated by a lever in a quadrant.

All wheels are detachable and interchangeable. It is only necessary to unscrew the detachable spindle from the drum plate, the wheel will then drop out, leaving all brake-drums, sprockets, etc., in place. There are no extra nuts, bolts or other attachments. Wheels can be changed with ease in two minutes.

In spite of its advantages, this outfit is not expensive. The sidecar chassis is our reinforced competition model with four point connections, and is supplied with drive complete, with all drive gear, sidecar body, mudguard, tyre, etc., and detachable wheels, ready for the road at £30 more than the price of the solo model. In fact very little more than is usually paid for an ordinary competition model sidecar.

The ideal outfit for home and the colonies.

Components of the detachable wheel

SPECIFICATIONS.

250cc S.V.   250cc O.H.V.

Frame. Built throughout of highest quality steel tube reinforced at the lugs, with steel bridge to top tube. All clips and lugs are built in. Specially designed to give good ground clearance, low position and a machine that "handles" perfectly.

Forks. Druid, single spring, adjustable shock absorbers, steering damper and adjustable handlebar lugs.

Gears. Three speed Burman, with pivot fixing and the means of adjusting chains is accessible. Long gear lever, or kick control.

Transmission. Front chain is totally enclosed and the rear chain protected by heavy guard.

Brakes. 5" x 1" front, 6" x 1" rear, finger adjustment and the rear brake pedal is adjustable for position.

Tank. Saddle petrol tank capacity two gallons. Finished in Black and Gold or optional colour panels. Oil tank is mounted on frame under saddle.

Adjustments. Handlebars, footrests, saddle, brake pedal, are all adjustable to suit riders.

Equipment. Front and rear stands, Avon tyres 26 x 3.25. B.T.H. magneto or lighting set, Amal carburetter, twist grip or lever controls, Dunlop saddle. Large tool box and kit of tools.

Engines. Every engine is tuned and has to give a definite standard of performance.

250cc S.V. Blackburne, with downswept exhaust pipes and effective silencer.

250cc O.H.V. Blackburne, single port, enclosed push rods and valve gear and special magneto drive. Dry sump lubrication. Down or upswept chromium exhaust pipe to choice. Magneto ignition. Bore 63 mm. Stroke 79 mm.

G Fisher collection.

This photograph of a 350cc Sturmey Archer powered Baughan was 'Tipped' in the sales brochure rather than being printed. Edwin C. Peckham FRPS visited Piccadilly Mill where these photos were taken. The rare brochures that do exist contain a blank page where this photo was placed. Most photos featured Fisher's machine, others were used that displayed the inlay red, white and green panels on the petrol tank.

SPECIFICATIONS.

250cc S.V.   250cc O.H.V.

Frame. Built throughout of highest quality steel tube reinforced at the lugs, with steel bridge to top tube. All clips and lugs are built in. Specially designed to give good ground clearance, low position and a machine that "handles" perfectly.

Forks. Druid, single spring, adjustable shock absorbers, steering damper and adjustable handlebar lugs.

Gears. Three speed Burman, with pivot fixing and the means of adjusting chains is accessible. Long gear lever, or kick control.

Transmission. Front chain is totally enclosed and the rear chain protected by heavy guard.

Brakes. 5" x 1" front, 6" x 1" rear, finger adjustment and the rear brake pedal is adjustable for position.

Tank. Saddle petrol tank capacity two gallons. Finished in Black and Gold or optional colour panels. Oil tank is mounted on frame under saddle.

Adjustments. Handlebars, footrests, saddle, brake pedal, are all adjustable to suit riders.

Equipment. Front and rear stands, Avon tyres 26 x 3.25, B.T.H. magneto or lighting set, Amal carburetter, twist grip or lever controls, Dunlop saddle. Large tool box and kit of tools.

Engines. Every engine is tuned and has to give a definite standard of performance.

250cc S.V. Blackburne, with downswept exhaust pipes and effective silencer.

250cc O.H.V. Blackburne, single port, enclosed push rods and valve gear and special magneto drive. Dry sump lubrication. Down or upswept chromium exhaust pipe to choice. Magneto ignition.
Bore 63 mm. Stroke 79 mm.

Authors collection.

G Fisher collection.

This superb photo of the 350cc ohv Sturmey Archer engined Baughan gives an insight to the care that Baughan Motors went to when building their motor cycles. As they were all hand built it reflects the craftsmanship that Chris Stagg and Bill Hayward employed. All the enamel was hand brushed by Bill in conditions that were far from ideal. Some later models featured a tool box on the off-side reaf forks. (See page 120).

The upswept pipes were a common feature of their trials models. For the publicity shot the exhaust pipes featured the more attractive low level pipe runs. The silencers were chrome plated as opposed to their normal matt black finish. Fisher's first trials machine featured the high level system, these rather exposed pipes gave Geoff some cause for grief when he was trapped underneath the machine and badly burnt the inside of his thigh. He soon wrapped asbestos string around both pipes in case of a further mishap.

G Fisher collection.

Harry Baughan in local trials. Peter Falconer, Guy Babbage observes HPBs spectacular driving of the Red Car. HPB greater involvement with the Stroud and District Motor Club and organization.

With Baughan Motors now established Harry Baughan pressed ahead with his motor cycles and in their first year of manufacture (1923) saw just three machines leave Lower Street. The last of the cyclecars went in January of that year but the movement still had its advocates and they continued to be produced in quantity by various other people willing to chance their arm. By this time Harry Baughan no longer thought in terms of cyclecars as a viable proposition in a commercial sense he still devoted his attention to competition and his Red Car became a familiar sight in local events. These were organized by the Stroud and District Motor Cycle Club of which Harry Baughan was a very enthusiastic member, there was always a class for cyclecars in their local trials which also embraced threewheeler Morgans with a capacity limit of 1,100cc. One person who had an early impression of Harry Baughan's press-on style of driving was a very young Peter Falconer whose architectural partnership at 'The Hill,' in Stroud still continues. He was taken to the very steep section of Gyddynap. This was approached from the bottom of the Nailsworth/Woodchester valley (A46) and wound its way up from the rear of what was then Newman Hender engineers.

From this vantage point at Gyddynap the young Falconer had a grandstand view of this difficult section. "When I was a small boy I was taken there by my Nanny to see motor cycles and light cars climbing up from the valley below and this created a great impression with me, but the talk was of this man Baughan and there was great excitement when he arrived. He shot up this straight track and crossed over the adverse camber to Gyddynap and the front wheels came right up in the air and were flapping everywhere. That was Harry Baughan, and from this first impression gave me the incentive in later years to try motor cycles and eventually cars in competition."

The Stroud club in its early years indulged in distance reliability trials that extended from its base in Stroud to Bath, Bristol and as far east as Berkshire. The Welsh area was not neglected either and runs to Carmarthen, Ross, Monmouth and the Brecon Beacons. These early years in the club history formulated a strong policy towards these reliability trials and when Harry Baughan joined this was very much to his liking, in fact almost an extension of what the Motor Cycling Club promoted with their own long distance reliability trials, albeit on a much smaller scale. Even with this local activity Harry Baughan's interest in long distance events was as strong as ever and in 1925 rode one of his own 350cc creations in the London and District MCC London to Holyhead and won a Gold Medal despite inclement weather. While all this activity was taking

Courtesy: Mike Budd.

The steep approach to Gyddynap that led up from Newman Hender on the A46. This climb increased from 1 in 6 to 1 in 4 just before it crossed the road at Gyddynap. It was here that Peter Falconer first saw HPB with the Red Car and gave him the inspiration to follow competition both on motor cycles and cars. Gyddynap in those days was just grass and exited onto Culver Hill, just below the Amberley Inn.

place at Baughan Motors the S and DMCC was enjoying good health with all manner of functions taking place. Over the years since its inception competition was always at the forefront of its activities. Hill climbs were organized at Stratford Park, Stanley Park and Miserden, all these events were run over private land as speed events on public roads were being frowned on by the local constabulary. There were already restrictions imposed by the Police in various counties throughout the country and many local authorities in Worcestershire, Warwickshire and Staffordshire were quick to ban speed events taking place on the public highway, Gloucestershire was not far behind. With these events becoming ever more difficult on public roads there were other venues that would accommodate such activities and Harry Baughan, Bill Hayward and Chris Stagg were involved with all these and they travelled to the following counties, Worcestershire and Monmouthshire where private roads were available that allowed such competition, often situated in large country estates; eventu-

The Baughan pictured on the Western Centre Team Trial, 1922. The mudguards have been removed along with the lights, Parsons chains adorn the rear wheels which combined with a solid back axle was a combination that became unbeatable. *The Light Car and Cyclecar* was moved to comment, 'climbing the hills with an absence of fuss.' Ernie Knee was his early passenger.

Courtesy: Mike Budd.

ally even these were later abandoned due to the damage caused by spectators. Although Harry Baughan's Red Car was perhaps best remembered for its trials success he was often tempted to try speed events, even going as far as changing the engine on occasions from its original Blackburne to a British Anzani.

The one person who remembered it at the time was Fred Halliday who rode a 250cc Baughan in local trials and those which were 'Open to Centre' with support from the works. This engine swap he recalls was often undertaken for just these occasions. Although Fred rode a works supported Baughan on a regular basis and was closely associated with the factory research does not substantiate these engine changes. This does not mean, however, that they never took place for he was quite adamant that they did. Harry Baughan through his involvement with trials, came into contact with George Goodall whose exploits with a threewheeler Morgan were the talk of the Western Centre. A great friendship developed between Harry Baughan and 'Uncle George' which eventually led to Harry being offered a JAP engine from Morgans courtesy of Goodall. The original Blackburne in MD264 suffered a piston failure while dropping down the Slad Valley just after finishing a local trial. With all this sporting activity enjoyed by the local club other events were also available to members within the Western Centre for the Stroud Club had affiliated with the Auto Cycle Union in 1910. This gave the members a greater variety and scope for competition where they could try other events out of the county. The Baughan Red Car was out on many of these events for clubs catered not only for solo motor cycles and combinations, they also ran classes for Morgan type three wheelers and four wheeled cyclecars to a limit of 1,100cc.

This continued right up until 1933 when the cyclecars in competition had all but disappeared and it was left to the Morgans to compete against themselves, eventually being placed in the sidecar class. Although Harry Baughan's main interest was with his motor cycles his forte lay with the car. Despite this he was not averse in riding his own products in competition. 1925 saw him out on the London-Holyhead trial riding a 350cc solo which again produced a gold medal and *Motor Cycling* was moved to comment that Baughan, riding his own creation was a newcomer to motor cycle trials. The reliability of these early machines was quite remarkable for this trial produced a 93% finishing rate and practically all the riders were on time. Given the condition of the roads up through Rhayader, Llanidloes, Bwlch-y-Groes and Betws-y-Coed was nothing short of remarkable. All these long distance trials featured a night run and any weakness in lighting sets was soon discovered. Baughan Motors used Powell and Hanmer Ltd, acetylene lamps right up until 1927, machine (No.16) No.25/207 then moved on to BTH and Miller equipment. By the middle of the 1920s Baughan Motors like many other garages supplemented their income with recharging these sets with carbide.

Just as Harry Baughan indulged in long distance events, Bill Hayward's enthusiasm for these reliability trials was as great as the Gaffers and in 1926 took on the challenge of the London-Lands End, and like his employer came away with a gold award riding a 350cc machine (No.19) No.26/210. These long distance trials proved their worth and many a company benefited from the publicity that was generated. In the 1920s machines were becoming much more reliable but the one thing they all suffered from was the poor state of the roads. Punctures were common place and any self-respecting rider of the time carried several spare inner tubes and puncture repair outfit, plus tyre levers for such an eventuality, any distance riding could almost guarantee such a misfortune. This spurred the tyre companies to pursue a strategy that made them far more reliable as every year passed. These self-same roads were always bringing business to Baughan Motors in an indirect way, many a machine was brought to Lower Street for repairs, not only to the wheels, but the forks as well. One of the more notorious hills in Gloucestershire was the descent from the Air Balloon public house near Birdlip to the Cross Hands on the valley floor at Shurdington. The

Courtesy: Mike Budd.

The 'Chockers' always played an important part on the Nailsworth 'Ladder' when many of the vehicles lacked sufficient power to make the climb. Harry Baughan was glad of them when the chain snapped on the steepest part of the climb on this very trial. In the early part of the 1920s the Ladder extended through a small farm on the upper reaches, this was later abandoned when the farmer complained.

potholes were plentiful and deep. Chris Stagg remembers them for the wheel rebuilding he had to undertake for their unhappy owners. "This drop down from the Air Balloon often brought bent bikes to the works. They were more often than not front wheel damage. At times they were so badly buckled that the front forks needed replacing; not only that the riders were in a pretty poor state as well."

However, motor cyclists of the day were hardy creatures and they were forced to tolerate these sub-standard roads and if their bikes were damaged as a result then Baughans were only too happy to carry out the repairs. As the local trials became firmly established with the S and DMCC there were opportunities for the enthusiast to take on greater things that were on offer in the Western Centre. The affiliation of the S and DMCC to the ACU allowed members to enter other events run by neighbouring clubs such as the Cheltenham MCC, and this enabled people to not only try out new ground but also to sample organization that differed from their own club. Harry Baughan was certainly in this category. Trials organization was fast developing for him and his interest became ever greater. He undoubtedly enjoyed his trials with the cyclecar and was as keen as ever, also the much rarer appearances astride his motor cycles. HPB soon realized that the very top level of competition was beyond him and this was the beginning of his formative years as regards organization. Bill Hayward remembers that when the Gaffer rode in a trial he was always delighted with the participation, not so much the winning of an award; just the involvement. He found that with a trial his mind was always focused on the organizational side of things and this appealed to his deep thinking on the subject. (Later to be firmly established when it came to the British Experts and the International Six Days Trial.) Life at Lower Street, with its cramped conditions carried on despite the confinements.

The working conditions were far from ideal and the endurance displayed on behalf of Bill and Chris was part and parcel of the job. HPB on the other hand had no option for it was his business and as he was working under the same conditions as his employees he had very little choice in the matter. The Star engine still provided the motive power for all the overhead shafts and belting but suffered from bouts of indigestion over the fuel it was fed. Initially, this engine was adequate for an independent power source but was not really up to the job when the loadings increased from the additional engineering machinery that the Gaffer bought. To take its place a four cylinder Mors engine of doubtful ancestry was found, and installed, again this was fed on a very suspect diet of just whatever was available at the time. The old Star being single cylinder utilized a large flywheel that gave it a degree of stability when under load. The Mors on the other hand was a revelation with its four cylinders and gave a far smoother output when several machines were driven from it. The cooling system, if it could be called that, proved to be more than adequate, and extremely cheap as well . . . a forty gallon oil drum.

Using the thermo syphon principle to good effect the engine ran very cool, even after many hours running the water in the tank was just warm, in the winter a fine mist of condensation issued from the open top. Anyone on the shop floor in these cold months found this a boon whereby they could always warm their hands on its side. The exhaust system was routed up and through the wall to exit several feet above the ground. Like most things, if it runs well, leave it alone, undoubtedly a fine principle and Baughan Motors followed it to the letter, but that was not always the case as Chris Stagg remembers. "This old Mors did very well for us at the works, much better than the Star. Even so it had this tendency to leak fuel and under the sump there was this old oil tray a few inches deep which collected all the drips. The trouble was it used to burst into flames at regular intervals for we were loath to empty the damn thing. We always kept a bucket or two of sand along side of it for just such a flare-up: and we needed it! When it burst into flames, whoever was nearest carried out the fire drill." This state of affairs went on for some time and eventually, Bill Hayward could stand no more of it for being a prolific Woodbine smoker he was in imminent danger of immolation. Finally he set to and fixed all the leaks which seemed to

Authors collection.

Harry Baughan swings his Red Car off Bagpath Lane into the bottom section of Ham Mill. Just inside the entrance was quite a large step of natural stone. Sidecars and cyclecars were required to stop and restart, solos carried on without stopping. This obstacle caught out even the best riders, damaged front forks, handlebars and front wheels all suffered. Jimmy Simpson came off his solo works Norton here and damaged his hand so badly with the wall on the left, he retired on the spot.

settle everyone's nerves. (With the Latin connotation of Mors to 'Death' and Bill Hayward with his weakness for the WD and HO Wills product along with the Gaffer, his repairs may well have been timely). The ground floor was becoming increasingly crowded with several additions of machinery and the space was becoming scarce. However, they pressed on and still continued to produce motor cycles under far from ideal conditions.

The whole ethos of trials gradually drew in Harry Baughan. Both Bill Hayward and Chris Stagg noted this subtle change in the Gaffers approach to trials and competition. By 1924 he was becoming more deeply involved with events that the S and DMCC ran, but more importantly with the Western Centre and the local clubs that it comprised of. Within the Western Centre these clubs also favoured long distance events run by the MCC and within the space of a few years would lead to great friction within the Centre. Eventually the members of the various clubs within the Centre staged something of a revolt that was to have repercussions at all levels in the Centre, and with the ACU. At Lower Street, the business kept all three men fully occupied with general engineering, servicing, and repairing all manner of vehicles, from humble farm machinery to the local Vicar's Bugatti. The initial year of motor cycle building (1923) just one left the factory. Not a startling amount and in comparison to Cottons just fourteen miles away, this was insignificant indeed. Although this increase in sales was in part due to local knowledge of the marque. It was only in later years that Baughans started to build machines that would be far more suitable for trials. In the 1920s there were few if any specialists machines made for this purpose. Invariably the only concession to anything 'sporting' was a high level exhaust system and very occasionally a close ratio gearbox and quickly detachable wheels. The sales ledger gives an indication of this sports leaning on their first motor cycle (No.5) MC.24/196 actually refers to it as a 'Baughan Sports' and (No.6) MC.24/197 relates to a close ratio gearbox with racing pistons and cams which took part in Chatcombe Pitch then famous for its use of a public highway for a speed hill climb. Out of their first three machines that they built, two of them were of a sporting nature, No.6 was equipped for perhaps more than just road use.

The racing piston and cams were a feature of Blackburnes at the time for they could be readily supplied on any of their engines if required. Gradually the Baughan reputation for building motor cycles had become well known and numerous local people had more than a passing interest in them. One such person was Fred Halliday who at the time was enjoying trials riding on a variety of machines. Through his interest in trials he came into contact with Harry Baughan and a friendship was soon established. Fred purchased a second-hand Baughan that featured a 250cc sv Sturmey Archer engine with outside flywheel. Fred exhibited a natural flare when it came to competition work and HPB, ever a shrewd judge of character and talent, elected to support Halliday with maintenance of the machine but was also willing to pay his entry fees in open to centre events. There was one proviso, however. To enjoy this support Harry wanted Fred to give a helping hand to the young Chris Stagg who was getting more and more involved with trials and showing great promise. Rather than have Bill Hayward looking after Chris, HPB decided that a more independent person would be good for the parties involved.

This in effect would give Bill a free hand to concentrate on the event without having to look after his compatriot. Both Fred and Chris found this to their mutual advantage and they worked very well together in S and DMCC trials where Baughan riders were given sequential numbers so Fred led, followed by Chris and Bill. How this state of affairs came about was that HPB was often assistant to the secretary of the meeting and the issue of competition numbers fell to him; a little bit of poetic licence applied one feels? With HPB on the committee of the S and DMCC often helping out the competitions secretary and arranging these sequential numbers for his runners took but a moment. This may not be strictly true but the inference is there and it was not until 1925 that HPB had a hand in the official organization side of things for he started out as assistant secretary of the meeting and this allowed him the flexibility to issue consecutive numbers. One of his first involvements was the Open Stroud Team Trial of 1926 where he played second fiddle to the Hon Trials Sec, RJ Hillman. This issuing of concurrent competition numbers may have smacked of favouritism,

Route surveyor H. P. Baughan. Later taken over by. Max Young.

Owing to Nore: not finding route Course was altered.
Owing to the route selected by Stroud Club being altered by Mr Young without Police permission. route was altered in this district.
Final route as card.

This is just part of the final written report by Harry Baughan of the Western Centre One Day Open Reliability Trial, June 26th 1926. As can be seen the ever watchful eye of the constabulary was in attendance. Harry Baughan was responsible for the route along with Max Young. In the course of marking one hundredweight of red powder was used. Each section of the various hills was marked by blue powder where the observers were to be stationed. As usual with Harry Baughan a sketch of every hill was given to the various marshals indicating their positions for correct observation. Each observers card and book was colour coded for easy identification for the results officials.

in club trials. This was perhaps not a consideration, when it came to Open to Centre events, things were a little different for entries were accepted on a first come first served postal basis. Early entries received early numbers. This was not always the case, however, when it came to the Inter Centre Team Trial, teams often requested consecutive numbers and more often than not were allocated them. This policy made a fair amount of sense for not only could each member of a team render assistance to each other when the need arose, but equally as important the opposition could be observed and give some indication of how much success was being achieved, or not as the case maybe.

Fred Halliday came into contact with Harry Baughan in 1924 when he was in charge of the British Petroleum Depot at the LMS railway siding in Stroud. They soon discovered their mutual interest in motor cycles and they hit it off straight away. Fred Halliday showed a natural talent for trials riding which did not escape Baughan's notice and within a short time a 250cc Baughan was placed at his disposal. (This machine does not appear in the sales ledger and Fred Halliday was most insistent that it was produced specially for him.)* His services to Baughan Motors netted him the princely sum of £10 (nearly £400 at 1990s value), a considerable amount of money at the time. This procedure of Chris following Fred was soon dropped when Chris showed considerable prom-

*Probably built from the many spares that were plentyful at the factory

ise in trials and started to pass Fred on ability. Fred Halliday's observations on Bill and Harry are interesting, on the former he found that his ability on a solo machine was nothing outstanding for he never featured strongly in that department. Only when he moved onto a combination did he shine and was to prove he had outstanding ability.

On HPB he had strong views. Here he found a man whose brain was sharp and incisive and had this wonderful ability to solve the most difficult and complex problems; certainly when it came to engineering. Later when he developed his skill with trials organization he found him absolutely outstanding. Nothing it seemed would distract him and he had every eventuality covered. Fred's comments were certainly enlightening on HPB when it came to trials. "Mr. Baughan (everyone addressed him as such) was not a good rider on a solo, but in the Red Car he really came alive and when in competition with George Goodall in the Morgan it was always entertaining stuff. George and HPB were great friends away from competition but it was a different matter when they were in a trial together, for in the back of HPBs mind was this strong urge to beat the might of the Morgans and this was always fun to watch." As Chris Stagg gained ever more experience the need for Fred Halliday's overseeing eye was gradually dispensed with and there was no longer the necessity for Chris to follow in his tyre tracks. Eventually, Fred went his own way but still carried with him a degree of support from Baughan Motors.

From the time that Harry Baughan had settled into rural life which was far removed from suburban Pinner, his interest in trials remained as strong as ever and at almost every opportunity the Red Car was out competing in his hands, mostly in local club events. In 1922 Harry found a willing passenger who was prepared to be subjected to the very strenuous and forceful efforts that marked his style. Ernie Knee was employed at Baughan Motors on a casual basis and this state of affairs lasted for a few years. As soon as Harry Baughan expressed his intentions towards trials, Ernie was very keen to join in. This partnership carried on until Chris took over when Ernie was not available and eventually Knee stood down and was later to be replaced by a delightful female passenger. In these early years Ernie became a familiar sight sitting in the dicky seat behind the Gaffer and one could hardly mistake him for the seating/kneeling position he occupied was almost head and shoulders above the driver. Towards the latter part of the 1920s the Red Car was involved with the essential part of any trial in those days, that of route marking. Instead of Ernie going out on these trips it was Chris who took his place. This part of the decade HPB was occasionally assisting the Secretary of the Meeting and was primarily responsible for its accurate marking. Chris being keen to get in any mileage which would add to his trials knowledge, so he offered his services. As with any trial in those days planning was paramount, accuracy of road mileage was essential and all the turns required the correct coloured dyes. Chris remembers the problems associated with it. "The dyes were carried on the floor of the dickey compartment and were usually red and blue for solos, and on occasions, yellow for sidecars. When I first started with the Gaffer I thought it would be a fairly easy job. When we came to an important turn I would hop out with a scoop and mark the corner. The colour depended on whether it was for the solos or sidecars for often they never always followed the same route.

"The Gaffer always insisted that the dye was placed the same distance before and after every corner, something in the order of twenty feet. On the floor of the dickey were these sacks of dye half a hundredweight each and it was a struggle to get them in there without the contents spilling everywhere. When it was a dry day (the Friday before a Saturday trial was the usual time for this important task, then checked again an hour before the trial started) the job was not too bad, but if it was raining, what a mess! Very often the Gaffer and me would arrive back at the works looking like a couple of Red Indians, the dye was everywhere. Our faces, hands, clothes, were all covered with the stuff and for days afterwards we still had this red and bluish tinge about us; it was the devil's own job to wash off. Now I know why Ernie was never around when it came to route marking."

The Baughan method for route marking never varied. Once he was convinced that the competitors fully understood his methods they remained the same. In his mind there was no room for ambiguity and the resultant protests that would follow if competitors were confused at any point along the route. Harry Baughan devoted a great deal of time to perfecting his trials organization and he drew up a set of instructions that were issued to anyone who sought to undertake such a venture. Simple standardization, that was his secret. Also his observers cards and books with their various colours was something that he pioneered. In the programme for the 1925 fourth Inter-Team Trial it stated that Mr. Baughan would conduct any rider or riders around the course if they wished to do so. However, an error crept into the programme stating that he would undertake this on the Saturday afternoon. In actual fact it should have stated Friday. This practice, or familiarization for any trial that HPB organized was primarily for any rider without knowledge of the district and the locations of the hills and sections. Riders with the experience of Jack Williams, George Rowley, and Bert Perrigo etc, would hardly be swayed by this offer for they knew the sections almost as well as Baughan himself.* In actual fact Jack Williams and HPB worked together very closely and when HPB wanted an answer to a specific question concerning any aspect of one of his trials then Williams gave him a truthful reply. In later years when HPB was Chairman of the ISDT Sub-Committee he had the same rapport and understanding with Allan Jefferies.

* They still went out, just in case a mid-week trial by the Stroud club had used these hills and left them in a very churned-up state. It was not uncommon for the Cheltenham and Gloucester clubs used them as well.

This close understanding with riders was always something that Harry Baughan encouraged with his various officials and entirely depended on which particular trial in his locality was taking place. In the 'Experts' this was not always appropriate. Early in the 1920s solos and sidecars often used different sections and each route was marked with standard coloured dyes. These were red and blue denoting left and right hand turns. At this time BB1 was the first hill for the solos, the sidecar crews followed the same route through Middleyard but instead of passing through on their way to King's Stanley as the solos did they turned left and climbed the steep ascent to Penn Woods. This turn was usually marked with yellow dye indicating sidecars only. Later Penn Woods was dropped completely due to the local residents complaining about the noise and disturbance. This brought in the police and ended what was a very difficult and demanding climb for the crews. While all this activity was going on at Lower Street, Harry Baughan was as enthusiastic as ever for local trials in the mid 1920s. HPB was noted for his press-on style, often at times spectacular, never cautious; every hill was a great challenge. Those far-off days any trial in the locality was an excuse for the public to turn out in their thousands, watching intrepid riders trying to climb hills that few would care to walk up.

One person who witnessed the rise of the fledgling Baughan Motors was Guy Babbage. Here he relates fond memories of his connections with the Gaffer, Bill and Chris. Guy first saw Harry Baughan in 1925 when he was twelve years old. "I was out with my next door neighbour who had a son the same age as myself. They asked me one day if I would like to watch a motor cycle trial. So I hopped on my bike and we all cycled along Bagpath Lane and just before you get to Ham Mill there's a steep track that leads up to Bownham Common. Well, my friend's father knew all about these trials and pointed out the various 'stars'. There was one I remember who was very fast; this was George Dance. I thought that was wonderful until I saw this person called Harry Baughan. What a sight his Red Car was! Spectacular driving, full of excitement for a young lad like me. From that moment I was hooked on anything to do with motor cycles. At the time we lived in Bisley Road, not far from Bill Hayward as I later found out. Not only that Baughan Motors was just a few hundred yards away. A little later I went down to the works just to hang around, look through the doors to see what was going on. One day I was outside and Mr. Baughan came out when he saw me and motioned, 'come on in youngster'. I needed no second bidding. Well they were all very friendly and in the end I went down a lot, sweeping the floors, doing odd jobs for them. I remember at the time I desperately wanted a radio as I saw an *Echo* in one of the shops in Stroud. I could only afford it on hire purchase but I did not want to ask my parents to sign the forms. Well, Mr. Baughan got to hear about it from Chris and he signed as guarantor. Being on the inside I was able to see Chris bending the tubes for the motor cycle frames after they came out of the hearth. They had discarded the old wooden jigs and replaced them with metal and new adjusters. In the early years months would pass before an order came in for a bike and as these wooden jigs had been stored away they found that they had warped or stretched, depending on the time of the year, so out they went. The one thing that I do remember was this old Mors four cylinder engine that drove all the overhead shafting and belts. The cooling system used a forty gallon oil drum and on the sides were countless oily hand prints, especially in the winter. The exhaust pipe went up the wall some ten to twelve feet and out through and extended a couple of feet outside. There was no silencer but it ran very quietly, there was just one problem though, after it had been running for a few hours oily drips started to find their way out. Well one day I forgot all about this and came past with a light coloured coat on I collected a good dose; boy did I get into trouble when I got home!" On the bike building he saw the trouble Chris had with the exhaust pipe bending. "Nobody wanted the job, in the end poor old Chris was lumbered with it. The times he wrestled with these, bending them under the short stairs that led up to the office. In the end Chris and Mr. Baughan devised a method so that they could be bent on a former which was a vast improvement.

"Every so often I was lucky to get a ride in a sidecar with Chris when he went out on test. Not far away was a family called Wheatley (Later to buy machine (No.26) No.27/219) and they had a V twin Enfield, the only thing was the brakes weren't up to much. Well, out we went. Chris sorted the engine out and we returned. He swept in through the open doors and promptly collided with this huge pillar drill just inside. Fortunately the damage was slight and Chris soon repaired it. As I grew older things changed. One of the most popular happenings that took place was the 'unofficial' runs across the common. The best place for a long sustained run was the road outside the Aston Down airfield. This straight extended past the White Horse pub and gave plenty of distance for flat out runs. The two people who indulged in this were Bill Hayward and Bill Peters. Hayward had a very fast 250cc Blackburne Baughan which he used for hill climbs and was quite a special. I remember seeing the engine in pieces at Lower Street and the internals just gleamed, they were so highly polished. These runs usually took place on a Sunday morning. In those days there was hardly any traffic, certainly not at that time in the morning. What happened was that Hayward would start his run from the Cirencester side of the pub and as he passed another helper would drop his arm with a white handkerchief as the signal. Peters had the watch and was stationed just past the airfield runway. In that distance Hayward reached over 70mph on that 250. Then the roles changed. Peters had a very special 500cc sprint Sunbeam with a little wedge tank and a huge exhaust pipe. Hayward took over the timing using the same position, Peters clocked well over 100mph. Even though there were very few houses in the area, one run each was enough, any more would have the locals up in arms over the noise as both machines were unsilenced." Babbage followed them round on their various escapades. One favourite spot was the hill leading up from the Daneway Inn right outside the Sapperton Canal tunnel entrance. "This was Bill Peters favourite spot to give the Sunbeam full bore. Hayward was on the watch and Chris Stagg often helped. It was strange to see Peters decked out in plus-fours and glasses, cap on back to front which I thought brought a gentlemanly influence to this whole business. Well it was all great fun until the police got to hear of it, then it finished. Mr. Baughan I think turned a deaf ear to all this. He was not in favour of having his employees racing about on public roads, especially with his standing in the community. Mr. Baughan's Red Car was eagerly awaited on any trial that took place in the district. His first passenger was Ernie Knee who drove one of the Co-op vans in Stroud. One thing, Bill Hayward's father was their vehicle manager and that's how the connection was made." Ernie Knee lived in Bisley Old Road and often went in to Baughan Motors. He was also dead keen on motor cycles and purchased several (The sales ledger lists the following: (No.10) No.24/201. (No.17) No.25/208 and (No.21) No.26/212.) and started to trial them in local events, then ventured further afield with limited success.

Knee passengered for HPB in the early years, eventually concentrating entirely on motor cycles when the Grant Heelas sisters came on the scene. "I think Ernie got a little fed-up with the Red Car" recalls Guy. "Mr. Baughan expected him to help out with the route marking involving the dyes. That did not suit him at all and they parted company, on good terms as I recall. These sisters had a very calming influence at Lower Street and Bill Hayward had to curb his language when they were around; even Mr. Baughan commented on it for I never heard him swear." On the subject of profanities Graham Stagg has this to say. "When a trial was planned with the Gaffer at Lansdown, and with the the rest of us looking and with the rain pouring down outside, HPB was dropping Woodbine ash over the map. With one sweep of his arm he exclaimed: 'damn the weather and the Kaiser!' That was as close as he got to swearing." Guy again. "Baughan Motors always had plenty of motor cycles and cars in for service. The Reverend Dean brought his Trojan in which caused Mr. Baughan a few problems in the ignition department which tried his patience, as did the farmers who wanted the impossible; but Mr. Baughan was always very affable to them all. The Carter brothers (WT and H) who had a milk round were also in and out regularly and bought new machines from the works (No.8) No.24/199 and later (No.29) No.28/222. They ran the first machine with straight through exhaust pipes with gauze stuffed in them as PC Greenslade often caught them and tried to poke his truncheon up the end." Years later Guy competed in trials with a Brough Superior SS80 (he also bought two second hand Baughan trials bikes from Lower Street), and had great fun with this rather unsuitable machine. "I always wanted a Brough and eventually one came along, but at a price!" He used this both for work and competition. "It was great fun, but a handful, especially on some of the very tight sections that made up Breakheart. The right hander was a nightmare and I could never quite manage that one. The bike was just too big. Then came Fisher's, which was very tight and twisty and could be divided into small sub-sections which if it was at all wet attracted a lot of locals. The longest climb if I remember right was BB, it changed over the years. The usual was BB 1 and 2. I remember 3,* but to my knowledge it was only used once (1931 Experts), at the behest of Graham Goodman. It was far too difficult and the bikes often got well and truly stuck, it was far too much trouble even for Mr. Baughan and his helpers. The second part was the Gravestones. The climb was a long one with the spring at the bottom which if it had been raining the week before the trial was always running across the track and everything churned up after the first few bikes passed through. When I used the Brough this long climb was hard on your arms and by the time I reached the 'stones' I was pretty tired. In those days they were a swine and required some very careful riding. Even the big boys came off here. On the left were bramble bushes which caught a rider or two who was not paying attention. Mr. Baughan often included a dog-leg just after them if the going was dry on the first circuit, and was littered with boulders; that really sorted them out! Hodgecombe was very difficult, a long climb which you had to use full throttle; and hang on.

"This track was usually covered in deep leaf mould which hid some big stones. If they had been exposed as the bikes passed through, the locals would cover them up again. If there had been logging they used this track which often cleared many of them out. The spectators soon found them again and very often the second ascent was even more difficult than the first one. There was one hill, Ferris Court, it looked simple enough but suffered from fine limestone, almost like marbles at times. At first many riders used the left hand bank to find better grip. Mr. Baughan was quick to spot that and placed tapes to narrow the climb. This made a big difference for you had to pick your way very carefully, or down you went. The Nailsworth Ladder was always a popular choice for the spectators; and there were hundreds. What they always wanted to see was the cyclecars and sidecars having to stop and re-start at the step. Mr. Baughan was very clever here. He instructed his marshals and observers that it had to be conducted in a certain way with poles and tapes marking the correct position. Most locals practised it many times. Certainly Bill Hayward with the swd; even he got it wrong at times and nearly looped it." After using the Brough for a few seasons Guy

*This was a *downhill* section which became narrower and steeper, machines became wedged requiring a rope and many helpers to retrieve it.

Courtesy: Mike Budd.

The Nailsworth Ladder was very popular with the Hampton Car Company and many of their vehicles were tested here. As a demonstration they fitted one car with an extra low axle ratio and ascended with some ten people aboard, this Hampton though is a stock item.

bought the first of his Baughans,* with a 250cc Blackburne engine with tapered push rods. As this was a little under powered he moved onto another one. This time it was a 350cc with the less common parallel push rods. Of the latter he found this was more to his liking and found it a beautifully balanced machine. "I rode many bikes over the years in competition but this Baughan was excellent, lightweight, with lovely steering; but then, it was designed for trials." Later, Guy rode in scrambles and replaced the Blackburne engine with a Velocette KSS and found, as Chris Stagg did, went like the wind. "I soon found out as Chris did that the engine was a revelation and with such a lightweight frame I often got into trouble. I remember Martyn Rich riding Chris's machine in scrambles and found that it was not up to the increased performance, but he made it fly." Guy remembers with great affection his connection with Mr. Baughan and Lower Street. As to the organization side of things he was more than generous in his praise. "Mr. Baughan did wonderful things on that side. His great assets were the sisters, and Geoff Fisher. Fisher was always behind the scenes. He somehow had the ear of all the landowners and farmers in the district and came up with new hills that were only available on certain trials. These proved outstanding and I don't think many people understood that."

* These were second hand machines, refurbished at the factory.

Geoff Fisher's knowledge of Stroud district and bridle paths. Fisher's famous note books. Harry Baughan and the MCC-ACU affiliation and great upheaval in the Western Centre of the ACU.

When Harry Baughan ventured into the Stroud valleys in the early 1920s to watch various trials he had very little knowledge of the surrounding country-side. However, he was destined to meet someone who did indeed have a very comprehensive understanding of the district; a certain Geoff Fisher. It would be prudent at this stage to give a brief background to these valleys that played such an important part in the trials that were run in the Stroud district. The southern part of the Cotswolds which comprise the area surrounding Stroud and has many fine and picturesque valleys and Stroud is at the centre of five of them. All these valleys since the 18th century have seen a succession of businesses thrive within them.

The adequate supply of fast flowing water proved ideal to power the water-wheels for the many factories that sprang up. The area famous for its woollen industry used this free source of power to good effect. Around the early part of the 18th century any form of transport had enormous difficulty in negotiating the valley floors for they were extensively covered in marsh or bogs. The hamlets that eventually sprang up were usually centred on a plentiful supply of spring water and in the majority of cases were situated half-way up the hillsides. Lines of communication were slowly established by the cutting of roads that would take a horse and cart between these settlements. The best established roads and the ones that had most use were from Stroud to Thrupp, then to the Bourne at Brimscombe. The other from Stroud, went out towards Nailsworth and on through Tetbury, again situated half-way up the south side of the valley and on to Bath. As the century progressed and development in business increased, a need arose for better communications from the nation's capital to the west where commercial connections to Bristol, Bath and Gloucester were vital. Gradually, the roads improved and became a much more permanent feature with crushed stone making up a semblance to what in later years was to become metalled ones.

As the floor of the valleys still remained water-logged, no serious drainage had been undertaken and these roads became the only access. Eventually the woollen mills were built on the valley floor, some at considerable expense considering the difficulty of building in what was almost a river bed. By 1795 there was still no road running along these valley floors. Nevertheless a coaching route was well established from London to Stroud, which utilized the roads that connected these tiny villages. A coach leaving the London terminus at Ludgate Hill at 3am would arrive (barring mishaps and many changes of horses) at Stroud around 10 pm the same day. The key stops for the passengers were Oxford, Cirencester,

G Fisher collection.

Warren Fisher was the inspiration to his brother in exploring all the byways and bridle paths that abounded in the Stroud district. Geoff noted all these down and soon became the basis for all Harry Baughan's trials.

Stroud and eventually Gloucester. The latter part of the route from Cirencester dropped down through the Toadsmoor Valley and into the Bourne, Thrupp and eventually Stroud. The final part of this journey was level and gave the passengers a splendid view of what was to be known as the western end of the Golden Valley. As early as 1715 the road from Stroud through Cirencester to London was turned into a Turnpike and things steadily improved both for the coach and the passengers. By the early 1800s springs started to appear on both the coaches and the coachman's seats which made life a little more tolerable. In 1815 the first road had been driven slightly above the valley floor from Stroud, through Brimscombe to Chalford where it eventually climbed out of the valley via Cowcombe Hill, then north east to Cirencester. As industrialization gathered pace the Great Western Railway pushed west and 1845 saw its appearance in Stroud, and virtually overnight the Stroud Water Canal Company that had been established in 1785 was dealt a mortal blow which would see its gradual decline. They were not alone, wayside Inns that had sprung up as the routes developed felt the loss of trade and many closed along with the stables and hostelries that offered a change of horses and refreshment.

This background information gives a little indication as to the many interconnecting roads, or rather tracks that had served the many villages that had been built, often precariously halfway up the hillsides. There were a few sections that can be traced to one of these roads in the Brimscombe valley. The famous 'Ham Mill,' still in use even today when the Cotswold Clouds production car trial takes place in February.* One man who made a great study of these old roads and bridle ways etc, was Geoff Fisher and although the kudos went to Harry Baughan for discovering new hills on which to run many trials sections, it was Fisher's great and intimate knowledge of the district that had been handed down from what he liked to describe as his 'Ancestors'. Geoffrey Warren Fisher was born and bred in Gloucestershire in contrast to Harry Baughan with his Welsh connections and they were destined to work together in terms of motor cycling

*The other notable hill was 'Ashmeads,' this could be divided into many sub-sections. Almost opposite was another famous climb, 'Station Lane'. This was two separate hills, with sub-sections.

for the best part of forty years. Both men were resolute bachelors but their enthusiasm for motor cycles and the associated sport drew them together. Fisher was born in 1906. The youngest of three brothers and a sister, he was a countryman at heart following the lead that was given to him by his father and his father before him. Fisher's grandfather (Paul Hawkins Fisher. 1779-1873) was greatly interested in Stroud and the surrounding district and Geoff Fisher's long lasting Christian faith was initiated by the grandfather and passed on to his father where his son was brought up to follow Christianity from an early age. He was a great believer and for seventy years of his life was spent, appropriately enough in Rectory Cottage; just a stone's throw from his beloved Minchinhampton Church which he was closely associated. Paul Fisher wrote an intriguing book on

G Fisher collection.

Geoff Fisher aboard his brothers bike. Later Geoff bought a Scott two-stroke and rode this in competition in the mid 1920s.

the Stroud district that went into amazing detail, certainly when it came to many buildings in Stroud. Perhaps some of the more interesting features in the book deal with the road systems that were in use at the time.

The turnpikes and the old coaching roads are recorded and give a fascinating insight into just how the primitive road systems developed in the Stroud district. This in turn was gradually brought to Geoff's attention by his father who took his young sons out walking these many roads and bridle ways that had been established at the end of the 18th century. These old tracks held particular fascination to the young Fisher for many had long been forgotten and had almost become fully overgrown and almost invisible. Later, Hugh Warren Fisher, Geoff's elder brother, went a stage further in searching the district and found the need for something more swiftly to carry on the explorations, Geoff rapidly joined in. Bicycles were the next step and with this new transport they ranged further afield and followed the old tracks that were still rideable. Both brothers kept notebooks on their many excursions and during these formative years Geoff Fisher started a discipline that was to occupy him for over sixty years. Fisher, a cultured, intelligent and articulate man with a great sense of diplomacy was also an amateur meteorologist, from an early age kept meticulous records of rainfall, hours of sunshine, winds, along with temperatures that

G Fisher collection.

Refreshments on the Cotswold Cups Trial 1933. The lunch break was quite a feature of the Cotswold and always found favour with the riders. From the left, George Stannard, third, fourth and fifth from the left, are, Bob Foster, Chris Stagg and Geoff Fisher. It was past this pub that Bill Hayward and Bill Peters raced their machines against the stop watch on Sunday mornings, then disappeared just as quickly before the law appeared. For a number of years the 'Bear' on Rodborough Common was the usual lunch halt as was the start. Riders decided that thirty minutes was enough for a quick stop.

were to form the basis of what these conditions would have on the hills in the district. This attention to detail was to prove significant when he started to ride motor cycles along with his brother. However, it was to have far greater influence on trials when his and Harry Baughan's paths crossed in the middle 1920s. Hugh made the first move to motor cycles and Geoff sat on the pillion for their many expeditions throughout the county. Eventually they both shared the riding (shades of Harry and his brother) and covered many miles in their travels. Soon Geoff became discontented with having to share the motor cycle and made due arrangement to purchase his own machine after meeting with approval from his father. The two young men set about their explorations with vigour and at every opportunity they were out riding. Gradually they explored further and further 'off' road to such good effect that one of them had to extract the other's machine from some dense undergrowth that had never been penetrated by a motor cycle before. Once home Geoff had some explaining to do about the torn trousers and jacket, but like Harry Baughan, managed to get away with it. Very soon they joined the S and DMCC and found people who shared their passion for riding motor cycles. They indulged in all the social events that the club ran and all the

Geoff Fisher vigorously footing on his 350cc Rudge climbing Mount Vernon in the 1931 Kickham Memorial Trial. This section was nearly always slimey, comprising loose slabs of limestone. All the the top factory riders found the greatest difficulty in staying upright even when it was fairly dry.

reliability trials; but the fast emerging competition attracted their attention the most. Speed hill climbs were a particular fascination and helped out with the organization at Stratford Park. Stanley Park and other local events that took place on private land. Chatcombe Pitch was one of Geoff's favourite attractions which was located a few miles north of Cheltenham where he watched great riders such as George Dance and Wal Handley tackle the very dusty climb. Modest competition followed, the purchase of a Scott saw Geoff riding the hills that he had so carefully investigated over the previous years. In these competitions he soon came into contact with an equally enthusiastic Harry Baughan in 1926. Their personalities were not that dissimilar. Both were enthusiastic motor cyclists and deep thinkers. The common ground was trials. They found riding motor cycles up hills, through streams and water courses in all manner of weather conditions immensely satisfying. Competition against the clock and the elements captured them completely and remained throughout their lives. HPB was some ten years older than Fisher and had accumulated far more trials experience than his younger counterpart. Fisher soon caught up and became a very competent trials rider indeed and soon qualified for 'Open' events. In Fisher, HPB saw a man whose outlook on trials and the benefits that could be obtained were akin to his own philosophy. Not only that he saw a person with a nice even temperament and excellent negotiating skills. The latter is an asset to any motor cycle club. So Harry Baughan's influence was brought to bear and Fisher was persuaded to stand for the Stroud and District Motor Cycle Club committee, to which he was successful and gave years of faithful service, often through difficult times. Harry Baughan was concerned that very few trials catered for the first time rider, the pure novice in fact. He recalled his army days when he saw the limited amount of training given to their motor cycle riders to improve their riding techniques. Away from the structured discipline of the army he recognized that any civilian would find it hard to gain any sort of entry outside their own club to gain trials riding experience, and would perhaps feel intimidated in the process; he was determined to re-dress the balance.

There were many riders in the Stroud club who had considered trials as an interesting pastime but were put off at the thought of making fools of themselves. This concerned HPB greatly and he had a few thoughts on a possible remedy. He outlined a plan to Fisher. Strange to relate Fisher had given this some thought himself and once they had discovered their mutual feelings they discussed it further and came up with what they saw as a solution. In the end HPB asked Fisher if he would like to organize such an event. He wanted to give the complete novice the opportunity to try his or her motor cycle in competition that would serve as a gentle introduction and give them an insight to just what was involved with the necessary rules and regulations and understanding them. So was born the Minchinhampton Cup Trial, an event that was to prove quite a success in the years to come. Geoff Fisher used his comprehensive and detailed knowledge of the surrounding district to come up with a trial that would be approved by the club committee. Many club members often entered in reliability runs that the Stroud club organized, and this gave them a taste for straightforward, no nonsense rides against the clock at speeds that would not tax either the machine or the individual. This trial gave the novice an insight to map reading. Fisher and Baughan showed them how to judge gradients from the contour lines and distance etc; in fact they were probably given more information than they perhaps needed. Later, all this had greater relevance when these 'novices' were seconded to help with all aspects of marshalling and the needs of other competitors which allowed the trials to run on time, and smoothly as well. Gradually Harry Baughan built up a nucleus of members who were willing to give up their spare time to carry out these important functions. As the years passed under HPBs guidance they became superbly effective and Baughan's

G Fisher collection.

The 1932 Kickham was something of a nightmare with days of rain before the trial. Here Fisher is struggling to maintain forward momentum. Many Centre organizers thought copious amounts of mud would add spice to any event. Harry Baughan was not one of them. He preferred hills that had difficult turns and tight sections which would show the skill of the best riders, mud — was certainly out.

reputation increased as a trials organizer. Baughan was always at pains to point out that it was the volunteers who did the job efficiently, and not him. This was something that Peter Chamberlain pointed out to many people years later, especially when HPB was Chairman of the ACU-ISDT sub-committee. He knew that without HPBs leadership the ACU would have a very difficult task on its hands when the trial was held in Great Britain. Many people in the Western Centre found it fascinating that HPB could attract so many people to give assistance, and willingly to trials, scrambles, speed events and motor cycle football. Very few people refused and if Mr. Baughan asked for volunteers there were many willing hands. As one would expect Sunday trials never went down very well with him or Geoff Fisher. Also the many Centres in the ACU frowned upon such activity. Gradually, Fisher built up his skills and collected many 1st, 2nd and 3rd class awards and was an enthusiastic supporter of all Western Centre activities. Geoff Fisher pointed out to HPB that simply riding motor cycles up and down hills would not necessarily give him the true picture. His recommendations were to drive out in his cyclecar, then walk the hills and see just where it could be

G Fisher collection.

G Fisher collection.

Geoff Fisher's first trials Baughan bought in 1933 fitted with a 350cc ohv Sturmey Archer. His second was another 350cc, this time Blackburne powered. The photo was taken just after its completion. This was his everyday transport for quite a number of years. The hand control position for the gear change on the petrol tank was very popular, a great improvement on the old type. Registered, 18/4/1933. Compare this photo to the ones on pages 95 and 96. There are quite a few alterations. The exhaust pipes have been rerouted and the silencers are now the standard Baughan pattern, smaller versions of the famous Brooklands 'Cans.' The mudguards have changed and there is now a lighting system. A small tool box has also been added.

divided into sub-sections; this in his opinion was the only way to understand the topography. To the average trials rider this would not have been given a second's thought. In later years this became standard practice. Geoff Fisher knowing the extent of the water table in the area could put his finger on all the natural springs and just how they would be affected by days of light and sometimes constant rain. The amount of direct sunshine at certain times in the winter would make climbing in deep shadow difficult, knowledge of rock outcrops, low branches, this was essential if the rider became temporarily blinded by the sun. Fisher observed it all, the wind speed and direction, often giving quick drying of certain exposed sections that were south–west facing, frost that would remain all day in sheltered spots, unaffected until the temperature rose. All this minutiae was recorded. Geoff Fisher may not have been closely involved in trials as Harry Baughan was, nevertheless he was a keen observer of commercial trends in both motor cycles and cars and fully appreciated that competition improved the product. When HPB introduced his swd it was Fisher who voiced his opinion that he could see very little, if any, commercial use in it especially as the light car was becoming very popular, but still thought it was a very progressive step in motor cycle development.

Fisher ran a Cotton for a few years, and this served for both everyday transport and competition. Later he progressed to a Rudge, firstly to a 350cc and then a 500. In 1933 he bought his first Baughan. He found the Rudge a little on the heavy side, and was surprised that his close friend Jack Williams expressed the same feelings. Fisher had hankered after a Baughan for a while, and finally he had one made. Geoff expressed his thoughts. "It was a revelation, so completely different to the Rudge, it was lighter, steered beautifully and proved excellent on hills. I ordered their trials/sports model and it was so easy to ride, too easy in fact. I took it to Ashmeads along the Chalford Valley and went up one of my favourite sections, but my enthusiasm got the better of me and I fell off. That was a real lesson and one I will never forget for it proved very painful." In this spill Geoff suffered burns to the inside of his thigh from the high level exhaust which trapped him when he went over. A visit to the doctor was the result, but he suffered no long lasting effects, except a scar to remind him for the rest of his life. "The first thing I did was to wrap both exhaust pipes in asbestos string to avoid embarrassment in the future." The Rudge it seems was fine for trials, very solid and reliable but not really suited to some of the very tight spots. Geoff raised this with Jack Williams and to his surprise found the same shortcomings with his. In the end he defected to Norton despite his limited support from Rudge. "I could see why he was in such demand for he was a superb natural rider, whether it was trials, scrambles or grass track, besides he was such a very nice person; both he and Harry had a close affinity and understanding when it

G Fisher collection.

The only time Harry Baughan indulged in alcohol was when the royal toast was taken at a club dinner. On his left are: Auriol Marjorie Grant Heelas, Geoff Fisher, Marjorie Auriol Grant Heelas. The twin sisters by this time had slightly changed their hair styles and could be better identified.

came to trials and was a wonderful source of inspiration." As Harry Baughan became more deeply involved with trials organization he was always on the look out for new hills that might produce some tricky sections. Baughan was never a man who looked for hills that were covered in mud. His idea was that sections should be difficult in the extreme, but not impossible which was a feature of the Kickham Memorial Trial that often involved spindle deep mud on occasions. Harry Baughan was much more subtle, not wishing to follow the practice that a lot of clubs used whereby copious amounts of mud were considered essential for a trial. He wanted the skills of the top private and factory riders to be tested to the maximum. The latter could readily be described as 'Professional' riders who were out almost every weekend at some open trial or another. This applied to solo and sidecar riders alike. Good balance, the ability to 'read' a section without prior knowledge of it and coupled with the mental agility as the course changed if adverse weather conditions prevailed. Once Harry Baughan discovered Fisher's extensive local knowledge, and this combined with his study of weather patterns he found that the conditions of the hills in many places were in part closely associated with rainfall and strong winds. Fisher knew just how rainfall would change conditions on certain hills and hardly affect others. The same applied to strong south–westerly winds on sections in the Dursley area and parts of Crickley Hill at Birdlip. He based his judgment on the many years, he, along with his brother walked and rode the district. As befits the man, he kept meticulous note books on just how the weather would affect certain areas. This along

The London-Gloucester Trial, 1929. Geoff Fisher is on the extreme left and enjoyed a trouble free run as did Harry Daniels. They were the only members from the Stroud club to enter. Fisher recorded the fastest climb of Ferris Court beating all the works riders; local knowledge comes in handy at times.

with the frequent use of small local trials that often used hills like the Nailsworth Ladder, Ashmeads and Ham Mill. One particular section that ran over private land was the Weighbridge Inn on the Nailsworth to Avening road. If there was heavy rainfall prior to a trial the first part of this section benefited from it, keeping all the rocks clean. However, it was a different matter on the level ground after this first observed section for the route divided, solos went straight ahead through a pond, while the sidecars turned 90° left and ascended Hazelwood. The heavy rain increased the size of this pond and was always a great source of amusement to the spectators when the solos passed through it, many taking an 'early bath' in the process. With the combinations diverted they found Hazelwood/Rowden almost as difficult as the first section was easy. Harry Baughan in his capacity as Clerk of the Course knew that he could rely on Fisher and his judgment for the planning of the trials route that took place between October and March, for every Friday night at Lower Street these hills and sections were planned in great detail. On the day if the first circuit of the route proved to be easy then the supplementary regulations allowed a change in the sections so local knowledge might in some cases not be of very much help, for Harry Baughan was astute enough to alter parts of them completely. His planning was meticulous and an alternative was always an option for him and any rider who entered trials in the Western Centre knew that there was never an easy trial in the Stroud area when Harry Baughan was Clerk of the Course. In the early years of motor cycle trials public attention in certain quarters had been unwelcome. Editors of local newspapers often received letters in the following vein . . . one example from Mr. C Roy Sanders who writes about public opinion of club road trials and their effect in general. This letter was published in the *Littleworth Argus*, entitled 'Disgusted.' Sir. "When is our National Government going to put a stop to all this dashing about the countryside on the part of crowds of hare-brained lunatics on motor cycles? Every Sunday hoards of these irresponsible youngsters dash up the hill by my home at 70 miles an hour and so on" . . . This type of activity may not have been conducted by the various clubs within the Western Centre but there was considerable discontent by the public along the routes of many trials and it was always going to be a problem for the organizers. HPB was keenly aware of these feelings and did his best to keep it to a minimum. The Cotswold Cups Trial suffered from such complaints and when the residents informed the Police then pressure was brought to bear. Harry Baughan was at great pains to ensure that the public was not outraged or inconvenienced by passing trials. On one such occasion Fisher was approached by HPB in order for him to visit the residents whose houses bordered the steep approach from Middle Yard to Penn Woods which proved to be a particular sensitive spot. Sadly, it was a cause too far and Fisher had to concede on this one, ever mindful of the BB section in Stanley Woods which held one of the best climbs in the area. Fortunately the rough track that led from King's Stanley to the foot of BB only featured one isolated house and they were quite happy to see some activity, especially if they were motor cyclists. When it came to the Penn Woods section HPB was forced to comply with the constabulary's wishes and drop this controversial section. It was only used by the sidecars amounting at the most to 12 competitors once a year, even this was too much for the residents and the best efforts of Geoff Fisher were thwarted. So local pressure eventually killed off this very difficult and tight section. A real pity for this was a stiff test for even the most experienced crews. It would have been folly in the extreme for HPB to continue and bowed to their wishes, many of the road sections between the various hills were routed away from villages as far as it was possible. At times this was not always practical for it made excessive road mileages that just extended the time a trial took to run. When the Cotswold Cups and the Inter Centre Team Trial started it was usually at 10 or 10.30am and on rare occasions even later. This late start ensured that villagers were not disturbed too early and helped reduce public alienation, or at least to keep it as low as possible. In this respect Geoff Fisher came into his own, ever the diplomat he went out and ensured valuable PR work was carried out on behalf of the organizing club.

Geoff Fisher proudly displaying the No.1 plate about to start at midnight on the London-Gloucester Trial in 1932. It departed from Slough trading estate and ran through Berkshire and many passage controls to the Air Balloon, Birdlip, then south to the Stroud area where all the observed hills were located.

Harry Baughan did his fair share of this increasingly valuable function and as he was often C of C it was his responsibility. More sensitive areas were left to Fisher. Where Fisher scored in later years was with the private land owners and through his extensive connections he was the prime mover to opening up some wonderful sections on previously inaccessible land.* Harry Baughan, ever the visionary always wanted better and better sections to stretch the increasingly more competent rider along with developing machinery by the more astute manufactures. In Geoff he found an outlet. Fisher approached many land owners to persuade them to allow a trial to pass over their property. However, they were rightly concerned about damage that might be incurred, so Fisher had to persuade them otherwise. Initially, he complied with their wishes to limit access to

*Fisher excelled here. He gradually rose up through the estate agent, Davis Champion and Payne to become a land valuer and auctioneer. From this position he knew all the farmers and landowners.

G Fisher collection.

Geoff Fisher, fifth from the right with fellow competitors gathered at the start of the London-Gloucester Trial, 1932. The run through the night comprised mainly passage control checks for early or late arrivals. The Stroud club under HPB's leadership followed this practice for long distance reliability runs.

the public and roped off areas were first tried. Once the word had spread of these early successes then Fisher found his task a lot easier. All this was reminiscent of the early troubles when the public could roam free on the public roads when speed events were run without restriction and little control, but the incident at Princes Risborough where a spectator was injured at a speed hill climb in 1926, competition on public roads came to an end. Speed events then moved to private land, many thought it would be the solution to all the difficulties. It was not to be. These private grounds soon suffered untold damage from spectators and eventually even this avenue was closed. The local land owners in the Stroud district hearing of these at first limited access, however, they were finally persuaded by Fisher to allow them to take place on a trial basis. Geoff Fisher could not give a cast iron guarantee that the public would not damage their property and after the success of the first Cotswold Scramble at Througham he successfully negotiated the use of land at Lypiatt Park. The first scramble at Througham proved a great success for there was no significant damage to property, the many hundreds that did turn up hardly made an impression on the grass that withstood six hours of trampling. From then on Geoff Fisher went from strength to strength, gradually making greater and more important contacts that furthered the cause of motor cycle competition in the Western Centre. This, however, was a little way in the future. Other things of a more serious nature were beginning to disturb the tranquil waters of the Western Centre.

GREAT UPHEAVAL IN THE WESTERN CENTRE

The Western Centre and all the clubs it comprised had happily existed together since its inception. The competitions that took place within its jurisdiction ran without any serious fault or dispute. In the early days of motor cycling the pioneering spirit was uppermost and the opportunities were not lost on these early motor cyclists; soon this convivial state was about to change. In December 1925 the Auto Cycle Union decided once and for all that they would be the only body that would officially sanction motor cycle competition. The Motor Cycling Club that had enjoyed the reputation as the founding organization of motor cycling in the country was about to be challenged. In that December, the ACU adopted a new set of competition rules which provided for the government of all forms of motor cycle competition and restrict the holding of such competitions to clubs affiliated to the Union. These rules were not aimed at the MCC, which everybody agreed had a reputation for the successful organization of motor cycle events that was second to none; but that their effect was that either the MCC had to affiliate or its competitions would be unauthorized. It was felt that the friendly relations between these two bodies were somewhat precarious and a year passed before serious efforts were made to get them on a better footing. These coincided with another necessity, the general tightening up by the ACU of its control of the sport, into which several abuses had crept, notably in connection with the holding of closed trials by unaffiliated clubs over which the Union had no control.

What the ACU had overlooked was the outcry that was to follow from its members in affiliated clubs. At first the implications were not immediately recognized by its members. Initially there were rumblings from the South Eastern Centre, who spotted possible repercussions, but the strongest reaction came from the Western Centre and the following letters give some idea just what affect this had. Harry Baughan was clearly upset over the ACU attitude and the possible draconian measures they implied. The Motor Cycling Club and the Auto Cycle Union had co-existed for years and both bodies had run competitions with hardly any disagreement, but the ACU statement in December proved to be very unpopular indeed. What had sparked off this confrontation was the new set of competition rules the ACU had published that December (1925). The gist of the matter was that the ACU would govern all forms of motor cycle competition and restrict the holding of such competitions to clubs affiliated to the Union. These rules were not aimed specifically at the MCC which had an outstanding reputation of successful organization unequalled by any other body, but there was no denying the implication The effect was that either the MCC should affiliate or its competitions would be unauthorized. These were the bare facts; in essence any MCC member or club that was not affiliated to the ACU would be subject to reprisals by the Union. This business of reprisals was the crux of the matter and had the immediate effect of alienation to the ACU by riders who indulged in MCC events and objected to the proposed restrictive power of the ACU. The MCC ran events, both in trials and speed where members had enjoyed their delights for years, the latter mostly at Brooklands where all manner of renowned riders and drivers took part in them. The Trade might suffer at first from this MCC-ACU disagreement when it came to record attempts. These were very carefully regulated by the Trade when maximum publicity was required. As Brooklands was the only venue suitable for record attempts a strict rationing policy was enforced. It was very unproductive for riders and drivers sponsored by various parts of the Trade to aim for a certain record all on the same day for the resultant publicity would have little impact. Far better for the individuals to be spaced more than a month apart or longer to give greater coverage and returns on their investment to all the parties involved; which was often considerable. The Trade looked upon these record attempts as money well spent, not only for the rider and the manufacturer who were well reimbursed in financial and material terms. This interconnection within the Trade was an important consideration as record attempts could be spaced throughout the summer months, thus ensuring that the circuit would be available well in advance for record attempts. Consideration also had to be given to the availability of the time keepers and the most prominent of these was 'Ebby' Eblewhite who, despite his standing in such circles was also a business man and needed to be booked in advance.

It was not long before the riders and drivers cottoned on as to just how valuable record breaking could be. If the ACU insisted on its affiliation policy there would be considerable ill feeling, and possibly long term consequences in those speed events held at Brooklands, with its excellent reputation might have to look at the fixtures which both these respected bodies used. The problem with riders who undertook MCC events came to a head in 1926. Those riders involved with the MCC promotions came to the notice of the ACU, none more so than in the Western Centre. Eventually the ACU was not prepared to have its members, either on an individual or club basis competing in events run by a rival club. (A closed event.) This warning certainly angered a great many members who made up the Western Centre, namely the Gloucester MCC, Cheltenham MCC and the S and DMCC. There was so much discontent within the Cheltenham club concerning the MCC-ACU that certainly put the wind up those with strong loyalties towards the MCC, so much so that a new Cheltenham club was formed so as to circumnavigate the problem (no MCC members). Also keeping a watching brief were the clubs in the Worcester and Hereford area that were affiliated to the Western Centre. This new club was hurriedly formed and comprised of members whose sympathies lay with the ACU. If the old Cheltenham club decided to disaffiliate from the ACU that along with Gloucester and Stroud the Western Centre would hardly exist. The move was to form a new Cheltenham club that would be securely affiliated to the ACU. The Centre would still be in a viable position, but perhaps not so effective. This new Cheltenham club was a good ploy from the ACU point of view for they would only recognize one Club in the town, as was the ACU policy at the time. Perhaps the deciding factor in all this was Mr. E Featherstone. (At the time Mr. Featherstone was an ACU Steward in the Western Centre and had considerable influence. A few years later he again figured in this capacity when the problems of motor cycle football was to split the S and DMCC.) In mid-March the MCC had circulated its members, all 1,500 of them for an extraordinary meeting in London where the topic was the possible MCC-ACU affiliation. It was disappointing from the MCC point of view for only 140 turned up. After a long discussion a vote was taken and the upshot was that the MCC would not affiliate with the ACU. The Whitsuntide Trial promoted by the MCC and any other events so promoted by the MCC would go ahead as planned, even if they were considered rogue events and any ACU members competing in them may suffer as a result and action taken against them by the ACU.

All this activity was doing nothing to resolve the matter. Both organizations enjoyed support in their various enterprizes by the Trade and in their eyes had little to concern them. The very few trials that the MCC indulged in attracted a good deal of support. On the other hand events at Brooklands were a different matter. The MCC had a very large following at the former and attracted great support from the Trade, which was essential, certainly when it came to record breaking. Reliability trials came into this category, simply the need to emphasize just how good a motor cycle or car was. Initially, motor cycles led the way by the pioneering Motor Cycling Club who started to organize long distance reliability trials that would not only give the motor cyclist a spirit of adventure, but would also give an incentive for the manufacturers to increase the quality of their products. In 1904 the MCC started its London-Edinburgh Reliability Run for motor cycles at Whitsuntide and incorporated cyclecars and then, light cars two years later, lasting a full twenty-four hours and it gradually increased in popularity. The two elements of time and distance proved their worth and gradually more and more riders found great satisfaction in these long distance events. These trials, popular as they were with the entrants lacked one ingredient; that of competition. Certainly time and distance was quite a discipline and the reward of a trophy, gold or silver was much sought after, but there was something lacking . . . excitement! Once the Auto Cycle Union was formed out of the Royal Automobile Club to look after the interests of the motor cyclists. The one thing they spotted at the outset was the revenue available to them if all the motor cycle clubs were under their control. Money was to be made from individual members who in turn paid their dues to their club, not to mention competition fees and permits that they sanctioned throughout the centres. Thereafter the RAC controlled the motor sport side of things. The MCC long distance events remained popular and retained their individuality. However, there was no direct competition between individuals, it was still a time and distance affair.

The newly–formed clubs that sprang up in great profusion started to affiliate themselves to the ACU and then close competition intensified. Very quickly the ACU responded with dividing the country into various Centres that would collectively coordinate all forms of motor cycle sport and as a result led to uniform stability. While all this official organization was going on with the ACU, riders carried on with their allegiance to the MCC and its long distance events. This status quo existed for many years, over twenty in fact and there was no inkling of any serious undercurrent or division between these two bodies. Gradually the old style of twenty–four hours on the road highlighted by the MCC London-Edinburgh trial slightly lost its popularity. Nevertheless, there were still many willing to have a crack at this classic event that was always challenging. The clubs that formed the Western Centre still had many members who were game to spend a whole day in the saddle, often under inclement weather conditions just for the satisfaction of riding in one of the great events that would more than tax the individual and motor cycle alike. These clubmen were willing to forfeit many a club event just for this great adventure. These, one to half-day local trials certainly gave plenty of competition and there were many evening trials lasting but a few hours which gave the clubman, who was perhaps on a restricted budget, a little flavour of climbing a variety of local hills without the problem of travelling long distance with its greatly increased expense.

The mid 1920s saw Harry Baughan and Bill Hayward fully immersed with these local trials, not only riding but helping with the organization. Even so they both rode in the MCC London-Edinburgh and the Lands End-John o' Groats as and when time and money would allow. There were other like minded riders from the Hereford clubs who felt the same way, and, like their Stroud counterparts indulged whenever they could. Up to that time the MCC and the ACU hardly had any conflict of interest, but things were about to change and the ACU was about to have its feathers severely ruffled when the question of its riders riding in competition events being run by a non-affiliated organization; that of the Motor Cycling Club. Gradually relations within the Western Centre deteriorated. Officials of the many individual clubs that comprised the Western Centre were finding that their members whose allegiance they had perhaps taken for granted was suddenly put in a different perspective. Open hostility towards the ACU was something they were not accustomed to and HPB had just been elected as the Honorary Secretary of the Stroud club and later that year became the Hon Sec of the Western Centre, ACU. As can be seen in the following correspondence he was very upset with this MCC and ACU rivalry and was determined to see it resolved. After the ACU made the announcement in December 1925 HPB sounded out the feelings of the many members within the Western Centre. The strongest of these was from the Gloucester and Cheltenham clubs along with some support from Hereford and Worcester. He then sent a letter to the ACU in April requesting an explanation, . . . things then started to move!

ACU to HPB. April 19th, 1926. *

Dear Sir,
I should like to take this opportunity of briefly stating the reasons why the General Council of the Auto Cycle Union is not prepared to recognize the Motor Cycling Club unless that Club becomes affiliated to this Union.

For twenty-three years the ACU has been recognized by the RAC and the International Federation as the governing body of the sport of motor cycling. Today it is composed of over 300 Clubs representing every district in England. No fewer than 34 new Clubs have joined the ACU this year. Until the end of last year the ACU had no Rules for closed competitions. These, however, became so numerous that not only did they clash with each other, but some of them interfered with open competitions. Closed competitions were run by various bodies, including newspaper proprietors, and there being no fixed rules, the Union was often asked to decide difficult questions.

The whole question was referred by the Council to a special committee of experienced competition men from various parts of England, and that committee reported unanimously in favour of the ACU taking over the control of all motor cycling competitions. They recommended that closed competitions should be controlled by the 17 Local Centres of the Union, and as a necessary corollary, that permits should be issued only to affiliated Clubs. If permits were issued to other bodies, the door was left open to abuse. The Council adopted the report of its committee, and the new rules came into force this year. The MCC has announced that it is prepared to be governed by these rules, if the question of affiliation is not insisted on.

If affiliation imposed any hardship on a Club, this attitude could be understood. But the fees are nominal, every Club gets representation, and there is absolutely no interference with any Club's own affairs. All the Union asks is that every Club shall formally recognize the principle that there should be *one* ruling authority for the sport, as there is in every other sport in the United Kingdom, and signify its allegiance to the great majority of Clubs, and run its competitions under accepted rules. That, in the opinion of the General Council, is the only

*MCC and ACU letters are from the Pat Mather collection.

way in which the sport can be satisfactorily governed. The MCC has refused, and prefers to remain independent. We must show them that they are wrong. The success of any sport depends on loyal co-operation, and on recognition of the rule of the majority. As the MCC has defined the organized motor cycling clubs of England, they are not entitled to any encouragement or assistance from outside their own ranks.

As Chairman of the General Council of the Union, I appeal to all our Centres, Clubs and members to stand firm for the principle of unified control.

Yours faithfully, JR Potter, Chairman.

One can only assume what Harry Baughan thought of the above letter, especially the last line.

HPB to
JA Masters, Esq. Hon Sec, MCC,
Lower St, Stroud. 19/4/26.

Dears Sir.
As the enclosed report seems to take for granted that all ACU members will leave the MCC it has been suggested that it would be good policy for the MCC to sound its members and if the majority of the well known members will remain loyal, to organize a trial with a very small entrance fee and specially ask every member to enter (even if not intending to actually ride). If the ACU continued in its policy to disqualify every entrant it would find its own trials would be almost washed out and it would be forced to climb down.

I forward this on to you for your consideration..

Immediately after HPB wrote the above letter his attention was drawn to an article in the local newspaper which prompted HPB to write again to Masters.

HPB to JA Masters, Esq.
22/4/26.
Hon Sec, MCC.

Dear Sir.
As a member of the MCC I should like to draw your attention to the enclosed cutting from the *Gloucestershire Echo*, of Saturday, April 17th. Incidentally I understand that 'Criticus' is Captain Phillips of the ACU.

The Cheltenham club which is just being reformed adjourned its meeting and decided to await the results of the MCC general meeting before re-affiliating to the ACU and it seems that the enclosed report has been somewhat inspired and try to weigh the balance in favour. I wonder if some reply from the MCC could be sent to the *Echo* this week. I am Hon, Sec, of the S and DMCC and have called a committee for Wednesday next, April 21st, to discuss the advisability of the Stroud Club continuing to affiliate as long as the ACU controls closed competitions.

Should the Stroud and Cheltenham clubs decide not to affiliate the Western Centre will then become almost defunct. The whole matter will be brought up at the next board meeting.

As the report seems to take it for granted that all ACU members will leave the MCC it has been suggested that it would be good policy for the MCC to carefully sound its members and especially the well known competition riders to organize a small trial with a very small entrance fee and specially ask every member to enter. (Even if not intending to ride.) If the ACU continued in its ruling to disqualify every entrant it would find that its own trials would be compromised and be forced to climb down. If you have any inside knowledge of any large clubs following the lead of the MCC it would greatly strengthen my hand in our own centre.

In this letter there are these comments: Carefully sound its members and especially the well known competition riders . . . With reference to the paragraph by 'Criticus' re, motor cycling in the *Echo* of Saturday. 'Criticus' states by remaining unaffiliated to the ACU the MCC will lose more than half its members and all the ACU-RAC licence holders (this may not be correct) will resign. This is certainly very misleading. The MCC is standing up for the principle that the ACU should not force itself on private club life and a large number of clubs are already on their side and also a large number of MCC members are resigning from the ACU.

By not affiliating to the ACU the new Cheltenham Club will be showing its disapproval of the high handed attitude of the ACU in forcing its control upon them, and will probably find it has a larger membership and a better backing by so doing. When the ACU realize that a club should be allowed to rule its own destinies without being compelled by the mailed fist, it will be time for the Cheltenham club to affiliate.

Mr. Paynter. (Western Centre Official) to HPB.   Lower St, Stroud. (no date).

Have been thinking things over and I think there is one very important point not quite ok. I believe the notice you are sending to the press is not clear to anyone who is not in the know of the Cheltenham Club's attitude. It simply objects to rules of the ACU and does not state what rule.

How about something as follows:

The Cheltenham Motor Club refuse to affiliate to the ACU until the rule which a person taking part in a competition organized by an unaffiliated club is penalized by the ACU is rescinded. I am sending a letter to Max Young today telling him that you are elected as delegate for the Stroud club. I fancy that I personally shall want all the support that can be given at the next meeting at Ledbury. I think it is certain that the 'parent body' will make a dead set at me and probably tell the meeting that I am guilty of disloyalty to the centre etc: He may even try to disqualify me for an act prejudicial to the interests of competitions and the sport. We shall go in force, and if you have a good chap who can speak lets take him as a member of the S and DMCC as well. I think the really important thing however, is to get Glos on our side over this, so if you see Ware or any of them, you know what to do.

Cheerio now.

HPB to JM Masters.
Dear Mr. Masters.   Lower St, Stroud. (no date)

I am taking advantage of your kind offer to help us, and am writing to know if you will be good enough to give us some information.

The Cheltenham Motor Club definitely decided not to affiliate until there was an understanding between the ACU and the MCC. Our friend Mr. Featherstone* then called another meeting with his friends and formed another Cheltenham club. Several persons attended who were not in affiliation but they were ordered out of the room by Mr. F, who would not conduct further business until they had left.

This new club therefore decided to affiliate, and we are told as Mr. Featherstone and the Hon Sec of the Western Centre was present this was done immediately. A notice appeared in the local press saying that the new club was affiliated and that it would not now be possible for the Cheltenham club to affiliate even if they wished to do so as the ACU only allowed one affiliated club in one town.

The Western Centre Board meeting takes place on Friday evening and we are very anxious to know:

1. Whether this club of Mr. F's, is entitled to call itself affiliated at the present time (without the matter going before the Western Centre Board, of the ACU).

2. Is this new club entitled to send its delegates to our

---

* Featherstone was to feature prominently a few years later when he was to officiate at the S and DMCC when it called an extraordinary meeting in 1929 to resolve the crisis that emerged with its motor cycle football team.

board meeting on Friday, with the right to vote?

               3. Is there any rule against there being two affiliated clubs in one town?

Can I purchase a set of rules of the ACU relating to the formation and conduct of Local Centres, and the general rules of the ACU (I have a copy on the competition rules). We require these very urgently as we are at a great disadvantage with Mr. F, without them. Would it trouble you too much to get copies sent to me at once? Can you let me have latest official news of the RAC action with ref to the ACU-MCC. I am very sorry to trouble you so much, but unless we can quote definite rules our opponents will probably twist the facts and the ACU rules to suit circumstances.

Thanking you, yours sincerely, HPB.

As can be seen from the above letter the new club that was formed in hurried circumstances in Cheltenham was to help preserve the Western Centre, for if things went badly for the ACU their influence would be greatly diminished. The vital question was, how many clubs would it support? The ACU stated it would only recognize just one club in any town. Things were getting more complicated as the days passed and no wonder Harry Baughan was requesting more specific information on item 3.

W Smith,
Secretary,
Worc & DMCC. (no date).
Dear Sir.

I beg to inform you that at a meeting of the S and DMCC held on Wed: 21st inst 'the following resolutions were carried unanimously . . .'

"The basic principle of the ACU in refusing to approve unaffiliated clubs for closed competitions interferes with the liberty of clubs and individuals, and works to the detriment of clubs, the centres, the ACU and the sport generally. The S and DMCC, calls on the Western Centre to use every effort to get this clause rescinded.

If by reason of entering, riding or assisting with an unauthorized closed competition, any member of the S and DMCC, is penalized by the ACU, the S and DMCC, will immediately disaffiliate.

I understand that the Gloucester MCC has passed a similar resolution. We have requested that the matter be put on the agenda at the next board meeting, at Hereford."

Yours sincerely, HPB.

Up to this point the S and DMCC had been a loyal supporter of the ACU since 1910 and members were getting to the stage where serious action was contemplated.

The Secretary,
Western Centre, ACU.   April 24th, 1926.

Dear Sir.
The S and DMCC, wish that the following be placed on the agenda of the Board meeting to be held at Hereford on Tuesday next the 27st inst.
Discussion on the application of the closed competition rules of the Auto Cycle Union.
Yours faithfully Hon Sec, HPB.

The letter below gives more details, this time directed specifically to the motor cycle faction, the issue of cyclecars and Morgan type threewheelers was skilfully avoided; or specifically passed over.

MCC to HPB.
1, Queen Victoria Street, EC4.   24th April, 1926.

Dear Sir.
Now that the members of the Club have, by an overwhelming majority, decided not to be affiliated to the Auto Cycle Union, it becomes necessary to point out to those members who were unable to be present at the Meeting last week, the position of individual members of the Club.
As regards car members, provide that the Royal Automobile Club does not vary the attitude it has adopted heretofore, nothing will be altered, the position being affected only as regards motor cycle members.
The Royal Automobile Club, the parent body from which the Auto Cycle Union derives its authority, do not demand affiliation from clubs to which they issue permits, and it is possible it may not endorse the action of its branch body the Auto Cycle Union in its efforts to enforce affiliation on clubs in connection with their motor cycling members.
However, until the position develops, motor cycle members of the Motor Cycling Club, if they continue to partake in any MCC competitions, run the risk of being banned from taking part in any competitions promoted by clubs affiliated to the Auto Cycle Union. How far such a ban can be made effective your Committee cannot forecast, but they consider it extremely likely that, if members of the Motor Cycling Club strongly support their Club, such a ban

must become inoperative.

Your Committee feels that there must be other clubs unwilling to be dictated to by the ACU as regards their own closed club competitions, and that the number of such clubs is sufficient to provide ample sport.

The following events, as already announced, will be promoted by the Motor Cycling Club as usual—

> The London-Edinburgh Run.
>
> The Inter-Club Team Trial.
>
> The Land's End-John o'Groats Run.
>
> The Lugano Run.
>
> The One-Day Sporting Trial.
>
> The Winter Run.

Should it be the wish of the members to have other events promoted during the season, your Committee are prepared to act, and would be pleased to receive any suggestions from members for such events. The Committee is already in possession of the outlines of several attractive events which have only been shelved owing to the difficulty of including them in an already full programme.

Your Committee wish to thank the members for the whole-hearted support that has been accorded to them in the difficult position that has arisen, and are convinced that if such support is continued the success of the Club will be maintained.

Yours faithfully,
LA Baddeley,
Chairman.

HPB to
FT Ridlake, Esq.
North End Road,
London.

Dear Sir.

Thank you for your telegram of yesterday with ref: to the RAC and ACU attitude to the Edinburgh run, it may interest you to know that at the meeting of the S and DMCC yesterday evening the following resolution was proposed and carried . . . "If by any reason of entering, riding, or assisting with a closed trial, organized by an approved but unaffiliated club, any member of the S and DMCC is penalized in any way by the ACU the S and DMCC will instantly disaffiliate." I have also brought the matter before the Gloucester MCC and at their meeting the following resolution was passed. 'By any reason of any of the GMCC members riding in an MCC trial they are in any way penalized the GMCC will immediately join the ranks of the unaffiliated clubs.' A meeting of the Western Centre Board is held next week and I have great hopes of persuading the Western Centre itself to adopt a similar resolution. In that case we shall insist on the Centre delegate bringing the matter before the ACU. The Worcester Club delegate is Mr. Featherstone of the ACU Competitions Committee. I will advise you of any further developments.

Yours faithfully, HP Baughan.

Geoff Fisher remembers that Featherstone certainly had a rough time at the Western Centre meeting for his fellow club members had the same strong feelings as Harry Baughan.

JA Masters,
Hon Secretary,
The Motor Cycling Club Ltd,
22 Norland Square,
Kensington, W11. 22/4/26.

Dear Mr. Baughan.

As I was away from home when your letter arrived it was a surprise to hear that Bidlake invited you. As you will see the RAC has not endorsed the action of the ACU, and it is not likely that they will do so. Captain Phillips, very misleading and one sided attack was obviously written before the local club but I hope it will not have any effect. There are indications that in the South Eastern Centre, many of the leading clubs will break away. As a matter of fact the Centre was very nearly dissolved at a special Branch meeting to the determination of the clubs to look as interference by the ACU with their chief event.

The MCC are prepared to give any encouragement to clubs who like themselves resent this interference and it is probable that an association of unaffiliated clubs will shortly be formed. If your local club stands firm and support the MCC attitude it will greatly assist us in our fight for those who wish to carry on the sport without interference from a respected and elite organization such as the ACU now has become. I have been on the ACU Committee and Council for the past seven years (until recently) so I am speaking with inside knowledge.

Yours sincerely,
JA Masters.

At the Western Centre level these important matters raised by Harry Baughan were left in abeyance and members who supported the MCC were free to pursue their events. The matter of affiliation was of such importance that immediate negotiation at national level was instigated.

With such strong feelings within a Centre serious repercussions would follow unless a solution was found. The first paragraph of the previous letter gives an indication that the Western Centre was not alone with the proposed changes.

JA Masters.
Hon Secretary,
The Motor Cycling Club Ltd,
22 Norland Square,
Kensington, W11.

Dear Mr. Baughan. 12/5/26.
I only received your letter last night so thought it best to write you today in case this does not reach you in time. It is actually irregular for a club to be affiliated or claim to be affiliated until the matter has been dealt with by the Centre and the ACU Council. Until the Centre approve the club could claim to be affiliated or its members sit on the Centre Board. There is no rule whatever against two or more clubs in one town becoming affiliated.

I am trying to get a copy of the local Centre bye laws also for you, but in the meantime I should accept nothing that F states unless he can show you the rule in print, no other statements are binding on the ACU. The latest MCC-ACU position is that we have applied for a permit for Edinburgh (as an unaffiliated club) as deemed by the RAC but we have not heard from the ACU. They have previously hung up on the matter so that the permit when issued will be too late to make use of and we shall probably run the Edinburgh run without it.

Yours sincerely,
                    JA Masters.

Very few people remember this upheaval, Harry Baughan was at the centre of it and these letters give a very good indication of the strength of feeling of the clubs in the Western Centre and elsewhere. Harry Baughan and many others had great affection for MCC events, to be regarded as renegades was too much to stomach; their stand was instrumental in the final outcome. In late August the whole sorry business of affiliation was finally resolved, the ACU could have partly claimed victory, if indeed that was their intention. The MCC on the other hand, not wishing to prolong the issue finally sanctioned its affiliation to the ACU and members of both organizations could then get on with the business of enjoying their sport without fear or favour.

Eventually the following statement was issued by the ACU, entitled:

Peace at last. August 1926.

After many months of negotiation the difficult question of relations between the ACU and the MCC has been happily settled. The General Council of the Union on July 19th last unanimously approved the general terms of the settlement, which has also been approved by the MCC, and those were translated into agreed terms at a joint meeting of the two bodies held under the chairmanship of Lt. Colonel Mervyn O'Gorman, the chairman of the Competitions Committee of the Royal Automobile Club, at a meeting last Friday. There now only remains the formal sanction by the Council of the necessary amendments to the ACU competition rules.

The London-Edinburgh Ban

The refusal of the MCC to become affiliated and the consequent ban on its London-Edinburgh run is past history to which it is unnecessary to refer, except to point out that the penalties which the MCC officials then incurred were technical in character and in no way reflect on these gentlemen's characters as sportsmen. In one case in particular, that of Mr. Bidlake, the trials secretary of the MCC, and the well known timekeeper, there appears to have been some misunderstanding on the part of the public.

Mr. Bidlake was, and is, an appointed timekeeper of the ACU. His appointment necessarily lapsed so long as he was connected with the promotion of a competition declared to be unauthorized, but immediately the ban on the London-Edinburgh was lifted Mr. Bidlake was again in a position to act as an official timekeeper, his capabilities for which work has never been in question. The lifting of the ban on the London-Edinburgh run was largely due to Col. O'Gorman's insistence on the difficulties between the two bodies being rediscussed. He and the Competitions committee of the RAC felt that there must be some way by which, without detracting from the authority of the ACU, such an event could be regularized. The way was found by the institution of a new class of club — the approved club to which permits would only be issued by the ACU after it had satisfied itself that such a club was prepared to run under its rules. The distinction between the affiliated and the approved but non-constituent club is all to the advantage of the former. The permit fees to be paid by an approved club are heavier, and they have no share in the government of the sport. The MCC admits ACU authority. The MCC, however, has never as a club wished to control the sport outside its own ranks; many of its officials are closely identified with the ACU through other clubs, and they find their hands already full. By admitting the authority throughout the country of the ACU, the MCC has shown a very proper regard for constitutional government, whilst the Auto Cycle Union

Courtesy: Ken Rogers.

Bert Rogers with his 1926 350cc ohv Blackburne powered Baughan, No.27/214 (No.23 in the sales ledger). Registered DF2280 on the 13/4/1927.

may also be congratulated on securing as its supporters the representatives of a body older, in fact, than itself.

The outcome of this bitter wrangle between the two bodies was well received throughout the Centres and not just from the Western one. Geoff Fisher remembers that the feelings ran high and thought the ACU had seriously under estimated this. Just how strong the feeling was with MCC members within the Western Centre they were quite willing to sever all connections with the Centre and the ACU attitude that they must 'toe the line'. Geoff Fisher remembers there was great bitterness towards the ACU, especially from the clubs in Worcestershire and Herefordshire which is not immediately obvious in these previous letters.

BATTY-SMITH, H. L., Bridewell House,
Bridewell Place, E.C.4.
BAUGHAN, H. P., Lower Street, Stroud, Glos.
BAXTER, G. E., Cumberland House, Park Lane,
Wembley.

Harry Baughan's entry as a member of the the Motor Cycling Club in 1922. It was quite understandable that HPB was very upset with all the trouble that went on between the ACU and the MCC. Like a large number of riders in the Western Centre he had great loyalty to the MCC. When he attended Western Centre meetings as their spokes person he had tremendous support from the clubs within the Centre.

JM Baughan collection.

Harry Baughan's medals from The Motor Cycling Club when he started on his trials involvement. HPB was a great supporter of this pioneering club from the beginning. The reasons for his disenchantment with the ACU attitude is obvious from the preceding letters.

Start of motor cycle football in Stroud. Problems with commercialization and money. MCFC causes great division within the Stroud and District Motor Cycle Club. Fred Halliday's serious accident. S&DMCC disband due to motor cycle football. Stroud Valley Motor Club formed.

By 1926 many riders in the Stroud and District Motor Cycle Club had heard of a new craze, motor cycle football and a small band of these curious enthusiasts decided to investigate its potential further. To them this offered a new venture and they wanted to be part of it. The chief players in these formative days were the Powles, Tom, Leslie and John, along with Harry Daniels, Cyril Hughes, Johnny Beak, Fred Halliday and later Eddie Mills. They paid a visit to the Cheltenham Athletic ground to find out first hand just what motor cycle football was all about. The match was between Cheltenham Motor Cycle Club and Gloucester Motor Cycle Club. What they witnessed that day fired them with such enthusiasm for the game they were totally convinced that this sport offered great new opportunities for motor cycling.

At this point these keen members of the S and DMCC approached their committee to be allowed to form the Stroud Motor Cycle Football Club. The committee could see no reason to refuse their request and the SMCFC came into being in name only; answerable to the committee itself. No one could have seen the possible outcome of this new extension of motor cycle sport in the Stroud club; a can of worms was about to be opened! From that first meeting they started to practise in earnest, gradually sorting themselves out, repairing the damaged machines in the process, and up to that point no one had suffered any serious injury. After a few months of practice and in a somewhat bold move Tom Powles suggested that Stroud should challenge the Gloucester Club to a match. This was received to such good effect that the Gloucester Club even put up a special award for the winners that would be played over two legs. So the Gibb Challenge Shield came into being.

The first leg was to be played at Gloucester where Harry Daniels led out the, then, unofficial Stroud side as Captain. Despite their complete lack of experience they came away with just two goals against them. Not down hearted they arranged the return leg at Fromehall Park, the very first time motor cycle football had been played there. This match caused considerable interest in the Stroud area and over two thousand paying spectators passed through the turnstiles, and more to the point, Stroud reversed their original defeat and beat Gloucester on goal average and won the Gibb Shield; the die was well and truly cast for the Stroud side. From that moment this group of enthusiasts went from strength to strength and played at Coventry, Melksham, Shepton Mallet, North Hants, Bristol, Worcester and also the locals, Gloucester and Cheltenham. Eventually the Western Centre introduced a league for motor cycle football. In due course the SMCFC consolidated their position within the Western Centre and won the League Cup four years in succession. Despite all this success there were to be a few ups and downs from time to time which were not considered serious. Motor cycle football to many motor cyclists is a strange sport, so why should anyone wish to play a game of football while riding a motor cycle? Strange to relate, there were hundreds that did. Up to this point trials had dominated just about all motor cycle activity. Motor cycle football offered something completely different. Many clubs ran evening events that gave a modicum of competition and this was the only chance the public had to witness such activity.

Throughout the 1920s and 1930s many thousands of people who turned out in the winter to witness the performances of the best trials riders in the country, were prepared to travel considerable distances to do so. Take for instance the early version of the Cotswold Cup Trial, perhaps the premier event of the Western Centre. From Sandy Lane on the Cheltenham outskirts to all the hills surrounding Stroud involved a fair amount of road miles between the many hills. Even in the 1920s there were thousands of spectators on the Nailsworth Ladder witnessing the eighty or so riders and drivers giving their all. Those onlookers were willing to stand for hours, often in poor weather conditions to see riding skills not only displayed by enthusiastic clubmen who were often local from the spectators point of view, but the factory supported riders on the latest machines who came down from the Midlands. Motor cycle football on the other hand drew a different crowd, not the mainstream competition orientated clubman, but the general public looking for entertainment, who were in all honesty, not terribly disposed to motor cycle sport at all. It was just pure entertainment as far as they were concerned. Perhaps the most important factor in its popularity was the time of year it was held. Usually it started in May and finished in September, a very comfortable time of year for everyone, especially families.

The one thing that swayed the attendance figures was an established location, usually within a short bus ride and then a few hundred yards walk. Stroud had an excellent venue at Fromehall Park; now the home of Stroud Rugby Football Club. This was situated less than a mile from the town centre, just off the A46. This proved ideal, the ground being flat, and gave the riders an excellent surface. The paying spectators had ample space to spread around the ground; and the emphasis was on paying. Since the inception of the S and DMCC the members had existed without any serious conflict of interest. The social side had its followers as did the mildly sporting side, distance reliability trials attracted many as did those keen on pillion trials. The trials riders were well catered for as were the speed merchants. This happy state of affairs carried through until 1926 when things started to change, nothing too dramatic at first but after two more years there was increasing discontent that finally became a serious prob-

Stroud Motor Cycle Club Football Team 1928. L to R, Fred Halliday, Eddie Mills, Johnny Powles, Chris Stagg, Johnny Beak and Cyril Hughes. This photo was taken after the first practice session. Twenty minutes later Halliday was in a serious condition with multiple injuries after a collision with the opposition. Ironically the bike he was riding at the time can be just seen behind Fred, this belonged to Harry Daniels.

lem; motor cycle football was about to give many people sleepless nights. The S and DMCC gradually became involved with this fast growing sport and the members within the Club formed a nucleus that became ever more enthusiastic as the months passed. Baughan Motors soon became drawn into it, not perhaps by any particular enthusiasm on Harry Baughan's part, but just because of motor cycling developing into a new aspect of the sport. But in 1928 motor cycle football had greatly increased in popularity and in the Western Centre this was no exception. Motor cycle clubs always tried to give its members as much a choice and variety as circumstances would allow. The Stroud Club saw the increase of this new sport develop through all its aspects. Initial enthusiasm by its own members to push for a suitable site to stage these events, some form of commercial sponsorship, the inevitable monetary problems, great anguish, and then the eventual ruination of the S and DMCC. The faction that favoured motor cycle football may not have been great in number. Their presence became ever more of a problem that eventually created great internal friction which became difficult to contain. Harry Baughan was never entirely convinced of the value in motor cycle football but did not actually oppose it. However, he could not see any possible development that would benefit motor cycling in the future. At the time Fred Halliday was still riding his Baughan in trials to good effect and was paid a small retainer by the Baughan concern. In this capacity he also had competition insurance that was to prove in the not too distant future, very valuable indeed. Despite this, Fred also found motor cycle football to his liking and as challenging as any trials he had competed in; within a few months he was a regular member of the team. Soon motor cycle football started to develop into a serious business. Geoff Fisher was drawn into this circle, but not out of choice.

He was approached in an attempt to find a suitable field on which to play matches, and more importantly, to practise. Fisher soon found an outlet for the latter and it was only a few miles from Stroud and conveniently situated behind a public house, the Ragged Cot, at Hyde. This was completely flat, of ample size and on Sunday mornings the Stroud team were out in force, earnestly practising. This assortment of riders with an equally diverse selection of bikes spent a couple of hours honing their skills. Later this practice time was reduced to just over an hour for open exhausts may have been sweet music to the dedicated enthusiast, but the locals, sparse as they were, did not share their passion. This band of riders were the same that initially formed the SMCFC and included a small number of new officials. These intrepid souls went from strength to strength and as the success increased so did the concern within the S and DMCC. With these riders who were totally engrossed in this new sport the remainder of the club carried on with its activities in trials, long distance runs, treasure hunts, etc. This state of affairs did not exist for long and dissent was soon apparent. The SMCFC were gathering an increasing audience that paid to pass through the turnstiles and this income then found its way into the club coffers.

Discontent soon reared its head when money was requested to repair their machines and carry out essential maintenance along with the running costs. Initially it was for fuel (mostly 'dope') chains and clutches, but it did not stop there. Gradually the demands increased. Engines that had 'blown up,' broken gearboxes and bent wheels started to be submitted to the treasurer. At one stage the SMCFC approached HPB to supply a complete set of machines (free) for their activities. As can be imagined this fell on stony ground. The SMCFC made their case to the committee for reimbursement, in their opinion they had made significant contribution to the finances that the Club was enjoying. At first the Club complied with their wishes and for a while things smoothed themselves out, but this ambience was not to last and when the motor cycle footballers started to make further overtures that complete motor cycles should be purchased it almost led to total anarchy within the Club. There was a degree of sympathy expressed by the committee as to the case they put forward. A solution had to be found or there would be an impasse that was going to be difficult to resolve. The committee knew that if they showed any procrastination they would have open revolt on their hands. The only solution they could see was to call an extraordinary general meeting to resolve the matter which hopefully would be acceptable to all parties. This extraordinary general meeting was indeed called. The committee decided that it required an impartial arbiter and they approached the Western Centre Chairman, Mr. E Featherstone who was well known to the club in general and Harry Baughan in particular. Featherstone had found himself at odds with the Stroud Club in 1926 as he did with the Cheltenham and Gloucester ones over the business of the MCC-ACU affiliation and was certainly at pains to prove there was no ill feeling in his arbitration role. That aside, Featherstone, in his capacity as an ACU Steward was to sit and hear the evidence and then to reach a conclusion.

The two parties expressed their points of view, there were long discussions in great detail. However, things were not moving forward. Geoff Fisher proposed a motion, seconded by Harry Baughan that the old Club should be dissolved and two separate ones be formed. Geoff Fisher and Harry Baughan could see no end to the SMCFC problems and between them brought forward this vital motion that would effectively see the disillusion of the S and DMCC in its present form. A new club could be formed in the fullness of time that would take away the commercial aspect that was growing increasingly troublesome. Both men were true enthusiasts in terms of motor cycle sport and this 'off-shoot' into the realms of blatant financial gain was not in the true interests of motor cycling. This was not their style and they became spokesmen for like minded men and women in the club. One club should be formed solely to deal with all the matters relating to motor cycle football, the other, if formed, should be along the lines as previous with competition and social events.

There was one provision, neither club should encroach on each other's territory. This was accepted in principle by Mr. Featherstone, who patiently listened to all the arguments and grievances from both sides and according to Geoff Fisher was the epitome of impartiality. Then the thorny aspects of assets was brought up, who would own what? Geoff Fisher once more came up with a possible solution, the footballers would go their way while the cups and trophies for the trials would be held over for the new club when formed and the remainder sold off. This was agreed and any monies that would be accrued should be presented to Stroud General Hospital. It was also agreed that the new clubs would affiliate to the Auto Cycle Union and be incorporated within the Western Centre. So the S and DMCC that saw its foundation in 1910 was dissolved in 1930, only to rise, Phoenix like, in a different guise at a meeting that Geoff Fisher called at the Bear Hotel, Rodborough a few weeks later. Fisher had circulated all the old members in an effort to keep those that had opposed the football aspect and have a new chance to continue as before, leaving the bitter feelings behind. A special meeting was called at The Bear Hotel and was well attended. Archibald Hay Grant Heelas, was elected to the Chair, and Geoff Fisher acted as Minuting Secretary. Mr. Fisher proposed that the Club should be renamed the STROUD VALLEY MOTOR CLUB, and should re-affiliate with the ACU. Club rules were suggested and discussed. Rules were accepted, officers and committee were nominated. AH Grant Heelas was installed as President and GW Fisher was General Secretary.

The first meeting of the Committee followed seven days later. Members were approved and elected, soon Harry Baughan and Geoff Fisher started to organize competitions that would be suitable to all abilities. With all the unsavoury business of motor cycle football finally resolved, the new club started in good spirits and continues to this day. The SMCFC carried on with its independent status and continued until the late 1940s when motor cycle football gradually lost its attraction, and finally the club ceased to exist. There was a sad aside to the SMCFC which involved Fred Halliday. Although Fred was riding a Baughan (with assistance from Baughan Motors) in trials he started to take a keen interest in motor cycle football and joined the Stroud team and quickly fitted in very well.

They rode their own bikes as much as possible, but on the odd occasions they did swop. On September 29th 1928, Fred was playing for Stroud at Fromehall. Due to trouble in practice with his 348cc Baughan, borrowed Harry Daniels spare machine; it proved to be a near fatal move. Daniels had modified his machine with two rear brake pedals, one on either side of the bike. Fred was informed of it, but in the heat of battle it was forgotten. Fred was making a fast move onto the ball in an effort to beat his opponent, made to change up and his right foot stamped on the rear brake completely losing control of it. Fred collided with the rider he was trying to cut out; the impact was very heavy and resulted in a smashed pelvis, broken right leg in two places, a broken right arm and collar bone. If this was not enough he was severely concussed and passed out. This enormous accident put him in hospital for months and was to finish his competition days. The one important thing in Fred's favour was the insurance that Harry Baughan had taken out when Fred had started to ride for the factory. It took many months, leading into years before Fred was fully mobile again; but it did not come without its hardships. A leg calliper had to be worn for two years, eventually it was dispensed with. However, Fred had to suffer with his right leg slightly shorter than his left, leaving him with a slight limp. Fred Halliday was indeed lucky to have had competition insurance thoughtfully provided by Baughan Motors. His pay out was £350 (over £13,000 at todays value). This was

F Halliday collection.

Stroud Motor Cycle Football Club. This was the the team that became the Western Centre football league champions of 1930-31. By this time Fred Halliday had taken on the duties of trainer and secretary. L to R, Johnny Beak, Harry Daniels, Tom Powles (captain), Fred Cudmore (chairman), Fred Halliday, Ron Johnson, Johnny Powles and Eddie Mills. Motor cycle football was to divide the parent club, eventually they went their separate ways.

very comforting to Fred for he was a long time recuperating and gave him great peace of mind. Eventually he came back to motor cycle football for the Stroud club, but in a different capacity, that of their trainer. This proved very valuable to the club for now they had a person who could devote time to planning and tactics giving the fixtures secretary an easier time who was trying to do both jobs.

At one stage Chris Stagg played motor cycle football. This aside his first allegiance was to trials and the factory, and he found that accidents in motor cycle football were more than just the odd knock or two many leading to spells in hospital that prevented him from earning a living, insurance aside. Two machines were bought for motor cycle football and Baughan Motors supplied one of them. This was (No.33) No.29/227 on the 19th June 1929. Chris Stagg rode it most of the time when he played for the team. His commitment was not that great for he concentrated mostly on trials in his early days, later expanding into grass track and scrambling. This machine was built entirely by Chris and received no help from Bill or the Gaffer. This was a very basic bike built in the trials jig and was little more than the usual trials machine with the minimum of equipment. Initially there was protection around the engine comprising of two bars. The top one was bolted to the front down tube, the bottom one was attached to the engine mounting plates and the two were joined together. At first it worked fine, but later as experience was gained, it proved to be too restrictive for the rider and they were taken off. The team members all felt that using this type of protection was never a very good idea. Chris does remember that all the machines were fitted with stronger throttle return springs for a fast shut-off; essential in football events. Some were equipped with an ignition 'cut-out' that if the rider was unseated the engine would stop.

There were incidents of machines in the early days before these safety devices were fitted with competitors running into the spectators. The brake shoes were removed from the front hub (there was no time for the luxury of front wheel braking) and the engine and gearbox plates were drilled for lightness. Castrol 'R' lubricated it and Singer sewing machine oil kept the gearbox happy and dope was the fuel that was fed through larger jets in the carb. The 350cc Blackburne was a twin port affair and featured a great amount of fettling by Chris and throughout its life ran faultlessly. As to engines, there were a number of them at Lower Street which had been placed aside from various machines that had been bought in over the years. These were very often modified when Bill or Chris had time on their hands. The engines, like many Baughan Motors had lying about the factory received attention from either Chris or Bill. Both spent hours polishing the internals and were destined only for competition. On a few occasions HPB relented and allowed the SMCFC to use one if they fitted it themselves, the proviso being, 'it was just on loan'. The exhausts on this machine were 'straight through' and instead of the usual sweep up either side of the bike and running just under the petrol tank, they came together just two inches apart under the frame and flared either side of the rear wheel out of harm's way. They made a note that many a rider had been trapped under his machine for a few seconds after the odd collision, time enough for burns to the inside of the thigh and was not to be recommended. Reproduced here is the front page of the programme (overleaf) for what was the culmination of Stroud's Motor Cycle Football Club. Inside was a potted history of the club. Nowhere does it give an account of the anguish that the original S and DMCC suffered before the parties went their separate ways, and needless to say both clubs flourished.

Eventually the motor cycle football lost its following in the area. This was reflected throughout the country and in the end the Stroud Club was wound up. Even so they did play an important part in the development of motor cycle football in the West of England and it gave great entertainment to both spectators and riders alike. The business of finances was touched upon in their programme and states, "our turnover in cash exceeds three figures", This gives an indication and puts into perspective the total outlay that would have been required to buy seven machines for the riders; no wonder the S and DMCC blanched at the suggestion. There was not only the monies that the riders tried to claim back from the S and DMCC but they also had it brought to their attention that cash had changed hands in a rather 'unofficial' way and from there on dealings became very difficult. This undercurrent gave further ammunition to finish the matter once and for all. A glance at the 1948 programme and the list of names gives a good indication of the organization involved when running and promoting an event such as this. The paper work was just as time consuming as any closed to club trial; financially it was far more rewarding.

The SMCFC was successful and despite the inaccuracies in the programme one name remains outstanding, that of George Goodall. Although Goodall had very little connection with the football even though he was the President of the Western Centre ACU. George Goodall will always be remembered as one of the great Morgan exponents in the 1920s and 1930s and featured prominently in all the 'Open' trade supported trials of the time and ran the competition side of things for Morgans. Just what he thought of motor cycle football is not recorded, presumably along the lines of his long time friend Harry Baughan. Despite 'Uncle' George's unquenchable enthusiasm for competition he did have a parsimonious side to him when it came to business for he was not adverse to sending out an invoice for trivial amounts like 'tuppence' (old money) if warranted . . . but that was George as Chris Stagg remembers.

Presentation of the League Championship Cup will be made
to Stroud on conclusion of the match, by G. H. GOODALL,
Esq., President of the Western Centre, A.C.U.

STROUD

Colours: BLUE & WHITE.

1st Reserve: WALT. GRIFFITHS
2nd Reserve: FRANK FINCH

EDDIE TURNER
Goal

N. BURROWS
No. 4. Back.

HARRY DANIELS   **TOM POWLES**   **JACK HOGG**
No. 2. R. Wing   No. 1. Centre   No. 3. L. Wing

Referee: E. J. JARVIS
(Nuneaton)

HAROLD BREECH   **S. BARNETT**   **CYRIL LORD**
(Gloucester)   (Cheltenham)   (Coventry)
No. 3. L. Wing   No. 1. Centre   No. 2. R. Wing

ERIC LITTLE
(Antelope)
No. 4. Back.

Goal
TINY JONES
(Gloucester)

1st Reserve: E. GORE (Cheltenham)

The level of competition that the Stroud Motor Cycle Football Club enjoyed can
be judged by this 1946 programme when Stroud played the Rest of England.
The location was Fromehall Park on the 12th of August 1948. Soon the popularity disappeared and eventually the Club was wound up. Nevertheless it had
many exciting matches around the country and at home.

Sidecar-wheel drives. Richard Woods Patent. Bill Bradley's swd Felix. Howard Uzzell BSA swd. Harry Baughan's first swd with differential. Second Baughan swd with dog-clutch. Details of the Hayward swd and the changes made. Details of the drives.

When the editor of *The Motor Cycle*, Harry Louis interviewed Harry Baughan after his presentation for fifty premier events in 1947, he mentioned the sidecar-wheel drive saga and considered that he had been responsible for all the trouble that followed. Surprisingly, HPB agreed. There is no question that the Baughan swd attracted considerable attention from 1929 to 1932, even though it was in some isolation; then other riders joined in. Bill and Marjorie last used their outfit despite the 50% mark-up penalty, to win the opposite class in the 1946 Cotswold Cups; no doubt this was still fresh in Louis's mind at the time.

Harry Baughan was seen as the chief instigator of the sidecar-wheel drive. By the 1970s and 1980s many motor cycle scribes, through their lack of knowledge always made great play of the Baughan outfit being banned; this was far from the truth. The popular misconception was that the machine *was* banned. In actual fact it was the use of the drive that outlawed it by many clubs within the various ACU Centres. Even those redoubtable journalists Bob Currie and Ralph Venables MBE were convinced this was the case until enlightened by the author. It would be nice to think that Harry Baughan was the sole designer of such a device and claim that his invention started what was to become something that attracted considerable attention in the early to mid 1930s. However, it goes further back than that. Louis, in his position as editor would seem to have overlooked the swds that preceded the Baughan, or conveniently forgot them. As sidecar-wheel drive was such an important part of Baughan Motors history, it is worth recalling some of the events that surrounds this most radical and logical development. Throughout sidecar trials there have been very few revolutionary designs, the only significant factor that had any profound influence was the introduction of sidecar-wheel drive.

This is by no means a definitive treatise on the subject, just that something as contentious as swd should rate more than a passing reference for such an interesting device which caused so much bitterness with many competitors and Centres. Harry Baughan may not have invented swd, just that he seems to be the whipping boy when the clubmen made their feelings known, which in the end almost led to open revolt within the Centres that allowed them to compete. With such an important milestone in trials development, perhaps the only one, in the past seventy years it has never been resurrected and nothing has come remotely close to change things. Its relationship to trials was very interesting and controversial. Swds were a unique development that caused much soul searching by many people, it came at a time in motor cycle history when great inventiveness was the norm. Nevertheless, it caused quite a stir for a number of years before it was finally smothered by penalty marking, or completely outlawed. Despite the interest it generated, very little in the way of documented evidence exists, and amazingly the journalists of the day hardly recorded such a great leap forward in motor cycle transmission. Experiments with swd came in the early 1920s when advancement in motorcycle design was starting to make itself felt. The humble sidecar which gave the family man a method of transport did not quite attain the supposed leg-up the social scale to the light car. In the scheme of things Harry Baughan was perhaps vilified for his leaning towards swd. His influence within the Western Centre may have contributed to its acceptance. However, it was a democratic decision by that committee to allow swd free rein without penalty mark-up for in 1929 it had not been considered necessary. Only a few years later (1936) when under some pressure, did they impose it. Even so, they were the last Centre to do so. I'm sure the reader will draw their own conclusions on this interesting subject.

In 1922 a certain Mr. Richard Wood from Manchester designed and built a swd that incorporated a differential, and duly filed a Patent for it. Wood, it seems did not use this transmission device in trials, so it remains in isolation; but it may have been the inspiration for later developments. A drawing was published (see opposite page) and an explanation accompanies it. The dimensions are not revealed in the Wood invention but a general idea can be gained by looking at the spokes. (Later there is an interesting comparison to the first Baughan swd design on pages 164/165.) Although Wood went on to file a Patent little has come to light as to its eventual outcome. The timing was perhaps right for general sidecar use as they were gaining in popularity with the public. Like a good many other inventions money was needed to develop it. In Wood's case this may have been a serious consideration if production was to be the end result. Tooling, machining and all the associated disciplines that needed to be addressed may have been far more than Wood was prepared to go, and perhaps the reality was that no manufacturer had the foresight to undertake such a speculative venture, or a bank willing to support him. Wood, with his differential was certainly ahead of his time and not until Harry Baughan designed his own swd differential in 1927 (but only part built as Geoff Fisher remembers) was there any attempt to modify motor cycle combination transmission commercially.

The Baughan differential was remarkably compact and one has only to glance at some of those that appear in the 500/600cc racing car class in today's hill climbs to appreciate its size. In eighty years or more after their device little has changed, the only discernible difference with the racing car ones being a slight increase in overall size to accommodate bigger internals due to the considerable increase in power and torque. The Western Centre it seems was looked on as the

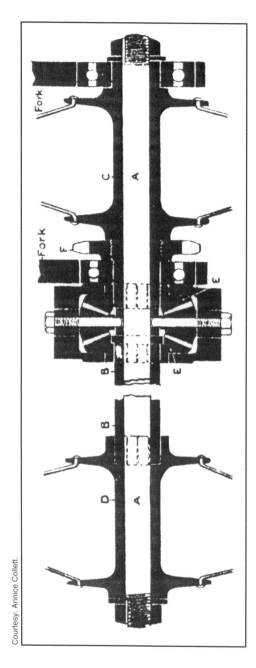

Courtesy: Annice Collett.

Wood's S.-W.D. Differential. Motor Commerce, June 10th, 1922.

Wood's Patent differential for Motorcycle sidecar combination: The axle here shown in section is interesting as marking a step towards constituting the motorcycle and sidecar combination a permanent *two-wheels* driven car. The patentee is Mr. R.S. Wood, at 62, Boston Street, Manchester, who also has applied the feature of the layout for other vehicles. The shaft A is a solid stay with nutted outer-ends, and serves to hold the outer revolving parts in position. The hubs C and D revolve about A, being kept in step by the differential gear E, the power drive being through the chain wheel F secured to the cycle hub C, and thence through the differential and sleeve B (shown broken to reduce the size of the illustration) to the sidecar hub D. Thus both wheels are driven and use is made of the adhesion available through the sidecar's weight, combined with the advantages peculiar to a differential gear when turning corners.

prime mover for all that was to follow concerning swds. This was not entirely the case for it was the Yorkshire equivalent where a certain Bill Bradley lived that a serious and successful attempt at building a sidecar-wheel drive specifically designed for climbing freak hills that the breakthrough was made in 1925, eventually moving on to sporting trials in general. The great difference between the Bradley swd and the Baughan device was that Bradley did not view a commercial outcome as did Baughan Motors. Bradley was content to climb impossibly steep hills as a pure engineering exercise. At this time the Bradford Club had a new hill of their own, known as Hepolite Scar at Manningham, just outside the city. It had a maximum gradient of 1 in 1.5, which comprised a surface of quarry tippings, slabs of flat stones varying in size along with rocks and sand, which would have shocked most people on the level. Bill Bradley turned his attention to this 'Freak' hill which had foiled all previous attempts to ascend by mechanical means. This was a challenge too good to miss.

Bradley was a gifted textile engineer who had great enthusiasm for motor cycles and the sport. His fertile brain came up with some wonderful designs for motor cycles that remained unchallenged for years. Being a Yorkshireman, Bradley's choice of motor cycle was not, unsurprisingly, a Scott, bought on April 2nd, 1925, which he extensively modified. It was in something of a dilapidated state. However, he soon got to work on it and it proved to be the ideal basis for an experimental combination. After some redesigning, 'Felix' was re-born and registered WT 9789. (The original Felix was a solo Raleigh which featured a chain drive to the front as well as the rear wheel.) At this time Bill had his own business at Beacon Works, Addingham, near Ilkley. The name 'Felix,' meaning happy or fortunate, as well as the 'unstoppable cat' who kept on walking turned out to be very appropriate. Once completed he took it to Hepolite Scar on May 29th, 1926 where his ambition was fulfilled at his first attempt and with Bert Ward in the sidecar. This was four years before Bill Hayward's debut with his swd. Felix was a hybrid, powered by a 2 cylinder water-cooled two stroke Scott Squirrel engine of 596cc, fitted with an original two-port exhaust manifold made by the Scott Motor Company of Shipley.

The crank pins overhang the central flywheel, driving sprockets and bearings. Lubrication is by separate oil tank and two sight drip feeds to the two separate crankcases. The carburettor is a Cox and Thomas No. E24 155109. Two chains connect the power unit to the normal 2 speed Scott gearbox driven by expanding bands to the output shaft. The right hand side high gear driven sprocket driving the magneto by chain drive. A chain drives a 3 speed Sturmey Archer gearbox with clutch and kick start, the rear wheel driven by the normal chain. The two speed gear is operated by Bowden cable and lever on the right hand side of the machine. Overall gear ratios are 22.4.5 to 1. Direct lubrication of the chains is

'Felix' description: Courtesy of the Bradford Industrial Museum.

PATENT SPECIFICATION

Application Date: Nov. 17, 1920.   No. 27,711 / 20.   **174,682**

Complete Accepted : Feb. 9, 1922.

COMPLETE SPECIFICATION.

Improvements relating to Differential Gear for Motor Vehicles.

I, RICHARD SAMUEL WOOD, of 62, Boston Street, Manchester, in the County of Lancaster, Mechanical Engineer, English, do hereby declare the nature of
5 this invention and in what manner the same is to be performed, to be particularly described and ascertained in and by the following statement:—

In order that my invention, an im-
10 proved differential gear for motor vehicles that can be used with a solid axle for motor cars, motor lurrys, motor cycles with side cars, may be readily understood, I send with this specification a
15 sheet of drawings illustrative thereof, to which, by figures and letters, reference is made in the following description.
Fig. 1 shows an example of my improved differential gear fitted on a solid
20 axle of a motor car, with the driving gear connected at each side by means of tubes which are attached to the gear and road wheels, by means of dog clutch connections or other suitable means, and revolve
25 on the solid axle.
Fig. 2 shows bevel wheel with square hole as fitted on axle of Fig. 7 and is part of my differential gear.
Fig. 3 shows frame that carries the
30 pinions that mesh into the bevel wheels Fig. 6 and Fig. 1 when in place upon their axles.
Fig. 4 shows the tubes with dog clutch ends.
35 Fig. 5 shows frame that carries the pinions that mesh into the bevel wheels Fig. 2 and Fig. 6 when on the axle of Fig. 7 and geared up with other part of gear.
40 Fig. 6 shows bevel wheels fitted on axle Fig. 1 at each side, showing pinions in frame meshed into them, and con-

nected to the road wheels by means of the dog clutch tubes at each side running on the solid axle.   45
Fig. 7 shows an example of my improved differential gear on a solid axle with tube, with dog clutch ends fitted at one side only and connected with gear and road wheel, the other side being con-   50
nected through the square hole in bevel wheel Fig. 2 and square on the axle to fit with another square on axle to fit flanges of road wheel.
Fig. 8 shows pinions that revolve in   55
frames Fig. 3 and in frame Fig. 5 and mesh into the bevel wheels Fig. 2 and Fig. 6.
To attain the object of my invention is to make a suitable differential gear   60
that can be fitted on a solid axle, and will vary the speeds of the road wheels of a motor car, motor lurry, or motor cycle with side car.
Fig. 1 shows motor car axle fitted with   65
my improved differential gear, with tubes at each side, with dog clutch ends that connects the gear with road wheels, a is the first mover crown wheel, b is the flange of gear, c is the bevel wheels of   70
gear, d is the bolts that bind gear together e is the pinions in frame f is the spindles that pinions revolve on in frame g is the frame that carries the pinions h is the tubes with dog clutch ends j the   75
solid axle k flange of wheel for tube with dog clutch end to fit l the road wheel m flange of wheel n washer with square hole p nut q bolts that bind flanges to wheel.
Fig. 2 shows bevel wheel with square   80
hole in gear that fits on shaft or axle of Fig. 7.
Fig. 3 shows frame that carries the pinions g the frame e the pinions f the spindles.   85

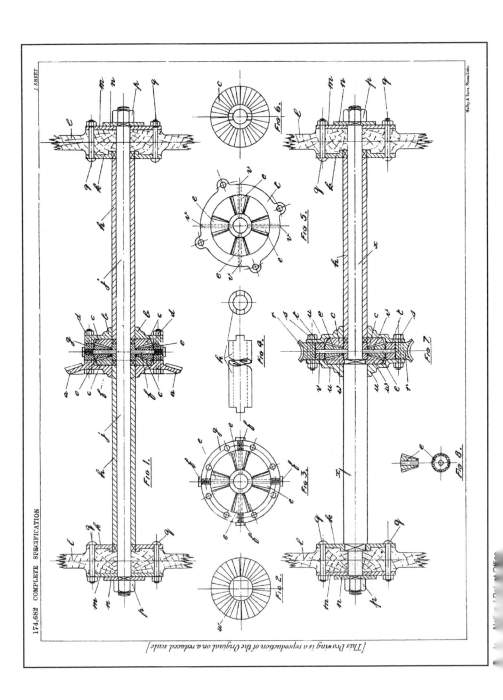

2 174,682

Fig. 4 shows the tubes with dog clutch ends *h* the dog clutch ends.

Fig. 5 shows frame that carries pinions in gear of Fig. 7 *e* is the pinions *t* is the 5 frame *v* the spindles that pinions revolve upon.

Fig. 6 shows bevel wheels as fitted in gear Fig. 1 with. the slots for dog clutch ends of tubes.

10 Fig. 7 shows motor car axle fitted with my improved differential gear, fitted with tube, with dog clutch end at one side only *e* is the pinions in frame *t* is the frame *u* is the flanges of gear *v* spindles 15 for pinions to revolve in frame *r* worm wheel *s* bolts *c* bevel wheels *h* tube with dog clutch end *k* flange for dog clutch end of tube *l* wheel *m* flange *n* washer with square hole *p* nut *q* bolts that bind 20 flanges to wheel *x* solid axle.

Fig. 8 shows pinions *e* that revolve in frame of gear.

Having now particularly described and ascertained the nature of my said invention, and in what manner the same is 25 to be performed, I declare that what I claim is:—

1. A differential gear that will revolve upon a solid axle as described in my specification and shown in my drawings 30 Fig. 1.

2. A differential gear that will revolve upon a solid axle as described in my specification and shown in my drawings Fig. 7. 35

Dated the 16th day of November, 1920.

RICHARD SAMUEL WOOD.

Reference has been directed, in pursuance of Section 7, Sub-section 4, of the Patents and Designs Acts, 1907 and 1919, 40 to Specifications No. 4236 of 1883, No. 21,147 of 1892, No. 24,196 of 1906, No. 28,106 of 1906, No. 480 of 1909, and No. 107,486.

Rodhill: Printed for His Majesty's Stationery Office, by Love & Malcomson, Ltd.—1922.

The original patent documents for Richard Wood's sidecar-wheel drive from 1922. Woods was probably the first person to submit such a design specifically for motor cycles.

by tap on the oil tank and suitable piping. Brakes were improved by the fitting of a hand brake on the left hand side of the machine and had a mechanical duo-servo coupling of the rear brake to the front. This was achieved by removing the rear brake back plate anchor pin and substituting a lever with a limited forward and backward movement. When the foot brake was applied the reaction from the back plate was used to operate the front brake by means of levers and cables. Two levers are used, one attached to the inner cable, the other to the outer cable which operates the front brake. When the machine moves forwards or backwards the reaction operates the front brake by one lever or the other. The Felix frame is of special pyramidal construction, all tubes being straight and subject to compression or tension only.

An undershield of sheet steel protects the crank case. The transmission is effected by the combination of a Scott two-speed foot controlled countershaft gear, driven by two chains from the engine crankshaft, and a SA three-speed gearbox, type LSLW, with handlebar controlled clutch. The drive from the former is taken from an extension of the hollow shaft carrying a sprocket well to the left of the machine, in such a way that the three-speed may take its position centrally within the frame. A special clutch chain wheel takes the place of the standard

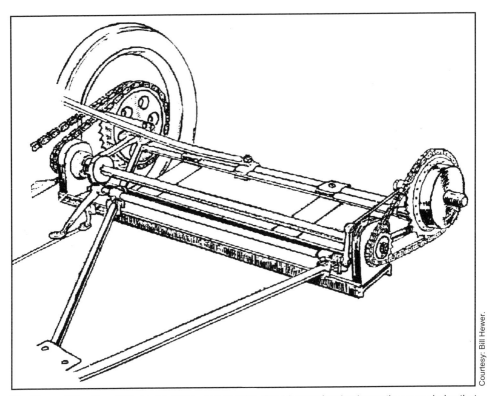

The Howard Uzzell swd fitted to his 998cc, V twin BSA. The biggest drawback was the open chains that were a constant source of trouble to Uzzell. The **I** beams that support either end of the transmission shaft was its Achilles heel and the torque fractured them frequently. The bars that were welded into place to counter this and can be seen extending from the front to the rear of the chassis. Uzzell used it for about a year, finally abandoning it. A few years later Harold Taylor used the same principle, this time as the Williams drive. Taylor experienced the same problems as Uzzell.

pattern. No shock absorber has been found necessary. The final drive is taken from the three-speed in the usual manner. The chain line would accommodate a 23 x 4 inch tyre which was sufficient to allow the use of Parsons chains, as did the sidecar wheel when needed. Parsons chains were still used in the late 1920s and early 1930s, Morgans were a prime example; eventually they *were* banned. Six speeds are available, the ratios being 4.03, 5.8, 7.25, 10.44, and 20.88 to 1. On each of these gears the hand or foot clutches may be used. A standard BTH magneto is mounted directly above the two-speed gear, from which it is driven. The sidecar is also 'special,' has 10 inches of ground clearance, and is fitted with a driven sidecar wheel. The transmission for this is by means of two chains and a light high speed countershaft, which is supported by Skefko bearings, and fitted

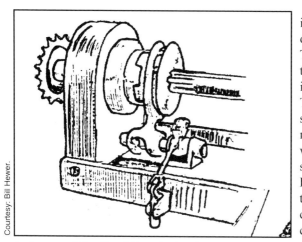

Courtesy: Bill Hewer.

A close-up of the Uzzell Dog-clutch. The principle followed Bradley's Felix where the rider made the decision instead of the passenger who could concentrate on balancing the outfit.

in the ends of a large diameter torque tube. This tube is arranged to withstand the driving and braking forces. The dog-clutch for the sidecar-wheel engagement was situated half way along the cross shaft and operated by Bradley with a lever on the left hand handle bar connected to a Bowden cable. There was also a mechanism for locking this lever in or out of drive. This was removed when the swd was changed sometime in the 1950s from chain to friction discs. Although Bradley used chains to drive his swd they were remarkably short, only an inch or so between the sprocket teeth. With Felix there was less danger of anything getting trapped in these short chain runs. The sprocket from the bike rear spindle was approximately 6/7 inches in diameter and through the chain drove another sprocket 3 inches in diameter on the cross shaft with corresponding ones to the sidecar-wheel. Later Howard Uzzell followed the same principle but with far longer chains, which proved to be its downfall. Bradley, with his torque tube never experienced Uzzell's **I** beam problems, perhaps due in the main to different conditions in local trials that the BSA user experienced.

Like most perfectionists Bill Bradley continued to modify Felix over the years, incorporating new ideas such as the magneto being pressurized by the compression of the saddle cushion which fed a pipe to the back plate to keep out stray water when trialling. Then followed the whole outfit banking in either, left or right hand corners, thus going one better than Freddie Dixon's banking sidecar. In this respect Bill Bradley was years in front of Hans Haldemann who used the same fully banking principle on his road racing outfit in the 1950s. He then continued for many more years trialling over his beloved Wharfdale. Without question Bradley will be remembered as the true pioneer of swd and was just a few years in front of Harry Baughan with his offering. Four months after Bradley's successful ascent of Hepolite Scar, Stanley Bellhouse of Ben Rhydding, Ilkley, had this to say about Felix. *"After I had inspected Felix, played with his six gears, admired the sidecar drive, and jumped hard on the immovable chas-*

Bill Bradley with an anxious looking Bert Ward in the chair climbing Hepolite Scar on the 29th of May, 1926. This was the second successful climb by any mechanical device and was in the back of Bill's mind when he built 'Felix' and his effort was duly rewarded.

The climbing ability of Felix is amply demonstrated by Bill Bradley at the Clifton Fair in 1928. A careful count reveals there are six people aboard. Bill often used Felix this way in order to show what sidecar-wheel drive could achieve.

The first ascent of the Scar by car was Captain A G Frazer–Nash in an 1.9cc Frazer–Nash, October 1925.

Just how forward thinking Bill Bradley was is well illustrated here with a banking outfit. Felix the cat sits proudly on the nose of the sidecar no doubt enjoying the ride. The gentleman on the right is suitably impressed.

sis, I was swirled from Addingham up to the point where the track left the road and started to climb up the Beacon side. It was a nice trip, but I wished I had been smaller and could have sat in and not on the needle pointed sidecar. I got off, put a roll of film in the camera and watched 'Bert' pack himself scientifically aboard. Bradley gave me a hundred yards start–at which point the real tiger country begins–and then started the climb.

"The first two hundred yards were comparatively easy, a mere nothing of a one in six, surfaced with tufts of coarse grass relieved with patches of shingle. Then Felix had his throttle closed and everyone got out and reconnoitred. The track began to rear itself seriously on end, and was composed chiefly of those bucket–like boulders mentioned in an earlier paragraph. After this came a section on which the buckets gave place to barrels–stones so large and so sheer that nothing except a tank could ever hope of getting over them. This lasted about fifty yards and then the buckets became fashionable again and continued until the foot of the cairn was reached." Exploration having finished, the crew got aboard and Felix was kicked into life. A restart was made easily and without a trace of wheel spin. A steady climb was accomplished, the advantage of the double drive being most evident. When the precipice of barrel–like boulders was reached, the Scott was guided off the track into the heather. Here things were softer, but still notably uneven. The track was regained some fifty yards

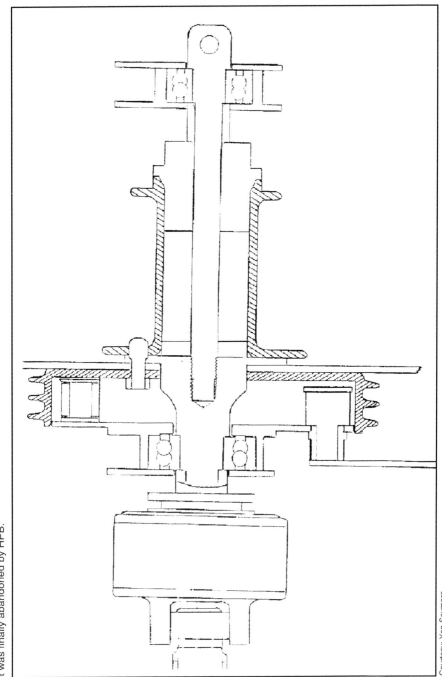

The first Baughan sidecar-wheel drive circa 1927/8. The differential can be clearly seen on the left and measures two inches by four. This was only partly built as the cost of developing and machining was going to be high. The drive was intended to be in a straight line, spindle to spindle. it was finally abandoned by HPB.

Courtesy: Yan Seymore

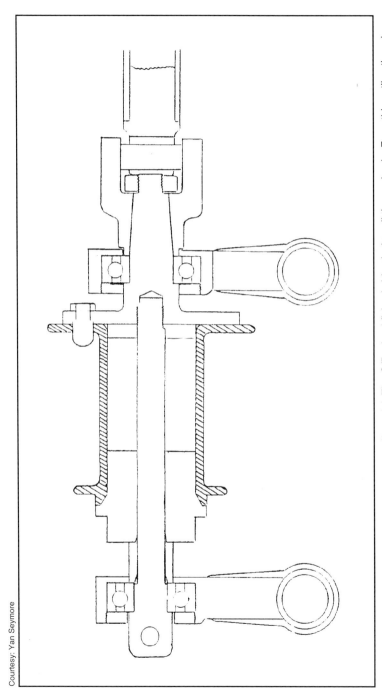

Courtesy: Yan Seymore

The sidecar-wheel detail of the first Baughan with differential. The Q/D wheel fixing is identical to all three wheels. From this outline there is no indication as to how any lateral movement was accommodated in the drive train. Bill Hayward could not remember if this was indeed the case. The similarity to the Wood device is evident. Neither Chris nor Bill recall any connection with the 1922 design.

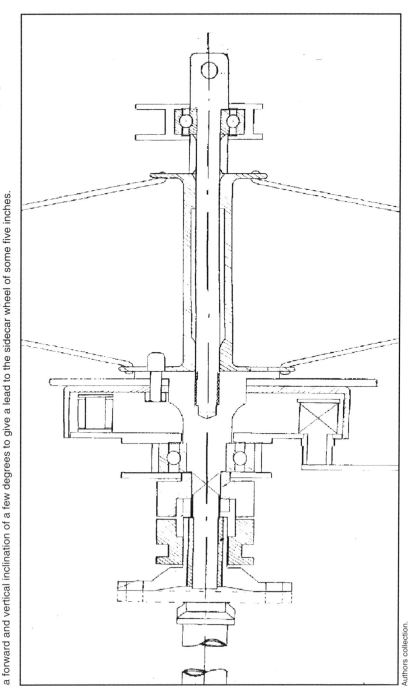

The second Baughan sidecar-wheel drive without the differential. This was the most simple solution of all the swds that were produced for trials, uncomplicated, reliable and efficient. The dotted line on this and the opposite page indicates the position of the flexible coupling which allowed a forward and vertical inclination of a few degrees to give a lead to the sidecar wheel of some five inches.

Authors collection.

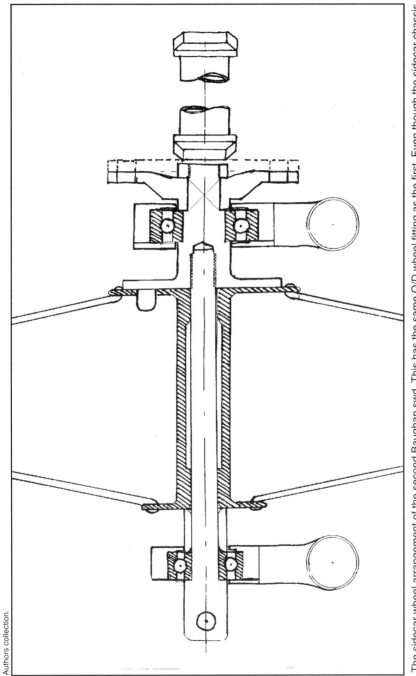

The sidecar wheel arrangement of the second Baughan swd, This has the same Q/D wheel fitting as the first. Even though the sidecar chassis movement could be dealt with by the flexible joints the dog-clutch with its wide teeth could also take up any movement with their generous clearance. The shaft that the dog-clutch ran on was four flats, an easy engineering solution.

higher up and in a few minutes the cairn was reached. *"Our triumphal advance had been watched by some half-dozen walkers who were perched on the cairn's sides. Their amazement grew even greater when, with a tremendous loud buzz, Felix assaulted the very cairn itself. He bucked his front wheel some four feet up its almost vertical side, and then droned into silence. Petrol had conquered Beamsley for the first time. The whole performance, including the survey of the route, took some twenty minutes. The descent was as convincing as the climb, and as free from wheel spin. At the bottom we looked Felix over to see what he had thought of the adventure. One footrest was missing, and one exhaust pipe slightly bent. That was the sum total of the damage occasioned by the climb. In the pride of his strength Felix challenges all comers to repeat the climb, with or without a sidecar passenger."*

Around this time, HPB, Bill and Chris entered trials in and occasionally out of the Western Centre. Only Chris ventured further afield for the odd grass track meeting in the late 1920s. HPB was still giving his Red Car an airing whenever the opportunity arose mostly in the Stroud district. Hayward was still riding solo but as Fred Halliday remarked, "Bill was never a great solo competitor." Things were about to change when Harry outlined his plans to build a sidecar outfit, not just a straightforward one. This was to incorporate a sidecar-wheel drive which the public could buy as a stock item straight out of their sales catalogue; Hayward was immediately interested. Despite grabbing Bill's attention his feelings were mixed for no other manufacturer that he could think of in the country, or anywhere else for that matter, had ever taken such a bold step before. Bill voiced concern to just how they would produce in numbers if the design was a success.

That was the question he put to HPB. The Gaffer outlined his plans to Bill and Chris. His intended market was the farmer, explaining there were plenty of hills in Gloucestershire and throughout the country where feed was needed to be transported in the dead of winter, when snow and frost made life difficult for those trying to scratch a living from the soil. Bill was in agreement with the general concept but advised caution. Why not prove the device in trials before things became too serious and the company found itself in a position that could have embarrassing consequences trying to deliver such a radical machine. At the time Bill had not given any serious thought to trialling a threewheeler but was willing to give it a go just to prove something as unorthodox as a driven third wheel. HPB considered Bill's advice but in the back of his mind was his Red Car which lacked a differential and years before he had contemplated building one in order to give his machine greater driveability . . . and there the matter rested. (As will be revealed later HPB never gave up on the differential theme.) For the swd he was keen to incorporate some type of differential and long dis-

This is perhaps the very first photo of the Baughan swd. Was this how Harry Baughan envisaged his creation? The sidecar is almost a work of art with its beautifully polished mahogany decking in front of the aeroscreen. In this form it was used in a few trials, and eventually the boat shape was abandoned for a more practical design. At this stage there are no springs on the front of the sidecar chassis.

cussions took place at Lower Street between the three of them. As Chris relates. "The Gaffer was always very enthusiastic initially. Once the technical details had been worked out, the thing designed, built and proved, he immediately lost interest and moved on to other things," the swd was no exception. From the design point of view it was in the same vein as Richard Wood's device and used a countershaft running inside a torque tube as did Bill Bradley with Felix. All this discussion took place in late 1927 and nothing more serious was done until the following year. But what followed was not what Bill expected. Over the winter months HPB had designed a differential for the swd and revealed his sketches to Bill. Once he saw them his first reaction was the amount of precision engineering involved. Undaunted, he set about drawing the external dimensions. Just how compact it was can be seen on page 164. Geoff Fisher remembers that HPB wanted to incorporate some degree of slip in it. The drawing does not reveal any method of taking up the movement laterally from the sidecar wheel to the differential. Sliding splines or similar could have been used but this vital detail is not evident in the drawing. This being an external one no internals are shown, sadly this drawing of the internal dimensions has never been discovered. One can only assume the sidecar chassis must have had a very high degree of rigidity otherwise lateral loads would have been transmitted to the differential

Stagg collection.

Bill Hayward with Marjorie Grant Heelas in the sidecar photographed outside Stroud Hospital. The factory was just yards away from this location. The sidecar has changed. No longer is there wooden decking in front of the screen having been replaced with aluminium. The sidecar mudguard has gained a light to comply with the road traffic act. Still no springing under the sidecar nose.

mechanism. There may, however, have been some method of allowing for lateral movement in the transmission. This might have been on the same principle as the later dog-clutch (page166). Here the round cross-shaft had four flats machined on it which was a simpler solution than splines to manufacture. Bill Hayward does not remember if this was considered.

The first Baughan swd (differential) was a direct drive from the spindle of the bike to the spindle of the sidecar wheel in a straight line. This first Baughan swd may have been a step too far incorporating a differential, some of the machining did take place. Due to the small internal dimensions a great deal of time and effort was needed. Other things at the time took priority as Geoff Fisher remembers. "I saw it on several occasions and it seemed that very little progress had been made, but that was how things were at Lower Street." In the end it was only part built by Bill and never progressed any further. Bill Hayward's son Edwin, recalls that his father said it was unfinished. Perhaps the reason that it remained so was the great amount of precision engineering involved, with the size of this

Stagg collection.

Bill and Marjorie climb Ferris Court in the Stroud Team Trial, Oct 12th, 1929. Although Hayward was a member of the Baughan Team he collected nothing due to HPB's magneto failure in the Red Car. Bill and Marjorie were also members of the JB Watsdon Team, comprising Jack Williams and Len Vale-Onslow who came away with 1st class awards. The swd certainly attracted one keen spectator attention. On some later trials this section was marked with tapes to confine riders to a tighter line.

differential being so small it was no wonder that the work involved outweighed the time and effort, to say nothing of the expense. In the end HPB abandoned it and settled on the far simpler, and easier to manufacture, dog-clutch.*

While Harry Baughan decided on his second much less sophisticated design with the flexible couplings and dog-clutch there was another swd being developed, this time by Howard Uzzell. His 998cc V twin BSA has the same mystery surrounding it as the Baughan offering at the time, again little evidence is available and only one drawing was published. It seems that Uzzell was very secretive. Hayward and Baughan were not aware of its existence until it was ridden for the first time in the 1929 Power Trial. The involvement of BSA seems tenuous. When Hayward questioned Uzzell late in 1929 as to the factory input, he denied it. Later Hayward came to know the BSA more intimately when Uzzell was always asking him for chain links or complete chains when foreign material became tangled in its vitals with disastrous results. Hayward pushed Uzzell further on the BSA connection and their influence. Bill was not sure if Uzzell

*London-Coventry 1929. First appearance of the Baughan swd in competition. Hayward/Heelas, s/c, finished with a 1st class award.

These photos show the dog-clutch engaged. The engagement dog slid on four flats, easier to make than splines. The forward deflection of the cross-shaft is apparent. The lower photo shows the location of the lever for in/out engagement. In practice it does require some skill and effort to make the operation successful. The whole concept of the Baughan swd was simplicity.

Authors collection.

With the dog-clutch disengaged the teeth are clearly visible. At first it was thought that a chamfer on the teeth would be necessary for easier connection, but proved unfounded. If the mechanism became caked in mud, a splash of paraffin or petrol by Bill would be enough to clean it.

was really truthful when the question was raised. Bill had a point, he could never understand how BSA, if they were involved, would allow their star rider to enter a trial so poorly equipped in this department. Bill was very wary when Uzzell was in the same trial. He could almost guarantee he would be on the scrounge for a spare chain or links.* So bad was the situation that in the 1929 British Experts, Uzzell had to finally disengage his swd when the chains became detached by stones and branches. This in turn damaged the cross shaft bearings and he found it impossible to carry on.

This was the one and only time that a swd was used in this most prestigious of trials. As Howard Uzzell received short shrift from Bill he diverted his attention to Chris for chains, but that approach was not forthcoming either. Chris tried to avoid Uzzell on every occassion, eventually the BSA man directed his quest elseware. Both machines used a simple dog-clutch, the Baughan version used a lever operating transversely by the passenger. The Uzzell BSA did away with this and used a more useful arrangement, foot operation by cable on the left side of the bike. This foot operated dog-clutch was unquestionably the best method of all the swds. A finger slid into an open slotted cam that must have given Uzzell a very smooth and progressive engagement compared to the Baughan

*A number of years later Harold Flook also pestered Hayward for chains and links for his Norton. He received the same treatment as Uzzell.

The hub of the sidecar wheel with its quick release operation. The wheel could be removed in less than thirty seconds without disturbing the drive. As the sidecar chassis encloses the wheel it gave very good protection against any collision in a trial. Hayward and Morris were grateful for this on many occasions.

which required a fair amount of effort to make the connection. However, the initial design was flawed and gave considerable trouble to Uzzell, and in the end the aggravation was too much and he abandoned it completely. It all stemmed from the cross shaft not running in a torque tube, and the I beam that supported this cross shaft at both ends was constantly being subjected to so much stress that even in a half day trial the I beam started to fracture and rendered the drive useless.

As if this was not enough he had to contend with the lateral loads on the cross shaft bearings when things started to go out of alignment. The amount of frustration he suffered, according to Bill Hayward, was more than enough to ditch the whole thing. This weakness was responsible for him missing several trials and a solution needed to be found. In the end two sheets of metal were brazed to the underside of the I beam which extended to the rear of the sidecar chassis and also had to incorporate some method of adjustment in order to keep the two swd chains in correct tension. The first attempt was not successful and thicker steel was used, but even then there were still problems which resulted in yet more missed trials. Finally it disappeared, later to rise like the proverbial Phoenix in the guise of the Williams drive (four years after the Baughan swd).

The substantial 'C' springs give adequate movement in trials. Smaller versions were used on the front, later to be replaced with four coil types. In all the years this outfit was used in trials (1929-46) the only damage it suffered was to the head stock. This was only discovered when the machine was rebuilt.

This was ridden by Harold Taylor; he too experienced Uzzell's frustration with chains. With Harold Taylor having only one leg, it was doubly frustrating for him when it came to adjusting the chains fore and aft, which his passenger had to do frequently. Bill Hayward was convinced that the drive arrangement design was flawed with so many open chains, to say nothing of the **I** beams and as a result both gave up on it.

In later swds the passenger was responsible for the dog-clutch operation which often led to some difficulties with understanding the driver's intention, the poor old passenger often getting it wrong. Anything that did away with this was to be welcomed. Uzzell, with his foot control of the swd engagement had the perfect answer when it came to timing, thus relieving the passenger of this chore, who could then divert his attention to balancing the outfit. If Uzzell's swd design was flawed with the **I** beams then his thinking on the dog-clutch operation was beyond reproach. Bill Bradley's 'Felix' had its dog-clutch control sited half-way along this torque tube which was controlled by a lever similar to the clutch one. This was complete with locking catch on the left side of the handle bar which again relieved the passenger of this essential timing. Howard Uzzell must have given this careful thought and his solution was the best. As he was

Authors collection.

The last version for the sidecar suspension. It was Marjorie's insistence that persuaded Bill to use coils and they proved to be far more practical than the C type and could be easily replaced.

driving the outfit he was in the perfect position to make the judgement on something as crucial as this. Uzzell's left foot controlled the dog-clutch engagement, both in and out. Just what method he employed to ensure that the foot control was locked in position is uncertain. The dog-clutch control exercised by Uzzell must have been quite a revelation and took out all the guesswork from the passenger in difficult situations. If the driver got it wrong he had only himself to blame. Marjorie Grant Heelas found timing of the swd critical and the most difficult thing to judge. Only after many trials was she really confident of Bill's intentions on certain hills (primarily through familiarity).

The BSA used a fore and aft movement which was then translated to a transverse one to engage the dogs. The Baughan was just a transverse action. Of the two it looks like the Uzzell device was far easier in practice. In Hayward's case it was left to his passenger to judge the moment often encouraged by a shouted instruction over the noise of the engine. This took the best part of two years experience on Marjorie's part to fully master it. The Baughan required much more effort on the part of the passenger for the engagement. One of the more interesting features of the Uzzell outfit was its use of a sidecar wheel brake operated as normal by the left foot. This was right in front of the dog-clutch and well away from the normal rear brake and was only used when the swd was disconnected. Bill Hayward's machine was eventually fitted with such a brake but not on his swd chassis. When the swd chassis was removed and a conventional one

The sidecar chassis rear adjustment which was infinitely variable for any set-up that was required. Marjorie remembers that Bill always checked this along with the front before every trial.

fitted (around 1936) it also took the cross shaft and the two flexible couplings attached to it. This did not include the dog-clutch mechanism which stayed in place. Work was started initially by the Gaffer and Bill. However, Chris did the bulk of the build, bending the tubes for the bike and the sidecar chassis. This came about in the latter part of 1928. Too much time had been wasted on the ill fated swd differential, and it was never pursued with much vigour by HPB. Many interruptions had prolonged the work and at times the day to day business suffered.

The Gaffer finally admitted defeat. It was essential to keep the company solvent. There was one small addition to this first drawing. This was outlined in pencil on the flanges at either end of the torque tube and gives an indication of what was to follow. A complete re-design by HPB gave a new layout, still using a cross shaft, but not enclosed. This time the thinking was more clear and not so far reaching which turned out to be the simplest of all the swds. The swd was based on the frame of their 500cc solo and would use a sidecar chassis to be built in conjunction with the drive. The more difficult part was to marry them together. Harry Baughan designed the outfit not as an add-on affair, but a complete machine from scratch with all the calculations to ensure that it was rugged enough to climb anything it was confronted with. In later years many people thought this swd was an accessory that could be purchased and fitted retrospectively. This was certainly not the case, and indeed the solo frame was a standard item up until the rear forks; there the resemblance ended. Both rear forks were dispensed with and stronger ones fitted for these had to accommodate substantial fork ends to take the drive and load reversals of the swd. There is one interesting feature of this swd chassis which can be clearly seen in the photo on pages 169/170 and shows that it completely encloses the sidecar wheel and gives excellent protection to the vulnerable sidecar wheel and the support bearing which also carried a quickly detachable fitting. In later years Bill was grateful for this foresight on the Gaffers part when many a tree and wall was 'contacted' in a trial. In the event of a puncture this wheel could be detached within a few seconds thanks to this q/d fixing. The only hitch was that the outfit had to be tipped on its side to enable the wheel to be removed.

The attachment of the rear forks by bolts where the top tube ends and meets the rear down tube. At the base of the down tube further bolts are used to connect up the bottom forks. The width of the top and bottom forks were designed to allow enough space to use a Parsons chain if needed. The rear fork end was made up from eight pieces (four for each side) of sheet steel one quarter to one sixteenth inch thick. Chris then cut to Bill's pattern. All this cutting and shaping was done by hand and the top photo on page 179 shows how it all fitted together complete with adjustment for the rear wheel. Once the eight pieces were pinned they were brazed, then the hard work began. The greatest difficulty for Chris was rounding off the ends that had to fit into the bottom fork ends. This had to be completed with a large file until the right size diameter had been achieved. Once this was finished mitred sleeves were inserted in the fork tubes, pinned and brazed. The dog-clutch was simple enough with three teeth which did not feature any chamfer to allow ease of engagement/disengagement and remained so throughout its life. At first Bill thought that with the solo wheel spinning the engagement might be a little brutal and result in damage; practice proved to be different and his worries unfounded. Sidecar-wheel drive still comes to light on occasions in spite of a gap of some forty or more years. In the February edition of *Motor Cycle Sport*, 1988 'Titch' Allen* covered the Baughan and described it as 'crude' but effective. He goes on to cover the mechanism as gear driven from within the bike brake plate which was akin to the old type of speedo drive with constant mesh. The dog-clutch provided the means to drive the cross shaft to the sidecar wheel, again in the hub using the same constant mesh gears. This cross shaft was said to be straight and devoid of any flexible coupling. However, a paragraph later he admits that he never saw or heard the Baughan in action. Fortunately in the April issue Peter Roydhouse corrected this most obvious mistake

---

* The late CE'Titch' Allen OBE, BEM, who was the man primarily responsible for the founding of the Vintage Motor Cycle Club, later to become Life President.

Authors collection.

Top: The rear fork end of Bill's swd that comprised of four pieces of sheet steel, hand cut by Chris Stagg. Where the two lower ends enter the lower forks this had to be rounded by hand, a very long process that Chris found very difficult. **Below**: Hayward modified the original hand change gear box to a positive stop mechanism. This greatly improved performance in trials. This took place around 1934.

Authors collection.

The positive stop mechanism with its debris cover removed. Hayward never suffered any clutch or gearbox failures in all the years with the extra stress of the constant engaging and disengaging of the dog-clutch. The one component that required frequent changing was the final drive chain.

to the Baughan swd configuration. But Titch never stopped there. In the same article he sites Fred Stevenson's Brough Superior SS80 which he said was using a chain system to drive a cross shaft to the sidecar wheel, similar to Uzzell's BSA. Again this is in variance to the machine that featured in *Motor Cycling* of August 15th, 1934. Two of the three photos clearly show a straight cross shaft from spindle to spindle using a dog-clutch sited between the sidecar and the sidecar wheel which required the passenger to use his left hand to operate it.

This SS80 is devoid of rear forks both top and bottom so there is no means of attaching a rear wheel in the normal method as a driven item. A completely separate sidecar chassis is bolted to the solo complete with the rear wheel. All that remains is the final drive chain to be attached to complete things. The sidecar chassis was normal tubing but featured two large triangular metal plates each 3/8 of an inch thick separated by a small gap that provided immense rigidity to carry the rear hub even before it was bolted to the solo frame. One unusual feature was the two rear brakes. The first was conventional 8 inch internal expanding within the hub. The second was another 8 inch, this time an external contracting band type 2 inches wide. This drum alone must have added considerably to the overall weight. Once this chassis is bolted up the rear wheel adopts its usual position in the solo frame with the correct chain line. The one outstanding advantage was that the rear wheel (car type) could be freely removed without the slightest trouble, requiring just three nuts to be undone and the wheel pulled off.* Originally the exhaust pipes prevented free access to this unique innovation and were rapidly re-routed. With the spare wheel located between the bike and sidecar it could be quickly removed and changed either for the sidecar or the bike side as both were interchangeable. The adjustment for the one chain (final drive) was accomplished by two bolts and the whole of the sidecar chassis could be moved fore and aft. Two large 'C' springs similar to the Baughan supported the rear of the sidecar. The whole machine was big and heavy and must have required considerable physical effort to control it in tight sections. Stevenson must have been quite exhausted after a difficult trial. The two interchangeable wheels used the biggest tyre width available at the time. The sidecar wheel did not have the protection from the chassis frame as in the Baughan swd and would have been vulnerable when sections were narrow. In the case of the Baughan swd all three wheels are interchangeable and until the mishap with the spare wheel hitting Marjorie in the back Hayward, like most of the top charioteers, carried a spare. The Baughan drive was simplicity itself and totally reliable throughout its competition life. Howard Uzzell suffered so much frustration he abandoned it after a year. Towards the mid 1930s Harold Taylor tried his luck with the same principle as Uzzell with the Williams swd. Once again the basic flaw in the design let him down. It is also interesting to note that Harold who had lost his left leg years before, mounted the sidecar right alongside the bike frame which made the outfit very narrow indeed, ideal for tight sections like the first part of the Weighbridge climb and also those notorious hills, 'Breakheart' and 'Fisher's' which defeated many a combination.

As swd attracted such attention (belatedly as it turned out) when it first appeared, very little thought was given to its impact on trials sport. Many at the time dismissed it out of hand and could not see any future for it . The most ardent critic was Harry Perrey who voiced his opinion in no uncertain terms: 'It would never be a commercial success.' His prediction was spot on. As to the enthusiast these outfits generated great interest and the more knowledgeable found them quite compelling. After the initial response to the introduction of swd the journalists of the day commented favourably on the interest generated. After Howard Uzzell left the scene with his somewhat unreliable BSA conversion it was left to Bill Hayward to plough a lone furrow for nearly eighteen months until the Norton company decided to enter the fray. Things then changed, Stuart Waycott and Peter Bradley then followed suit with their offerings. Up to that time the motor cycle press had been content to cover the trials in the normal scheme of things. However, the Scottish Six Days Trial changed everything. Once it had been reported that Ted Morris had won with his Baughan equipped with swd journalists took a closer interest in this unique advantage to climbing

*See page 268

steep muddy hills. One journal, *Motor Cycling*, decided to investigate further. *Motor Cycling* first made the approach to Harry Baughan in 1933, just after the 'Scottish' with a view to testing Hayward's machine that Baughans described as an 'Interesting Experiment'. Their journalist, 'Castor,' no doubt mindful of Morris in Scotland made arrangements to visit Lower Street to try it first hand. After a couple of false starts over dates things finally resolved themselves in May. The arrangement was that Bill Hayward would conduct the proceedings with Castor in the chair to allow himself the dubious pleasure of understanding the dog-clutch operation. As Bill had enjoyed Marjorie's understanding and timing of engagement/disengagement of the drive he was not expecting the same from a journalist . . . he soon found out the difference. In defence to his lack of knowledge of any form of swd Castor elected to observe Bill's skill and technique from the sidecar. Harry Baughan was on hand to oversee things and suggested that 'Crickley Back' would be a good place to start. This hill is not very far from the 'Air Balloon' pub at Birdlip. In the Cotswold Cup Trial of 1933 this was the fourth hill after the Gloucester start. Bill first demonstrated the use of two wheel drive to his passenger, then handed over.

Castor took the start cautiously, then Bill shouted he would push out the drive. Slowly the outfit bogged down, sinking deeper. Quick as a flash the drive was thrown in. A complete revelation! The Baughan pulled itself out of the grave it had dug, and the difference was amazing. After this initiation HPB suggested 'Juniper.' This hill when seen by Graham Goodman as a possible inclusion for the British Experts Trial decided it was too difficult, certainly in the wet. Castor tried this very steep, boulder strewn climb with conventional drive, but this time in the dry. At the steepest part things went badly awry. Forward momentum ceased and the revs rose alarmingly. Within seconds the outfit was backing down at an increasing pace. The final drive chain had snapped resulting in the undignified bale-out of Bill and Castor. Fortunately the flight of the Baughan was arrested by a small tree stopping the outfit from somersaulting down a very steep bank. Bill immediately looked in the sidecar rear compartment only to discover there was no spare chain. This was indeed an oversight as he always carried a comprehensive tool kit along with all manner of spares. Bill was quick to point out that "This would never happen on a proper trial." There was nothing for it but to retire to the Bear Inn on Rodborough Common and summon assistance from the factory. A short while later Chris Stagg arrived with a new chain, and he also could not believe that Bill had made such an mistake. After the enforced lunch the trio went back and made the repair. With the swd restored to health HPB thought that Castor should get a taste of some 'Experts' hills. First up was that old favourite BB 1 and 2. For Castor this first part of the climb (BB 1) was the long haul from the stream covered start. After that it was dry and his confidence rose. He was soon brought back to earth when BB 2 appeared–the famous 'Gravestones.' This part of the section involved the use of the swd and in complete contrast with the preceding climb when single wheel drive was used. Castor found BB 1 made the Baughan wander all over the place and needed all his concentration to make the outfit obey his commands, all this was about to change. As soon as Bill pulled the drive in the whole outfit changed quite quickly. No longer was it wayward. Instead it adopted its famous 'straight on complex.' The trip over the gravestones was easier than the first half of the section and Castor was suitably impressed. Once clear of this famous hill, it was just a matter of a mile or two for the next on the itinerary. This time 'Camp' would be more of a test and give Castor a true feeling for swd. Camp wound itself around an escarpment and exited at the top of Crawley Hill on the way out from Uley.

Here the entire hill was covered in leaf mould and hid many large boulders and defeated all the sidecar drivers in the Experts trial that year. Bill started the ball rolling using the single drive first. He just managed to clear the top. After returning to the bottom it was a change of places and still with the single drive in operation Castor started. Half way up the Baughan was in danger of stalling, Bill quickly engaged the dogs without telling the driver. Castor was taken by surprise, and immediately the outfit gained almost instant grip accompanied by the SO attitude. Castor gained the section end and was almost lost for words according to Bill. As if this was not enough HPB said it would be a good idea to tackle 'Hodgecombe' as the exit was just yards from Camp. In the Experts this hill was solos only, but in later years sidecars used it. Their alternative was the famous Penn Woods climb until the locals turned belligerent and ended it all.

Hodgecombe was one of the all time great climbs, almost flat out from start to finish. This old logging track was feet deep in places with leaf mould, covering old logs, boulders and all manner of detritus. It started just after the local farmyard and had a firmish surface with a left hand curve after which it was almost straight, and steep. Rarely were the outfits on an even keel. If anything the boulders were even larger than on Camp and BB 2. Castor had full reign with the third wheel driving and found it remarkably easy. The Baughan with the SO handling pulled all the way to the top with ease. After the climb he thought Bill should have a go without the use of the drive. So back down they went, not through the section but the long way around on the main road. Bill knew it would be tempting providence to actually go back down the hill having witnessed a few outfits turning turtle in past years. This time Castor sat in the chair and was given a virtuoso performance of just how to climb with just one wheel drive by a top notch driver. The Baughan went just about everywhere but straight, hidden stones deflecting the machine from the chosen path and it took

Form P. Acc. 2.

Any further communication on this subject
should be addressed to—
THE COMPTROLLER,
THE PATENT OFFICE,
25, SOUTHAMPTON BUILDINGS,
LONDON, W.C.2.
(*Telegraphic Address :* PATENT OFFICE, LONDON.)
(*Telephone No. :* HOLBORN 8721.)
and the following number should be quoted in
the communication :—

36822/32

THE PATENT OFFICE,

25, SOUTHAMPTON BUILDINGS,

LONDON, W.C.2.

12th January, 1933.

In conformity with the provisions of Section 3 (6) of the Patents and Designs Acts, 1907 to 1932, the Comptroller hereby gives you notice of the acceptance of your Application with a Provisional Specification for a Patent for **Improvement of transmission of motor cycle and sidecar.**

No.36822 dated 30th December, 1932.

A <u>Complete Specification</u> must be left at the Patent Office within twelve months from the date of the <u>application</u>, if a patent is desired. <u>One month's extension</u> of this period may be obtained by application upon Patents Form No: 6, stamped £2. <u>No further extension is obtainable</u> and if, at the end of thirteen months, no complete specification has been filed, the application is deemed to be abandoned.

The Complete Specification must be commenced upon Patents Form No. 3, stamped £4, must bear the number and date of the application, and must end with a distinct, clear and succinct statement of the invention claimed. <u>Claims should not be made for the efficiency or advantages of the invention</u>, but should form a brief and clear statement of what are regarded by the applicant as the novel features of the invention.

Stamped Patents Forms cannot be sent by post from the Patent Office, but may be obtained on <u>personal</u> application at the Inland Revenue Office (Room 28), The Patent Office, 25, Southampton Buildings, London, W.C.2, or, at a few days' notice, and upon pre-payment of the value of the stamp, at any Money Order Office in Great Britain or Northern Ireland.

Messrs.H.P.Baughan and W.E.Hayward,

[B1143] Wt 13801/2247 75,000(2) 10/32 H & SP Gp 112

See last paragraph opposite for more details.

Stagg collection.

Just to the left and right of the centre pillar are the tyres to be used by Chris Stagg when he competed at Red Marley hill climb in the 1930s. These still have the coach bolts in place. Any old worn-out tyre was suitable, in just one climb they would barely make the top, then promptly disintegrated. Very often they destroyed themselves half-way up. As Chris remarked, "It was great fun."

all Bill's skill to *just* make the top. After this demonstration Castor was a complete convert to swd and found the grip amazing and viewed them in a totally different light. If this test drive made him supportive of swd he eventually came to recognize that the traction swd demonstrated would give a huge advantage over a conventional drive. In the end the single wheel drive was to win the day as more and more protests came in from the clubs within the various Centres. The likes of Mansell, Hayward, Peter Bradley, Stuart Waycott, Freddy Stevenson and Harold Taylor with these devices were unbeatable. Even without their swds they were still the best combination crews and demonstrated as much in all the premier events that they entered. In the following years many letters were received by both motor cycle journals implying that they were 'Freak' machines and should be banned . . . which is exactly how the Baughan is remembered. As a matter of interest Castor also tested Geoff Fisher's trials Baughan, but sadly it was never published.*

The patent application opposite was submitted by the Baughan Motor Company to give them their correct title in 1932. It took some persuasion on the part of Geoff Fisher to take this step. Bill Hayward encouraged HPB even more. The date is fully four years after the swd appeared in the Cotswold Cup Trial. When Dennis Mansell approached HPB to have his drive fitted, Bill Mewis was convinced that a patent existed and advised caution. History relates differently. Bill Mewis was a lot more sceptical than Mansell, as far as he was aware Howard Uzzell never applied for a patent for his swd conversion to his BSA. Speculation abounded at the time when other swds were introduced as to patent infringements. The swd that Harold Taylor used on his Norton was almost identical to Uzzell's design and designed by a Mr. Williams. Harold, despite his handicap he was able to use a sidecar that was very close to the bike and there was just

*I am grateful to the late Geoff Fisher and his note books that recorded Castor's visit to the Baughan-works. Fisher heard all about the swd escapade from Bill Hayward and the embarrassment when there was no final drive chain to be found in the rear compartment of the sidecar.

Authors collection.

The front adjustment of the chassis immediately identifies it as the swd. The threewheeler that Chris Stagg built for the Gaffer had a swan neck which lacked adjustment. There was ample ground clearance for the swd. The primary chain was left exposed and could be replaced quickly once the guard was removed.

enough space for the passenger to operate the dog-clutch lever when required. Little seems to be known about Williams, perhaps the restrictions imposed on swds by the various Centres was enough to finish any development at the time. So passed into history the swd. It was indeed a controversial time in sidecar trials and caused considerable upset. The motor cycle journalists never really revealed the true story, many editorials in the motor cycle journals never came to any hard and fast decision over them either. It would seem they were quite willing to sit on the fence and not take sides (was readership at stake?). Perhaps swd was a step too far, Harry Perrey certainly thought so, based no doubt on his considerable threewheeler experience. Geoff Fisher could not see any commercial future in the device, and told Harry so. Today, retrospective analysis is always accurate. History proved them right.

The Baughan/Norton sidecar-wheel drive conversion. One of
Baughans best kept secrets. Mansell refers to lesser drivers using
these hill climbing devices. Norton build their own swd. Mansell, Mewis
and Arthur Carroll design their first official works swd machine.

Although Baughan launched his swd to an unsuspecting trials world in early
1929, months later Howard Uzzell introduced his 998cc swd BSA, it was fully
two years before another factory of note followed this route and it turned out to
be perhaps the manufacturer who had the highest profile in Great Britain, Norton
Motors. The Bracebridge Street marque was establishing a reputation on the
race tracks of Europe. Norton, famous for their road racing ability had developed their race department to the envy of all others and boasted a staff that were
both inventive, skilful and diverse. Their successes on the race tracks throughout
the continent were certainly familiar to the enthusiast and the public. The latter
may not have had the insight as did the enthusiast, but the word Norton was synonymous with quality in road racing, mention of trials in connection with this
famous marque may have drawn a blank with the public at large.

Trials did not play such a high profile in Nortons strategy. They were satisfied with their growing reputation in racing and the increased sales that resulted,
much to the envy of lesser manufacturers. At Norton in the late 1920s there was
a pairing who were racing in the European Sidecar Championships and were
destined to move into trials and challenge the established stars. These two were
Dennis Mansell and Bill Mewis. Mansell, the son of Nortons managing director,
and Mewis who worked at Bracebridge Street eventually being seconded into
the race shop after serving his apprenticeship with the London-Midland and
Scottish Railway. These two over the coming years formed a partnership that
was almost as good as a marriage and as enduring. They rode together for over
thirty years and became one of the most successful crews in terms of awards
and outright wins in trials, both club and national. Mansell was perhaps in a
somewhat privileged position which allowed him to indulge in these activities
with the backing of Norton that would have been denied to other people, but his
enthusiasm was the driving force and he found a kindred spirit in Bill Mewis.

Both men were motor cycle enthusiasts from an early age which developed
over the years as competition became a major part of their lives. Their attempts
at racing on the Continent turned out to be brief for they soon found the long
trips both expensive in time and money, receiving little financial support from
the factory, Nortons concern was that their solos should have the utmost support and the threewheeler it seemed would hardly feature in their mainstream
racing. This lack of support is perhaps understandable from Nortons point of
view. Their main thrust was to their solo riders and in this they were more than
successful. So Mansell and Mewis abandoned the race circuits and moved on
to the delights of snow, frost, fog, rain and mud in the depths of winter. In 1929

Mansell and Mewis started to make great inroads into trials and began to win not only first class awards but premier victories as well. At first everyone put this down to their position as factory riders. To many people this may have seemed obvious but in actual fact they received very little support from Nortons (shades of their road racing efforts). The autocratic Joe Craig was never enamoured with trials, his allegiance lay elsewhere but when the managing director's son was riding in what was to all intent and purpose a 'works' machine he was hardly in a position to criticize; as Mewis pointed out he was just an employee himself.

So the Mansell/Mewis partnership flourished and they made great progress in just two seasons on the hills. Dennis was very stocky at the time. He was the archetypal threewheeler driver with a lot of upper body strength and was well suited to handle the waywardness of a trials outfit. By contrast, Bill Mewis was the opposite, just a few inches over five feet tall and weighing around nine stone was perfect for a sidecar passenger. He was fit, naturally agile with an excellent sense of balance; a perfect foil for Mansell. By 1930 the business of swd had not escaped the notice of the Norton pairing. In the previous year they had become aware of the Hayward/Grant Heelas patnership and their reputation with the Baughan swd, not that they were a direct threat to the Birmingham crew for Hayward and his passenger hardly ventured outside the Western Centre at that time, with only the odd outing into Midland territory. What did precede the Stroud crew was the fast growing advantage that the sidecar wheel-drive supposedly offered and they were convinced that as their reputation increased, they would have serious opposition to contend with if they decided to enter events on a regular basis, especially outside their Centre.

It must be stated that Mansell and Mewis were out every weekend in one trial or another, and certainly mid-week, so their experience was far superior to the Baughan pairing who only managed perhaps four open trials a season backed up by the occasional mid-week event. Bill Mewis recalls that Dennis was getting increasingly depressed by the two swds that were romping up difficult sections driven by people, who in his opinion, were not as good as he was! This was around 1929 when Howard Uzzell first appeared with his 998cc BSA and Bill Hayward with his swd. Perhaps what rankled Mansell most was that Hayward had never ridden any type of combination in competition before and was making fools of riders with conventional single wheel drive. As Mansell was a shrewd observer of motor cycle development he discussed with Mewis the possibility of having a Baughan swd fitted to their trials outfit; Mewis was astounded. The reason given by Mansell was that he was getting fed up by *lesser* crews who were using swd and found himself playing second fiddle to them. This spurred him to make the approach to Lower Street. It seems rather ironic that he made this move for Hayward and Heelas must have been one of these 'lesser' crews he referred to. Mansell was quick to spot the obvious advantage that swds possessed and told Mewis that they would have to do something about it. The approach to Baughan Motors was made. This must have been one of the best kept secrets in motor cycling, for unknown to the Norton management, Mansell set the wheels in motion resulting in the Baughan swd being grafted onto a Norton solo.

Bill Mewis was certainly impressed by the climbing ability of Howard Uzzell's swd BSA and came, somewhat reluctantly, to the same conclusion as Mansell. To stand any sort of chance they would have to join them. At this time in trials competition there was no separate cup awarded for swds; only later did this become a feature. Both Mansell and Mewis knew all about Harry Baughan's reputation as an engineer and the builder of trials motor cycles. For him to introduce a sidecar wheel-drive it must have some merit, so both came to a mutual agreement and decided to investigate the practical advantages of swd. Bill Mewis recalls: "We both knew that if Bill Hayward maintained his progress with his swd then it was only a matter of time before he was winning on a regular basis." So Bill and Dennis got together and had many discussions over the advantages and disadvantages of such a drive. "It was out of the question at that time to build our own device in the race department" recalls Bill. "I was always making up special bits and pieces for the race machines. To drop everything and build a swd was completely out of the question. My time was too precious." However, a possible solution was at hand, and on Mansell's suggestion they were to approach Harry Baughan and have a swd fitted to a solo Norton frame.

If this swd had proved its worth Bill Mewis was not sure how this was going to be squared with the board of directors when a factory such as Norton had to involve a tiny company in Stroud to produce a device that might give them an advantage in winning trials. Mewis knew that if they progressed with the Baughan conversion they would have great trouble in keeping it secret. This way there would be no direct involvement by Norton and both men were keen to see just what a swd could offer them with a performance increase. So Mansell made direct contact with Harry Baughan and an outline plan was approved; at least by Mansell. Even today there is some vagueness surrounding this alliance. From the Baughan side of things there was never any question as to the outcome. Chris Stagg remembers it well: "I was amazed when the Gaffer told me that Mansell was going to bring down a solo frame so that we could fit our swd to it, that would mean that the sidecar chassis would somehow have to be grafted to the Norton." This was the only explanation that the Gaffer offered to Chris and Bill. For a Baughan swd to be fitted to another machine was just not a simple job. In their case the machine was designed as a whole unit, not just an add on and bolt up device. This was explained to Dennis. "This made no difference as far as he was concerned," Chris recalls, "So the Gaffer gave the go-ahead."

Now for Dennis Mansell to take such a decision without prior knowledge of the factory was extreme as it was risky and a great deal of secrecy was vital if the venture was to succeed. (On the question of the patent they did have to redesign their Norton swd two years later.) At that time both Mansell and Mewis were certainly well known throughout Birmingham by the trade, and the journalists of the day. To see either Mansell or Mewis driving, or riding around always aroused suspicion, where were they going? What were they up to?

Bill could relate many stories of being followed for miles by test riders from other factories, and if not them, it was the journalists. One such was Bob Currie. He always referred to it as 'fair game' for many in his position were well placed to find out if the factories surrounding Birmingham were up to anything remotely suspicious. Not to be discouraged by this Mansell would deliver a solo frame as and when it was convenient. Chris Stagg remembers the episode. "Only three of us at the time knew about it, the Gaffer, Bill and myself; we were well aware that it was all very unofficial and needed to be kept quiet. (Unknown to Chris at the time Harry had included Geoff Fisher in his confidence.) Everything was ready for the arrival of Dennis and the only warning we were given was a phone call just before he left Birmingham." Mansell made Lower Street in the late evening and the frame was unloaded after a lot of fiddling. Sacks covered the whole thing to avoid arousing too much interest from any casual glance on his way out of the Midlands. Chris was concerned about the conversion for within a few minutes of examining the frame, found that it was not going to be as straight forward as they all thought. "All three of us looked at it after Dennis departed and we soon discovered that it would be impossible to fit our drive without major alterations." After a brief discussion they came to the same conclusion; the rear forks, top and bottom, would have to be cut off and the Baughan ones brazed into place. This was not a matter of a moment for there was a substantial amount of difficult work involved.

Both Mansell and Mewis had studied the Baughan drive over the previous couple of seasons and to them it seemed a simple enough device, which in essence it was. The one thing that had escaped their notice was that the swd chassis had been designed as a one-piece fitment and the whole machine was carefully thought out with this in mind. In fairness to the Norton pair it must be said that in those far off days it was not the done thing to be seen expressing too much interest in opponents machinery even if they desperately wanted to; even placing ones gloves on a rival's machine quickly aroused suspicion. In later years when Mansell and Mewis stopped for a lunch halt with their 'official' swd machine built at Nortons, the first thing they always did was to throw a lightweight tarpaulin over the rear of their outfit just to keep out prying eyes, not only from rivals, but the journalists keen to report on developments for their readers. The only recourse in HPB's mind was major surgery to the frame with new lugs etc, then braze on their attachments to make it complete. But another problem was lurking, that of modifying the old jig that they used for the build of Bill Hayward's machine. The Baughan swd was a very sturdy affair and the whole rear hub with the dog-clutch mechanism was a complete unit along with the swd chassis. The fork ends comprised of four sheets of mild sheet steel (each side) which required pinning and brazing to complete the assembly.

The rear hub with its QD fitting and the back plate to take the thrust bearings was a very solid piece of work that took very careful machining. Where the side-car chassis joins the bike frame there is provision for two adjustments to ensure the angles are correct for setting up the steering.* When the drive was engaged the steering characteristics changed quite markedly and was a different machine to ride, so the set up was bordering on a compromise. There was an increase in weight of some 25/30lbs, and this helped considerably with the traction. There was also weight in the toolbox when fully equipped for a trial, with chains, fuel etc; this was balanced nicely between the two driven wheels. In actual fact this was a basic 500cc solo one with the special top and bottom rear forks that would take the swd. As all the frames were hand built to customer order none were ever built for stock and then stored. Chris at the time was responsible for nearly all the solo builds and this extra work was an interesting aside. "It wasn't too difficult a job," explains Chris. "The biggest problem I had was with the solo frame, getting it into position before Bill and me brazed it. Once that was done the whole thing was finished and then the Gaffer got his camera out and took a photo" (page 192). The only trouble was it suffers from a double exposure from a previous or latter picture; a common fault in those days when cameras relied on the photographer's memory as to whether he had, or had not, wound on the film.

Nevertheless, it is a rare photograph indeed and despite the fault it gives a unique insight to a wonderful piece of motor cycling history. With the secrecy surrounding this operation two other people got wind of it, Fred Halliday and Geoff Fisher. Fred was on excellent terms with Harry Baughan, as in the past he had ridden one of his early trials models and received a modicum of financial support from the factory. During the course of his business being the local representative for BP oil products, he often called at Whitehall. "I was always popping in to Lower Street for despite my motor cycle football accident I kept a keen interest on what Baughans were up to. This day I just chanced upon Bill and Chris in the middle of trying to get the swd chassis to marry up with the Norton solo. I arrived to find Bill getting more and more annoyed with the difficulty in trying to adapt the jig to line everything up before the pinning and the brazing started. Of course they could not disguise the fact that something

* The Norton conversion did not have the front sidecar chassis adjustment, just the Swan Neck attachment seen on page192.

Stagg collection.

A rare photograph. The Baughan/Norton swd conversion immediately after it was completed. Even though it suffers from a double exposure the lever for the dog-clutch operation is clearly visible and positioned alongside the left rear fork down tube. Bill Hayward's machine used it in the upright position which was more difficult for Marjorie to use. It was Mansell's insistance that it should be located on the forks. Compare the Hayward swd and the difference is obvious.

unusual was going on for I had seen the original swd being built for Bill by Chris; so they knew immediately that I would never be fooled and fobbed off with any old story." This indeed was true for Fred had a lot of competition experience riding all manner of machines. So his arrival at the works forced a ready explanation from Chris, although Bill was reluctant to divulge much at the time when he saw Fred arrive.

Geoff Fisher on the other hand learnt about it directly from Harry himself. These two had a close working relationship on all trials matters. Because of this Harry Baughan knew that he could rely on Fisher's integrity in confidential matters. "I heard about it from the very start when Mansell made the phone call to Harry weeks before any action was even contemplated. At first I was amazed and outlined the legal side of the matter that perhaps he had overlooked. I also pointed out why Norton, with their reputation would never get involved in such a venture." Harry explained to Fisher the circumstances, and even then he was somewhat sceptical. "At first I thought Baughans were carrying out sub-contract work for them as at the time I had no idea of the politics involved and Harry explained fully why a great degree of secrecy was essential." Geoff Fisher's first sight of the machine was in the evening out of working hours when he was invited down to view it. "I arrived just after Chris and Bill had finished the pinning and brazing. It was still in a rough state for the work had only taken place that day and was to be cleaned the following one prior to enamelling.

Geoff Fisher was quite surprised that Mansell had made such a move, and without informing the company. It was a risky undertaking to say the least but he appreciated Mansell's standing within the company and felt he had a fair amount of leeway in these things. Geoff recalls some other aspects: "Even years after, nothing was ever mentioned in the trade, or the press at the time, and if they ever discovered it I'm sure things would have been entirely different." Another thing that concerned Baughan Motors was the protection of his device in the long term by a Patent application and this took place a year after the Mansell conversion. This time it was Bill Hayward who pushed the Gaffer in that direction and he felt that if Baughan Motors moved ahead with the swd then they should be adequately protected in case anyone decided to 'pirate' it; after all it was Bill who drew up the original layout and felt he had a claim in it as well. Eventually HPB did apply and everything was submitted to the Patent Office (see page 184) at Queen Ann's Gate and there it resided for the best part of a year. Although Harry Baughan was given the opportunity to take up his Patent application he failed to do so. An explanation as to this lapse comes again from Geoff Fisher: "I think Harry's failure to fully patent it was perhaps influenced by what I had said when they built Bill's machine, 'not a viable commercial proposition', I was no engineer but even I could see the limitation to the drive and the extra cost would be enough to put off the public, and then there was the more serious problem of the drive being used on the road."

In reality this just confirmed what other people were either thinking or telling each other and gradually this filtered back to Lower Street. In the end it never saw the light of day as a practical road going machine. Even the original Baughan concept as a combination that the farmer could use in taking feed to his livestock never materialized either and no sales were recorded. In a way it was all very disappointing for HPB for the countryside around Stroud abounded with steep hills; just the right environment for such a machine. But it was never to be the farmers choice and the tractor won the day. In the wake of all this the conversion undertaken for Mansell also came to nought. It was used but briefly in a test drive. Bill Mewis remembers it well: "I knew that Dennis had taken the frame to Baughans and we managed to stuff it into the back of his car. Then we threw a few old sacks over it just to keep the prying eyes away and he left late in the afternoon, which helped. We had a lot of trouble around Birmingham in those days with 'spies' for they followed us everywhere, either in cars or on motor cycles. Some were journalists, more often than not rival manufacturers keen to find out what we were up to. Once Dennis and me drove for a long time around Birmingham with three cars following us in convoy. We went for miles, eventually ending back at the factory where we pulled up and switched off. After a few minutes they twigged on that they had been 'rumbled,' and pushed off." Bob Currie has the same story when testing bikes for motor cycle papers for they were all up to such tricks: "We went for miles following some of the factory staff, especially from the competition departments, and to be honest it was fair game for we had a genuine excuse to be out testing and we were on fairly good terms with most of the lads. They knew the score as well as us." Then came the time for the conversion to be collected. Mewis again, "After Baughans had completed the work I went down with Dennis and we took the trailer. We loaded up and this time we had an old tarpaulin to cover the chassis, then back to Birmingham, only not to the factory for obvious reasons; instead we left it with Arthur Carroll (chief designer at Nortons) who knew the nature of the affair. Dennis and I fitted all the running gear until we had a complete machine that was ready for a run."

All this activity was undertaken in great secrecy and away from the works. Finally when everything was finished it was decided to give it a serious test and find out just what advantage Bill Hayward enjoyed. "We took the machine down to the sections that were used on the 'Victory' to give it a good workout over ground that we both knew like the back of our hands. Well! It was a terrible disappointment and not what we were expecting at all. In fact it was *bloody* awful. Dennis at the time thought it was undriveable. In a straight line it was marvellous when the drive was in engagement but turning corners was almost impossible and after a few trips into the bushes, Dennis gave up." In this very short try out they both discovered what Bill and Marjorie had encountered two years before . . . the straight on complex took the Norton pair completely by surprise. Bill elaborates further:

"To be fair to Harry Baughan we never gave it a proper test. I think we should have tried it over a longer period; and as it caused Dennis so much difficulty I just took his word for it. I suppose we both thought it would give us an immediate advantage just like Hayward had, but we never believed it would be as bad as it was. To be honest I could only marvel at Hayward's passenger getting to grips with the operation with the dog-clutch, and getting the *timing* just right. It took me the best part of a season to master it." So that first introduction by the Norton crew changed their thinking completely. From that moment on they both took a different view of just how good Bill Hayward and his passenger were. "We thought it would be plain sailing and prove to be the answer on the hills that were often deep in mud. After this Dennis's views towards Hayward changed and we both realized just how good he was for it was a very difficult machine to drive. Only later when we designed and built our own swd did we discover the technique on just how to ride a swd that the Baughan crew had found out years before." Both Mansell and Mewis took a while to overcome their apprehension to swd in general, and the Baughan device in particular for by 1933 there were several other machines equipped with some form of swd. At the time Peter Bradley* was rumoured to be experimenting with swd on his Rudge whereas Stuart Waycott with his Sunbeam had his equally experimental swd which had no connection with the factory. Freddie Stevenson built his own swd version based on a Brough Superior which George Brough often rode when it suited him. With these top crews who regularly featured in Open to Centre trials, winning on a regular basis was not lost on the Birmingham pair. So, this time their machine was built in the competition department under the gaze of Craig who hardly passed comment on it. He was not at all enamoured with such a machine taking up space in a race shop that had first call on his precious solos.

This time it was tackled differently. There was no clandestine operations under cover of darkness, everything was all above board and fitted in, as, and when commitments allowed in the race shop. Bill being a cautious engineer, decided their drive would be different for he thought a Patent for the Baughan drive was pending (he was partly right) and there would be acute embarrassment suffered by Norton if they infringed it. The one man who Bill did have a fine rapport with was their chief designer, Arthur Carroll who on many occasions penned the drawings that Mewis sketched out for the racing machines. (Bill Mewis and his wife were very close friends of Carroll. Late one Sunday night a policeman called on them with sad news, Carroll was due for tea at six o' clock that evening. On the way he lost control of his motor cycle in very wet conditions and collided with a bridge parapet and lost his life. Mewis said it took quite a while for the staff in the experimental department to get over his death). Dennis Mansell was particularly affected. Mewis outlined what he thought was a solution and Mansell confirmed. Mewis then passed it on to Carroll who drew up the plans with corresponding dimensions so that he could start the engineering. In principle their device was not far removed from the Baughan. It employed the same method of engagement . . . the simple dog-clutch. The cross driving shaft to the sidecar wheel was almost identical as the Baughan; the difference was, it never came off the centre of the rear wheel spindle but slightly displaced by a few inches forward and was driven by a constant mesh gear inside the hub and a similar one was employed in the sidecar wheel to make the drive complete. Here the drive across the sidecar chassis differed from the Baughan slightly. Instead of a forward deflection the cross shaft was straight and the sidecar wheel ran in-line with the rear wheel of the bike. The dog clutch engagement handle was sited between the sidecar and the bike, almost identical to the Baughan. Bill Mewis had this to say on *their* drive. "Because the two wheels were in-line the outfit never handled very well, especially when the drive was in, the SO effect

*Bradley eventually changed to Sunbeam and produced his own version of swd.

Courtesy: Bob Light.

Mansell and Mewis may have been the first British Experts, but they went to Baughans for their first swd. When they tested the Baughan drive they found it very difficult to use and abandoned it immediately. Later they manufactured their own.

was considerable and we only used it in difficult conditions. Our conventional machine was far more manoeuvrable, certainly when I started cutting the tread blocks on the rear tyre. To be honest this cutting of the tread was more useful than the swd at times, in the end Dennis decided to abandon the swd. One other thing, clubs were starting to ban the use of swd, or place a 50% mark-up on their use, so that finished it." When I visited Bill he explained in some detail the workings of this constant-mesh gear, then he disappeared under the stairs in the hall way. After a few minutes rummaging around he returned and placed on the coffee table some waxed paper. Inside were two pristine gears, beautifully machined, as good as the day they were manufactured. "These were the spares that I cut when I made the originals for the drive. Arthur when he designed them made sufficient tolerance for the high loadings he knew would be encountered in trials and made allowances for it. Well as you can see we never used them, and I carried them as spares in the sidecar. At a push I could have probably changed them at the side of the road if necessary. We never did though." In the end Bill spent more time on tread cutting and making modifications to cleaning the tread grooves which resulted in better performance from their results point of view. So ended the swd from the Norton competition department. A later development of this swd was the Big4 built for the army.

The Baughan/Yorkshire connection. Ted Morris, early interest in motor cycles. Competition with solos. Move to threewheelers. Competes in ISDT. Exploits with Harrogate and Ilkley trials events.

Although Harry Baughan's products were more associated with the Western Centre from the early 1920s and nearly all of the 1930s, there was one rider from Yorkshire who towards the end of his trials career made history on a Baughan sidecar-wheel drive riding in the 1933 Scottish Six Days Trial, and subsequently scupperd all swd entries in that trial thereafter. Ted Morris had an early attraction to motor cycles and built up his skills and knowledge long before he could obtain a driving licence. In many ways he mirrored Harry Baughan in his early days when all things mechanical held a great fascination for him. By the time he was fifteen the mysteries of motor cycle and car engines posed no difficulty and when he qualified for a licence he was as quick off the mark as HPB, although this time there was no brother of like minded ilk.

Ted Morris was the son of a successful Harrogate builder and had been an enthusiastic motor cyclist from a very early age. By the time he was seventeen he had already competed in the Motor Cycling Club, London to Edinburgh trial. As a youngster Ted took part in many speed hill climbs on a variety of motor cycles. His first serious outings were speed events either on the flat or up the numerous hills in Yorkshire, and two of his favourites were climbs of Post Hill and Hepolite Scar. On numerous occasions he often came away with the fastest time of the day in his class. All manner of secondhand motor cycles came his way, even some 'borrowed' from friends that almost turned out to be on permanent loan, such was his enthusiasm for riding. As a young man starting out in the working world he undoubtedly had something of an advantage over the other lads of his age, namely, a fairly well-off father. When Ted was fifteen his father naturally enough wished him to enter the family business.

Ted signed his indentures as an apprentice and he was shown no favouritism on his behalf just because he was the boss's son. He was expected to give a good day's work for a good day's pay, just like any other employee. In this respect he was treated somewhat harsher than the other workers, just to emphasize the point a prompt start from him was expected. This sense of loyalty was instilled in him which came to a head many years later. Like many young men Ted started with solos. Initially it was in speed hill climbs and then sprints and the odd grass track event, then moving on to trials with his trusty Phelan and Moore, later fitting a sidecar and finally settling on three wheels for the rest of his competition career. Post Hill near Leeds was a popular venue for motor cycles in the 1920s. It was purchased by *The Yorkshire Evening Post* and was presented to The Leeds Motor Club. Famed as a 'freak' climb, a description which seems to have migrated from across the Atlantic, the steepest part of Post Hill was a

Morris collection.

Ted Morris at the start of Post Hill. He was a frequent visitor to this venue, at times took FTD in his class. In his early competition career he excelled at hills climbs, moving on later to sidecar trials.

shade under 1 in 2 at the top. This was one competition that Ted really enjoyed before he switched to trials on a regular basis. Ted's father was not very enamoured with his son's passion for motor cycle sport. Instead he was keen for him to take his place within the firm and eventually take over the business when he saw fit. Like many fathers he was indulgent to his son's sport up to a point. To show willing he was always up at seven in the morning and ready to start work, demonstrating that his motor cycling activities was not detrimental to his work. Then, like many young men he discovered the delights of young ladies and started to take them on the pillion. This was fine, but did not offer any real comfort so a move was made to threewheelers.

Through this change he met a girl, Gladys, who was later to become his wife. She too was keen on motor cycles and the associated sport, and with their friendship becoming stronger they entered many trials together. He did the driving while she looked after the navigation. Ted's competition spirit instead of diminishing, took on a new lease of life as he became more involved and successful with his threewheeler exploits. He changed his machines for better models that would increase his chance of winning. As competition gripped him ever tighter it became more serious, and Gladys found that it was becoming a little too serious, so she gracefully retired and that made way for passengers who did not mind getting soaking wet, covered in mud and generally knocked about. In their early days with the threewheeler the emphasis was on road reliability trials that ran against the clock, and at best were often leisurely affairs. Most took place mid-week but the more serious stuff was on the Saturday. Cars, motor cycles and sidecars often competed together for a road trial in the late 1920s and early 1930s which became a very popular pastime. Television did not rule the roost. Radio was in its infancy and the same could be said for the cinemas; in those far off days entertainment was mostly self made. Gradually, Ted with his skills of riding threewheelers fast improving, so did his machines. Gladys had fond memories of these club activities.

"The whole of the local club got involved with trials. Wives and girl friends all mucked in to help with the refreshments, ham and eggs along with many pints of beer. Sunday trials, some on the Saturday afternoon and most Wednesday nights were up at Ripon, Pateley Bridge, Blubberhouses, Ilkley, Leeds, Bradford and Middlesbrough. Every week end there was a trial you could enter in." Theirs was a partnership and they shared the joys of riding sidecars. They also had a small boat on the York canal which they used frequently. Gladys recalls that it was not all plain sailing. "Ted's father was not very sympathetic at first about the trials riding. He was spending a lot of time restoring and repairing them between one event and the next. After a while he came round and Ted worked very hard in between times and learned the business from the ground up; a complete apprenticeship in fact. Also included was the fine art of costing and estimating that was equally necessary. His father took him on as any other person he would employ and had to take the rough with the smooth, favouritism was not an option when he became indentured."

With this dedication to motor cycles he had some help in the preparation with them from a long time friend, Bert Topham, later to be his best man when he married. When Ted abandoned the solos Bert was his first passenger in trials. Then came Keith Dodson and Eric Oddy. Oddy was a work colleague and did a lot of sub-contract work for Ted's father in painting and decorating. Then Ted made contact with Alec Hill who turned out to have a lot of competition experience. Of the four passengers it was Oddy and Hill who were mostly involved with Morris when he bought his first Baughan swd. Alec Hill and Ted Morris met in the mid 1920s for both were members of the Harrogate Motor Club and keen on motor cycle competition. Later Hill set up his own business repairing motor cycles at his small shop in Park Road, Harrogate. The events in Yorkshire were not dissimilar to those that were being held in Gloucestershire. Evening get togethers included pillion trials, treasure hunts, time and distance trials, and of course social runs. Ted and Gladys continued supporting their local club for a number of years, but as Ted became more experienced he expanded his hori-

Morris astride his Phelon and Moore at Post Hill. This 'Freak' climb was a favourite of his with this machine along with Sutton Bank and Hepolite Scar.

Morris collection.

Rosedale Abbey Bank drew a great many spectators in all weathers. Ted and Gladys climb the Chimney section on Whit Monday, June 6th, 1927 with the 499cc P and M. Ted was also a member of the Harrogate Club Team comprising FH Smithies, 499cc James and Alec Hill riding his 498cc Scott. Alec Hill later became Ted's passenger on many a local trial. Six years later they won the 'Scottish'.

zons with ever more difficult events that did not suit his wife. Mrs. Morris well recalls this change. "Ted was getting better and better with these weekend trials but I found them ever more uncomfortable and the sections became much more difficult and bumpier so I felt it was time for me to finish and for him to find a passenger who was much better at it than I was." Mrs. Morris remembers her husband's skill with the mechanical side of things. "Ted would spend hours taking apart engines and tuning them. Mostly he did it himself but there were other riders who gave him a helping hand.

"One was Bill Cross. They spent hours in the garage in the early years working on the bikes, Ted was always trying to find ways of making them better. He always prided himself on their reliability for he hated breaking down in a trial; finishing was very important to him." Morris soon found that the P and M was not the ideal threewheeler for trials and changed it for a machine that raised a few eyebrows amongst his friends, some thought it was a backward step. Ted had other ideas. A two year old Brough Superior SS80* replaced the P and M and was fitted with a hefty sidecar to match the bike. (See pages 203/4) The Brough undoubtedly had prestige value, just how it would perform in trials was another

* See page 351 for a copy of the Brough Superior works record card specification.

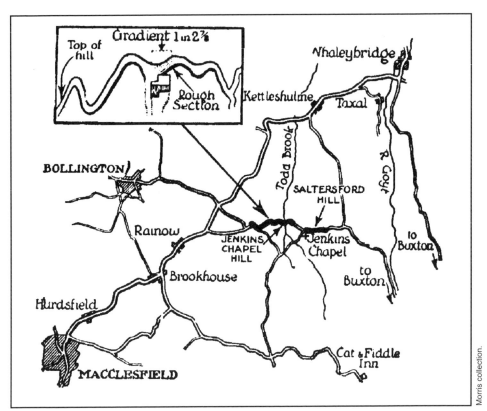

The area around Jenkins Chapel which saw the first four days of the International. Many observed hills were used in reverse order which resulted in many damaged machines, backed by more protests.

matter entirely. Certainly the Brough would be a hefty beast to handle around some of the hills in the Dales. The Yorkshire Centre in the 1920s may not have had sections that were quite as severe compared to the Cotswolds. The Western Centre around 1932 underwent a change as new hills were introduced which were much narrower with far more difficult gradients and acute turns as were to be found in the British Experts and the Cotswold Cups. One can just visualize Morris trying 'Breakheart' with George Brough's finest. Morris was made of sterner stuff to worry about the bulk of the Brough and in 1926 decided to have a crack at an event that had fascinated him for a number of years, the International Six Days Trial; based for four of the six days in Buxton, Derbyshire. Like many riders before him the appeal of long distance events was strong and after his initial experience with the London-Edinburgh he was keen to repeat the exercise, but six days was somewhat different to a half day local trial. The SS80

Morris collection.

Ted Morris climbing 'Jenkins Chapel' in the 1926 International Six Days Trial. The poor road conditions led to many punctures, some being eliminated through lateness. Some of the hills proved very difficult to many riders, and poor organization led to a stream of protests mostly addressed to 'Baulking'.

was robust enough for the job in hand, and with his tall build he was more than confident he could handle it. Although the Brough was just over two years old and in good condition he still gave the outfit a complete check over realizing that six days would be no picnic and with such a heavy machine weak spots would soon be found. Not only that it would be a test of his own stamina.

Ted Morris had his first taste of really serious competition in 1926 when he entered the International Six Days Trial. This trial was run on similar lines to the old reliability one day events. As befitting a six days trial there was some strenuous climbs in prospect for the 114 competitors and a total of 797 road miles to look forward to. The trial was not strictly a male preserve either. Seven ladies were entered in the solo class, the most prominent being Marjorie Cottle riding her works supported Raleigh. This was her *seventh* ISDT and she had the greatest experience, in many cases more than the men. Not to be left out were the sidecars. They featured five lady passengers; enthusiasts all. Ted Morris thought long and hard before he embarked on a trial that would extend both him and his

A well contented Morris after the final run on the Brooklands banking. The SS80 never missed a beat throughout the six days and finished without collecting a puncture. In the mid 1920s spare tyres were always a feature along with several tubes stuffed in the sidecar. Many competitors lost marks through dirty machines. The Brough looks like it could do with a bit of a clean-up.

passenger over six arduous days that would finish at Brooklands. This challenge he found irresistible. He only had limited experience of both sidecars and trials that extended over half a day. He thought that this would broaden his outlook for serious competition in the years to come and give him a standard in performance to achieve. Riding his Brough Superior SS80 may not have been the ideal machine but its rugged build would ensure a finish. With a trial of such prestige there were many names that later would become well known in the years to come, George Dance, Graham Walker, Vic Anstice, Len Crisp, Jack Amott and George Rowley. The sidecars saw HG Uzzell, Harry Perrey and EA Morris, whose last long distance experience was the Motor Cycling Club London-Edinburgh. Uzzell was 500cc BSA mounted, Perrey on his 500cc Ariel and Morris astride his Brough.

The Morris outfit was something of a handful, nothing perhaps compared to the SS100 ridden in solo form by FJR (Joe) Heath. Despite its size he was to win a gold medal for his skill and perseverance. The International flavour may not have been as strong as it should have. The International Trophy saw only three teams entered, two by England and one by Germany. However, things were a little different in the International Silver Vase—a more respectable seven teams were entered. Three each by England and Holland and one from Germany. One of the English Teams comprised entirely of ladies, Marjorie Cottle, Edith Fowley and Lucia Ball. The Saturday, prior to the Monday start, saw almost the entire contingent out for a spot of practice on two of the most difficult climbs, Jenkins Chapel and Blacker Mill. There were so many riders that things turned almost farcical. The regulations allowed practice for the competitors, but no officials were there to oversee things and exercise some control. Under this 'free day' on which to practise, both hills became clogged with riders and at times tempers became frayed when so many had the greatest difficulty climbing, often having to abandon their machines on the hill. Eventually all the riders made it back to Buxton and then spent the Sunday carrying out final checks, or repairing the damage sustained from the previous day's outing.

The four days in Derbyshire centred around these two famous climbs, Blacker Mill and Jenkins Chapel, great difficulty was experienced by many riders and tested the organizers almost to breaking point. Baulking on these climbs became so acute that riders filed protest after protest in order to establish some accurate marking. This affected the solos. The sidecar crews managed to avoid most of the serious confusion. Descents became a feature of Blacker Mill and Jenkins Chapel which resulted in damaged machines, and at one stage a rope was used to enable some solos to reach the bottom. All in all, a very unsatisfactory state of affairs. Ted Morris along with the other threewheelers played a waiting game to allow these hills to be cleared, then claiming *force majeure* for lateness.

Morris collection.

Morris in some difficulty with his Phelan and Moore, while Eric Oddy tries desperately to balance the outfit. Oddy was passenger with Morris on many trials and was the first passenger to experience the difficult technique of using the swd when Ted bought the Baughan. Eric freely admitted he never came to terms with the problem of the swd. Oddy went on to become the Mayor of Harrogate in 1946.

Friday: 186 Miles. With the four days finished at Buxton all the competitors packed their bags, and prepared to head for Weighbridge, and then Brooklands for the Saturday and final speed test. Marjorie Cottle's 348cc Raleigh was not as swift as the owner would have liked due to a stretched valve stem that took place early in the week; perhaps her thoughts were more occupied with the final run on the Saturday. Ted Morris's progress was unspectacular and the Brough, despite its bulk was performing reliably. Heading south they passed through Lichfield, Coleshill, Stonebridge, Kenilworth, Warwick and then Banbury for lunch. There was some frantic work seen at this midday break when the riders effected adjustments and some even found time to clean their machines.

Alms Hill proved to be clean for the sidecar crews but the real star was the climb of George Goodall with his works Morgan. Such was his speed and spectacular climb the spectators had to dive for cover when they were showered with stones. Needless to say he made the fastest ascent with a passenger looking none too happy. Goodall, even with his considerable experience resorted to Parsons chains on a few occasions, and the two other Morgan crews were quick to follow suit. After all this excitement the remaining 93 riders checked in at Weighbridge. Saturday: Brooklands. (Full circuit). With all the frustration of the previous five

Morris collection.

Ted Morris on his Scott Flying Squirrel with a happy Dodson in the chair. 'Pa' Monkhouse wearing his characteristic plus fours was the ACU Yorkshire Centre President in 1926 and a stalwart of the ACU for years. The photo was taken on an evening trial, one of the many in the Ilkley district.

days over the competitors had a chance of a number of laps on the two and three quarter mile lap of the famous banking. The motor cycles were placed in various classes. The 175cc class were to complete 18 laps at an average speed of 30mph. The 250cc class was 21 laps with a minimum of 35mph. The 375cc class were set to complete 24 laps at an average of 40mph. All these classes were conducted in the morning session and after the lunch break it was the time for the larger capacities and at four o' clock the 500cc and 750cc solos had to average 45mph and the 1000cc solos 50mph. Before the sidecar men attempted the high speed runs many replaced their tyres that must have suffered badly in the previous days climbing flint strewn hills.

So the sidecars were divided into 600cc and 1000cc classes and were down to average 35mph and 40mph respectively. Once these runs were completed all riders were required to assemble at the bottom of the test hill for the final climb. At the top they were subjected to scrutiny by Dr. Low. One of the requirements was for the rear wheel to be raised off the ground and the gear box examined for drive and all the gears to be in working order (penalties were handed out for missing gears). As if this was not enough tests were conducted on exhaust sys-

Morris collection.

Pa Monkhouse in the centre overseeing an evening trial run by the Ilkley and District Motor Club. Keith Dodson is second from the right and Ted Morris fourth.

tems and condition of machines. The exhaust systems came in for criticism, not exactly being well 'silenced' and perhaps this was fair comment. The other was that of machine condition and this raised a few hackles. Marks were deducted for poor condition and this seemed a little harsh, for nobody would expect competition machines to be exactly concours after five hard ridden days over hills, that when wet were almost unridable and their riders suffered almost as much as their machines and were equally as filthy. With the final tests completed there just remained the awards. The solos recorded 62 Golds, of these 16 were without loss of marks, there were just 7 silvers.

The sidecars had 19 Golds, 5 of them completed the event with no loss of marks and there was only 1 silver awarded. Ted Morris lost 8 marks and was just pipped by Phil Pike on his 600cc Norton with 5 marks lost. Harry Perrey was more than pleased to come away without losing a mark. Out of the 20 sidecars entered 8 retired with mechanical problems which was a greater mortality rate than the solos, who lost just 12 out of 91. According to Eric Oddy, Ted found the whole week a wonderful experience and though he found the Brough Superior a handful, it was rugged enough to take him through the week without a moments worry. It would be another seven years before he tackled a six day event again, and this time he would be mounted on a far more suitable outfit.

Morris buys first Baughan swd, wins SSDT. Buys a second swd
Baughan. Western Centre exploits. Wins Cotswold Cups. Ted Morris
finally finishes with competition. Takes over his father's building business. Over one hundered and fifty awards in his career.

By the end of 1932 the Stroud company had greatly increased in stature, the
solos were well used by local riders and Bill Hayward was enjoying success
with the swd. For three years Hayward's exploits had been brought to the readers attention by the popular motor cycling journals. Harry Baughan was well
known in this respect as was his position within the ACU Western Centre as
Secretary. All this had not escaped the notice of a certain Ted Morris and when
their paths crossed the talk soon turned to the swd. Ted visited Lower Street and
there examined Bill Hayward's machine in great detail, not to miss a chance
of selling a swd, Bill extolled the virtues of the driven third wheel. Ted Morris
being a member of the Harrogate MC had witnessed the climbing ability of Bill
Bradley's 'Felix' on Hepolite Scar and with his close connection with the Ilkley
club knew Bradley well.

This unique machine stuck in Morris's mind and when the Baughan swd
became available he was more than interested, he did not rush in to buy one but
made several enquiries before he finally decided it was the way to go. Morris
hardly needed convincing as to the merits of such a machine. He took the opportunity to drive the swd and came back suitably impressed, the order was placed
there and then. At that time Bill was using the ex-works TT engine from Blackburnes and pointed out that this type of engine would not be available. Unde-
terred, Ted mentioned that he was going to use a Rudge Python TT replica and
could they accommodate it? They certainly could! Within a couple of weeks Ted
collected the engine direct from the factory and delivered it in his Railton, Chris
then set about to build the first official sale of their sidecar-wheel drive. The
construction took just over two weeks to complete, the cycle parts were standard
Baughan, virtually a copy of Bill's machine.

As soon as Ted supplied the engine and gearbox the mounting plates for both
were cut and drilled, then the final drive chain length could be determined.* Once
this was in place Chris set about the bending the exhaust pipes and cutting the
sheet steel for the 'Brooklands Cans,' albeit, smaller and less elaborate than the
normal wear for the circuit. On the Hayward machine the original gearbox was
hand change this led to foot operation by the mid 1930s. The Morris swd used
foot change at the outset and is recorded as (No.49) No33/243 in the Baughan
sales ledger and 498cc was the capacity. The gearbox was Sturmey Archer and
featured positive stop mechanism, and like the previous threewheeler followed
the same build pattern. When looking at both of the swds they look seem almost
identical from a distance, the same interchangeable wheels, rear and front drop
stands and the same exhaust pipe runs. When Ted ordered his second machine

* See sketch on page 230.

Stagg collection.

The first Baughan swd that Ted Morris bought in 1933 (No.49) No.33/243. Chris Stagg took this photo just hours before Morris was due to collect it from Lower Street. He managed to put a few road miles on to check everything was in working order. Just weeks later Morris and Hill won the Scottish Six Days Trial with it. Sidecar adjustment is identical to Hayward's. The location above is Lower Littleworth, Amberley. Just a few yards in the opposite direction is 'Hillslie', the home of the Grant Heelas sisters.

(No.51) No35/245 he specified a Blackburne of 600cc and this was coupled to a Burman gearbox with foot change. This second outfit with the big Blackburne was a follow on from Bill's machine. The engine plates were identical as the crankcases were the same for the 500cc engine. There was no miss-match on chain runs as with the Python and Chris said the build was "almost routine." The engine featured twin exhaust ports and was supplied direct from Bookham which was a standard catalogue item, later subjected to extensive tuning by Morris. It could be that Ted insisted on that size as there were numerous trials in his area that gave awards over the 500cc limit, Dennis Mansell's Norton regularly used the bigger size for that very purpose.

It was not unknown for riders of sidecars to change engines from 500cc to 350cc, and visa-versa in an effort to win in that particular capacity class. For Ted Morris to buy not just one, but two swds would appear to border on sheer indulgence for less than three years later he was to finish serious trials riding. The Baughan swd was not cheap and to set things into context a price comparison is worth mentioning. In 1933 their 500cc model WH with twin port Blackburne was £62.10/-, the SW (swd) again with the same engine was retailed at £92.10/-,

The prices on this and the next page give a sixty year gap comparison. The price of motor cycles remained very stable from year to year, inflation had not yet reared its ugly head.

Stagg collection.

Morris never used any form of lighting on his Baughans. The sidecar has the helical springs under the nose of the sidecar, the spare wheel attached to the rear. Morris soon removed it and ran as Bill Hayward did almost at the outset. Spare wheels were losing favour with sidecar drivers by this time. The sidecar adjustment fore and aft is identical to Bill Hayward's machine.

A £30. increase. The value of the pound in 1933 to 1993 is £38. The WH at £62. 10/-, = £2,375. and the swd was £3,515, which is an increase of £1,140 over the standard 500cc solo. A glance at the sales ledger on page 333 reveals that Morris paid under one hundred pounds for this first machine, the price of the Rudge engine was deducted, nevertheless to spend over £7,000 was a little over the top, no wonder his father was concerned.

In Morris's case it seems rather decadent to have two swds of different capacities on which to ring the changes, if indeed that was the intention. Strange to relate Ted hardly ever used this second machine for his father made it clear to him that he should spend more time concentrating on the family building business instead of trialling every weekend. At the time of his purchasing his first swd he was already the father of a small son some three years old. He responded to his fathers wishes and made it clear that when he had won a hundred first class awards, he would quit. In the end one hundred and three came his way and then Ted hung up his trials gear some fifteen years after he started

Within days of collecting the Baughan, Morris posted an entry for the 'Scottish.' This time he had a suitable machine for his talents. Soon he and Oddy

Stagg collection.

When Ted Morris ordered his Baughan he emphasised that he did not want a screen in front of the passenger, Hayward had related the experience that Marjorie had on one of their early trials when she suffered a cut face when the spare wheel came away from its mountings when they collided heavily with a bank which resulted in a trip to hospital. The chassis frame gives good protection to the sidecar wheel. Morris was glad of this when he collided with a wall on the 'Scottish.'

were out on the Dales investigating the intricacy of sidecar-wheel drive. Oddy had no idea as to the technique involved with this additional drive and between them struggled through. As Oddy undertook subcontract painting and decorating for Ted's father he had pressing work to do, so reluctantly had to pass up the opportunity to compete in the prestigious Scottish event. Alec Hill had no such problems and jumped at the chance. Then began a few weeks of intensive acclimatization with the swd. Hill was far more adept than Oddy and his competition experience came to the fore. In later years Oddy admitted that he only stood in as passenger if Ted was short of ballast and knew that Hill was far better in that department. Undoubtedly, Ted's greatest achievement and Baughans free publicity came when he and Alec Hill, his long time passenger, took the sidecar class in the Scottish Six Days Trial in 1933. History does not relate that Ted purchased the swd just to enter the Scottish but this must have been uppermost in his mind for the machine was purchased in March of that year and the Scottish was in mid April. Unquestionably, the swd gave Ted and Alec some advantage in that class for at the time there was no restriction on a driven third wheel. The

Ted Morris and Eric Oddy trying out the swd Baughan. Morris was concerned about the handling of the Baughan and had been instructed by Hayward on just how the swd could take over if concentration wandered. Morris was keen to get as much mileage as he could before the Scottish. As much a Oddy was willing he found the swd difficult to master. Fortunately Alec Hill filled this vital role in Scotland.

Morris collection.

Ted Morris and Alec Hill immediately after their return from their victory in the Scottish. This Baughan swd is almost an exact copy of Bill's outfit, the only difference is a slight change in the sidecar shape. Compare this to the photo on page 265

Morris collection.

The author in conversation with Mrs. Morris. When she finished as passenger to her husband she still went with him to all the trials he was involved with. The Stroud area was a great favourite with them.

entry list relates to a very low number of sidecar crews. Harry Perrey, Harold Flook and Ted Morris. The solos were always up to the maximum, but in the 1933 event the sidecars ran in a separate class as in previous years they had been lumped in with the cars. Despite the low turn out for the sidecars Ted Morris was up against two of the finest threewheeler experts in the business. The one crew who were missing was that of Mansell/Mewis who at that time were perhaps the best trials crew in the country. Flook was later to take no less than five British Experts titles and four more wins in the Scottish, he and his brother were just starting to become a formidable pairing. The 1933 Scottish Six Days Trial was organized by the Edinburgh and District Motor Club, this time cars were being admitted for the first time since 1925.

Cars were something of a novelty and would stretch the organizational powers of the host club. Despite the inclusion of the cars the entry for the sidecars was very low; just three. This apart these crews were well established in their own right. At number 57 Harry Perrey weighed in with his 493cc Triumph, then came Ted Morris at 58 with his brand new Baughan swd powered by a 499cc Rudge Python, and finally the Flook brothers at 59 with their 490cc Norton. The reason given for the non–appearance of the Norton pairing of Mansell and Mewis was that they were required for the ISDT later in the year when they would represent Great Britain. Perrey, a long time exponent of sidecars had little to prove when it came to three wheelers. On the other hand the one person who perhaps did not rank as highly as Perrey, was Morris. Just a few months before the Scottish he had purchased a machine from the Lower Street concern that up until then had

Hill collection.

Ted Morris with Alec Hill in the chair on what appears to be the Pyton engined swd Baughan. The location is Dob Park Splash. The water did not pose a problem for their cigarettes.

been surrounded in controversy caused by its driven third wheel. For Morris, this caused him little concern. He was well aware of all the friction this device had caused and the ACU blanket ban when considered for the British Experts. Harold Flooks reputation preceded him in respect of the SSDT.

The previous year saw the introduction of a sidecar class in this endurance event and Flook was the first winner of it, so his credentials were well known. In this respect his prior knowledge of the hills they were likely to encounter, would, without question, give Morris with his limited experience of swd and the trial a hard time. Morris, however, knew that Flook and his brother were difficult characters for they had crossed swords in the past and the prospect of six days in direct competition with each other may not be something they would savour. Despite these previous disputes both Morris and the Flooks got through the week without further embitterment. Ted, the ever shrewd Yorkshire man had read the SSDT regulations very carefully taking note that this long distance event placed no restriction on the driven sidecar wheel. The original Baughan swd had been around from 1929 in the hands of Bill Hayward and had never been extended in anything other than a one day trial and in this respect it was an unknown quantity. To put things in perspective both Morris and Hill were in this category as well. The only experience that Morris could call on was his

Eric Oddy brings back many memories while looking at Ted's photo of his many awards. Oddy was Morris's first passenger to try the swd before Alec Hill took over for the 'Scottish'.

The above photo was taken on their return from the Scottish Six Days Trial, happy men both. Despite their limited knowledge of swd they came away with the sidecar trophy. One can only speculate just what Morris could have done with the Baughan if he had bought it years before.

What a collection! Ted Morris displayed his trophies with one of his earliest passengers, Bert Cross. Morris said he would retire when he won a hundred first class awards. In the end he made a hundred and three. Illustrated here there are over one hundred and fifty awards that Morris collected.

ride in 1926 when he rode his Brough Superior, SS80 in the International Six Days Trial. That was eight years before, things had moved on considerably in that time. Morris, with his variety of passengers had no real previous experience of swd in competition and it was a gamble not only on his own ability but the reliability surrounding the Baughan on such a prestigious event lasting a week. Morris, knowing full well that at times certain hills could be tackled with the drive in engagement, on others this had to be pulled out of drive very quickly indeed if they were to keep forward momentum. At times some sections would be better tackled without the drive being used, especially with its 'straight on complex.' Bill Hayward found this out at his cost before he got the technique perfected. Morris had to make these decisions as and when he confronted them for the first time, slowly learning by experience. This was perhaps not the best

Morris collection.

A very sad picture. Three year old Derek Morris, Ted's only son pictured on his father's outfit, months later he died of leukemia. Ted later had two daughters.

way to tackle your first Scottish. It is very doubtful if any prior practice could prepare them for anything they would encounter in Scotland. They were not sure if the Baughan would last the distance given the early troubles that Bill Hayward encountered with the flexible couplings on his first trial. One of the crucial points concerning the Baughan swd was how well these flexible couplings would stand up to six days of continuous trialling and road mileage. The initial problems that Bill Hayward encountered on his first trial were eventually overcome. Four years of development had seen the introduction of new flexible material, but a full and rugged six days was another matter altogether. Changing an inner tube to Morris and Hill would be small beer; a coupling was going to take considerably longer and time was of the essence, penalties would be high and expensive. Even if both couplings had failed at the same time they could simply disengage the dog-clutch and carry on after removing the cross-shaft. To help overcome Ted's lack of experience with swd which to all intents and purposes was almost nil, in the few weeks prior to the Scottish, he had very few trials in which to fully understand the technique required to get the best out of it

Hill collection.

Alec Hill was no stranger to sidecar trials and speed events. Here he powers his Scott demonstrating a nice touch of controlled oversteer.

in the short time available. Bill Hayward admits it took a whole season to get to know about his machine and in this time he had only one regular passenger, as he did throughout his trials career. Prior to the Scottish Alec Hill had no experience of it whatsoever. Eric Oddy had ridden with Ted when he first acquired the Baughan but was unable to get the time off for the trip to Scotland. Despite these drawbacks both Morris and Hill experimented with the drive and were very keen to accept the challenge and prepared to make many mistakes along the way . . . things turned out to be rather different.

Harry Perrey at the time was a very respected member of the sidecar fraternity and featured prominently throughout the country, not limiting himself to any particular Centre. His views were always sought after, not only by fellow competitors but by the journalists of both *The Motor Cycle* and *Motor Cycling*. He was always forthright and honest in his opinion; at times bordering on the offensive if the person he was levelling his criticism at was at all sensitive, for he pulled no punches did Perrey. At the sight of Morris with his brand new swd Baughan entered, gave him cause for concern for he was not an aficionado of such devices; quite the opposite in fact. These swds had been dubbed freak machines and in his eyes would serve no useful purpose if they were ever considered as a commercial proposition. In short he detested them. Flook on the other hand reserved judgement for he was thinking about transferring his allegiance from his present Norton mount to a BSA and was on the verge of becoming embroiled with the Small Heath concern who were considering using a swd themselves.

So the scene was set for six lively days in Scotland that would see just how

Authors collection.

Mrs. Morris proudly displays her husband's silverware. When she visited Lower Street and met HPB she was amazed that such wonderful machines were made in such a small factory. She said that the swd he rode was the finest machine he ever used in trials. He must have been impressed, he bought two of them.

a swd would acquit itself in the hands of a crew with precious little experience of it. As in previous years late entries were accepted on the day when the trial officially started, the threewheelers benefited from this when HJ Finden arrived with his 498cc, James twin. Finden, like Ted Morris and Harry Perrey had met before in 1926 when they all competed in the ISDT. The difference then was that Finden was riding his James, as a solo. So all four knew just what was required of them and their passengers in terms of distance and stamina when they entered the Scottish. Finden, however, knowing full well what six rigorous days on the Scottish hills would be like, entered his James sidecar for the London-Exeter the previous December, possibly to give himself a taster for the rugged April event. Hugh Arnott's job as Clerk of the Course was even bigger than usual with the cars and there was so many competitors that the 'weighing in' was moved from Semple Street Garage, to the more spacious Waverley Market. All the solo and sidecar machines without exception were 'competition' models, and what must have been the first time on record every machine was devoid of lights, and fully equipped with sump guards and what seemed the highest exhaust systems possible. There was surprisingly no comment on the Baughan swd when it came to scrutineering, the regulations did not make a stipulation against this device.

Only one lady was entered, that was the irrepressible Marjorie Cottle on her works supported BSA. The older hands such as Povey and Perrigo had been in Scotland for several days prior to the event, and they reportedly went fishing with Bob MacGregor, but was this the only reason for their early visit? Teams were entered from Rudge, Ariel, Triumph, Royal Enfield and BSA. Much was made of Harry Perrey's Triumph with its QD rear wheel that was due to be incorporated in their new models the following year. There was a comment from one of the motor cycle journals of the day regarding the Baughan as, 'a most interesting model designed on the same lines as Bill Hayward's device.' Nothing was mentioned about Ted Morris's outfit with all three wheels that were quickly detachable, and fully interchangeable. It seems strange how the reporters of the day missed such an important feature as this, but then Perrey was more of a household name than Morris and commanded more attention as well as being supported by the factory.

Day 1. Monday 15th, May. 206 miles, 8.30 am start. Average speed 24 mph. Start: Edinburgh.

Observed Hills: Bolderston, Sheriffmuir, Amulree, Trinafour, Inverfarigaig.

Inverness. This was to prove the easiest first day ever. Kinchyle was cut out due to forestry activity but the full 206 miles was still covered. All the sidecar riders completed without loss of marks. The Bolderston section saw the sidecars clean, but Morris had to look at his time keeping for he was late on this one and in danger of incurring penalty marks.

The road average of 24 mph caught many riders out, and certainly Ted Morris found he could not afford to loiter between sections. Then on to Sheriffmuir where only the cars were observed. Lunch was taken at Kingussie and then on to Inverness. This first day was indeed to be the easiest for many years. The Forestry management put paid to Kinchlyle and robbed the first day of its most difficult hill. With that over it did not spring any surprises and all the sidecars found it little more than a fun day out with no marks lost in the process. At the finish in Inverness there were still 21 clean sheets.

Day 2. Tuesday 16th, 194 Miles. Average speed 24 mph. Start: Inverness.

(OHs): Hive Brae, Tornapress, Applecross, Balbeg, Abriachan.

Twenty miles out, Hive Brae sorted out many of the solo men but the sidecar drivers never had a problem. Ted Morris, becoming more confident by the mile with his Baughan and found the going easy despite his unfamiliarity with swd. Applecross: This proved to be nothing special and was reached via Tornapress the famous pass with a six mile climb which was thought to give a few engines a hard time in the overheating department as there was hardly any air moving. Only one solo suffered the indignity of a seizure. The sidecars climbed without a moments hesitation. Morris was most impressive and the Baughan tackled the

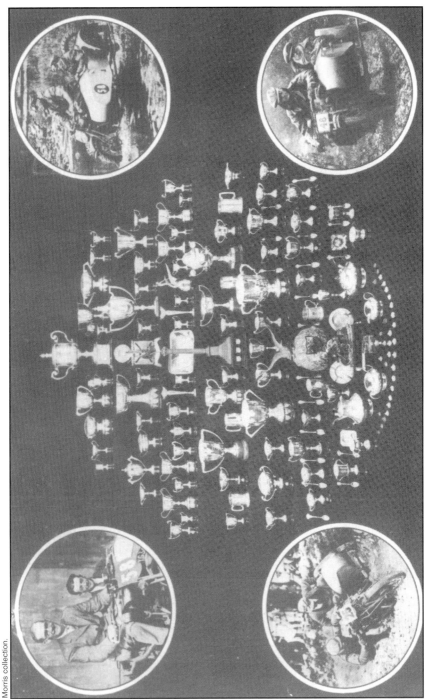

Morris collection.

A fine montage of Ted Morris's career. When he bought his swd Baughan he came down to the Western Centre for the Cotswold Cups, the Inter Centre Team Trial and the British Experts. Always a formidable competitor he rode against the best in the country and beat many of the 'names'.

loose surface with almost disdain.

The remainder of the day passed without incident. Morris and Flook finished without a blemish on their cards; not so fortunate was Finden who recoursed to footing, and even more surprising was Perrey with all his experience, it did not save him from putting a foot down as well. So it was down to rivals Morris and Flook to go into the third day without penalty. Finden, with his James sidecar, despite his earlier indiscretion, found the going as easy as the rest of the sidecars crews. With a higher average speed on the return run to Inverness there was a sense of urgency amongst the solos, Harry Perrey was not to be left behind and he was observed on quite a few occasions with the front wheel of his outfit well in the air. No doubt he had witnessed Morris's lateness on the first day. The final check time was from Drumdrochit to Inverness and this stretch was a slightly lower average speed at 24 mph. As Balbeg and Abriachan had to be climbed there was little time for relaxation and this was reflected in the lower than morning average speed. Flook and Morris were clean, and the latter were rapidly coming to terms with riding a sidecar-wheel driven machine on the observed sections. On the open road Morris no doubt had the words of Bill Hayward ringing in his ears: "do not use the drive on the road."

Day 3. Wednesday. 17th, 151 Miles. Start: Inverness.

(OHs) Abriachan, Mamore. So far the sidecars had faired well and found the going over the solo sections better than expected. Morris and Hill were finding their feet very quickly with the vagaries of swd. Perrey, no supporter of these devices expressed his amazement that Morris had not succumbed to its difficulties. One surprise for the riders was the 20 miles between Drumnadrochit and Fort Augustus, described at the time 'as the worst in the world' due to the surface receiving treatment from the local authority. When the riders arrived at the next hill they were completely covered in fine dust that was not greatly appreciated. To make up for this, the run from Fort Augustus to Fort William allowed all the riders to really 'extend' their machines as conditions would allow. The Mamore section with its very difficult cross gullies required the riders to average 15mph. This hill caught out even the most experienced of riders, all supported by factories. The 'Cheltenham Flyer,' Jack Williams, was forced to foot as was George Rowley on his works AJS. Even the great Bert Perrigo was docked 2 marks for a touch, although he strongly protested it. Later he was proved to be right and retained his clean sheet. The sidecars finished the day as they did on the previous one, no change.

Day 4. Thursday. 18th, 180 miles solos, 191 miles. Start: Oban.

(OHs) Ford Hill, Glen Douglas, Taymouth.

There was more trouble in store for Finden on Taymouth and recorded a failure; the three other crews climbed it without drama after which they all returned to Perth. For the four sidecar crews things had not been too severe and all the locals said that the really serious part of the trial started on the Thursday. They were to be proved right. The hills were described as 'the worst encountered in any six days before.'

At the end of the day Flook and Morris were still there unpenalized. There was a sensation after the midnight posting of the day's results when Bert Perrigo was disqualified when it was discovered he had changed a fork spring on the Tuesday. Man that he was he accepted the decision without rancour. In today's climate of rules and regulation and where the cult of the personality seems to take preference, things would be different, especially if he was a works rider. In Perrigo's position he was just that. Fully supported by BSA, he was their top competitor and was fully aware of the regulations when he signed on at the start of the trial. Someone had spotted this indiscretion on his part and was duly reported. In those far-off days a sense of fair play was considered gentlemanly, but rules were rules and applied to everyone. Perrigo, with his vast experience of trials knew full well that changing such an item would be difficult to disguise, not only from officials, but fellow riders as well; just who spotted it was never disclosed.

Day 5. Friday. 19th, 123 Miles. Start: Perth.

(OHs) Tullgmet, Hudson Hill, Weem, Taymouth, Cambusurich, Stony Brae.

The solos had plenty to contend with. On the Thursday night all the locals were saying that there would be a big sort out on the Friday and any clean sheets would disappear. They were not wrong. Bob MacGregor who knew the course intimately finally lost his clean sheet.

On Hudson, MacGregor found that his rear sprocket was about to depart its correct position, and from there on in he started to lose marks. Taymouth proved to be the final barrier to the clean sheets. MacGregor (Rudge), Edward's (Ariel), Len Heath and Bert Perrigo (BSA) finally succumbed. So the last clean sheets in the solo category finally went. On Cambusurich, Morris and Hill lost their only points in the trial and conceded seven marks. Just before Morris lost his marks, he had a fright when the old problem encountered with all swds, that of the 'straight on complex'. This lack of concentration on Morris's part caught him out and before he could respond the outfit collided with a wall. The Baughan only suffered superficial damage to the sidecar wheel mudguard and bent it onto the tyre. It only took a few moments by Hill to free it and they were soon on their way.

This was to be the only incident throughout the trial that caused any embarrassment to Morris and only his pride suffered at the time. Ted and Alec directed their attention to Flooks climb. Was he going to take the lead in the sidecar class? Flook, knowing that Morris had footed gave his Norton the gun and with the outfit leaping all over the place, his brother did his best to keep the machine stable. It nearly paid off. Refusing to put a foot down Flook lost control of it and the combination went over on its side; a complete stop. Perhaps a wry smile may have crossed the faces of the Baughan pairing at the predicament of the Flooks for they could hardly believe their good fortune. Either way Flook was in second place. Another well known rider, Jack Amott suffered the indignity of being disqualified when his machine was inspected at the finish at Perth. The rear brake rod was missing and the officials had no alternative but to exclude him. Machine condition was still catching out riders with damaged parts.

Day 6. 20th, Saturday. 132 Miles. Start: Edinburgh.

(OHs) Kenmore, Brick Hill, Balderston, then special tests on Blackford Hill.

There was very little to disturb the riders on the last day, the only observed hills being Kenmore, Brick, Balderston, and finally, Blackford. There was no last minute excitement and all the competitors wound their way through Stirling and back to Edinburgh. After all the sections on the Saturday there was no change to the overall order of things, only the odd mark or two being lost. The final hill, Blackford just might change things in the lower order.

So, the whole cavalcade following the yellow dye placed so accurately by George Grinton and his faithful band of helpers swept down Princes Street with what seemed every constable out controlling the sideroads to allow an unhindered passage. After the stop-and-go, plus the slow riding to act as tie deciders, it all came to a conclusion. The weather had been fine all the way through and everyone agreed that it had been the best 'Scottish' ever. There were a few marks added here and there, not enough though to change the final standings. George Grinton got to work with his team and the results were duly published; subject to official confirmation. The awards, suitably inscribed, were presented by Mrs. Grinton and everyone expressed satisfaction with the route marking and organization for the week. At the finish, Len Heath had made the best performance on his 499cc works Ariel with a loss of only two marks, a quite remarkable performance. Jack Williams took the 350cc class on his works camshaft Norton with just four marks lost. In the opposite class Ted Morris and Alec Hill ran out the winners with seven marks lost. Right behind was the previous year's winner, Harold Flook with his brother as passenger with twelve marks gone. Finden was next up on his James just beating Harry Perrey by one mark. Perrey, despite all his knowledge clocked twenty–seven marks, and finished last.

So the Baughan with its extra drive proved that it did have an advantage when it came to difficult conditions. Despite that, Morris and Hill were very quick to learn about the secrets of how to control a swd, over the six days it never gave the slightest trouble. As far as the 'Scottish' organizers were concerned they had learned a valuable lesson, sidecar-wheel drive was something they had not encountered before and were surprised by its performance. At the end of the trial all machines were examined for parts that had been changed, and as if this was not enough, there were penalty marks lost for machine damage and some riders were treated harshly, not enough though to affect the overall standing. So ended a 'Scottish' that broke new ground in which saw the appearance of the first sidecar-wheel driven machine and the officials no doubt felt that an advantage had been gained by Morris and his passenger. This was noted and filed away for the following year. In 1934 when the regulations were published the organizers went to great lengths to inform potential swd crews that their entries would no longer be accepted. Nothing was mentioned about the drive being locked out of engagement, just that they would not accept the machine. Morris and Hill proved their worth and with the swd in operation, they went through five of the six days without penalty. Damage to the sidecar mudguard was only slight and it was soon repaired before the machine was placed in *parc ferme* overnight. It looked like Ted and Alec would complete the six days without losing a mark, but despite their careful riding they collected seven points on the fifth hill on the Friday and beat Harold Flook into first place for a memorable win in the sidecar class. The very first for a swd in a six day event which also turned out to be the last.

Baughan Motors earned a unique place in motor cycling history in one of the great classic trials, but sadly, this was never to be repeated. One can only imagine Flooks feelings knowing that he had been beaten by a sidecar that had a distinct advantage despite the Baughan crew having very little experience of it. Considering this outstanding achievement by Morris and Hill, the Lower Street concern never capitalized on such wonderful potential publicity. If a Norton crew had won under the same circumstances there would have been full-page adverts in both motor cycle journals. Perhaps the reason that Baughan Motors never used this win to enhance their standing was the feeling at the time by the staunch clubman concerning the use of swd, and in the Baughan device all they saw was an unfair advantage to its crew. That indeed may have been the case. However, other riders were also using these devices that were certainly the equal of the product from Lower Street.

In many eyes Baughans were the instigators of this type of machine and were never viewed in a favourable light for that very reason. Keeping such a low profile with their win in the SSDT, Harry Baughan was more than a little sensitive towards this issue. The performance of Morris and Hill gave ample evidence, if any were needed, the advantage the driven third wheel could bring. The ACU had banned the use of swds in the British Experts and the Scots followed suit with their six day event. So, Baughans scored a remarkable success, one that was never to be repeated. The somewhat bitter feeling that the Baughan swd aroused was all too clear to HPB and with his position in the Western Centre, many thought he had too much influence in that quarter. In actual fact Baughan had no axe to grind. He never set out with the intention of producing a machine that would sweep all before it and it was never more than a technical exercise in his eyes to prove its worth. If he had really been serious in pursuing swd in trials it was certainly not beyond his means to produce another machine identical to Hayward's and get a rider such as Peter Bradley to ride it. The offer of a 'free' machine along with running costs would be hard to refuse. Bradley himself was fully conversant with swd, after all he had two seasons behind him riding his Sunbeam with a drive of his own design. If the Morris victory in the 'Scottish' surprised a few people, Eric Oddy was not one of them. "Ted was an exceptional rider and I was never in any doubt as to his ability in that event covering six days." This was what he said forty years later. "To be really honest I was glad that Alec rode with him. I don't think I would have been up to the job; Alec had far more experience than I had in sidecars." Oddy did cover many miles with Ted on local trials but knew his limitations, Morris, he recalled had quite a 'press-on' style when it mattered, something that was evident when he rode in the Cotswold Cups and the Stroud Team Trials.

Bill Hayward watched Morris from close quarters and remarked how quickly he mastered swd. Chris Stagg was of the same opinion. "If Ted had bought his Baughan in 1931 then Bill would have had a real fight on his hands. He was a very quick learner and if he had ventured into the Western Centre earlier and rode in the 'Experts' I think he could have won it." Geoff Fisher, always one to closely observe any rider, solo or threewheeler with any talent had this to say. "I met Morris soon after he bought his first swd. His attention to detail was like Harry's. Once when I was at the start helping the sisters I had a chance to look over his machine, especially in the sidecar. This had been modified in the nose and a small closed shelf had been added, when I queried what was wrapped in a very oily rag he carefully unwrapped it revealing a complete carburettor with all manner of jets and needles; . . . I never enquired what was in the rear compartment." Morris, now with a machine that was equal to his talent certainly used swd to its full potential. If he had bought his machine two years before then the Western Centre might have had considerably more disgruntled clubmen on their hands. The antagonism that swd generated in certain circles was bad enough. If there had been two from Harry Baughan, things might had been very different. Many Centres by 1934 had banned their use, or at least their drives. To have two from the same factory would have caused much hand wringing. The poor old clubman must have felt a very poor relation to such riders with their undoubted advantage. Efforts were made to redress the balance when Centres restricted swd machines to standard tyres, thinking this would allow the single wheel drives to continue with competition ones. The idea was full of promise, alas, they soon found it was of limited use.

Within a few months swds were winning again and more severe measures had to be concocted. Ted Morris still continued his winning ways for the next few years as the next chapter reveals. In 1933 swds were almost at their peak, and by the following year their ranks had increased. Hayward was always there along with Mansell and Peter Bradley. The BSA of Uzzell had long gone, and soon Freddie Stevenson's contribution when he modified George Brough's finest, then Harold Taylor came up with the Williams drive. With Morris now having two swds the opposition was beaten before they had turned a wheel . . . well almost.

The Flook brothers had other ideas. They were certainly not intimidated by these extra drives as they were fast becoming a serious challenge to the established drivers of the day. Soon they were to excel in the trial that gave every sidecarist an equal chance, the British Experts. At this time (1933) many Centres were giving serious thought to swds. The clubman saw no end to them in competition and even if the Flooks could win without them, they were still concerned. One measure that was introduced by the ACU was to limit the swds to standard trials tyres and leave the single wheel drives to continue with 'knobblies'. Many thought this was a solution, however, it was not long before swds were winning on 'standard' tyres; another think was in order by the organizers.

Before long swds met their nemisis, severe restrictions either by the clubs within the Centres, or the Centres themselves. Vic Anstice the Hon Sec of the Wessex Centre railed against them and for a while refused their entries, pressure was brought to bear and he relented, he even put up a separate cup for swds paid out of his own pocket.

Geoff Fisher suspected, as did many other riders that Anstice bowed to the Trade for swds to be included, bonuses and publicity were at stake.

Hill collection.

Alec Hill was a fine all-round competitor, whether in grass track, speedway, hill climbs, sidecar passenger in grass track or trials. Here seen taking Dob Park Splash in his stride while competing in the 1926 Scott Trial . . . on a Scott.

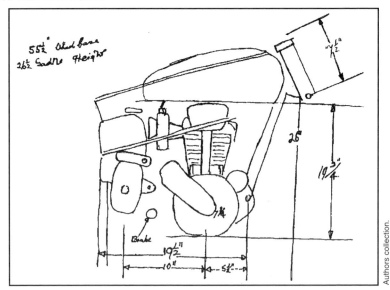

Authors collection.

The sketch that Chris Stagg used as an outline for the general dimensions when Ted Morris informed Harry Baughan that he would be using the Rudge Python TT replica. He preferred this engine instead of the 500cc Blackburne as used by Hayward. As soon as the blueprints were delivered Chris was able to make a start on the overall dimensions. The difference between the engines was minimal.

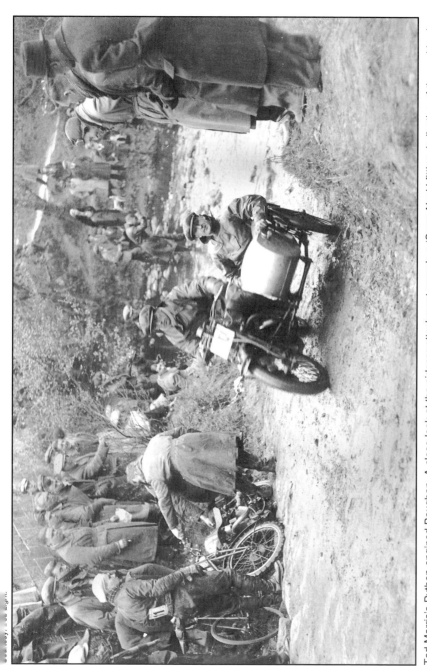

Ted Morris's Python engined Baughan. A close look at the sidecar attachment reveals a 'Swan Neck' fitting, indicative of the swd having been removed. When Chris Stagg built both Ted's swds they had the same attachment to the bike frame as Bill Hayward's with full adjustment front and rear. The location is unknown as is the trial. This machine appeared as late as 1947, then disappeared.

Hill collection.

Alec Hill was a great supporter of speedway competition. Here in the centre he lines up alongside Eric and Oliver Langton and Frank Varley at the Leeds stadium in 1929. Alec was also an excellent grass track rider and was a regular competitor at the Harrogate Cricket Ground.

The list of events that feature Baughan riders. Some awards are listed as, Gold, Silver or Bronze which later were often classified as 1st, 2nd or 3rd class depending on either of the trial organizers, MCC or ACU.

Baughan Competition Results

1921

N/A (no award) **N/S** (non starter) **N/F** (non finisher) **R** (retired) **N/E** (no entry). Unless otherwise stated, Marjorie Grant Heelas was Bill Hayward's passenger and her sister, Auriol Grant Heelas was passenger to Harry Baughan. Hayward's swd Blackburne engine was always 500cc.

MCC London-Edinburgh.
HPB, Red Car (MD264)* Retired when Woodruff key fails in rear axle.

From the *Light Car and Cyclecar* .
Trial on Nailsworth Ladder.
Although this was a test of hill climbing ability on just the famous 'Ladder' a number of other hills in the district were tried like 'Black Nest' just outside of Stroud but all the action was at Nailsworth. HPB, on his first, attempt broke his final drive chain. A second try, this time with two passengers successfully made it to the top of the 1 in 2.5 gradient. The locally built Hampton car (Dudbridge works) was also demonstrated with eight passengers on the first climb. On its second ascent there were no less than *fourteen* bodies aboard.

1922

MCC London-Edinburgh.
HPB, car. Silver Medal.

1923

MCC London-Edinburgh.
HPB, car. Gold Medal.

London-Lands End
HPB, car. Gold Medal.

1924

Western Centre Team Trial.
Hayward, 300cc, (solo). Silver Medal. Machine (No.14), No.25/206.

*Entries for (car) refer to the Red Car MD264.

1925

London-Holyhead.
HPB, 300cc, Silver Cup.

London-Edinburgh.
HPB, 300cc, Gold Cup.

Western Centre Inter Team Trial.
CW (Bill) Peters, 300cc, Gold Medal. HPB, Red Car 998cc, Gold Medal. Hayward, 348cc, Silver Medal. GE Isles 348, **N/A.** A Meeze, 348, **N/A.** C King, 348cc, **N/A.**

London-Lands End.
Hayward, 300cc (solo), Gold Medal. Machine (No.15), No.25/206 was ridden in the above four trials.

1926

Colmore Cup.
Bill Peters, 300cc, Silver Medal.

Victory Cup.
HPB, 300cc, Gold Medal.

London-Lands End.
HPB, 300cc, Gold Medal.
Machine (No.19), No.26/210 was used in the above three trials.

1927

Cotswold Cup.
Hayward, 348cc, Gold. Halliday, 348cc, Gold. J Butt, 348cc, Silver. HPB, car, 998cc, Gold. There were no Baughan riders entered as a team to compete for the nine Open awards or for the five Closed awards.

Stroud Team and Individual Entry Trial.
Baughan Team. HPB, car, 998cc, 1st class. Hayward, 348cc, 3rd class. CWS Peters, 348cc, 2nd class. They finished in 3rd place. Stroud Motor Cycle Club also entered three teams, 'S,' 'M' and 'C.' (S), HPB and Hayward accompanied by Fred Halliday on his 348cc Cotton. (M), J Butt, 348cc, Peters, 348cc and Tom Powles, 348cc, Douglas. 'C,' George Isles, 348cc, ran with Harry Daniels, 349cc, BSA and F Meadows, 249cc, Dunelt.

Officials gather around the famous Red Car. L to R. Alf Williams, Treasurer of the Western Centre. Max Young, Western Centre Steward. HPB, Secretary Western Centre. William Box. Charlie Baughan and AU Zimmerman, ACU Official. Looking at the kick start poking through the bodywork it would seem the SA motor cycle gear box was still being used. Aluminium covers the scuttle and the aero screen is still being used. Around 1925 when this photograph was taken the mudguards have been removed.

1928

Cotswold Cup.

HPB, **N/E**. Hayward, 248cc, wins William Box Trophy (Open Award) for best under 250cc. Fred Halliday, 348cc, 1st class. FJ Hind, 348cc, 2nd class. J Butt, 348cc, 2nd class. Halliday, Hayward and Hind made up the Baughan Team and finished in 3rd place. *

Stroud Open Team and Individual Entry Trial.

Hayward, 248cc, 1st class. Bill Peters, 348cc, 1st class. FJ Hind, 348cc, 1st class. HPB, Red Car 998cc, 1st class. Stagg, **N/E**. The Stroud Motor Cycle Club entered a team of: HPB, Hayward, Butt, Halliday, F Meadows, 172cc, Baker. TM Powles, 348cc, Douglas. L Powles, 348cc, OK Supreme. H Daniels, 498cc, Ariel, and R Meadows; 249cc, Dunelt. They did not figure in the results.

---

*This trial must have proved very costly in terms of awards for the Western Centre. There were no less than a total of 148: 30 1st class, 50 2nd class and 68 3rd class.

1929

The 1929 results listed here are the personal records of Harry Baughan from his many long hand notes. Sadly the early minutes and results of the Stroud Motor Cycle Club no longer exist. The following list of riders are all Baughan mounted unless otherwise stated.

London-Coventry.
Hayward/Heelas, s/c, 1st class. (First appearance of the Baughan swd).

Presteign Auto Club Freak Hill Climb. Harley Bank.
Hayward/Auriol Grant Heelas,* s/c, 2nd class. F Hind, 250cc 1st class. Halliday, winner of the 250cc class.

Marklove Cup Trial.
HPB (Marklove Cup) car. F Hind 250cc, 1st class. Stagg, 300cc, 1st class.

John Bull Challenge Trophy.
HPB, car, 1st class. F Hind, 250cc, 2nd class. Stagg, 300cc, 1st class.

Wessex League Trial.
HPB, car, **N/A.** Hayward, s/c, 1st class. F Hind, 250cc, **N/A.** Stagg, 300cc, 1st class.

Wessex Autumn Trial.
HPB, car, 1st class. Hayward, s/c 1st class. Stagg, 300cc 1st class.

Meridith Cup Trial.
HPB, car, **N/S** (magneto trouble). Hayward, s/c, 1st class. F Hind, 250cc, 1st class. Team prize. **N/A.**

Triumph Cup Trial.
HPB, car, 1st class. Hayward, s/c, 2nd class. F Hind, 250cc, **N/A.** Stagg, 300cc, 3rd class.

Mallory Cup Trial.
Hayward, s/c, **N/A.** (broken sidecar spring, rear). F Hind, 250cc, 1st class. Stagg, 300cc, 1st class.

Worcester Motor Club.
HPB, car, **N/A.** Hayward, s/c, **N/A.**

*When it came to speed events Auriol took the place of her sister.

Mystery photo. Bill and Auriol at an unidentified location and event. This is Bill's swd but the registration is DG810. This registration was allocated to a Mr. P Selwyn on 23/5/1933, some four years after the swd was built. The event could possibly be Red Marley. Speed events required crash helmets.

Dunelt Trophy.
Stagg, 300cc, 1st class (no other Baughans entered).

Wye Valley Autumn Trial.
HPB, car, 1st class. Hayward, s/c, 3rd class. Stagg, 300cc, 2nd class.

Stroud Team Trial.
HPB, car, **R**, (magneto). Hayward,* s/c, 1st class. Stagg, 300cc, 1st class. Stroud Motor Cycle Club entered three teams: (S) Daniels, Hayward, HPB. **N/A** (M) P Meadows, Stagg, 1st class. Fisher, 2nd class. (C) HPB, RW Meadows, J Fawkes.

Cotswold Cup.
Hayward, s/c, Gold. Halliday, 348cc, Gold. J Butt, 348cc, Silver. HPB, Red Car, 998cc, Gold. There were no Baughan riders entered as a team to compete for the nine Open awards or for the five Closed awards.

*Denotes Premier Award, as a member of the JB Watson Team.

Worcester MC Half Day Trial.
HPB, car, 1st class. Hayward, s/c, 1st class. Stagg, 300cc, 1st class.

Drake Memorial Trial.
HPB, car, **N/A.** Hayward, s/c, wins Hardacre Cup. Stagg, 300cc, 3rd class.

Stroud Solo Trial.
Stagg, 300cc, 3rd class (no other Baughans entered).

London-Gloucester.
HPB, car, **N/A.** Hayward, s/c, 1st class.

1930

Victory Cup.
No Baughan entries.

Cotswold Cup.
HPB, car, **R**, (broken piston) Hayward, s/c, last position in the 2nd class awards. Stagg, 249cc, 1st class. HPB, Hayward and Stagg formed the Baughan Team, who failed when the Red Car suffered a damaged piston.

London-Gloucester.
No Baughan entries.

Stroud Team Trial.
Baughan Team winners of the Dunlop Trophy. HPB, car (now fitted with a new piston). Hayward, s/c. Stagg, 350cc, also 2nd class award. Hayward was also a member of the JB Watson team along with Jack Williams, 500cc Rudge and Len Vale-Onslow, 172, S-O-S, who won the White Trophy for the best performance by any team. Passenger awards went to the Grant Heelas sisters (these were certificates).

Kickham Memorial.
No Baughan entries.

Southern Trial.
Stagg, 350cc, 1st class.

Hayward collection.

Bill Hayward astride his Baughan hill climb and sprint special fitted with an outside flywheel 350cc twin port Blackburne. Bill, like Chris Stagg made these machines up from spares that were lying about at Lower Street. As they are specials they were never recorded in the sales ledger or registered.

Colmore Cup.
HPB, car, **R.** (broken front axle). Hayward, s/c, 2nd class.

Worcester Half Day Trial.
HPB, car, **N/A**. Hayward, s/c, **N/A**.

Wye Valley Traders Cup.
Hayward, s/c, **N/A**. No other Baughan entries.

Bath and Avon Trial.
Stagg, 300cc, 1st class. (April 12th).

Bath and Avon Trial.
Stagg, 300cc, **N/A**. (April 16th). (There were no other Baughan entries in these two trials).

1931
Colmore Cup.
Hayward, s/c, 2nd class. No other Baughan entries.

A wonderful photo of Chris Stagg cresting the top of Red Marley freak hill climb on Easter Monday 1933. He established a new hill record for his class. The rear tyre was greatly modified with 2 inch coach bolts through the cover which were spaced out by several inches and staggered across the tread. The grip generated was enormous. However, a price was paid when a cover lasted possibly two runs, and then destroyed itself. At times the tips were even ground down to points for increase grip.

Victory Cup.
Hayward, s/c, 2nd class. Stagg, 500cc, 2nd class.

Kickham Memorial.
Hayward, s/c, wins Wiltshire Cup (opposite class). Stagg, 350cc, 1st class.

Cotswold Cup.
HPB, car, wins John Bull Cup. 1st class. Hayward, s/c (Trier's Cup and Braham Cup). 1st class. Stagg, 350cc (Gotham Cup). 1st class. AJ Clarke, 350cc, 1st class.

Stroud Team Trial 1931

HPB and Auriol Grant Heelas win Hillslie Cup for the best individual performance. Red Car. Baughan Team win National Cup (HPB, Hayward, Stagg), Hayward and Stagg were also members of the Gloucester MC and LCC, 'B' team which collected the Dunlop Trophy. HPB, car, 1st class. Hayward, s/c, 2nd class. Stagg, 350cc, 3rd class.

The following report of the above trial gives an insight into Baughan Motors unique position in the history of trials competition; never to be repeated.*

The Stroud Team and Individual Trial attracted a reasonable entry, 34 in all. Just four of these were sidecars and the only cyclecar was Harry's Red Car fitted with a new engine. Chris Stagg had the dubious honour of running at the head of the field. Five behind came Jimmy Simpson on his works Norton. Harry Daniels at 10 on his 498cc Rudge with Geoff Fisher one minute in front of him on his Rudge, Ralph Dee similarly mounted at 15. Jack Williams at 18 also Rudge mounted. Two minutes behind him was Len Vale-Onslow on his 175cc water cooled S-O-S. George Stannard at 22 was one minute behind Bob Foster and George Pyecroft at 23, and the last of the solos at 28 was Bert Perrigo on his 348cc works BSA.

The weather was dry but the usual slime on the limestone was just enough to give problems to everyone with the exception of Bert Perrigo who cleared every hill, not just once but twice when he completed his second circuit. As Harry Baughan was the route surveyor this gave him great satisfaction for there was the usual special test included in the case of a tie; this time it was superfluous. Harry Baughan's aim on every trial was to plan a course that would be difficult, but not impossible as many trials frequently were. He wanted only one person to make it to the finish without any marks lost, and the best rider on the day would have the satisfaction of having the only clean sheet. In the sidecar class only four machines were entered. As the Red Car was the only cyclecar entered it was placed in with the sidecars and ran immediately behind Bill and Marjorie who were at 31. Dennis Mansell was one minute behind HPB, and once again Bill Mewis was in his rightful place. Sadly there were no Morgans present so HPB was competing against himself which he found rather pointless. The Red Car was to be used for a few more years when it was wheeled out for closed to club events. Otherwise it was used for route marking or the Gaffer's personal transport.

As a team event there were fourteen entries in all. Gloucester A, Stroud A, Stroud B, Stroud C, DK Mansell Norton Team, Tewkesbury A, Cheltenham Motor Club, Worcester Motor Club, Gloucester B, Stroud Baughan Team, JB Watson Team, Tewkesbury B, Wye Valley Auto Club and finally Birmingham

* The photo of Chris Stagg's cup for his winning ride in this team event is on page 276. Both the Gaffer and Bill Hayward received similar cups. This trophy is unique to Baughans.

Motor Club. *For the Stroud Baughan Team in this event was a very significant milestone. Chris rode his 348cc, ohv. Bill and Marjorie swd 498cc ohv and Harry and Auriol 998cc sv air-cooled V twin Blackburne Red Car. Never before, or after has there ever been an entry to match this from any other factory within the motorcycle industry, either in this country or abroad for that matter. When the spectators lined the many observed hills they were perhaps unaware that they were witnessing motor cycle history in the making. This tiny factory fielded a solo, a sidecar-wheel drive outfit and a cyclecar; and to make it absolutely unique the two female passengers were identical twins.*

Miss Ruby Slade on her Norton became a victim of the 'Gravestones' but managed to extricate herself. Despite the difficulties of BB, Ralph Dee, Len Vale-Onslow, Jack Williams and Bert Perrigo made it through clean, although Station Lane was a different matter. This proved to be very slippery but Bert Perrigo was on top form and demonstrated just why he was one of the top works riders in the country and cleaned it with ease. He was not alone for Harry Baughan gave the Red Car its head and shot up without a moment's hesitation for a clean. When everyone assembled at the Bear Hotel for the finish the Gaffer and Auriol were presented with the Hillslie Cup for the best individual performance. This was doubly pleasing for Auriol, this trophy had be presented to the Stroud Valley Motor Club by her father which incidentally was also the name of their house at Lower Littleworth just a few hundred yards from the Bear Hotel. There was a couple of notable retirements. Jimmy Simpson hit the large stone step at the bottom of Ham Mill and crashed into the stone wall which shook him up so badly that he took no further part in the trial and Jack Williams had the valve pull out of his rear tyre and failed to make the finish within the required time.

There was great elation for the Baughan Team which won the National Cup (presented by *The Yorkshire Post*). Once again the Red Car had proved its worth in spite of no other four wheeled competitor. Chris Stagg was delighted as he collected the Dunlop Trophy along with Bill Hayward and Marjorie and to complete the trio LW Hall on his Cotton made up the Gloucester B Team. Bill and his passenger also collected a 2nd class award along with Len Vale-Onslow and Dennis Mansell. Chris also picked up a 3rd class award as did another Baughan rider, AJ Clarke. All in all it was an excellent performance by Baughan Motors which was met with great approval by the partisan crowd at the finish. HPBs win may have cheered him immensely but he confessed that he would have liked to see a solo win. Even so it was a great tribute to his driving skill in his patent vehicle. HPB was justifiably proud of his riders achievements for it was a unique occasion, but the ever modest Harry Baughan passed this off and never looked upon the day as anything of a milestone. The result of the trial was an outstanding win for the Stroud factory, one that would never be repeated by a

Bill and Marjorie in the Victory Cup Trial, 1931. This is Bill's usual swd but with a few modifications. The sidecar aero screen has been removed along with the lights. The sidecar chassis is not the normal swd one, it was in fact a conventional one that Bill fitted from time to time just to ensure that swd had been removed to satisfy the organizers. This s/c is proably the one that HPB used on his 350cc outfit. The identifying feature for this is the absence of the chassis enclosing the sidecar wheel. The Swan Neck attaching the sidecar has no means of adjustment.

manufacturer with such uniqueness. As the Western Centre Secretary HPB was keenly aware just how much motoring had changed, motor cycles had gradually been evolving. The cyclecars on the other hand which had been designed and built out of necessity were no longer there. Serious developments had taken place with the introduction of the light cars and the once strong movement was well in decline. The era of motor cycle engines and transmissions was passed, even the threewheeler Morgans were being pushed into the sidecar class and were steadily being out-performed despite the gallant efforts of their owners. On some trials many sections hardly had any room to accommodate the width of combinations and Morgan drivers were finding things very difficult.

British Experts.
Hayward, s/c, **R.** Stagg, 350cc, 11th. (Bill Hayward's retirement was caused by the magneto bolts working loose, and by the time they were replaced he and

Marjorie were outside maximum lateness.)

Wye Valley.
Hayward, s/c, 1st class. AJ Clarke, 350cc, 1st class.

MCC Team Trial.
AJ Clarke, 500cc (Memento). Member of the Newport and Gwent MC.

London-Gloucester.
Stagg, 1st class.

London-Exeter.
Hayward, s/c, with Stagg as passenger, **R**.

Red Marley Hill Climb.
Hayward, s/c. Stagg, 350cc (Hill Climb Special). Both riders experienced engine problems (Hayward faulty magneto, Stagg, partial seizure). Stagg was Hayward's passenger on the climbs, swd was used on all the ascents.

1932

Colmore Cup.
Hayward, s/c, 1st class. No other Baughan entries.

Victory Cup.
Hayward, s/c, did not start due to damaged hand. Stagg, 350cc, 1st class.

Cotswold Cup.
Hayward, s/c, wins Cotswold Cup. Stagg, 350cc, 1st class. Bill Peters, 250cc, 2nd class.

Kickham Memorial.
Hayward, s/c, wins Kickham Memorial Cup and Therleigh Cup (opposite class). No other Baughan entries.

Wye Valley.
Hayward, s/c, wins HAC Challenge Bowl, (opposite class) and was a member of the Worcester Team which won the Hereford City Trophy.

Mather collection.

Auriol Marjorie Grant Heelas in the driving seat, a position she often occupied as secretary of the meeting when she drove HPB around the course checking that the marking dye was the correct colour and in the right position. The Red Car shows some alteration. The wind shield is now flexible and the fabric over the scuttle is tensioned by liberal amounts of aircraft dope. The rear compartment is open suggesting that the course was in the process of being checked. The cover was often removed as it proved far easier to get the scoop into the dye sacks. The location and trial remain a mystery.

Reliance Trial.
Hayward, s/c, forced to retire due to injury. HPB, s/c (350cc non-swd) also retires with Auriol Grant Heelas as passenger to help Hayward to hospital.

Mitchell Memorial.
Hayward, s/c, wins Mitchell Memorial Cup (opposite class). HPB, s/c, 350cc, non-swd, Hayward, s/c, and Stagg, 350cc, win the team prize.

Stroud Team Trial.
Dunlop Trophy won by the Stroud Valley Baughan Team. HPB, car, Hayward, s/c, Stagg, 350cc. Hayward and HPB were members of the Gloucester MC and LCC along with Jack Williams which won the National Cup.* Hayward and HPB, 1st class. Stagg, 350cc, 2nd class. Guy Babbage, 350cc, 3rd class. G Fisher, 350cc, 3rd class.

British Experts.
Hayward, s/c, 8th place. Stagg, 350 cc, 7th place.

*National Cup was the top award.

ACU Inter Centre Team Trial.
Hayward, s/c, and Stagg, 350cc, were members of the Western Centre Team who failed to finish through mechanical problems.

1933

Colmore Cup.
No Baughan entries.

Victory Cup.
Stagg, 350cc, 2nd class. No other Baughan entries.

Cotswold Cup.
Hayward, s/c, wins Gloucester Cup and 1st class award. Stagg, 350cc, **N/A**.

Mitchell Memorial.
HPB, s/c, 350cc, non-swd, **N/A**. Hayward, s/c, 1st class. Stagg, **N/E**.

Wye Valley Traders.
Hayward, s/c, 1st class. Stagg, **N/E**.

Kickham Memorial.
Hayward, s/c, wins Kickham Memorial Cup (opposite class). Stagg, 350cc, 1st class.

Scottish Six Days Trial.
Morris, s/c, 500cc, wins SSDT. (opposite class).

MCC Team Trial.
Hayward, s/c, and Stagg collect souvenirs.

Ilkley Grand National.
Morris, s/c, 500cc, wins Triumph Cup. No other Baughan entries.

Yorkshire Inter Centre Team Trial.
Morris, s/c, 500cc, member of the Ilkley and District MC which took *The Motor Cycle* Trophy.

Inter Centre Team Championships.
Hayward, s/c, and Fisher collect souvenirs. Stagg, **N/A**.

Chris Stagg riding in the 1931 Cotswold Cups Trial. Here he leads the Cotton works rider LN Hall with quite a rare Baughan. This was a customer machine which features a distinctive ivory inlay to the petrol tank. Chris registered this machine for the buyer on February 27th, 1931 (see page 332). This day Chris picked up a 1st class award and also the Gotham Cup. It was not unusual for Chris to ride a customers machine just to show him what it was capable of. The Gaffer was always very keen on this idea; waving the company flag was always good publicity.

HPB and Bill Hayward relax by the Scott Memorial on May 31st, 1925 after their ride in the MCC London-Edinburgh Trial. Both men look very tired after more than 24 hours in the saddle. They were true pioneering spirits for long distance trials.

Gloucester Grand National Scramble.
Stagg, 350cc, wins Gloucestershire Trophy.

ACU Inter Centre Team Championships.
Hayward, s/c, Stagg, 350, and Fisher, 350cc, were members of the Western Centre Team. They lost a member and were marked out of contention.

British Experts.
Hayward, s/c, Morris, s/c, 500cc, Fisher, 350cc, collected souvenirs. Chris Stagg rode as Hayward's passenger due to Marjorie being indisposed. This was the only time this happend in an open or premier event.

1934
Colmore Cup.
Morris, s/c, 500cc, 1st class. Fisher, 350cc, **R**. Hayward and Stagg, **N/E**.

Birmingham MCC Championship of the Clubs
Morris, s/c 499cc. HP Baughan s/c 500cc. Stagg 349cc, comprised the Stroud Team. All were awarded Souvenirs. HPB rode Haywards swd. This trial saw the

Hayward collection.

HPB and Bill take a break on a bridge over the river Clyde on their homeward run from Scotland.

one exception when Harry Baughan rode Bill Haywards swd. Marjorie was the passenger as her sister had no knowledge of the sidecar wheel drive and how it should be used in competition.

Kickham Memorial.
Hayward, s/c, 1st class. Fisher, 350cc, **R**.

Victory Cup.
Hayward, s/c, 1st class. Morris, s/c, 500cc, 1st class. Stagg, 350cc, 3rd class. Fisher, 350cc, 3rd class.

Cotswold Cup.
Hayward, s/c, Morris, s/c, 499cc, and Dennis Mansell, 490cc Norton s/c, tie for Cotswold Cup (opposite class). Team prize (Baughan, 'C'), comprising, Hayward, Morris and Stagg. Fisher, 350cc, wins Clift Cup*. Stagg, 350cc, also wins Gotham Cup*.

The following report of the above trial is also another first in trials history. This was the only trial that feature *three* swd outfits that tied for victory in the opposite class in a premier event; never to be repeated.

The 1934 Cotswold Cups Trial was as usual held in the Stroud district with Harry Baughan the Western Centre Secretary in charge. The familiar abundance of hills followed the usual 'Cotswold' pattern with Geoff Fisher giving his usual weather predictions and in the week prior to the trial warned HPB that there was the possibility of rain on the Friday or Saturday. A suitable course was planned in the event of a downpour. The rain put in an appearance on the Friday, and such was the force, it washed many of the sections clean. What nobody had envisaged was the closeness of the finishing order, HPB included. Seventy–one entries had been received, and only two failed to turn up. With so much rain the previous day no one thought there would be any chance of a tie. Events turned

* Denotes closed award.

The Marklove Cup presented to the Stroud Club as a closed award. The reverse is on page 258.

out differently, the best laid plans of mice and men . . . The start from the Bear Hotel was in fine weather in complete contrast to the previous day which was welcomed by volunteers and officials alike. At 10.30 the first rider headed off to BB where the long steady climb was washed clean of leaf mould and the gravestones gave few problems to the riders. The next hill, Camp, brought out the best in the works riders. Here, plenty of deep, greasy leaf mould hid many of the rocks. Bert Perrigo was outstanding, and due to the length of the section several observers were needed to keep an eye out for the odd 'dab'. Len Vale-Onslow, 175cc S-O-S came to grief when he discovered a hidden stone. Fred Povey, 499cc BSA was forced to foot and Ralph Dee, 346cc Rudge and Vic Brittain, 490cc Norton indulged in a dab. Jack Williams, 348cc Norton with all his experience fell off at the top of the hill, after he had cleared the section. George Rowley, 498cc AJS was another who demonstrated his skill that had earned him a works ride over many years. Tony Johnson 348cc Baughan fell off many times on Camp, and despite being a local rider on a machine purchased just months before, his lack of top class experience was all too evident. Tony Johnson relied heavily on HPB for guidance in trials. The only thing was that Harry Baughan was too tied up with other things to devote much attention his way. Later Chris Stagg helped him out, sadly Johnson never lived long enough to put this into practice. Camp claimed all the sidecars with conventional drive and not one cleared the hill. The swds on the other hand were in a different class altogether and Mansell 490cc Norton, Hayward 498cc Baughan, Morris 498cc Baughan and Peter Bradley 596cc Sunbeam all made it without penalty. George Stannard, 649cc Triumph inverted his outfit and was badly shaken up, but carried on in a very subdued mood.

Shadwell was next and only thirteen solos made it clean. Kilcott was the last observed hill before a welcome lunch break at the Bear, by which time only four riders had managed to keep a clean sheet. Jack Williams and Vic Brittain were two of them. The conversation at the halt was the state of the hills for the weather had taken its toll and the only people who were experiencing the least difficulty were the sidecar crews equipped with swd and this was the main talking point. The weather that was thought would make for a difficult trial was not turning out as predicted. After the much welcomed rest Station Lane was next on the list, then Trellis followed by Gulf and Henwood. The approach to Gulf and Henwood was barred to the riders by a number of felled trees. Permission was obtained for an alternative route, grudgingly this was given by the landowner. As soon as the solos had passed through the gate it was padlocked and access withdrawn; this was overseen by a substantial gentleman brandishing a riding crop. When the sidecars crews arrived the leading local sidecar exponent, Hayward, was quick to take charge of all the crews and with his intimate knowledge of the district, rapidly found an alternative route. Morris, whose first Cotswold this was, would have been totally lost without Hayward's help. The crews finally arrived at Henwood coming *down* the hill. This *force majeure* cost precious time, which was adjusted at the finish when formal protests were filed. This lateral thinking on Bill's part found great favour with the many of the crews whose understanding of the surrounding area was almost nil. The marshals and observers were very surprised when they were confronted by all the sidecar crews *en masse*. Gulf gave entertainment to the spectators especially when the 'Flyer' lost control of his 348cc works Norton, charging the bank at speed resulting in a failure. If this hill took a toll on the solos the swd outfits experienced little difficulty. Stuart Waycott on his newly acquired 411cc Velocette proved to be the best of the conventional drives and gave a demonstration to lesser crews of how to tackle this hill. Stinchcombe was where the special test was conducted, and this was to prove the only weak part of the trial, for up to this time the organization had been flawless. A large part of Juniper had to be divided into 50 yard sections in order to space the observers out to sight the whole climb. Libbys, the last hill of the trial saw just six solos clean it. Tiredness was creeping in and the conditions had taken their toll and when they arrived at the finish on Rodborough Common there were some very weary riders. The trial was judged a success despite the sidecar hold up and the weather had proved once again to be a factor for without the previous day's downpour the result may have been very different in the sidecar class.

Just after 7.30pm Harry Baughan's team published the provisional results and this produced something of a surprise. Five competitors had tied for two of the top awards; three in the sidecars and two from the solos. Two factory riders, Jack Williams 348cc Norton and Bert Perrigo's 348cc BSA were both on 16 marks and had to share the Cotton Trophy. More bizarre still, three sidecar drivers tied without loss of marks. Bill Hayward, Ted Morris and Dennis Mansell along with their passengers shared the opposite class for the Cotswold Cup; all equipped with swd. If this was astonishing it was perhaps a result of the special test which was far too short due to a misunderstanding on the officials part as to the distance to be used in the event of a tie. One thing, two Baughans finished without any marks lost, perhaps it was expected from Hayward and Mansell whose knowledge of the course over the years was comprehensive. It was not the same for Morris who was competing in his first Cotswold which he quickly mastered. There was no doubt who was the top solo rider; Vic Brittain on his 490cc Norton supplied by the factory lost just 9 marks. The Boaks and Harper Trophy went to Cheltenham with Bob Foster on a 148cc New Imperial with 26 marks. The Gibb Trophy for the best rider up to 500cc went to George Rowley on another works machine a 498cc AJS with 10 marks lost. There was little surprise over the Team Trophy going to Baughan Motors with Stagg, Hayward and Morris, the latter elected to ride his number one machine powered by the radial valved Python engine. There was another swd taking an award; the Triers Cup, which went to Freddie Stevenson on his 980cc Brough Superior swd for the best performance for a competitor who did not qualify for a special open award. Peter Bradley collected the John Bull Cup losing just 6 marks riding his 596cc Sunbeam, also with a swd. If any evidence was required as to the superiority of sidecar wheel drive, this was the trial, right throughout the event they were relentless in their climbing power and showed the complete mastery by the crews over their mounts in very poor conditions. It was not all dismay for the conventionally driven outfits, Stuart Waycott lifted the Haines and Strange Cup on his 411cc Velocette with 17 marks lost, and George Stannard 650cc Triumph took the Griffen Memorial Cup. There was more success for the Baughan riders, Chris Stagg finishing up with the Gotham Cup and Geoff Fisher came away with the Clift Cup; all in all, excellent publicity for the local firm which made up for HPBs disappointment over the tie decider test. First class awards went to Alan Jefferies 498cc Triumph, 12 marks. George Povey 499cc BSA 19 marks and Jack Amott 249cc Triumph, losing 22.

With such an overwhelming demonstration of what a sidecar wheel drive outfit in the right hands could do was plain for all to see. For five years these devices had been competing for top honours and the past two had seen more of them appear and opinion was starting to run against them. With such a result in an Open trial it was not long before more serious action was taken.There was a stop and go test at Stinchcombe which turned out to be too short and not on the most suitable part of the hill to allow a fair tie-breaking assessment. Later it turned out there was a lack of understanding on the officials part in the conducting of this important test. Oakridge had to be taken out as the conditions proved too difficult in the circumstances.The problem with the Henwood section was a fallen tree. No one was sure if this was by design or accident. Just when this was discovered has not been revealed, but the travelling marshal must have found it when he surveyed the route travelling as he was just ahead of the first solo man. This was relayed to Auriol Grant Heelas resulting in strenuous work on her part to obtain permission for an alternative route, this was obtained but was only partly successful, and short lived. Later the results were amended due to this unfortunate incident.

Mitchell Memorial.
Hayward,* s/c, and Stagg, 350cc, disqualified for non-payment of entry fees. Fisher, 350cc, 1st class.

Wye Valley.
Hayward, s/c, member of the Western Centre Team winning the HAC Challenge Bowl. Stagg, N/E. Fisher, 350cc, 2nd class.

Stroud Team Trial.
Hayward, s/c. Morris, s/c, 600cc, and Stagg, 350cc, win National Trophy (best team). Morris, s/c, 600cc, wins Hillslie Cup. Hayward, Stagg and Fisher, 1st class.

Scott Trial.
Stagg, 348cc, 1st class.

British Experts.
Hayward, s/c, 6th. Morris, s/c, 500cc, 7th. Fisher, 350cc, 27th. Stagg, 350cc, **R**.

Allan Trial (Lakeland).
Morris, s/c, 500cc, wins Barron Trophy (opposite Class).

1935

Kickham Memorial.
Hayward, s/c, **N/A**. Stagg, 350cc and Fisher, 350cc, 2nd class.

Victory Cup.
Hayward, s/c, wins Victory Cup (opposite class). Stagg, 350cc, 3rd class. Morris, s/c, 500cc, **N/A**.

Colmore Cup.
Morris, s/c, 500cc, 1st class. No other Baughan entries.

Mitchell Memorial.

*Due to a mix–up with the paper work and entry monies both Baughan riders were disqualified after the trial had finished. Harry Baughan was almost incandesent with the East South Wales Centre as he had submitted both entries a second time along with the fees, all went missing. Bill Hayward said he would never compete again in that Centre, eventually he did relent.

Hayward, s/c, Unlimited Award. Fisher, **N/A**. Morris, s/c and Stagg, **N/E**.

Cotswold Cup.
Hayward, s/c, wins Cotswold Cup (opposite class). Stagg, 350cc, Trier's Cup. Fisher, 350cc, 1st class.

Ilkley Grand National.
Morris, s/c, 500cc, wins National Trophy.

Travers Trial.
Morris, s/c, 500cc, wins NUT Trophy.

Wye Valley Traders.
Hayward, s/c, Stagg, 350cc, and Jack Williams, 490cc (works Norton) win HAC Challenge Bowl. (Western Centre Team). Fisher, 350cc, 2nd class.

British Experts.
Hayward, s/c, 3rd. Morris, s/c, 500cc, 4th (both in opposite class). Ralph Dee, 300cc, 16th. Stagg, 350cc, 19th.

Inter Centre Team Trial.
Hayward, s/c, Stagg, 350cc, Geoff Fisher, 350cc, were members of the Western Centre Team which finished in 2nd place. Morris, s/c, 500cc, was a member of the Yorkshire Centre Team which finished in 4th place.

Ilkley Grand National.
Morris, s/c, 500cc, wins opposite class.

Stroud Team Trial.
Baughan Team, Hayward, s/c, Morris, s/c, 600cc, Stagg, 350cc, **N/A**. Hayward, s/c, 1st class. Morris, s/c, 600cc, 1st class. Stagg, 350cc, 2nd class. Fisher, 350cc, 2nd class. Stroud Valley MC Baughan Team (Hayward, Morris, Stagg), **N/A**.

Scott Trial.
Stagg, 348cc, Certificate.

Cotswold Scramble.
Stagg, 350cc special, Valley Cup.

Gloucester Grand National.

Stagg, 350 special, **R**.

1936

Colmore Cup.
No Baughan entries.

Kickham Memorial.
Hayward, s/c, wins Kickham Memorial Cup (opposite class). Fisher, 350cc, 2nd class. Stagg, **N/E**.

Mitchell Memorial.
Hayward, s/c, 1st class. Fisher, 350cc, **R**. Stagg, **N/E**.

Cotswold Cup.
Morris, s/c, 600cc, wins Cotswold Cup (opposite class). Hayward, s/c, **R**. (damaged forks). Stagg, 350cc, 1st class. Fisher, 350cc, wins Cliff Cup. Butcher, 250cc, **N/A**.

Wye Valley.
Fisher, 350cc, 1st class. No other Baughan entries.

Stroud Team Trial.
Stroud Valley Team, and best performance by a Western Centre Team, comprising, Stagg, 350cc, Fisher, 350cc, and Ralph Dee, 350cc, OK Supreme, win the Dunlop Trophy. Hayward, s/c, 1st class. Fisher, 350cc, 1st class. Bedwell, 350cc, 2nd class. Butcher, 250cc, 2nd class.

Cotswold Scramble.
Stagg, 350cc, special, wins Culver Cup. No other Baughan entries.

British Experts.
Hayward, s/c, 3rd (opposite class). Stagg, 350cc, **N/A.**

1937

Colmore Cup.
No Baughan entries.

Kickham Memorial.
Hayward, s/c, 2nd class. Stagg, **N/E**. Fisher, 350cc, **N/A**. Butcher, 250cc, **N/A**.

1920. C.C.BEAVIS.
1921. W.B.GIBB.
1922. L.PAYNTER. | 1926. C.W.PETERS
1924. S.PETERS. | 1927. A.F.HALLIDAY.
1925. W.E.HAYWARD. | 1929. H.P.BAUGHAN.
1930. H.P.BAUGHAN. | 1932. H.P.BAUGHAN.

As Harry Baughan won this award on three occasions, he kept it for posterity. This was quite unique as he drove his Red Car to win all three.

Victory Cup.
Hayward, s/c, 2nd class. No other Baughan entries.

Mitchell Memorial.
No Baughan entries.

Wye Valley.
No Baughan entries.

Cotswold Cup.
Hayward, s/c, wins Cotswold Cup (opposite class). Stagg, 350cc, **N/A**.

Cotswold Scramble.
Stagg, 350cc, special wins Culver Cup.

Stroud Team Trial.
Stroud Valley 'A' Team win Dunlop Trophy, comprising, Hayward, s/c, R. Dee, 350cc, Royal Enfield, 350cc, and Peter Falconer, 350cc, Triumph. Hayward, s/c, wins Zimmerman Cup (opposite class). Butcher, 250cc, 3rd class.

Red Marley Hill Climb.
Stagg, 350, special, 3rd on the round course.

British Experts.
Hayward, s/c, runner-up in opposite class. No other Baughan entries.

The following report on the above trial shows that Bill Hayward and Marjorie Grant Heelas were up with the best without their swd.

Again the Birmingham MC ran the British Experts Trial in the Western Centre entrusting it to its Hon Sec, Harry Baughan. Again in conjunction with Geoff Fisher he came up with a course worthy of its name which many when they heard of the route remarked there would be some fun and games. After the reconnaissance on the Friday the riders came back with the same thoughts. It was going to be the severest test yet for the best trials riders in the country. At the Bear Hotel that night all the talk was about the three new hills; the Slide, Woodleigh and Millend. All the riders agreed that the one hill that might give the most trouble would be the Slide. This was a short distance from the famous Weighbridge climb and if the Gaffer had been present that night he might have had a wry smile on his face; instead he was at the factory esconced in the

Signal Box going over the final details with Fisher, Peters, Chris Stagg and Bill Hayward; the sisters were not present. From 1930 the 'Experts' had been run in the Western Centre and every year in conjunction with the Birmingham MC Harry Baughan and his faithful band of dedicated volunteers had proved their worth with exceptional hills and sections. 1937 was to be no exception. In the past the winner had come from a very well established number of works riders. However, 1937 was to see a new name that many people had overlooked, that of Charlie Rogers riding a 348cc ohv Royal Enfield. In the sidecar class not much had changed. Harold Flook with his brother in the sidecar were expected to take their sixth consecutive victory which would have been an outstanding achievement, but it was not to be. As in past years there was to be two laps with a break for lunch at the 'Bear' which would give all the riders a little idea of how things were going.

That Friday night there was quite a severe frost but on the following morning start at 10am the sun shone and the temperature was climbing. Instead of the drive down the Bear Hill the trial took a clockwise direction to the first observed hill, More Folly, just a quarter mile from the start. (Author: as I look out of my window I can see this section, alas, nature has reclaimed most of it.) This gave few problems despite its down hill approach, 180° adverse camber right turn and 1 in 6 climb out. In the past riders like Jack Williams, Fred Povey and Allan Jefferies had cause to remember it when they measured their length in the inches deep limestone. The next hill was the 'Slide' and here the fun started, at least for the spectators which according to many must have been half the population of Nailsworth. This hill was aptly named for it was used as a logging track with its access to the Nailsworth-Avening road. Once again it was a discovery of Geoff Fisher and he who gained the permission for its use. (private land, as was the Weighbridge). The ruts were considerable and still carried the overnight frost. Even the marshals and observers had trouble taking up their positions. Many riders who were early numbers expressed their feelings from 'ridiculous' to 'absurd'; those at least were the printable ones. Billie Tiffen and Jack Booker made splendid ascents, if not in complete control they made it without penalty. Joe Heath on his 497cc Ariel failed in spectacular fashion and flew into the assembled press corp who were bowled over like nine pins. Joe had to turn completely round to regain the track, and a fail. Fred Povey and Allan Jefferies made it but Jefferies, only by superb balance got to the section end card. The sidecars proved to be far more exciting than any of the solos. Flook was the rider they all came to see as this was to be for an unprecedented six in a row. It started badly, huge amounts of wheel spin which brought him to a halt. Willing hands soon had him going again over the deep ruts. By the time he reached the summit his 490cc camshaft Norton was under almost full power and he completely misjudged the turn and the outfit did a complete roll leaving both him and his brother lying in the ruts. This shaking detuned them both for the rest of the trial. Bill Hayward also failed but more drama was in store for Whittle on his 598cc Panther who almost made it to the top. Just as the Flooks before him he also lost control and his passenger rapidly flew out of the chair and promptly disappeared into the throng of spectators; they soon had him back in the sidecar, albeit carried there. The deep ruts, hard frozen, caused more trouble. EJ English, 499cc Royal Enfield almost looped his machine at the finish and once more a passenger was deposited on the hard ground. Even the experience of Stuart Waycott, 411cc Velocette failed and Harold Tozer, 498cc BSA managed to eject his passenger as well when the sidecar came up over the bike. The sidecar climb of the day went to the highly experienced duo, Mansell and Mewis on their works Norton. They showed consummate skill and understanding of the conditions and recorded a perfect climb which drew applause not only from the large crowd but fellow riders alike. On the exit of the Slide, thawed mud was carried for yards up the main road and with all the trouble in the past from the public and competition tyres together with the road traffic regulations it was imperative to have it cleaned up as soon as possible. Wisely, Harry Baughan enlisted a band of volunteers with brushes to sweep it all up, a good move for the constabulary, as always was keeping a watching brief on the conduct of the trial. With the Weighbridge proving to be almost straightforward the trial moved two valleys away to BB 2 where a stop-and-restart was sited, then to Coaley. Camp was for sidecars only. Flook's troubles were not over for he shed his chain on the first lap here and Harold Tozer suffered the same fate on the second lap. As the trial wore on so Flook was complaining of poor handling and his performance slowly deteriorated.

Only when the trial finished he discovered the reason, the rear fork end had broken which prevented a repeat of the previous year's winning ride. If the Slide was sorting them out then Millend gave even greater problems for not one rider cleaned it, a total defeat for both classes; Harry Baughan had done it again. Hodgecome, always a favourite with the spectators, had seen some logging in the previous weeks which resulted in quite a deep rut well hidden by the leaf mould and was to become a challenge that thwarted many. Once the bike had dropped into this frozen gully it was almost impossible to break free within the close confines of the banks. Those that did attempt it ran up the bank and stopped. The only successful sidecar was Mansell who knew this climb of old and the wily old Bill Mewis placed his weight in the right place at the right time to make a perfect climb in the conditions and the many spectators showed their appreciation. It was a different matter on the second circuit when not one of them cleaned it. However, the solos were better and no less than fifteen made it to the top without penalty. The penultimate hill was Stanley and Mansell was the best sidecar, but even he failed at the very top. Just as the marshals and observers were about to close the hill, Stuart Waycott arrived by which time darkness was beginning to fall and he proceeded to make a super climb in the class as Mansell; but just failed at the top. Due to a fair amount of delay towards the latter part of the trial the provisional results were not announced until 10.30pm. There was a little surprise when Charlie Rogers came out the winner with 48 marks lost and collected the Skefco Gold Cup. In doing so he changed the old order and the first time that a Royal Enfield had figured in the Experts winners. Fred Povey was runner up just 2 marks behind. In the opposite class the Norton pair of Mansell and Mewis lifted the Palmer Trophy, losing 93 marks in the process. This duo had won the very first 'Experts' back in 1929 but the really delighted crew was Hayward and Heelas who finished second with 138 marks lost which gives a very good indication of just how difficult the course was. This was the highest placing that the Baughan pairing had ever achieved in the Experts and the Gaffer was delighted for them both. At the Bear, all the talk was of just how difficult the course was, well worthy of the 'Experts' title and many expressed how it was possible to improve on what had passed before. The sheer variety of the sections had many of the riders shaking their heads, and many of them had been riding the Experts from its inception.

1938 1945

Stroud Team Trial.
Hayward, s/c, wins the Zimmerman Cup (opposite class). Stagg, 350cc, 1st class.

Cheltenham Scramble.
500cc Race, Stagg, 350cc special, 3rd place. Unlimited race: Stagg, 350cc, special, 3rd place. Stagg, retired with clutch-slip while riding Peter Falconer's Triumph speed twin in the standard machine race.

1946

Cotswold Cup.
Hayward, s/c, wins Cotswold Cup (opposite class). No marks lost despite the 50% mark-up penalty. Stagg, 350cc, 3rd class.

Stroud Team Trial.
Hayward, s/c, wins Badgery Cup (runner-up to Hillslie Cup winner). Guy Babbage, 350cc, 1st class.

1947

DK Mansell Trial.
C Kemp, 500cc, ex Ted Morris swd Baughan,* 1st class. This may have been the last trial for this machine. See the letter on page 348 As to the fate of the 600cc swd Baughan that belonged to Ted Morris. * swd had been removed.

The penultimate ride of the remarkable Bill Hayward/Marjorie Grant Heelas partnership. This is the Cotswold Cups of 1946, probably the last trial that a swd featured. By this time the Western Centre was the last one to allow the use of the driven third wheel. They still had to contend with the now mandatory 50% mark-up. It was a gamble that paid off; they won without a mark lost. A fitting end as the first Cotswold Cup trial they entered was in 1929 with swd, and won a gold award. The location is Rowden which was a sidecar only section. In the distance can be seen the Weighbridge Inn. Just to the left of Marjorie's shoulder is the 'Gaffer' with his 16mm cine camera recording the final climb. This famous swd still generated great interest from the spectators. At the start of this section was a large pond where the solos carried straight on and exited on the A46 overlooking Horsley. The sidecars at the end of this section went through the wood and onto the Nailsworth/Avening road.

Details of these awards that belonged to Bill Hayward are on the following page. Bill in his competition career must have won quite a few. His awards are documented in this chapter. However, they only amount to Open competition. Local results have sadly disappeared in the post-war period.

Authors collection.

Authors collection.

Authors collection.

The four awards on the previous page and the two above are all that remain of the many that Bill Hayward won from 1924-1946. These came to light at the Horsley refuse tip when discovered by a nephew of Bill Hewer while dumping rubbish in the 1980s. How they came to be there remains a mystery. When Baughan Motors moved from Lower Street to Lansdown, Bill packed all his trophies into several tea chests. All was forgotten when they thought they resided on the top floor of the new premises. In response to the author's plea for Baughan information through the motor cycle press, Bill Hewer kindly replied, as in the 1930 period he rode a secondhand 350cc Baughan. These awards were passed to the author, then to Edwin, Bill's son. This is in complete contrast to the awards that Ted Morris collected for his were complete. This is a sad reflection on Bill's achievements over the years that just these handful should end up in a council dump. On a slightly lighter note, Edwin still has his father's magnificent trophy for his win in the Kickham Memorial Trial of 1932. This is a beautiful figure of Mercury in black, reminiscent of the Isle-of-Man replicas for the TT winners.

Stagg collection.

Bill and Marjorie forcing on in the 1931 Kickham Memorial Trial. At the finish they collected the Wiltshire Cup for the best under 600cc outfit. The roughness of the climb is well illustrated by just how far the sidecar wheel is off the ground.

G Fisher collection.

Geoff Fisher riding his Scott in the 1926 Cotswold Cup Trial. The dryness can be judged by the amount of dust kicked up, and a little oil from the two-stroke. Leaning on the wall at the top right of the photo is Geoffrey Pavey Smith, one of the founder members of the original Stroud Motor Cycle Club. Fisher, half way up the climb which then exited at the very top of the famous 'W'.

Len Vale-Onslow

With the many riders that competed in the Western Centre from the mid 1920s, very few were alive in the late 1990s, but there was one who remembered those days; Len Vale-Onslow. Len first visited the hills around Stroud in 1924 and knew very little of Harry Baughan. HPB in those days was very much of a newcomer himself having just established his motor business two years before. Len remembered the many hills and sections that by the mid 1930s were not used or were in the throws of extinction. Isles and Knapp Lane being the most prominent, followed by Mutton and Station Lane. When Len first encountered Isles Lane it was just a cart track which increased in gradient and tightness in the last hundred yards. Knapp Lane was equally as bad and when Severn-Trent brought the mains water down this narrow lane in the 1990s it bore all the hall marks of the 1920s; deep ruts, pot holes which were a foot and a half deep (I know, I measured them: Author), this was just the conditions that the Stroud Team Trial encountered in October 1924. Many riders found it unclimbable, and Chris Stagg remembers it as the best place to ruin a pair of front forks. Len entered more and more trials in the Western Centre from the late 1920s right through until the outbreak of the war and saw a great many changes. Looking at the entry of the Stroud Team Trial of 1930 he was a member of the JB Watson Team along with Bill Hayward and Jack Williams when he rode his 172cc S-O-S. When asked what the attraction of the Western Centre was, the reply was straight to the point: "The best organization and wonderful hills."

G Fisher collection.

Geoff Fisher fording the 'Henwood Splash' in the 1936 Cotswold Cups Trial on his 350cc Blackburne powered Baughan. Immediately behind is TH Butcher 350cc BSA. Just about to pass through the stream is Chris Stagg, 350cc Baughan. Fisher went on to win the Clift Cup as a member of the Gloucester MC and LCC. Ted Morris with his swd 600cc Baughan won the opposite class. Two first class awards for the Baughan marque. Sadly Bill Hayward retired due to damaged front forks on this very same section when the SO swd complex caught him out just as it did Stuart Waycott with his swd, only he got away with it.

Authors collection.

Bill and Marjorie at the start ot the Weighbridge section in the 1945 Stroud Team Trial. They went on to win the Zimmerman Cup for the best sidecar. Today this section is hardly recognizable.

Courtesy: Bob Light.

Two versions of swd outfits. At the top is the Baughan, simple in design, completely reliable in competition. The bottom is Fred Stevenson's modified Brough Superior SS80, very complex, heavy and quite a handful in all conditions. Bill Hayward was astounded when this crew managed to get the machine to the top of 'Breakheart,' which was always a feature of Baughan territory. This Brough must have been the biggest combination in trials at the time.

Postscript

The results on the previous pages give just the bare facts as to Baughan achievements. There was, however, an under current that ran throughout the early part of the 1930s. Speculation was rife, bitter feelings and downright hostility in certain quarters. This came not only from fellow competitors, but ACU officials who really should have known better and perhaps should have had a more open mind at the time. In all manner of sports, regulations have always tried to be manipulated by the competitors. Parsons chains may well have received short shrift from the clubs and Centres; swds on the other hand was a different matter altogether as the meeting at the Bear Hotel in December 1934 (page 272), will testify. Then came the competition tyres which were another bone of contention. The use of Parsons chains can be traced back to the 1900s. The photo on page 99 shows the Red Car so equipped. This example may not have been an actual Parsons product, but their use was undeniable. When HPB designed his swd, due allowance was made to the bike frame and the sidecar chassis to allow chains along with oversize tyres.

On the London-Exeter Trial held on Boxing Day 1929, Dennis Welch was driving a works Morgan when he encountered wheel spin on Devonish Pit Hill. This loss of traction was pointed out to Goodall and thought twin rear-wheels might be a possible solution to this problem. George Goodall had already taken note of Lionel Creed's suggestion on the same lines when his transmission chain tangled with the Parsons chain on his Morgan. Creed had experienced this trouble a few years before and wondered whether the Parsons chain could be dispensed with altogether by having a greater area on the rear driving wheel. Theoretically, the extra grip this should have made up for the possible loss of the chain. In late 1929 Creed wrote to Dunlop asking whether they could produce a special rear wheel for him, consisting of two wheel rims slung side by side on a single hub. Dunlop came back with blueprints before Creed told HFS what he was up to. Once approached 'the old man' agreed to try out the idea. Very soon this twin rear wheel saga came to a head. For a number of years the Morgans had often used chains on their rear wheel in an effort to combat the solid rear axles of the cyclecars. Eventually clubs became wise to such additions and placed a complete ban on them in their supplementary regulations. This had to be accepted by the driver in order to enter. But a cunning move was in the offing and it proved to be just as controversial as the swd would be later. George Goodall, never a man to let the grass grow under his feet when it came to technical innovation, could see twin rear wheels as a novel solution to increase traction. When a Morgan appeared driven by Goodall with what at first glance was a fourth wheel, officials hurriedly consulted their current regulations in an effort to see just what the ruling was on the subject. It transpired that twin rear wheels in this category were indeed illegal and a smile crossed their collective faces at the thought of throwing out such a prestigious factory over a technicality. Goodall knew what to expect, he was no fool and pointed out with great delight to the various officials present from many clubs that they could not possibly ban him for his Morgan did not possess 'twin rear wheels'. He must have enjoyed the moment pointing out that they could indeed examine the rear end for he made it abundantly clear that he had nothing to hide. There was a little theatrical indulgence by 'Uncle' George when he lifted the tail for the organizers. Once examined, the truth was revealed. Indeed there were two tyres, and two rims! Closer inspection revealed they were laced to the usual single hub as in all Morgans; thus conforming to the regulations.

Competition Tyres

Towards the end of 1932 the trials reporters were beginning to notice the problems posed by the swds. This in itself was not surprising for the most prominent swd since 1929 (really the only drive in this intervening period to warrant serious consideration) was the Baughan. Certainly the period from 1929 to 1932 there was never any adverse publicity surrounding it. In actual fact there was only one other device so equipped, Uzzell's 998cc BSA, which soon disappeared. The swds may have attracted a certain amount of attention but there was a far more serious situation developing that was going to have an effect on the whole trials sport, and not just the sidecars, and it at all centred on competition tyres.

Competition tyres, better known as 'knobblies,' were universal by 1932 and they had developed steadily over the years and quickly became the norm in scrambles events, for their machines were at the forefront of this. Any rider who followed trials and indulged in competition, even at the very basic closed to club event, were fully acquainted with their phenomenal gripping power. Not every club rider could possibly afford the initial outlay and many relied on 'worn' covers from friendly riders who either purchased them at greatly reduced rates, or even better, were supplied free by the Trade. Baughan Motors certainly enjoyed the latter but were never overwhelmed by Trade generosity. Up until 1932 the question of competition tyres had hardly deserved comment. The riders were quite happy to use them and benefited from their advantage, and every clubman tried to aspire to them. The trouble came from the general public who were totally unconnected with the sport. Not only did the officials have to listen seriously to what the public had to say, they also had to consider the more pressing matter of the police. What concerned the public was the amount of mud that was being dragged onto the public highway and the possible consequences if this was responsible for an accident.* The sport functioned on the amicable relations with the public and any good trials secretary worth his or her salt would go to great lengths not to antagonise the public at large, but when the police became involved things took on a different complexion. At one stage the adverse

---

* Harry Baughan was always concerned about the debris that was deposited on the road after a trial, he made sure there was adequate marshalls available to sweep it all away. The constabulary would invariably be present at such spots.

publicity was so bad that an investigation was instigated by the ACU. This took place in late 1932. For trials, Trade support was very important to the governing body and certainly to the many factories that used competition as a shop window for their products. To keep any eye on what the public thought of motor cycle trials Harry Perrey was appointed and he selected a number of Trade officials to help him out. Perrey, along with the people he recommended visited trials at the many Centres where the complaints were the most numerous. Perrey was very well known throughout the trials fraternity; not so the other personnel. Some subtlety was used by Perrey who took on the role of spectator, as did his accomplices and mingled with the crowds where sections exited onto the public highway. What they witnessed was not supported by the general opinion of hostility towards trials. In reality the public reaction was somewhat different, generally they found them to be very supportive of these local and national events. Perrey and his companions after considerable investigation found there was little to answer for. The Trade, who were even more concerned about bad publicity were equally delighted with what they saw and heard. This continued for quite a few weeks and a report was submitted to the governing body. This was scrutinized in detail and the result was in complete variance with what the rumour mill had thrown up. Their conclusion was that the Centres they visited monitored their events very well indeed, and they found little cause for concern.

Len Crisp was one of the first to put pen to paper over the competition tyre issue. He was firmly of the opinion that it was all down to expense. Works riders had little to concern themselves over where price was concerned. They just rode the machines provided for them, and factory support in most cases followed this basic principle. Crisp, in his opinion, was all for trials that would cater for standard tyres so that the amateur would have a chance of a possible award. In the years prior to 1932 there was little, if any aggravation surrounding both competition tyres and sidecar-wheel drives, but after 1932 things started to change. Competition tyres became more of an issue for it affected all riders, whereas, the swd would have touched on less than three riders and was not so much of an issue. Competition tyres and trials were inseparable and the Trade became very concerned if a ban was proposed. In their opinion it would have a detrimental effect on the sport and was a retrograde step. Sidecar wheel-drive on the other hand would have the minimum effect with so few crews equipped, hardly an issue to concern the Trade unduly. With the competition tyre getting a very bad press; the public became very outspoken, or supposedly so, which led to the constabulary taking a much closer interest than the trials organisers would have liked. The next move many were convinced would involve some form of legislation that would severely limit their use, or worse still a complete ban which they were anxious to avoid at all costs. More letters started to appear in the columns of *The Motor Cycle* and *Motor Cycling*, some from much respected riders such as Stuart Waycott and Len Heath. They expressed concern over 'knobblies' and put forward reasoned arguments for their retention even though they knew that legislation might be the final sanction. With all this concern over competition tyres a move came from a quarter that had great influence in motor cycle circles; the Motor Cycling Club. On November 22nd 1932, the MCC general committee placed a complete ban on them and this was welcomed by many clubs; the journal *The Motor Cycle* embraced it whole-heartedly. Although this was approved in principle on the above date, its implementation would not take effect until the London-Lands End trial the following Easter.

The MCC may well have imposed this restriction on competition tyres. Despite their much respected position it was the ACU that the greatest majority of the clubmen were wedded to. The MCC movement was quick to follow public opinion but their trials were in the minority and would hardly have any great effect on the public at large. The hundreds of individual clubs throughout the country which were affiliated to the ACU through its many Centres was the governing body concerned with competition and who would undoubtedly lay the ground rules in all this business. The MCC were equally quick to respond and show sympathy for the public's concern over the amount of debris (or so they thought) that was still being carried onto the highway. The ACU were in a somewhat different position for their blanket coverage of motorcycle sport in the country merged with the Trade and its support of factory riders and selected private ones who enjoyed this luxury. Would the Trade continue its level of support if the ACU bowed to the public? Without question the MCC had made a bold step in banning all types of competition tyre; the true trials tyre would remain and this applied to motor cars as well. In the meantime the saga of the knobblies rumbled on without any clear indication as to what was going to happen. Things were about to come to a head.

On the Friday night (March 16th) before the Cotswold Cup Trial of 1934 these matters were raised in an 'open' forum. With all this letter writing in the various motor cycle journals from top works riders to the lowly clubmen, it was not surprising that HPB received his fair share through the post as well. He decided that the Bear Hotel would be a good venue to have a cross section of opinion on this matter. As the 'Cotswold' was one of *the* premier Trade supported events in the trials calendar it would be a good opportunity to find out the true feeling. Ostensibly it was to give an 'airing' to the problems surrounding the two previous items. Harry Baughan was not unsympathetic to these requests on the above subjects and decided that it was time to bring it into general discussion and really find out what the riders were thinking on these two very sensitive issues. First up was the sidecar-wheel drive. The various merits and drawbacks were discussed by many of the top riders of the day. As HPB was the secretary of the Western Centre he chaired this informal meeting. In the end there was no firm conclusion reached and as far as everyone was concerned, it was 'carry on as normal' for swds. When the attention was turned to competition tyres Dennis Mansell stood up and dropped something of a bombshell. This was to the effect that the Trade would withdraw support from trials if the various Centres placed a ban on competition tyres. What up to that time was a well conducted meeting suddenly degenerated into turmoil. Just why Mansell became the spokesman for the Trade has never been fully explained. (Bill Mewis gave this opinion to the author,) "Dennis at the time was perhaps the most respected figure in the trials scene and carried a good deal of authority and in him the Trade found an outlet that riders would listen to. After all his father was managing director of Norton Motors and carried a good deal of weight."

The meeting by this time was buzzing from this revelation and explanations were demanded from Mansell, to say nothing of Harry Baughan for he considered it a very serious matter indeed. However, Mansell was not to be drawn any further on the subject. Although there were a few Trade officials in the room they deemed it prudent not to comment. Later in the year the matter was raised once again, this time on the Friday night before the most prestigious event in the trials calendar, the British Experts. In the intervening period the ACU had time to digest this news that Mansell had revealed and must have a great many reservations on the subject.

Again it was an informal meeting comprising of riders, entrants, organizers and the technical press held at the 'Bear Hotel,' Rodborough Common (December 1934), to discuss the present position of trials. The instigator of the gathering was Harry Perrey, and the first topic he introduced was that of standard tyre versus competition covers. He argued that present courses had become too severe, with a result that riders often staged a debacle on observed sections, thereby bringing disgrace to themselves and the machines they rode. If standard tyres were compulsory it would enable trials to be run with more finesse.

Everyone present gave his opinion. Several, including Messrs, Rowley, Perrigo and Povey, were in favour of standard tyres providing suitable courses were used, but the majority, led by Mr Baughan, favoured retaining competition covers. Then Dennis Mansell stood up and stated that he had been given authority to say that tyre manufacturers would refuse to pay any bonus on standard tyres. This time Mansell's statement did not cause such a stir that his previous one did earlier in the year. On such a controversial subject a vote was taken and the advocates of competition tyres won easily. The ACU must have breathed a collective sigh of relief on this one. On the subject of sidecar-wheel drive, Mr. Perrey said he did not think such a machine would be regarded as a general

'British Experts' at the Bear Hotel in 1931. Famous names abound here. Bert Perrigo, Marjorie Cottle, Stuart Waycott, Jack Williams and perhaps the most famous name of all, Stanley Woods, sixth from the left. Bob Foster, second from the left and Geoff Fisher two more to the right. Chris Stagg is ninth from the right. Bill Hayward is missing and also Marjorie Grant Heelas. Chris commented that Bill was always late for most events and usually arrived just in time for the signing on. Marjorie was inside the Hotel with her sister and HPB making the final arrangements for the start of the trial.

utility outfit. He therefore could not see any useful purpose being served in allowing this device to be used. Mr. Baughan pointed out that in certain country districts where the roads were particularly bad; farmers could use sidecar-wheel drive because it may have been their only means of mechanical transport. He contended that sidecar-wheel drive was not terrifically expensive as most people supposed. As the meeting did not consider itself sufficiently representative to vote on this subject, no decision was taken. The meeting unanimously agreed that all trials courses should be of such a character that neither solos nor sidecars should find any section absolutely impassable, as had been the case in certain trials. (Like the 1932 Kickham Cup). Other decisions were that (1) the time factor should be made more use of–not to the split second, but in such a way that anyone experiencing trouble would be late at the next time check and thus the loser of marks; (2) that no open trials should be held on Sundays (the voting on this was 37 to 1 against Sunday open events) and (3) that more special stages could be introduced. It was agreed that copies of the resolutions should be sent to all organisers of both open trials and to the ACU in the hopes that the riders views should receive due attention from the proper quarters. With all this disagreement between the various factions, everything carried on much as it did in the past. There were a number of trials that used 'standard trials tyres' but the enthusiasm was not there and the old favourite 'knobbly' continued to dominate. The one thing the ACU was clear on, swd would not be used in the Experts.

WESTERN CENTRE, A. C. U.

Stroud Team & Individual Entry Trial.
October 10th, 1931.

YOUR NUMBER IS *2 - 33*   YOU START AT

Bear Hotel.	Start.	Standard Time 2 - 0.
		Your Time.........,....
		Downhill to main road, R, then L. R at fork. L at top. S O, & R to
B B 1.	OBSERVED.	S O to
B B 2.	OBSERVED. 2 sections	At top R. S O for 1 mile. R hairpin
		at cross roads. R to
Sandfords.	OBSERVED. 2 sections	At top R along main road, over
		previous route for 100 yds. then L to Nailsworth. S O. R at fork L up
Nailsworth Ladder.	OBSERVED.	at top S O. at 2nd signpost R. 4th L towards Chalford. L to
Mutton.	OBSERVED. 2 sections	at top R, behind Church, L to
Station Lane.	OBSERVED. 2 sections	at top L, main road R, turn L downhill, at bottom L at fork R, S O, cross roads, S O, down Bismore (CAUTION) S O up
Ferriscourt.	OBSERVED.	at cross roads L, R down Claypits, at main road R, L up Butterow, L at fork, R up
Ham Mill.	OBSERVED. 3 sections	at top S O to CHECK.
		Standard Time 3 - 25. Your Time.............

SECOND CIRCUIT AS ABOVE.

Standard Time 4 - 50.

Your Time

The route card for the event that made trials history. The results are on the following page. The report of the trial is on page 241. This is the route card for TDG Phillips who collected a 1st class award riding his 490cc Douglas. The secretary of the meeting was Auriol Grant Heelas and was navigator to HPB. In total there were fourteen teams entered. Bill Hayward was in five of them, Baughan, Stroud A, Gloucester B, JW Watson, and Tewkesbury B.

```
                    STROUD  TEAM  TRIAL.

                    Sat.October 10th.

                 Provisional Results.

THE NATIONAL CUP.-  Stroud Baughan Team.
                    1. C.W.Stagg      348cc Baughan   75 marks.
                    30. W.E.Hayward    498cc Baughan   90 marks.
                    31. H.P.Baughan    998cc Baughan  100 marks.

DUNLOP TROPHY.    - Gloucester M.C. & L.C.C."B" Team.
                    19. L.W.Hall      348cc Cotton   75 marks.
                    1. C.W.Stagg       348cc Baughan   75 marks.
                    30. W.E.Hayward    498cc Baughan   90 marks.

THE HILLSLIE CUP.-  H.P.Baughan        998cc Baughan.

FIRST CLASS AWARDS. 28.A.E.Perrigo     348cc B.S.A.
                    31.H.P.Baughan     998cc Baughan.
                    33.T.G.D.Phillips  490cc Douglas S/C.

SECOND CLASS AWARDS.21.L.H.Vale Onslow 172cc S.O.S.
                    29.R.Johnson       499cc Cotton.
                    30.W.E.Hayward     498cc Baughan S/C.
                    32.D.K.Mansell     490cc Norton S/C.

THIRD CLASS AWARDS. 1.C.W.Stagg        348cc Baughan.
                    19.L.W.Hall        348cc Cotton.
                    2.A.J.Clarke       348cc Baughan.
```

The above show the provisional results for a unique milestone in trials history (1931). Harry and passenger Auriol also carried off the Hillslie Cup as the best individual performance in the Trial. The cup on the left is incribed with Chris Stagg's name but Bill Hayward and HPB also received one. Sadly not Marjorie. It was to be another four years before she collected her first award along side Bill in the swd. This beautiful cup was presented by *The Yorkshire Post* and measures 3.4 inches high and 4 inches across.

Authors collection.

Authors collection.

First running of the Cotswold Scramble at Througham. Move to Miserden Estate, pre-war. Post war at Nympsfield. Thwarted International attempt in 1952. Great popularity throughout the 1950s and 1960s, eventual decline.

Scrambling in the early 1930s was new on the scene. It came as a derivative from trials. In the early years trials hills were not too plentiful and those that did exist hardly offered much of a challenge to the very serious clubman and certainly not to the works supported riders. As was inevitably the case when the trial finished, many riders tied on marks lost. It soon became evident that this state of affairs could not continue; something was required to act as a tie break. At first it was a run downhill over a certain distance and the rider braked the machine astride a white line. The elapsed time taken for this was how the tie was decided along with the distance measured from the spindle of the front wheel from the tape. The second method involved a set course some eighty to one hundred yards long and again used the shortest time taken, timed to the nearest one fifth of a second. This was not simply a race around a flat field but a very bumpy patch of ground where machine control could be exercised and was to a degree, performance related. Harry Baughan favoured the former method. This down hill run required no special engine tuned to high output; it was down to the skill of the rider alone. The latter method favoured the 'works men' whose factory prepared machines had a distinct advantage over the clubmen who competed just for the sport. From these tie break runs over rough ground formed the basis of scrambling, and inside of less than a year this rough riding caught on and soon clubs were asked by their members to provide a fixture for this new sport of 'scrambling.' As an extension to these tie deciders run over a rough piece of ground, this developed into a controlled event that on many occasions covered anything from a mile to nearly three.

The Western Centre, pushed enthusiastically by their secretary Harry Baughan, decided that a new event should be run on the lines of the Gloucester Grand National scramble and so the Cotswold Scramble was born. Harry Baughan made more enquiries and found strong support within the Centre. Geoff Fisher was brought in and given a free hand to sound out the numerous farmers and land owners that he had personal contact with through his employment. Many were sure if Fisher was given a brief it would not be long before he came up with a possible solution, sure enough a site was soon found. Througham Farm was the location and a few days later HPB and Fisher visited the owner. Both men went over the ground which was a long valley with quite steep sides, the great attraction as far as HPB was concerned was the stream that ran along the bottom. Harry was immediately taken, and within an hour he had roughed out a course that might appeal to both rider and spectator alike. Both men were not

Courtesy: Bob Light.

Bill Nicholson was probably the first man to establish a reputation in the Cotswold Scramble with his works BSA. He was one of the first riders to make Nympsfield a regular spot for a Midland factory.

competent to pass judgement on what the course had to offer fast riders so Chris Stagg was asked to evaluate it. He was also delighted, made a few suggestions and the thing was settled. Fisher made it clear to HPB that the owner would not be involved financially but would look favourably on a small 'reimbursement'. Harry Baughan was shrewd enough to have the spectator in mind. They would have to be well catered for viewing the course, especially as they were paying to be entertained. So HPB balanced out the course for the public along with what Chris had suggested. The Western Centre Committee paid a visit and gave its approval. Once the word got around that HPB was to be the C of C, things started to move. Througham is several miles from Stroud and not on a regular bus route so provision had to be made for transportation of spectators. The only thing that the Stroud Valley Club had to work on was the number who turned up to watch motor cycle football at Fromehall Park.

So they took a gamble and advertised that a coach would be run for their convenience. Many hours of volunteer labour prepared the course, and they even had to make a new entrance to allow an easy access for the public. As the event was an Open one, expectation was high as to who might enter. Jack Williams, always a crowd puller, was on the list with his works 500cc Norton and the 250cc class saw that ex–Sunbeam factory rider, Tommy Deadman. The 250cc class was a little disappointing when only eight were entered, but immediately reduced to five when Jack Amott (Triumph), Holdsworth (New Imp) and Harry Daniels failed to turn up. Six laps of the three mile course had to be covered, but

Courtesy: Bob Light.

Chris Stagg was perhaps best remembered for his trials exploits than scrambles. Here he enjoys an outing on his Baughan special with a Velocette KTT to power it. He ran it for a few seasons, sadly the frame was getting dated along with its girder forks and was only used in scrambles and grass track at odd times. The engine far outstripped the frame, also it was quite expensive to maintain, finally the engine was sold on.

the issue was never in doubt. Deadman (250cc, Stevens), finished ten seconds in front of Cotterell. It looked an easy victory for the Stevens rider. When he finished his race he took a quick trip to the St. Johns men to treat a blistered leg when the exhaust pipe burnt through his boot. If the 250cc race was rather short of riders, the unlimited promised to be better. Competitors came from the South-ern and South Eastern Centres. However, the spectators only had eyes for their local men. Chris Stagg was out with his special, but the 'star' was the 'flyer' himself, Jack Williams. Seventeen riders out of the twenty–one entered came to the line. At the drop of the flag the flyer lived up to his reputation and promptly disappeared into the distance. After the first lap his 350 works machine was nearly fifty seconds in front, and by four laps it had extended to a minute and a half. By half distance, Williams was lapping the back markers, Chris Stagg was in sixth place on his 350cc Baughan but suffered some baulking at the water splash and for his trouble was promptly covered in mud from head to foot. This water splash was the result of the locals who were always quick to spot any opportunity to make any event more exciting, quickly got about their business. First it was the children, then the adults joined in. Very soon a dam was built and

Courtesy: Bob Light.

Another Baughan trials machine this time in the hands of Guy Babbage. Guy rode in scrambles with his Baughan, eventually replacing the Blackburne engine with a Velocette KSS. This picture is from 1948 at the 'Cotswold'. Guy had great fun with this machine, but like Chris found the frame to be lacking, but still roadworthy as the registration plates indicate. Eventually it was sold.

a fair head of water backed up. The competitors found as much entertainment as the spectators and some skilful riding was the result . . . and avoidances. When he returned to the paddock the mud pack on his face would have done justice to any ladies beauty salon; all that was visible was a pair of eyes. Williams completed the eight laps in fifty–eight minutes, and on the last lap he eased off considerably and finished just under two minutes in front of GA Wolsey on his 497cc Ariel. After it was all over the officials were delighted with the result. Harry Baughan in his usual thoroughness had the Heelas sisters fully employed. This time they were in charge of the large lap score-board that kept the public informed of the positions. It was HPBs idea on the large score-board and was a feature of every Cotswold Scramble thereafter. Bill Hayward helped out with the scoring and rider positions along with the other Western Centre officials and Stewards. Not only was there the score-board, a public address system was employed. In the interval Christopher Stone's rendition of 'Momma don't want no peas, nor rice nor coco-nut oil', came through loud and clear. The ice cream seller had to go back to base for fresh supplies, the gate receipts were tallied up,

Martyn Rich on board Chris Stagg's Baughan special with the Velocette engine at Battlescombe Farm scramble in 1947. The front brake modification is still in place that Chris manufactured in the mid 1930s. Although Rich was very successful with this machine he found that the frame was no match for the engine and he moved on to other more suitable machines.

the farmer given a remuneration and Geoff Fisher was praised for his weather prediction; which was unremitting sunshine. The second running of the Stroud Valley Motor Club's Cotswold Scramble was to be held at Miserden. It moved there after the successful inauguration at Througham Farm. Once again Geoff Fisher was responsible for finding the new venue. This was again an Open event within the Western Centre and attracted another great crowd on par with the previous year. It was Fisher's connection with the Miserden Estate that allowed the scramble to go through. Througham proved the starting point and from this wonderful valley setting with its stream at the bottom and plenty of terraced viewing for the spectators, the same was to be had at this new location but on a longer course.

Geoff Fisher and Harry Baughan spent many weeks prior to the event surveying the best possible course that covered two and a half miles. The original Througham course was just over three miles in length and was to prove more popular. To give the crowd the best viewing advantage they laid it out cleverly so there was plenty of zig-zagging up the steep hills. Not only did it create interest for the viewing public but gave great sport for the riders. As with all motor

Hayward collection.

Some idea of the Nympsfield panorama can be judged from this photo of the start. The public had excellent viewing as the valley offered great vantage points to watch almost all of the course. Those who did decide to explore found that the wooded section was the place to be. Precise riding was essential; one wrong move and it was into the trees. As can be seen in the line-up quite a few of the machines were registered for the road. Many local riders competed and were heard to comment that they actually finished their event, such was the demands on the rider.

cycle events, preparation is all and Harry Baughan along with his many will-ing helpers created an excellent course. Miserden, due to its somewhat isolated position and almost non–existent public transport, still managed to attract an estimated three thousand spectators. Twenty–one entries had been received and the riders were split into two races; the up to 350cc limit with a sub-division for 250cc machines and the remainder were from 350cc to unlimited. The previous year's winner, Tom Deadman failed to put in an appearance, Jack Williams was entered for both events and was seen in the paddock but without his trusty Norton for it had failed to turn up from the Isle-of-Man and he was classified as a non-starter. There was local support, Bob Foster on his 348cc works New Imperial who was equally at home on grass as he was in the I-o-M. Chris Stagg was even more local and elected to ride his grass track bike for his home event. They all lined up for the first race in excellent weather. In the under 350cc class, the most conspicuous, was Foster decked out in a white riding suit. He was

Hayward collection.

The famous lap scoring board that was a feature of the Cotswold Scramble. It first appeared at Througham and continued for many years at Nympsfield. The Heelas sisters can be seen making the necessary alterations as the race progressed. Bill Hayward was usually at the lap scores bench.

quickly away, followed by arch rival Holdswoth on a 248cc New Imperial, by lap two Holdsworth's smaller New Imp was no match for Foster. Chris Stagg was closing rapidly and soon swept by. Even with his capacity advantage Chris could not shake off Holdsworth who was just feet behind giving an excellent demonstration of good power riding. Soon a white figure was seen walking, Foster was out with a slipping clutch, then Holdsworth failed to appear leaving Stagg with a clear lead. Riley was the only threat to the Baughan rider and on the last lap Chris eased off finishing eight seconds in front. There was a respectable interval before the second (unlimited) race which gave time for Foster to recover his machine and fit a new clutch plate.

This time seventeen starters lined up for the senior and once again all eyes were on Foster in his fetching garb. At the flag drop he was away into the lead and the outcome was never in dispute, Chris Stagg and Ralph Dee were engaged in a furious struggle and were met with huge encouragement right around the course. By lap five Foster had lapped half the field. Chris had slowed with a partial seizure, eventually retiring much to the crowd's disappointment. Dee on the other hand still received plenty of encouragement being a local man but

Courtesy: Bob Light.

Harry Baughan signals the end of the race for John Draper on his BSA in 1948. The background abounds with trees which the course passed through and gave great variety to a very open course. On many occasions this gave riders some difficulty adjusting to the sudden gloom on a bright day. These wooded sections proved many a downfall for even the most experienced rider.

could not get further than fourth place. At the end every one went away happy, the senior race winner, Foster, collected the Baughan Trophy on his 348cc works New Imperial and the Valley Cup went to Chris Stagg for the best 350cc machine. The Througham Cup was handed to Ralph Dee on his 498cc Rudge. So ended a good day's sport at the new location and the Miserden Estate was well pleased with the outcome. The public abided by the conditions laid down by the Stroud club and damage, always a problem when the public have access to private land, was minimal. Chris Stagg's machine was his grass track one and ran on dope. It was a bike that he had built up from the many spare parts that were always to be found at Lower Street, and featured a standard Baughan petrol tank. The finish was not the all black affair that immediately springs to mind for their machines. The tank was painted cream with an inch black outline was featured either side, finished off with the usual gold Baughan logo in the centre. The engine started life as a standard twin port Blackburne (not the one from his trials machine) and ran on dope. This allowed a higher compression ratio and the con-rod was machined from a solid billet of duralium which took him many hours of his spare time. If there was ever a lull in the work at the factory then Chris spent the time on this machining. This modification proved to be very effective

In the mid to late 1950s Dave Curtis dominated the 350 and 500cc classes at the Cotswold Scrambe. His stamina was legendary and won his many races there by huge margins and his style is well portrayed here. With the AMC marques of Matchless and AJS he gave faithful service to the company.

and lasted for years without giving the slightest trouble and was worked hard in hill climbs, scrambles and grass track. Miserden Park hosted the scramble until the out–break of the war, then resurrected in 1946 at Nympsfield. This postwar move was still high in the Cotswolds and was to prove an excellent move, not only for the Western Centre but the farmer whose land it ran over. As on the previous occasions it was Geoff Fisher who made the contact after due persuasion by the Stroud Valley Motor Club Committee. The site proved to be ideal. As with the previous venues a good sized valley was an essential ingredient. This time it was huge and the initial course was well over 2.5 miles per lap with variations for the smaller classes. With such an event the spectator wants a course that gives unlimited visibility and accessibility. At Nympsfield they had it all, steep rise and fall of hills with a stream running at the bottom which if required could be negotiated many times a lap. This course had this in abundance, and the spectators could view this unrestricted from both sides of the valley and could see almost the whole course with the exception of the wooded sections. As the popularity of scrambles increased throughout the 1930s the Western Centre was no exception and the public turned out in their thousands to witness this event, so much so that special coaches were laid on when Miserden Park was the venue. Nympsfield was a little more accessible to the public as Nailsworth was just a few miles away, well within walking distance. In the late 1940s the public were a lot more energetic and the road from Nailsworth to Nympsfield was scattered with people who had access to the north side of the valley. Transport was mainly by bicycle, (I know, I cycled there in the mid 1950s and dumped my bike in the hedge, amazingly it was still there hours later.) As the scramble increased in popularity with the competitors so the public followed, assured of a splendid day out, invariably in excellent weather. Throughout its time at Nympsfield the course was developed not in any vast way, just subtle changes that brought out the best in the top class riders. All this came under Harry Baughan's supervision as Western Centre Secretary along with the many clubs who helped out. The Cotswold Scramble became just as important as the Cotswold Cups and both attracted

After the era of Dave Curtis another Dave took over the winning at the Cotswold Scramble. This time it was Bickers. In the same mould as Curtis he also won race by large margins. Europen Moto-cross Champion in 1959/60, he was perhaps the true pioneer of the two-stroke after the loss of Brian Stonebridge. The Greeves factory was indeed fortunate to have a rider of Bickers calibre and became the rider to beat in the early 1960s. Of all the great scrambles riders this country has produced Bickers had a unique press-on style that became his trademark.

large followings, and gradually the support as the years passed became greater and Harry Baughan was looking to the future with an international flavour and made the approach to the ACU in 1952 with this intention. A permit was obtained to run this at Nympsfield and the Western Centre was delighted that they could rival anything that the continentals could offer. With something as important as this, Trade support was more than forthcoming which meant the finances would not be too stretched within the Western Centre. Alas!, The best laid plans of mice and men . . . foot and mouth disease forced the event to be cancelled to the great disappointment of Harry Baughan and everyone else who had shared his vision. Sadly, it never achieved international status and all the effort and goodwill went the way of all things. This was a great pity as Nympsfield had the capacity for the public and competitors alike. Undaunted, the Western Centre put it behind them and concentrated on making it a worthwhile national event. From its inception in 1934, to the last pre-war meeting in 1939 a few locals were prominent. Jack Williams, Bob Foster and Chris Stagg were all winners, and only post-war did it see a steady increase in works talent when Bill Nicholson from Ireland made a great impression in 1946. Looking at the list of winners on page 287 gives a clear indication of just who dominated the results in the 1950s. From 1951 to 1954 saw Geoff Ward, John Draper, Les Archer, John Avery and local man Tommy Barker who was to be a stalwart for the Stroud Valley MC in later years.

1955 saw one of the giants of the Cotswold Scramble begin a run of wins that was outstanding. Dave Curtis was a name synonymous with this event that carried on for almost a decade. Those who saw Curtis in those years were fortunate indeed. Here was a man whose stamina was legendary and riding ability second to none. In those years he was the complete master of the 350 and 500cc classes. Later came the two-stroke revolution headed by Dave Bickers the 1959/60 European Moto Cross champion. His run of success was akin to Curtis, demonstrated by great skill and wonderful machine control. What these two had in common was their 'press-on' style even if they had an unasable lead. a true reflection of their abilities. In later years there were other riders who will be remembered, Jeff Smith, Arthur Browning, Bryan Wade, Andy Roberton and many others who battled it out at Nympsfield. In the 1970s the course was made far more compact and a great deal shorter so the spectators had a short time to wait for a lap to be completed. Sadly, the 'Cotswold' lost its attraction and went into decline, the glory days had long passed.

PREVIOUS WINNERS

	SENIOR	JUNIOR	250 c.c.	200 c.c.
1934 ..	J. Williams			
1935 ..	A. R. Foster	C. W. Stagg	D. W. Nash	
1936 ..	S. R. Wise	K. D. Haynes	S. R. Wise	
1937 ..	W. A. West	K. D. Haynes	E. G. Wilmot	
1938 ..	K. D. Haynes	A. Briggs	A. C. Lane	
1939 ..	W. A. West	K. D. Haynes	J. Treseder	
1946 ..	W. Nicholson	W. Nicholson	G. Wakefield	S. R. Wise
1947 ..	W. Nicholson	W. Nicholson	F. M. Rist	B. Harris
1948 ..	B. W. Hall	F. M. Rist	W. Nicholson	J. Plowright
1949 ..	W. Nicholson	W. Nicholson	B. H. M. Viney	T. Barker
1950 ..	W. Nicholson	B. W. Hall	J. Avery	W. Nicholson
1951 ..	J. Draper	J. Draper	L. R. Archer	R. K. Pilling
1952 ..	J. Avery	G. H. Ward	L. R. Archer	R. Bolton
1953 ..	G. H. Ward	J. Draper	J. Avery	A. Vincent
1954 ..	P. A. Nex	G. H. Ward	J. Avery	W. Barugh
1955 ..	D. Curtis	D. Tye	B. Sharp	T. Sharp
1956 ..	D. Curtis	J. Draper	B. Sharp	D. Rickman
1957 ..	D. Curtis	D. Curtis	D. Rickman	J. Avery
1958 ..	D. Curtis	D. Curtis	D. Bickers	D. Bickers
1959 ..	D. Curtis	D. Curtis	J. V. Smith	D. Bickers
1960 ..	J. V. Smith	D. Curtis	J. V. Smith	J. Giles
1961 ..	D. Curtis	A. Lampkin	J. V. Smith	
1962 ..	D. Bickers	D. Bickers	D. Bickers	
1963 ..	J. Harris	W. Jackson	P. Lamper	
1964 ..	D. G. Curtis	D. Bickers	D. Bickers	
1965 ..	J. V. Smith	D. Bickers	D. Bickers	
1966 ..	M. Peach	B. Goss	B. Goss	

Just how sucessful Bill Nicholson, Dave Curtis and Dave Bickers were can be judged from the results above. What it does not reveal is the margins that they won by.

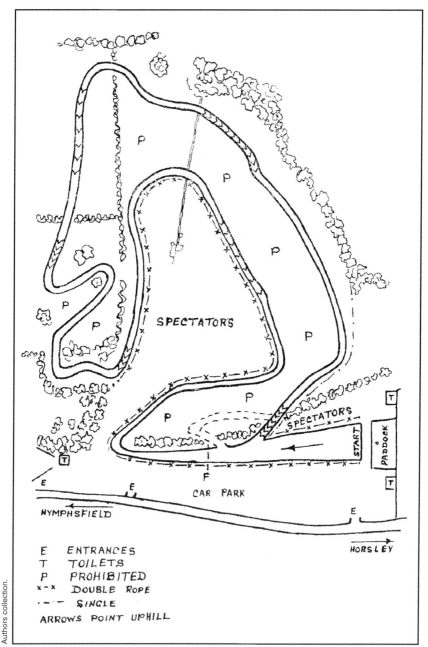

Authors collection.

Authors collection.

The 1962 Cotswold Scramble course, Nympsfield. Looking at the maps on the following pages gives a clear indication as to the variation over the years. In its final phase the course became very tight and difficult with steep climbs and equally deep drops. In the early post war years the course measured over three miles a lap.

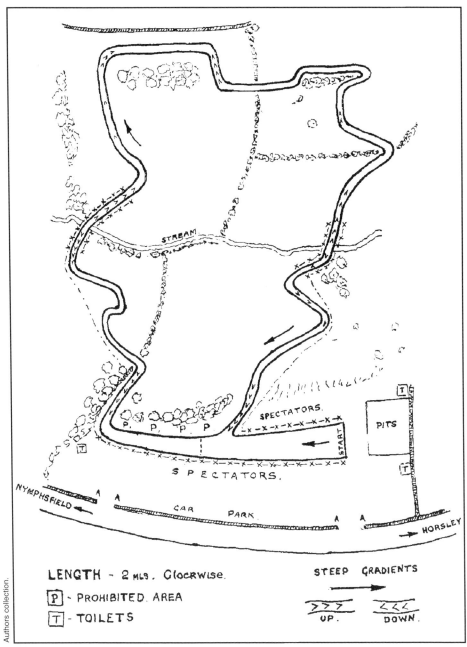

STREAM

SPECTATORS.

SPECTATORS.

P P P P

PITS

START

T

T

NYMPHSFIELD ←

A A

CAR PARK

A A

HORSLEY →

LENGTH - 2 MLS. Clockwise.

P - PROHIBITED. AREA

T - TOILETS

STEEP GRADIENTS

>>> UP.

<<< DOWN.

A further course change at Nympsfield, this time 1965.

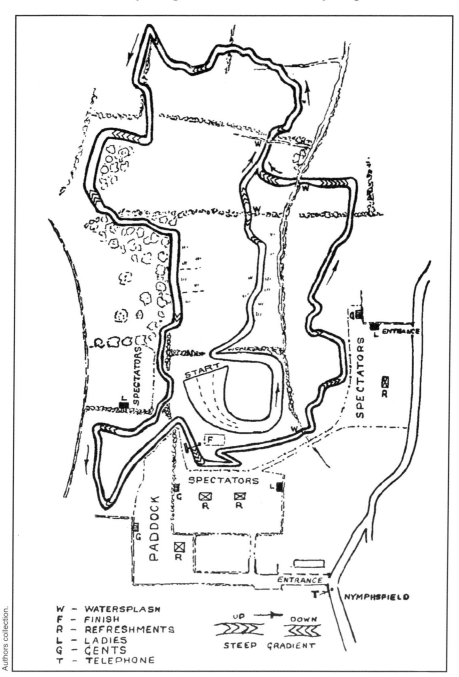

The 1967 course. Such was the scope at Nympsfield virtually any course could be mapped in an effort to please the paying public. It also found favour with the riders; if they had mechanical trouble they could recover their machines fairly quickly.

Cotswold Scramble Poem 1930?
With apologies to, Henry Wordsworth
Longfellow.

Through the leafy lanes of Cotswold.
On a fine and sunny morning,
Come the Jeep with Boss Baughan in it,
Came too, and Chris and Chrislets:
To the meeting place appointed,
To the place called Battlescombe:
Come a lorry steered by Bowley,
Bowley, with the ropes and trestles,
Bowley with the stakes and hammers;
To the meeting place called Battle,
To prepare for Cotswold Scramble.
Jeep was stopped lorry also;
Off they set armed with weapons;
Boss Baughan seized his trusty sickle,
With his axe, perspiring Peters,
Bowley came festooned with rope trails,
Chris and Chrislets followed after;
Bore the stakes and nails and hammers,
Bore the blue cards and the white cards;
To prepare the course for Cotswold.
For the Great Day, Cotswold Scramble.
As they hacked and slashed and muttered,
Cursing bough and branch and bramble,
Longing for a pint of bitter,
Dreaming of a pint of shandy,
Rose a shout, as on the skyline,
Silhouetted on the skyline,
Came a string of motor cycles,
Came the Suttons and Ron Wilkins,
Came the rest of the committee;
All to bear a hand for Cotswold,
All to clear a route for Cotswold;
So that riders, on the Great Day,
Halted not for briar or bramble;
"Turned it up" to pass the table,
To receive the Checkered Flag first,
Deftly waved by Big Boss Buffam.
As they laboured, putting stakes in,
Tying ropes and fixing blue cards,
See the eyes of Big Boss Buffam,
See them gleam, as at the gateway,

He espies the mud that glistens,
Deep and smooth and very slimy,
And he chuckles" That'll shake 'em!
If they try to 'drop their anchors',
They will 'hit the deck' for certain,
And the mud will be so slimy,
As they pass the gateway.
So they toiled until the nightfall,
Then, the last card in position,
And the tent and table ready,
Scrambled the tired committee homeward,
To the friendly Bear at Bisley;
There to drain a foaming tankard;
To the Great Day, the Cotswold Scramble,
Run the Club of Stroud Valley.
Fair the day dawned for the Cotswold,
Thick the mist lay in the valleys
Rose the sun, and mists retreated,
Hot it was and growing hotter,
'Proper' weather for the Cotswold.
All the morning, each was busy;
Tables placed and tents erected,
Tents where cold drinks and refresh-
ments,
Ice cream, tea and fizzy minerals,
Were arranged for all and sundry,
For spectators and for riders.
Soon the narrow lanes of Bisley,
Were athrong with bikes and motors,
First their riders and their keepers,
Bikes in cars and bikes on trailers,
Bikes of every make and pattern,
Being tried and tested,
Engines 'revved' and tyres deflated,
Helmets donned and belts adjusted,
For the practice lap of Cotswold,
For the trial run; er the marshal,
Lines them up before the Starter.
Some there were who in the practice,
Met disaster 'ere they started,
One brave fell and hurt his shoulder,
While a second flamed and burnt out…
By this time, the banks and hedges,
Deep were lined with keen spectators,
Came to see the braves and warriors,

The above poem takes a light hearted look at the first Cotswold Scramble run by the Stroud Valley
Motor Club at Througham Farm.

Battle for the cups and prizes,
Tommy Barker on his 'Beezer'
Won the babies race for Dursley.
Viney riding, cool as always,
Won the next race, the 250.
Then there followed the 350,
This was won by Nic from Ireland.
In the Senior or Unlimited,
Alves for two laps was a meteor,
Then he slowed, his tyre was punctured.
Hall chased Nic, but was unable,
To be first to past the table,
Space prevents from telling further
All the things that happened that day.
How one rider crashed and finished

On a stretcher quite unconscious.
How another struck a tree root,
And to climb the tree attempted.
Came the dusk and Cotswold ended.
Tents dismantled, ropes collected,
Rubbish burned and posts collected,
All removed and field left tidy.
Cotswold over till next year.
All the work and labour ended.
Homeward crept the weary workers,
Footsore, tired and thirsty,
Talking of friends and riderss,
They had met at this year's Meeting,
Planning routes for next year's Cotswold.

Chris Stagg's trophy at the 1935 Cotswold Scramble, the Valley Cup. Best 350cc performance on his Baughan special with Blackburne engine.

War and post war years. Engineering diversification. Still born
scooter. Building of specialist machines. Plastics extrusion.
Sub-contract work. Trials resumed. HPB Western Centre Secretary again. ISDT/ ACU Competition sub committee Secretary.
Selection of Vase and Trophy team riders. Welsh Two Days.

Towards the end of the 1930s Harry Baughan realized that motor cycle manufacture had little future for his company. The business had changed name, no
longer trading under Baughan Motors but became Baughan Engineers. This was
more in keeping with the company business. There was a growing demand for
engineering in all forms; gradually it became more and more specialized. The
situation in Europe was causing great concern; HPB having been involved in
the first conflict certainly understood that engineering would play a vital part
if it came to all out war. When the last motor cycle left Piccadilly Mill in 1936
the building that had served the company well had little scope for development;
certainly on the ground floor, there was no alternative but to move.

Once again Geoff Fisher was to prove his worth. HPB sought his advice.
Within a week Fisher invited Harry down to Lansdown at the bottom end of the
Slad valley. Here was a substantial building that had three storeys and a very
large basement, ideal for siting all the heavy machinery. Harry took to it immediately and the deal was done. When the time came to move from Lower Street
all the motor cycle frames were packed away, engines and spares placed in tea
chests. Bill Hayward got a company from Bristol to take all the spares. This
may explain the disappearance of his trophies which were also packed into a tea
chest. Could this have been taken by mistake and not returned? How strange to
find a few of them in a council rubbish dump over forty years later.

In the following years this building was to be so well known that the address
was HP Baughan, Lansdown, Stroud, Glos, very often it was just HP Baughan
ACU, Stroud, Glos.* No other description was necessary. After the war it was so
popular with sporting motor cyclists that the ACU used it as an official control/
check point when a national road trial passed through the Western Centre. This
site was to prove ideal in the coming years. There was a large car park and the
factory was always open, day and night, with 'Little' Joe Wright in attendance
who usually slept on the premises. In 1937 competition by Hayward and Stagg
had been reduced, the move from Lower Street to the bottom of Stroud taking
priority ensuring there was minimum disruption to the business, in less than a
month everything was back to normal. Even though they had far more room
they were still restricted to the overhead shafts and belting; this time without
the need of a recalcitrant car engine. From the previous cramped quarters there
was now sufficient room to plan everything in a logical fashion. Just prior to the
outbreak of the second world war Baughan Engineers were approached by the
War Department in connection with their sidecar-wheel drive. The army came

---

* So well known was HPB by the GPO that post cards often came addressed: HP Baughan, Stroud,
not even with Gloucestershire mentioned.

with a view to a possible production run which would give them an outfit with cross-country reconnaissance capability over difficult terrain. The contact came through HPBs involvement with the army. For a number of years he tried to encourage their dispatch riders to improve their skills in cross-country rough riding that was so lacking in the first conflict. The army had responded in a limited way to his approach but it did little to redress the balance. Only later when the likes of Jack Williams, Harold Flook and many other top trials riders joined the Corps of Mechanical Transport in WW2 did things change for the better. The initial contact with Harry Baughan for a batch of swd outfits was ambitious, and proved to be totally out of the question. He suggested that they approach Norton with the same request. As Baughan Engineers was such a small company it would have been impossible to undertake such a task. Bill Mewis did recall that Baughans were considered to build a prototype, then it was passed on to Bracebridge Street; the rest is history.

Harry Baughan with careful planning had extended his engineering base; subcontract work came in from everywhere. Hoffman bearings at Stonehouse and Gloucester Aircraft were just two notable companies that used their services. Parnell Aircraft at Yate also sent work in. Parnell were perhaps more famous for their Peto aircraft that they supplied to the Navy which was earmarked for the submarine M2. This was housed in a hanger in front of the conning tower to be used for reconnaissance duties. Sadly the M2 sank in over 120 feet of water with all hands on the 26th of November, 1932. (I have dived the M2 on many occasions in the 1970s and it is truly amazing that an aircraft with its wings folded could be stowed in an eight foot wide hanger space: Author.)

With the declaration of war Baughan Engineers were immediately given priority to steel stock and access to specialist equipment. Very soon additional machinery provided by the government for precision work was moved in at Lansdown and things were placed onto a more serious level. Skilled labour was in very short supply and along with many other engineering companies, were subject to manpower rotation. It was not uncommon for a person to spend two days at Baughans then complete the week at Hoffmans in Stonehouse, and so it went on. All this activity required an enormous amount of organization to juggle men and machines to comply with government contracts. In this department Harry was more than accomplished. His skills, developed over many years on countless trials, found a new lease of life at the factory. With a complete change of direction due to the war, all manner of things came their way. One, however, did give HPB a different slant on things, the arrival of Ministry inspectors, again to pass their eyes over the facilities at the factory. Their arrival was accompanied by a police constable which signalled something very unusual was going on. The official secrets act had already been invoked on the workforce;

Stagg collection.

Baughan Staff 1943

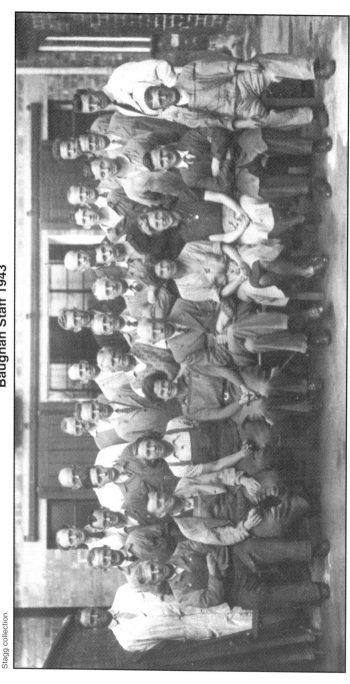

Back Row: All L to R. Frank Rendell. Bill Peters. Charlie Chambers. Len Butterworth. Wallace Hendry. King. Harry Field. Len Stone. Roy Vick. **Middle Row**: Chris Stagg. Frank Powell. Doug Andrews. Lionel Belcher. Alan Commander. Joe Hooper (Little Joe). Alan Cowmeadow. Alfie White. George Day. Roland Stagg. Bill Hayward. **Front Row**: Eric Lenley. Hobson. Mrs Ross. Auriol Marjorie Grant Heelas. HPB. Marjorie Auriol Grant Heelas. Gladys Stafford. Jack Seabright. Fred Davis. Due to the shortage of skilled labour during the war various other people were employed on a rotational basis. Many spent just a few hours at Baughan Engineers per week before moving on to other factories.

entirely understandable with the amount of diverse work for various aircraft factories and government agencies. Harry was no stranger to the methods of these inspectors having seen how they operated at de Havilland; what he witnessed did not fill him with confidence. Once the inspection (which was very thorough it seems), had been completed not very much thought was given to the outcome for very little information was forthcoming. However, it did indicate that something unusual was afoot. A few months later the officials returned without any announcement. Again they had a uniformed constable with them and this time a cardboard tube was produced and several blue prints were unrolled which bore the markings of the Gloucester Aircraft Company. At the time it made very little sense; nothing seemed to be related to anything else. They had no idea just what was to the left or right of their blue prints, but what they did have were details of two pumps, one for oil, the other paraffin; it was the latter that puzzled them. Who would want a pump for such a liquid, especially an aircraft company? Either side of the drawings remained a complete mystery. Once these items had been completed they were then taken over to Gloucester Aircraft by Bill Hayward with the inevitable armed escort. Before this took place Harry had to inform the police that a trip to Hucclecote was required. Very often an armed dispatch rider turned up and away they went. Harry hardly ever went as Bill was responsible for almost all the work on this highly secret engineering.

Eventually Hayward found out the truth of the matter. His arrival at GA was always planned by the constabulary and his official contact was waiting at the gatehouse. (Bill, despite his many visits was never allowed into the factory), this time greeted with more enthusiasm than he was used to. "I bet you're pleased with all your efforts these past months"? Bill had not the slightest idea what he was talking about. "What you blokes have been working on flew today." He then explained it in more detail. "The Whittle flew today." Bill was dumbfounded, he had not the slightest idea what the Whittle was. (the E28/39, Britain's first jet aircraft.) Eventually it all became clear; the paraffin pump now had a ready explanation. Bill Hayward was not the only person who came across the tight security in those troubled times. Peter Falconer, himself a fellow motor cyclist, was gradually extending his knowledge of motor cycle sport with encouragement from Chris Stagg. At the time the Whittle was being built at Hucclecote he was in charge of a Home Guard section that was responsible for the additional security at the factory. He rode in one evening for the usual parade and pulled up in the assembly area to find his small unit already 'fallen in,' he dismounted and took off his gloves . . . "In the distance I could hear this high pitched whine, which gradually grew louder. I looked up to see this aircraft approaching at considerable speed; it shot overhead and with a great roar disappeared towards the Severn. Well I was completely taken aback; the thing was so fast that I stood

The flexible coupling is clearly visible along with the distortion. The fixings are just as they were when HPB used it. The underbody has never been covered in and the exhaust pipes run underneath to the tail. On page 35 the exhaust pipe ran through the nearside mudguard as did the offside.

with my mouth open. Then I heard a ripple of laughter which grew louder. I must have been quite a sight still reeling from what I saw." A ready answer came from one of the lads. "We've been working on that for over eighteen months here." Such was the security, Falconer had not the slightest inclination as to what was going on in the factory or what they were building. Looking back it is quite remarkable that nothing was ever leaked. Hayward, who was very involved as was Harry Baughan, never had the slightest idea what they were manufacturing.

Baughan Post War

Once the crisis was over things started to approach normality. Labour that was in almost a constant state of flux gradually disappeared and new work was sought to make up the great short fall that the government left. Imposed restrictions became a way of life for a few years. Petrol rationing, along with food soon became the norm. The machinery that the government so willingly placed in the Lansdown factory did not quite disappear overnight. There was a brief period that allowed Harry Baughan to look at their long term resources in order to attract more work. Labour was shed, what was left fell to Chris and Bill to manage the best they could with a limited number of staff. One or two machines were left behind by the inspectors which gave the company some continuity in production, eventually these too were withdrawn. As Baughan Engineers tackled the post–war period a modicum of work still trickled in, and gradually things improved through the many and varied contacts that Harry had made in the previous six years. In the early 1950s plastics started to become popular for a great many products and eventually HPB started to design machines that could be used in the extrusion process. All manner of things from buttons to fountain pen blanks.

Their diversity in obtaining work was equal to the late 1920s when the depression was at its height. As Baughans garnered this reputation for versatility in engineering other companies in the district sought their advice. Three well established printing houses in the area who made contact were, Copeland-Chatterton, Frederick Steel, and Arthurs Press, all had various machines modified by Baughan Engineers. Many items were one-off's. Chris Stagg remembers that many of the reps from these companies often came in with strange requests, "Not knowing the process we had to make several visits to understand fully what they wanted. This way we made all manner of modification that did years of reliable service for them." There was one particular visit from Erinoid, who worked with Bakelite and plastics and Chris recalls what happened. "One Friday morning the Gaffer called me into the office. Bill was already there. The Gaffer said that Erinoid were about to manufacture buttons in all different sizes. They could produce the blanks and also the shapes but were at a loss as to how to drill the holes for sewing them on. The Gaffer asked if we had any idea how this could be done. Now Bill and I had many strange requests in engineering terms, but nothing like this. Anyway, the Boss could see we were on the spot and said, 'Have a think about it over the weekend and we'll have a talk about it on Monday.' When we left the office Bill looked at me and shook his head; he had no more idea than I did." On the Monday morning just after ten o' clock we were back in the office. "Neither Bill nor I had any idea as to a solution; I had wracked my brain all weekend, nothing"! While they sat there Harry opened a drawer and pulled out a foolscap sheet with his ideas on the subject. "What the Gaffer had drawn was simplicity itself. I had looked for an answer in a complex way, whereas the Gaffer reached a simple, logical conclusion, and it worked." Both men walked off without saying another word. As the years passed more and more diverse work found its way to Lansdown. One big name was TH and J Daniels at Lightpill. They manufactured Danarm chain saws and sub-contracted the barrels to Baughans. Here they inserted liners into the aluminum cylinders and finished them off in batches of three hundred at a time. (I remember printing the instruction/spares books for them at Arthurs Press in the 1960s: Author.)

Just after the war motor cycle competition resumed in a small way, petrol rationing restricting just about anything along these lines. The Western Centre was about to pick up the pieces and start again when rumours started that Harry Baughan had been less than honest with monies collected pre-war. All this emanated from members of an affiliated club within Cheltenham. The upshot was for them to call for a special general meeting of the Centre at Worcester. Word soon got around that certain factions wanted Harry Baughan out and they sited 'sharp' practice as the reason. Up to this time HPB had been the Hon Sec of the Western Centre since his election in 1926 and his credentials were impeccable, his honesty beyond question. This proposed action came as a bolt from the blue to a great many people. Peter Falconer gave this explanation. "When we heard this news about Mr. Baughan I could hardly believe it. Anybody who knew him found him, open, approachable, honest, sincere and trustworthy. His conduct was well known and would go to great lengths to see fair play; to have a possible slur on his character was astonishing. In a very short time there was a strong feeling that this special meeting should have the utmost backing to get to the bottom of such a serious accusation. In the Stroud district everyone wanted to go in support, there was just one problem, petrol! At the time I was very friendly with Ralph Dee who started his garage business in Nailsworth. Both of us were mad keen on competition and in fact he won the 1939 Cotswold Cups Trial on his New Imperial. His garage (now used by Trade Plas) had the dealership for Massey Ferguson and as such was allowed a generous petrol ration

Authors collection.

The suspension is about to be replaced on the offside after a rebuild. Twin float chambers were fitted, essential when severe cambers were encountered on some hills. The BTH magneto has been a constant problem over the years, it caused Pat Mather's retirement on 'Catswood' in the 1990 Cotswold Clouds Trial.

so that he could travel the county with the intent of selling farm machinery to help the economy back on its feet. It did not take long to rustle up the necessary fuel to allow for a good representation at Worcester. When the day arrived just about every member from all the clubs were gathered. After this indictment was brought up HPB was asked to respond. Well it was quite astonishing.

"Mr. Baughan not only tendered the money that was in question, but also the interest generated. He then produced the trophies that went with them (Cash often went with the award, especially if it was sponsored). Mr. Baughan had carefully placed them with his local bank and was waiting for the AGM he knew would be convened after the war when things had settled down. In actual fact Geoff Fisher knew all about this so called 'sharp' practice and was prepared to speak on Mr. Baughan's behalf, but he was not needed and the ACU found there was no case to answer." Shortly after, in 1947, HPB had organized over fifty premier events. The Trade, along with the ACU presented him with a Royal Enfield motor cycle at the Imperial Hotel in Stroud in recognition of his outstanding service to motor cycle sport. This was vindication enough from the Trade especially as he strived to involve the major factories in trials sport, thus hoping to

The asbestos string wrapped around the induction pipes give some protection from the heat to the incoming charge and has proved its worth, as does a new shield in front of the carburettor which protects the twin float chambers, The bulkhead has been changed from the original plywood to an aluminium one in deference to the current motor sport regulations. The BTH magneto has now become more reliable in the last few years.

better their products through competition.

Rebuilding the Cyclecar

The author in conversation with Pat Mather at his home in East Kirkby, Lincolnshire, 1980. Pat saw a different side of Baughan Engineers (Stroud) Co Ltd to what went on in the early 1950s, things had changed greatly in the 1960s.

"Harry was in charge, Bill Hayward who I imagine was the works manager and Chris Stagg was the shop foreman. Then the two sisters, the Miss Grant Heelas, who lived at Amberley, had a Lanchester I think? Geoff Fisher, Davis Champion and Payne, wonderful man to get on with. I never found Bill Hayward easy to converse with. Got on with Chris very well, super chap. Graham did the bush for the Red Car gearbox. HPB was not at all enthusiastic about the car being rebuilt. The Lansdown factory was not hostile to my intention. At the time they were doing quite a few barrels a week for Danarm chain saws, so they had little time for me; bit of a non–starter really. The time was not right, I then found another source who would do it on a one-off basis and that was fine. Then

Pat Mather with the author on the right make final preparations before loading the Red Car on the trailer for a trip to the 1980 Brooklands reunion the following day. On this occasion the engine never missed a beat throughout the weekend. Eventually mudguards had to be fitted to satisfy the constabulary.

I heard about the saga of the swd when HPB tried to get the War Office interested. Norton took it over, I think. There was no time deadline for the rebuild. I started to do some restoration on a shoe string. I just renovated until it got to be expensive. I built it up from scratch; the body was done and the engine was running and I had drive to the back wheels. I had new wheels made-up, got it wired and upholstered, and that was it. I had to shelve it for a while until I got some more money together.

"Also at the time I had a Morris Oxford that I rebuilt and later sold (£450, I think). Then I got involved with a friend with a racing Lotus 7 Climax* and that lasted about three years. I did a Cowley and also the father–in–law's Riley Gamecock and the brother–in–law's special (A7). Then I acquired an Austin Nippy. The Baughan was starting to cost money. I was not so keen on just restoring vehicles; the whole object was to get them roadworthy, I was always keen to drive them rather than just to look at them. The fun of driving vintage vehicles is that they should be as original as possible; no modern hydraulic brakes and fancy gear. The idea was to get it back on the road as it was in the 1920s, simple as that really. After getting divorced I moved up to Lincolnshire with a new wife who was as enthusiastic as I was about this vintage motoring. Then things moved on apace and I could concentrate more. The remaining jobs for

*The Author was also involved with the Lotus 7.

The lower brass plaque inscribed by Pat Mather when serious rebuilding started. The first full blooded run was a few years in the future. As Pat had other rebuilds in hand things took a little longer than anticipated. However, it was all worthwhile and the result is a fine example of a period cyclecar of the 1920s.

the cyclecar were finished there and a few exploratory events undertaken. Took it to Brooklands for the reunion meeting. While waiting in the queue for a run on the banking, just ticking over, it promptly seized-up. Thought it might be an expensive rebuild. Took the plugs out, poured in Castrol 'R' and after a while it freed up. The carburettor is interesting; it has twin float chambers because Harry was getting fuel starvation on severely cambered hills. This mod soon cured it. A valve lifter is employed.

"Originally had a kick start, now has a Dyno Start, wonderful, no trouble at all. Controls on the steering wheel. Throttle, advance and retard and the choke/mixture. Only two pedals on the floor, brake, for the left rear and the clutch. The brake lever on the offside of the cockpit for the right rear. The original Sturmey Archer gearbox was made specially for Baughans and was equipped with a reverse gear which featured a kick start on the off side by the brake lever. HPB said it dropped a valve one day and the result was a badly damaged engine and broken gearbox. A replacement for the latter was not available, and deemed far too expensive to rebuild anyway. The Blackburne engine was replaced with the current JAP Super Sports and this time a Morris Oxford gearbox was used, modified for the cyclecar. Shaft drive from the engine to the gearbox, with a coupling to a bevel box, then a short chain to a solid rear axle. The rear sprocket could

Excitement on the famous Nailsworth 'Ladder' in the 1990 Cotswold Clouds Trial. Pat Mather with wife Margaret in the passenger's seat encounter the dreaded stop-and-restart. It proved too much for the engine with standard gearing and a roll back was the result. Here, seventy years before Harry broke the drive chain and the 'Chockers' came to the rescue, no such luxury this time. Fortunately the Red Car remained upright, Pat's expression tells its own story.

Authors collection.

The Red Car after returning from the Derbyshire Trial in 1988 suitably covered in a liberal coating of mud. If HPB could see it in this state he would have been delighted. Even the cockpit is well covered. This is exactly what HPB envisaged in a trials cyclecar.

be changed so a lower ratio was available. The chain length can be adjusted by screw bolts in the rear radius arms. As the JAP was an odd size a special BTH mag was necessary. Bill Hayward found this out when he went to Birmingham for a replacement. They never had one so he waited while they rewound the old one. All this Baughan business started when I went down to Lansdown around 1963 with John Hayden and Mick Orr. (John Hayden volunteered his services to HPB for the 1953 ISDT and drew up a number of illustrations to help the competitors and marshals alike.)

"I met John in the late 1950s; he had bought a 1930 FIAT 501 from HPB. It was not a straightforward job at Lansdown. We had to take a partition down to get at it. Also there was Sunbeam Talbot 90, a Jeep, a Gold Star and sidecar. To get at this FIAT we had to move this cyclecar. There was also a Morris Oxford with a truck body; eventually I collected that with the intention of rebuilding and running it, but in the end it became too much so I sold it on for about £5. There was 1914 Enfield upstairs; sidecars were there, four if I remember rightly. Trials ones. There was a Baughan bike, solo. I know it had a beautiful sidecar that went with it, all thumbed, engineering turned. This was I found out later to be off Bill Hayward's swd. John took this away, at the time if I remember he had every intention of rebuilding it. I then bought an Austin 7, and rebuilt that.

Opposite: This is probably the last photo before the swd was placed in store at Lansdown. Over the years it has suffered from 'battle damage' judging from the state of the exhaust pipe. The bottom photo clearly shows the difference between the two sidecar chassis. The Swan Neck and the lack of frame around the sidecar wheel is immediately apparent. This was the chassis that Chris made for the Gaffer's 350 ohv Blackburne outfit. On this page the lower photo illustrates perfectly just how well the swd and QD mechanism is protected. This was welcomed on many a trial by both Bill and Ted Morris.

After, I thought it was a bit ridiculous; everyone was doing 7s at the time. In the end I gave a lot of thought to this cyclecar down at Lansdown. At the time John Hayden was involved with the Cotswold Scramble through Pete Daniels and I went along to help with the marshalling, and then went on to assistant scrutineer, finally scrutineer. I think that was for eight years or more. (I did help Pat as assistant scrutineer on a couple of occasions: Author.) I think 'Father' Baughan appreciated this because I was not part of the motor cycle club and I used to help mark out the course, do my job and then clean up afterwards. That was the accepted thing.

"This cyclecar at Lansdown really intrigued me. It was a bit ridiculous really, it was just lying there and was very unusual. So I went and saw Mr. Baughan at the shop at Walls Quarry, Brimscombe (Baughan Stores, belonging to Charlie). I just knocked on the door and asked him if he would part with it, and he agreed, no problem. 'You can have it. Help yourself; I've had my fun out of it.' He did not want anything for it; he gave it to me actually. The next day I took him 50 Woodbines in the old round tin, and that's what it cost me. I borrowed the father–in–law's lorry and he came with me. We got it out after shifting a great pile of cyanide. The front axle was there, just one wheel was attached, but it was a cup and cone type, the wrong one. Harry thought it was a Cheater-Lea and it had been taken off in the war for a trailer. Anyway we got it up on the gantry and then loaded the lorry. That was in 1964 I think. (Correct, I witnessed it being off-loaded at South Woodchester, Author.)

"It was in a fairly rotten state, the body was steel and full of holes, rusty and the entire alloy was pretty corroded. So I decided that it would be a bit ridiculous to try and use the original steel and I asked Harry about the body and he said he wanted to build it in aluminum, but the alloy at the time was of such poor quality that it would not stand up to much, very soft. But I rebuilt it in aluminium and used as much of the original steel as possible. I think that when I rebuilt it was done better than the original, I must say the original was pretty rough when I collected it." KJC: "Was there engine, gearbox, steering wheel, lights etc?" PLM: "When it had the Blackburne engine it had a high level exhaust that ran along the side of the body, but when I put the JAP in I ran it underneath. There were no silencers and the pipes were just joined together to make a single pipe that came out the back. This later changed to two pipes, one either side of the body. The pipes were just slid over each other and clamped to hold it all together. There was one light, the other one was damaged, there was no effective lighting system at all, and in the end I had to rewire the lot. The front number plate was still there and the rear number plate was painted on the back. No lights that worked, and no wings. Seats were just one and a half seater hole. It was just ordinary sacking upholstery back when I collected it. As I did not fancy being rammed up the back with the final drive chain as the driver's seat is directly in front of it, I put an alloy plate over it purely for safety's sake. The tandem set-up was made at Harrow. I think the upholstery fell to pieces because it was not very well built, then the whole thing changed to a one and a half seater along with the tail. The original, when I collected it, was covered in aircraft fabric over the scuttle. The photo on page 245 illustrates perfectly this fabric which was then covered with liberal amounts of red dope. This is now replaced with aluminium along with some steel to make it permanent as it was originally."

KJC: "Was he a forthcoming man, was he enthusiastic about the cyclecar being rebuilt?" PLM: "No, not at all. He looked at it as he had his fun out of it and that was it, he lost interest somewhat. It was a project that he had done and that was it as far as he was concerned. He did a bit of work for me. He machined a bush for the gearbox, but that was about it. I wanted some work done on the front axle but they were none too keen so Brian Mumford (Mumford Engineering, Nailsworth who built the three wheel Musketeer), did it all in the end. There was very little help forthcoming from Lansdown. If the factory was not busy than perhaps things might have been different. The enthusiasm was just not there. If they had been slack then it might have been different matter. Harry wasn't worried or interested in the job really. If I had rebuilt it and presented it to him it would have been a different matter and perhaps he might have been thrilled. As far as I was concerned I'd got it and that was that. He would help me out from time to time; he supplied a new set of rims for it. Bill Hayward ran the workshop there, things were left there but they were never done. They were going to do quite a lot, but things just went on and on, and it was never touched. The easy going attitude that existed in the 1930s when many a local motor cycle enthusiast availed themselves to Harry's generosity had long gone. Commercialization dictated time was money, also the factory inspector took a dim view of it as well. In the end I got Brian to do it. Harry still held the strings at the factory. One thing I do remember, everything was still belt driven from overhead shafting, just like going back into the past."

SWD rebuild

At the time Pat Mather collected the Red Car from Lansdown John Hayden took out the FIAT for rebuilding. Tucked away behind the partition that hid the Red Car was another gem . . . Bill's swd. This was in much the state when it finished the last trial (see page 306). Hayden had every intention of making a complete restoration of this famous combination. However, the best laid plans of mice and men . . . things never quite go to plan. John at the time was director of two companies and these took the majority of his time, restoration coming a poor third. Hayden took the swd from the factory with the blessing of both Bill and Harry. This freed up much needed space for things other than old vehicles. Hayden made a start, dismantling the sidecar chassis from the bike, and this turned out to be HPBs one without the swd. (The lower photo on page 306 shows it clearly). The petrol tank went to a specialist in London who made a first class restoration job, then the rest of the machine was gradually taken apart; then things ground to a halt. Shortly after Hayden moved his walking stick business from Chalford to South Woodchester, which was only a matter of yards from where Pat Mather (and the Author lived). If rebuilding old cars was not enough, John also indulged in narrow boats and stationary engines, usually of the local Lister variety. With steam fairs to attend things on the swd front suffered as a result. It was far too ambitious a project and became less and less a priority.

In the end Graham Stagg came to the rescue and took it off his hands. Once this had been handed over serious work began. Graham's father Chris then became involved, the man who had originally built it back in 1928/9. Just prior to the Stagg's involvement Graham finished restoring a 1918 fore and aft Douglas to concours condition, so it was perfect timing for something completely different and historic. Graham was the driving force, soon his father was as enthusiastic as his son and in very short time all the old enamel was taken off and the frame examined, which revealed a small crack in the head stock that was only a minor repair job. Apart from that it was in excellent condition. The engine and gearbox had been examined; the latter was perfect, right down to Bill's modification from hand change to foot control which he did in the early 1930s. The engine had suffered a seizure. Eventually this was freed but the piston had to be replaced. The barrel was honed by Graham and a replacement piston was hunted. This took a month or two, in the end an Ariel one was found to have the correct dimensions and slotted into place. The whole rebuild took the best part of eighteen months. The only things missing were parts of the sidecar wheel drive mechanism. Somehow these had gone missing, and new ones had to be manufactured. The original dog-clutch slid on four flats (see bottom photo of page 172), a simple solution compared to splines. When all this work was taking place, one thing that stirred Chris's memory was when it came to the lower rear fork ends (see top photo on page 179).

This fitting was made from four pieces of steel, cut by hand, pinned, brazed and the bottom hand ground to a round so it was a tight fit to insert into the bottom fork. Chris said it took him ages to get it just right, both sides are identical. The bare frame then had three coats of primer before the enamel was applied by brush, just as Bill did in the top floor at Piccadilly Mill. Some controls needed replacing along with the exhaust pipes which had to be re-bent as the original. This time it was left to Graham to complete the job. The small Brooklands type 'Cans' were carefully taken apart and a new buck made to match the original.

Courtesy: Bob Light

A complete contrast to the photo on page 305. The Red Car is a regular runner at VSCC speed hill climbs, both at Loton Park and Prescott. Here Pat Mather approaches the finish line at Prescott. The Red Car is perhaps more well known in the 1920s for trials work, it did take part in speed events on private land in Worcestershire and Herefordshire. Fred Halliday remembers that HPB often fitted a British Anzani V twin. At one time this engine was a possible customer option.

Once the outfit was finished Graham started on the sidecar. This was in a pretty poor condition, especially the interior which had suffered from rot and was near to collapse. The whole thing was carefully dismantled and as much salvaged as possible, later to be used as templates. Some of the aluminium was useable; certainly the strips on the side of the body were used again. A new rear compartment had to be made, the floor was completely gone. With much of the sidecar still intact, new wood frames were cut to match the original dimensions after the whole thing was dismantled.

Towards the end of the rebuild Chris was in poor health. Fortunately he saw the complete rebuild and running of what he constructed all those years before and expressed great satisfaction on the result. A wonderful piece of motor cycle history restored to pristine condition. Today Graham takes this unique swd to many local Fairs and is a wonderful ambassador for the long defunct Baughan Motor Company, and motor cycling in particular.* At these Fairs many people are amazed that there was a company manufacturing motor cycles in Stroud; they are even more astonished when it carried the title of 'Banned' as many journalists described it. There was some confusion around 1933 when Harry Baughan had his 350cc sidecar built by Chris Stagg in order to understand what the sidecars crews need when it came to competitive sections on certain hills. At the time journalists from the two popular magazines of the day jumped to the

*This unique Baughan is to be placed on display at The Museum in the Park, Stroud. This will allow the public to view a great piece of local history that has long been forgotten. www.museu-minthepark.org.uk

Authors collection.

In 1983 Pat Mather brought the Red Car back to where he originally collected it from in 1964 at Lansdown. Cliff Searle, then the owner of Baughan Engineers (Stroud) Ltd, (second left), kindly fitted a bush to the prop shaft to eliminate persistent vibration. The author is on the left, Pat Mather in the cockpit and Ken Rogers at the rear.

conclusion that this was another swd modelled on Bill's original and reported as such when it appeared in the 1933 Mitchell Memorial Trial. The photo shown is Bill and Marjorie and not Harry and Auriol for the picture clearly shows the swd chassis covering the sidecar wheel. These mistakes do crop up when reports on trials are written, especially where results are concerned. Once again it was concerning a swd Baughan, and this time it was Ted Morris riding in the Ilkley Grand National organized by the Ilkley and District Motor Club in 1935. Both *Motor Cycling* and *The Motor Cycle* were at odds with the final results. The former gave the opposite class win to Alec Hill driving Ted's Baughan. Ted was in the sidecar with an injury, allegedly, so Alec took over the entry. *The Motor Cycle* had the result the other way around; Ted driving, Alec in the chair. Now for two highly respected journals to be at odds over the finishing order gives rise to the question, who was actually watching the trial? Evidently not the former. In order to resolve the matter and have historical accuracy I contacted

The fitting room on the first floor at Lansdown. The photo shows only half the length, a far cry from the old premises at Lower Street. The next floor above contained the drawing office. All the light assembly work was carried out here.

the Ilkley and District MC. Their archivist and Vice President Janet Kitching delved through the club records; photocopied their official results which gave me the facts. It was Ted who was in the saddle. It is not always possible to corroborate results, and in this case it did need an answer and the record set right. The same thing applied to 'Titch' Allen with the article he wrote on the swd Baughan in *Motor Cycle Sport*; however, Peter Roydehouse soon corrected him. Once these things are written and published it is very difficult to get it redressed for historical accuracy . . . tablets of stone come to mind in these cases! (See page, 178). The sidecar chassis that Harry had fitted to this 350cc was built by Chris and resided at the Stagg household when Bill's was being restored; eventually this was sold on to someone in Wales. Incidentally, Harry was never fully at home with the outfit, just that he wanted to have an insight to what the crews wanted in competition, purely and simply an exercise for information. When Harry Baughan finished competing with his Red Car in 1933 it still came in useful for route marking. As there was little, if any four-wheel cyclecars in competition within the Western Centre he found it pointless continuing enter-

Stagg collection.

The ground floor at Lansdown still contained the overhead shafting and proved adequate for the production needs. Eventually changes were made to complete independence with electric motors.

ing trials. Cyclecars were, along with the threewheeler Morgans, placed in the sidecar class. As this was not a practical proposition he decided the threewheeler route was the better option. So Chris Stagg at Harry's request built up a 350cc ohv Blackburne powered Baughan from the many spare parts that littered the works. He also made a sidecar chassis that was a straightforward attachment, not a swd.* This was a very basic affair. Swan neck to the front down tube and an adjustable rear connection. This filled the need for HPB and allowed him to compete equally in the sidecar class which gave him a better insight to what the sidecar crews required when he planned sections exclusively for them. On occasions the sidecar competitors needed to have hills that were for their use only which gave a better chance for them to be marked on a fairer basis. From the 1920s there was a separate class for threewheelers. Most of the hills and their sections could accommodate both classes, he made sure of that. From time to time he added sidecar only hills that proved to be really difficult. All this planning was the Baughan trade mark; coupled with variations on many subsections was his forte. He rode this outfit in a few trials at odd times, but his greatest contribution with a sidecar was in the 1933 ISDT when he volunteered his services to the ACU for route surveying and marking. With his attention

*See the Mitchel Memorial Trial, page 312.

Harry Baughan in his familiar trench coat carries out observation in the Welsh Two Days Trial. Invariably these tests resulted in selection for the ISDT vase and trophy teams.

to the minutest detail he found the long sections of cross country right up his street. Initially Geoff Fisher accompanied him for the first few days, eventually returning home due to work commitments. However, an even more enthusiastic passenger volunteered his services, Peter Chamberlain. Here was a man imbued with motor cycling, he became the first 'Carbon' for *Motor Cycling*. So Chamberlain finished the week off with HPB. Harry Baughan was no stranger to him as their paths crossed in the mid 1920s when he rode in the Western Centre and the Stroud district in particular. They struck up an immediate and lasting friendship until Chamberlain died of a stroke at the early age of fifty. Ironically their greatest partnership was in the 1949/50/54 ISDT when run in Wales. HPBs name will always be associated with the ISDT in his capacity as Clerk of the Course, or Chairman of the ACU sub-committee when based in Llandrindod Wells. (In the hundreds of letters in my possession that passed between them not everything went smoothly: Author.) Whatever their differences they proved to be a very effective partnership. The one thing that placed Chamberlain aside and gave him a different aspect of trials competition was his journalistic ability, and a representation at the FIM through the ACU. Once they applied their talents to the ISDT, things 'took off.' Although Peter Chamberlain died at a very

A young Peter Chamberlain in a spot of bother in a Yorkshire trial. A water-cooled Scott undoubtelly. Peter Chamberlain and HPB became very close associates in the late1940s to early 1950s with the International Six Days Trial.

early age HPB carried out further duties for the ACU when the ISDT once again came back to Great Britain in 1961, then the Isle-of-Man in 1965. The latter year he conducted this event from his hospital bed in Stroud while suffering a chest infection. With Harry driving a sidecar he had a much better understanding of the difficulties the crews encountered, he always sought out their views and listened carefully to their comments and always championed their cause in competition. In the 1950s the sidecars were dropped from the ISDT, much to his disappointment, HPB had tried his best to influence the various committees to include them. Motor cycling was changing and the combination was slowly being replaced by the motor car buying public.

Peter Falconer was often reminded by Stuart Waycott just how interested Harry Baughan was in what everybody said about any trial he was responsible for, and the sidecar crews were no exception. HPBs enthusiasm for trials knew no bounds, either as a Western Centre secretary, or higher things with the ISDT. Even that much respected figure George Goodall was given to comment on Harry Baughan's contribution, "Mr. Baughan *is* the Western Centre!" In spite of the Chamberlain liaison, HPB was the man on the ground when it came to organizing things down in Wales, and worked in almost isolation when it came to making contacts. These were on a personal level when arranging things like accommodation, letters to traders, the local council, and the motor cycle clubs

Hayward collection.

HPB overseeing the start preparation of the British Team in the ISDT. The location is possibly San Remo.

for volunteers, the petrol companies, regional water boards, etc, etc. Without the assistance of the Grant Heelas sisters who were employed in the drawing office his work load would have been overwhelming; they often doubled as invaluable secretaries. When the ISDT was in full swing they typed hundreds of letters a week at Lansdown. Today we have almost instant communication with mobile phones and the internet; back in the late 1940s letters were the norm. Telephones were a little sparse in mid-Wales, anything urgent required a telegram. This long range communication was fraught with difficulties; willing individuals were often slow on responding to time critical issues which led to great frustration on Harry's part. This resulted in him departing to Llandrindod Wells on a Thursday afternoon with a departing comment to either Bill or Chris, "Keep an eye on the place; I'll be back about Tuesday." That's how it went week after week. Ralph Venables once remarked to me, "If the ACU had to pay for all of Harry's time they could never have afforded him." Although Geoff Fisher was not really connected to Baughan Motors in the direct sense he was more than instrumental in helping Harry Baughan with his intimate knowledge of the surrounding district. His interest and enthusiasm for trials was equal to Harry's and has never been given the recognition that he deserved. But then that was the nature of the man, very much in the background. The same applied to Marjorie Grant Heelas who was equally reticent and self effacing when it came to her exploits with Bill Hayward. Hayward's contribution with this controversial device is as unique as the length of time in competition with it. The partnership lasted longer than her sister Auriol with Harry and the Red Car. I missed interviewing her as she died ten years before her sister. Marjorie was at first very difficult to interview. She never considered herself, or her sister did anything extraordinary when it came to trials, she was at a loss to know why I was so interested all these years later. I am glad that I pursued with the interviews. At first I was very much the intruder, but once I mentioned Chris Stagg things changed completely and the floodgates opened. After several visits she was more forthcoming and proved to be a mine of information, far more that I expected. Her recall was remarkable despite a gap of almost forty–five years from the last time she rode in the outfit. She followed the advice of Geoff Fisher and along with her sister kept very detailed note books on just about every trial she rode in. The note books that she showed me were meticulous and comprehensive, just like Fisher's. I wonder where they are now, probably in a landfill somewhere?

Marjorie was of the opinion that her sisters input would have been more interesting than her own. Auriol as passenger to HPB had more variety with her trials. Although she had a shorter span in competition she was to see more of the organizational side of things. Route marking was one of the tasks and she never objected to the occasional dose of ochre covering her clothes; all part and parcel of the sport she said. Once the Red Car was no longer used in competition she accompanied Harry in the 350cc non-swd outfit that Chris Stagg built so he could still have a taste of competition and a far better understanding of what the sidecar crews would consider a real challenge. After HPB abandoned the sidecar he immersed himself deeper into the organization side of things. Auriol found a new role with the administration taking on the business of C of C, event secretary and all the signing on sheets, then producing the provisional results. Marjorie remarked that her sister knew HPB better than anyone else. Even at the end of a trial Marjorie had not finished. She then helped with the compilation of the results, a task that was often completed in less than two hours. HPBs insistence that results if possible should be in the hands of the competitors before they left for home. This was a feature of every trial in the Western Centre. Many a journalist made favourable comments over the years on this practice, but very few Centres matched it. At the end of a trial Marjorie gave her sister a hand in compiling a list of awards. By the time she entered the room that was used for the collection of the many section cards and books a rough check had already been compiled. How all this was achieved was down to careful planning. If an event required two circuits a position would have been worked out by the

Hayward collection.

HPB on ISDT duty. The riders have been given the signal to start their engines. This had to be completed within a specific time. Penalties were forthcoming otherwise. Third from the left is Pete Nortier, press officer for the FIM, fifth is Len Heath, sixth is Bernal Osborne of *The Motor Cycle*. The location is San Remo in 1948. I am indebted to the late Miss Olga Kevelos, herself an ex ISDT competitor with the works CZ factory for the identification.

lunch halt for the first one, and a provisional guide given as to how the trial was progressing. HPB had a marshal to relay the marks after the last competitor was through in the appropriate time. He then headed back to the start and the marks totted up. Every hill was the same, each had its own travelling marshal to relay the results and the system went like clockwork, the only failing came if a Marshal broke down on his return. Once the trial was finished the final analysis began. The room was out of bounds to all competitors and non officials. HPB carried overall responsibility. On hand was the appointed ACU Steward, the C of C and the Secretary of the meeting. There was a minimum of three sets of checkers to issue a provisional set of results. Protests had already been handed in at the various hills which allowed due consideration to take place rather than wait at the finish for them to be presented, this feature alone speeded up the process considerably.

My interviews with Marjorie came just two years before she died, at first she was very wary and information was difficult to come by. The second was completely different; she informed me that she had been in contact with Chris which undoubtedly paved the way. In the following weeks she unearthed all manner of

When the two-stroke engine was eventually built for the proposed scooter a rig similar to the above was used to determine basic torque output.

things; amongst them was a paper weight which was sitting on the mantelpiece which she invited me to pick up. It was an award for the Stroud Team Trial of 1935 and carried Bill Hayward's name on it. A two inch diameter Western Centre medal was attached to a 3 x 3.5 x 1 inch piece of onyx. She said it was the first award that she had ever received as a passenger in a trial, apart from the odd certificate. As Bill's name was engraved and not hers I enquired why. There was a ready reply. "Passengers in those early days were hardly recognized as being part of the crew, even though we had to sign on. You did not require a competition licence to be a passenger. Eventually things changed and awards came the way of the passenger. However, this was not true of every trial, even the big ones like the Kickham." She explained that when HPB handed her the award he said that they engraved two identical medals, hence Bill's name. As I admired it she immediately offered it to me. I was completely surprised at such a wonderful gesture and questioned her generosity, this being such a personal memento. She would hear nothing of it and insisted I take it. So today after all those years when they competed in the Stroud Team Trial along with Ted Morris and Chris Stagg, it still serves as an excellent paper weight. (See page 255 for the result.) Years later this expertise came to the fore when HPB was the ACU sub-committee Chairman for the ISDT.

Then he really expanded his talent for organization and at the core of all this were the Grant Heelas sisters. Although all the motor cycle building came to an end in 1936 HPB did not entirely give up on the idea of branching out again in the early 1950s. The motor cycle buying public had not seen great changes in previous years, the established factories were producing the same singles and twins much as they did pre–war. However, the European influence had started to penetrate these shores. The first scooters had started the public thinking of relative cheap transport. Not only were they easily affordable, they gave a degree of weather protection that the conventional motor cycle was lacking. The Lambretta and Vespa had a number of attractions for general use. Ease of parking, great manoeuvrability and even greater fuel economy. Carrying shopping was far simpler with generous luggage racks, often coming as standard equipment. Very soon these machines caught the attention of the public. Here was a mode of transport that afforded great potential. The true motor cycle enthusiast was never enamoured with them. As far as they were concerned, they were mere 'toys.' This change in motor cycling did not escape HPBs notice, and warranted further investigation. The Gaffer consulted with Chris and Bill about their worth. As they were both serious motor cycle riders their thoughts were much the same as the dyed in the wool riders; scooters were something of a novelty. Chris had this to say. "Well the Gaffer had this idea that scooters were the up and coming thing and decided to look at them in more detail. Nothing happened for a few months then he called us together and asked us what we thought about building a prototype. Well, knowing just how well the Gaffer worked I thought this would follow on with his other ideas he had in the past. Great interest at first, then disillusion and then abandoned. Well this time it was slightly different. The Boss seemed more serious than I anticipated. His thoughts turned to building an engine, using a proprietary gearbox and clutch and fitting it into our own frame. As to the frame and panels, I had no idea how this was to be done."

If this was a complete turn-around from previous thinking by HPB, both Chris and Bill were non-plussed over the idea. Over the years they had built motor cycles but it could never be considered a business even with a great stretch of the imagination. The workforce and the facilities were just not there. However, HPB was not to be dissuaded in his quest. There it rested for a while, to all intents and purposes, consigned to the shelf. In fact Chris had almost forgotten about it when the Gaffer brought it up again. Chris again. "With the Gaffer's involvement with the ISDT he came into contact with a great many factories and competition managers. He was quite aware of their many restrictions over money, and development costs in competition. In the 1950s two-strokes were making great in-roads, especially from the eastern bloc. CZ, MZ and Jawa developed their two-strokes and fielded teams in the ISDT where winning was uppermost and the prestige that went with it.

All this was not lost on HPB. His sense of awareness concerning this new development was the repercussions this might have with the Midland factories. He decided to investigate further. Around this time, Jack Durn was a regular visitor to Lansdown. He was keen on competition and helped out with many trials and scrambles when not competing himself. He was a good rider, tuning his own bikes quite often at the works in the ground floor machine shop. In those days Lansdown was always 'open house' so to speak. Anyone who had a keen interest in motor cycles often used the facilities. No one was ever charged for this and HPB was quite ambivalent to it all. As Chris soon found out, things were about to change. HPB may not have lct on to Chris and Bill but he had been in touch with Olga Kevelos who in the 1953 ISDT rode a 125cc CZ. Chris was in for a surprise. "The Gaffer asked me to go up to Birmingham to collect a CZ from Olga. I mentioned this to Jack who was very interested in going with me. He had just acquired an old Post Office van and suggested we could use it as transport for the bike. Well we brought it back to Lansdown and within a few

One of the specialist machines that Harry Baughan designed for making pins. HPB also started designing and building machines for the plastics industry in the early 1950s. Erinoid at Lightpill ordered several to produce fountain pen blanks. It was not popular with the workers as it was entirely automatic and one person could supervise several machines.

days we had it all dismantled. The engine was completely stripped and we had a close look at the internals. To be honest the thing was nothing special, just the inlet and exhaust ports that stood out, and the attention to detail. All this was done with the intention of forming the basis of what the Gaffer had in mind, building a two-stroke powered scooter. Eventually a set of castings were made for the engine along with a few barrels. All this was based on the porting of the CZ. Then we went even further, we built a very basic dynometer. This was based on first principles with weights and friction. In fact it was all too haphazard really. Nothing was ever pushed hard; the length of time involved was far too long to be of any serious value. We did build the engine; it was run, then it all went flat.* I'm sure the Gaffer was serious at first, then more and more work came in for the plastic machinery, and it all came to nothing." Whatever became of this engine and the dyno is another mystery. Searches in the 1980s revealed nothing to give any hard evidence. This was indeed the last attempt at anything resembling a motor cycle at Lansdown. Soon the premises became something

*Various people have confirmed that they saw the scooter, just what became of it is another Baughan conunderum. Chris Stagg remembers that the engine was lying around the works for quite a while. A number of people actually saw the finished machine, then it simply disappeared.

Authors collection.

The award that Marjorie Grant Heelas so generously donated to the author. This was the first that she received in her competition career. It is actually inscribed to Bill which was an oversight on the part of the Western Centre Committee. It should have had her name but two were made out to Bill. HPB apologized to Marjorie for the mistake, but it was accepted in good grace, after all it was the first time that she as a 'serious' passenger had been recognized as a competitor.

of a Mecca for local motor cyclists which became even more of an 'open house' for anyone who had a mechanical problem. Those who had sufficient knowledge could use the equipment; the factory doors were never locked. One aspect of Lansdown that everybody knew about was 'Little Joe.' He doubled up as caretaker and general helper, in today's parlance a 'Goffer', There were many stories surrounding Joe as he slept on the premises. One that did the rounds was when he decided to have a strip wash (read naked) in the sink late one evening. It was in the winter and Joe either forgot, or chose not to put out the light to carry out his ablutions. Sometime after he finished and extinguished the light the police arrived enquiring about a person standing in front of the window without any clothes. A lady neighbour witnessed the whole thing and reported it, but only after Joe had finished and the light went out . . . Harry Baughan sold the business in 1966. The company that he left went entirely over to producing plastic

J M Baughan collection.

This is probably the last photo taken of Harry Baughan, circa 1967/8. He died in Stroud Hospital with a lung related illness probably brought on by years of smoking. Many tributes flowed in from the Trade and the motor cycle press. One referred to HPB as 'The Grand Old Man of Motor Cycling.' A fitting tribute to a person who devoted almost his whole life to motor cycle trials sport.

extrusion machinery. In these latter years the public had some memories of the motor cycle business that had its roots in Lower Street in the 1920s and 1930s but little knowledge of the machines they produced and the competitions they entered. Harry, along with Chris and Bill were indeed pioneer motor cyclists. When Harry Baughan died the tributes were many. He brought the art of trials orginization to such a peak, it has never been surpassed, and and in many peoples eyes never will, as John Giles commented: "He was quite unique and we will probably never see his like again." This book, I hope, will make a lasting contribution to a piece of unique motor cycle history.

Baughan Cyclecars and Motor Cycles 1920-1936

BAUGHAN CYCLECARS
(Tyburn Lane, Middlesex.)

(No.1) Sept 20th, 1920.
John K. Baughan. 'Ivydell.' Southfield Park, Pinner, Middlesex. Deliver?
Remarks: Light Grey, Black Trimming, Supply at cost. 'Baughan 2/3 seater.'
Hood, screen, lamps, horn, tools, pump. Deposit paid £65. No.71. (**MD264**).

(No.2) Dec 2nd, 1920.
Anglo Scandinavian Agencies Ltd. 1, Arsenalogatan, Stockholm, Sweden. Delivery, approx, Feb 7th, 1921. Remarks: no deposit paid, advise when nearly ready for shipment. Hood, screen, electric lamps, horn, tools, pump. £229. No.72.

BAUGHAN CYCLECARS
(Stroud, Gloucestershire.)

(No.3) June 22nd, 1922.
J Newton. 14, Clarence Road, Withington, Manchester. Delivery, 3/4 weeks.
Remarks: demonstration model.
Baughan 2-3 seater, 'Standard.' Full equipment, special colour, side valve
Blackburne. TB428. £240. Less 15%, £36. July 28th, 1922. Total £204. Deposit
paid, £50. Balance: £152. Less 2.5%. No.73C673.

(No.4) Jan 1st, 1923.
W Tuck. King Street, Stroud, Glos. Delivery, 8 weeks. Remarks: special 5
seater. Baughan 2-3 seater (Special) 5 seater body and goods, with Blackburne
10hp engine, XM176. £180. Also included were spare wheel bracket, change of
colour, (£1). Electric horn (10/-), mirror (18/6), deposit paid £100. No.D674.
(**DD2169**).

BAUGHAN MOTOR CYCLES
(Stroud, Gloucestershire.)

(No.5) Aug 1923.
W Hayward. Bisley Road, Stroud, Glos. Delivery when ready. (Oct 26th, 1923).
Remarks: at cost. 1-2.75 hp Baughan sports sv motor cycle (£45). Lamp (£1.
17.6d), horn (8/6), knee grips (5/-). Licence (10/-). Engine No.DC1115. Frame
No.24196, deposit paid (£30). (These remarks appear on the rear of the origi-

The following pages are copied exactly from the sales ledger which logs all the cyclecars and motor cycles designed and built by Baughan Motors. This ledger was rescued by Graham Stagg when he worked at Baughan Engineers (Stroud) Co Ltd. This most valuable document almost went into the skip when there was a massive clear out at Lansdown.

nal). Renovated, January 1925. London-Edinburgh gold medal. No.MC24/196. (**DD3455**).

(No.6) Nov 1923.

Arthur Baxter. Lower Street, Stroud, Glos. Delivery as ready, Feb 28th, 1924. Remarks: supply at special price, close ratio gearbox. 2.75 hp ohv Baughan. (£65). Racing piston and cams. Engine No.CGL169. Frame No.24/197. Deposit paid (£32).
(These remarks appear on the rear of the original.)*
 Bought by Mr. Carter, Bisley Road, Stroud, Glos, in Oct 1924, (£50). Crankcase welded, new bushes and new timing cover fitted Feb 1925. No.MC24/197.

(No.7) Dec 10th, 1923.

C King. Central Hotel, Stroud, Glos. Delivery? (delivered Feb 22nd, 1924). Remarks: 2-75 hp sv Baughan MOK146 (£52.10/-). BTH Sparkright (5/-). Total (£57.10/-) (these remarks appear on the rear of the original). Sparkright taken off and ordinary magneto fitted. No.24/198.

(No.8) April 2nd, 1924.

WT Carter. 3, Glenroy, Bisley Road, Stroud, Glos. Delivery, as soon as ready. (Delivered June 7th, 1924). Remarks: not to exceed £50. 1-2.75 side valve Baughan (cut price model with silencer). (£49.10/-). Drip feed (10/-). Engine No.OFL785. Frame No? (Total £50). Deposit paid (£5). Paid: June 21st, 1924 (£45). (These remarks appear on the rear of the original.) Sold to Mr. Harris, Stroud in October for (£42.10/-). No.24/199. (**DD4866**), 6/6/24.

(No.9) April 8th, 1924.

Mr. H Hook. Fair View, Chalford, Glos. Delivery, as soon as ready. Delivered July 1st, 1924. Remarks: gate change, straight pipe. 1-2.75 side valve Baughan, straight through exhaust, short saddle (£57.10/-). Licence (£1). Horn (7/6). Engine No.DFL802, frame No.LW19884 (£58.17.6d). Deposit (£30). Balance paid (£28.17.6d). No.24/200.

(No.10) May 16th, 1924.

E Knee. Bisley Old Road, Stroud, Glos. Delivery, August. Delivered August 15th, 1924. Remarks: touring carb, touring bars, short saddle, footrests, straight through pipe, aluminium chain guard. 2.75 hp, side valve Baughan (cut price model). Engine No.DFL800. Settled in full. No.24/201. (**DD8301**).

---

　* No.24/197 took part in Chatcombe Pitch hill climb 5/4/1924.

(No.11) June 14th, 1924.
HM Goddard. Falcon Hotel, Painswick, Glos. (Trade). Deliver, as ready. Delivered July 23rd, 1924. Remarks: 2.75 ohv large port (£58). Sporting carb. CR, gearbox. Short peak saddle. 700 x 80 covers (14/8). Detachable carrier. Knee grips (3/4). Engine No.CGL961. Lamps (£1.10/-). Deposit paid (£28). (These remarks appear on the rear of the original.) Accident, fitted new front forks and front brake parts, September 1924. Accident, fitted new front forks (shock absorber), new tube in frame. New mudguard. No.24/202.

(No.12) November 12th, 1924.
Stroud Boot Co. Middle Street, Stroud, Glos. Deliver when ready. Remarks: footboards, 3.15/16 chain line. Sidecar to have detachable name panel. Sidecar finished in black and gold. 4.25 hp Baughan motor cycle with trade sidecar (£63). No.25/203.

(No.13) November 22nd, 1924.
C Vick. Paganhill, Stroud, Glos. Sold by E Knee. Delivery, January 1st, 1925. Remarks: chain guard, outside flywheel, foot boards, touring type bars, short peak saddle, silencer, N pipes, disc gear change, 3.1/2 chain line. 2.75 hp Baughan side valve 'A' (£56). Lucas horn (15/6), P & H lamps (£1.17.6d). Mechanical lubrication (15/-). 700 x 80 on rear wheel (9/6). Licence (£1.10/-). Fork extra (10/-). Engine No.OEL1263. Total (£61.17/6). Deposit paid (£1). January 5th, (£47). No.25/204.

(No.14). December 24th, 1924.
Miss. Harris. Kings Head, The Cross, Stroud, Glos. Sold by W Carter. Delivery, Feb 1st, 1925. (Delivered Feb 1st, 1925). Remarks: sports bars, straight through exhaust pipe, std gearbox, 3.1/2 chain line. 2.75 side valve 'A' Model (£56). Oversize on rear (9/6). Lamps, licence, horn, engine no.PA616. Deposit paid (£10). (These remarks appear on the rear of the original.) Accident, Crosshands. New footrests, front mudguard, oil pump, sold to C Clark. Accident, Coombe Hill. New front forks, new timing cover, mag, sprocket, footrests, brake pedal, handlebars, back into stock. WESTERN CENTRE TEAM TRIAL. Silver medal W E Hayward. Sold to O Phillips, April 20th, 1926. No.25/205.

(No.15) January 28th, 1925.
HP Baughan. Baughan Motors, Lower Street, Stroud, Glos. Delivery: as ready. Delivered, February. Remarks: sports bars, footrests, standard ratio gears, 3 chain line. 2.75 ohv model, oversize cover on rear. Engine No.CJ224. (These remarks appear on the rear of the original.) 1925 LONDON-HOLYHEAD. Silver cup,

(HPB). 1925 LONDON-EDINBURGH. Gold cup (HPB), 1925 WESTERN CENTRE TEAM TRIAL. Gold medal (CW Peters). 1926 COLEMORE CUP TRIAL. Silver medal (CW Peters). 1926 VICTORY CUP TRIAL. Gold medal (HPB). 1926 LONDON-LANDS END. Gold medal (HPB). No.25/206.

(No.16) May 18th, 1925.
Mr. Atkinson. Middle Lypiatt, Stroud, Glos. Delivery, June 15th. Delivered. Remarks: 1-2.75 Model 'B.' (£48). Footboards, standard gearbox, straight through pipe, acetylene lamps (£1.10/-), 700 x 80 tyre on rear (9/-). Horn (9/-). Licence (£1.4/9d). Engine No.PA1867. (These remarks appear on the rear of the original.) Taken back into stock January 1st, 1926. Sold to Mr. Shilman, January 11th, 1926. No.25/207.

(No.17) May 28th, 1925.
E Knee. Bisley Old Road, Stroud, Glos. Remarks: 1-2.75 Baughan 'A.' Model ohv, footrests, sports bars, gate change, engine No.CJ1387. (These remarks appear on the rear of the original.) Sold to Mr. J Melsome. No.25/208.

(No.18) June 6th, 1925.
Mr. Rine. Belmont Road, Stroud, Glos. Deliver, June 27th. Remarks: 1- 2.75 Baughan 348cc 'B.' Model (£48.10/-). Drip feed (9/-). Footrests, standard ratio, straight pipe. (These remarks appear on the rear of the original.) Sold to Mr. Palmer. No.25/209.

(No.19) (No date).
WE Hayward. Bideford, Bisley Road, Stroud, Glos. Delivery, delivered 20th, March. Remarks: 1-2.75 HV sports bars, footrests, standard ratios, straight pipe. (These remarks appear on the rear of the original.) 1926 LONDON-LANDS END. Gold medal. WEH. Sold to Mr. Brusden Winston. No.26/210 (**DD9125**), 17/3/26.

(No.20) (No. date).
Mr. G Walker. C/O Stroud General Hospital, Stroud, Glos. Delivery? Remarks: 1- 350cc. 'A.' model (£54.10/-). Lamps (£1.17.6d), horn (9/-), footrests, sports bars, straight ex pipe, standard gears, quadrant gate control, oversize tyre on back (9/-). Total (£57.5.6d). No.26/211.

(No.21) (1926).
E Knee. Bisley Old Road, Stroud, Glos. Delivery, June (1926). Remarks: 1- 350cc ohv complete. Oversize on the back. No.26/212. (**s**), 19/5/26.)

(No.22) April 20th, 1926.
HP Baughan. Delivery? Remarks: 350cc ohv complete. (These remarks appear on the rear of the original.) Sold to, A Andrews. H Purchase, collected. Sold to L Long, Middle Hill, Stroud. No.27/213.

(No.23) September 8th, 1926.
Mr. Rogers. 11, Bisley Old Road, Stroud, Glos. Delivery, about March. Remarks: 1-350cc. ohv (£58). Footrests, sports h/bars, B and B carb, standard gears, 145. P and H lamp and generator (£1.10/-). 700 x 80, carrier (£1.2.6d). Rear tyre (10/6). Ordered on the 8th September, 1926. To be delivered at date to be named later. Signed-Bert Rogers. Licence (£1.4.6d), insurance, (£3.17/-) Total: (£66.4.9d). Received, 21st April, (£31.4.9d). Balance, (£31.4.9d). No.27/214. **DF2280**.

(No.24) May 17th 1927.
Mr. A Gardiner. Woodbine Cottage, Oakridge, Stroud, Glos. Deliver, soon as ready. Delivered 23rd, July. 1- 350cc. Remarks: 'B.' Model (£48.10/-). Footrests, straight through pipe, standard ratio. 700 x 80 rear cover ((9/-). No.27/216. (**DF3244**), 23/7/26.

(No.25) June 4th, 1927.
Mr. L Gardiner. Vale View, Oakridge, Stroud, Glos. Delivery, soon as possible. Remarks: 1-350cc. Baughan side valve 'B.' (£46.10/-). Footrests, standard ratio, sports bars, straight through pipe (plated), (6/-). 700 x 80 cover (9/-). Drip feed, (7/3). Frame No.27218. Engine No.PC4060. I agree to take the above m/c to specifications when ready. Lionel Gardiner. No.27/218. (**DF3300**), 2/8/26.

(No.26) August 6th 1927.
Mr. Dennis Wheatley. 17, Chapel Street, Stroud, Glos. Delivery. Remarks: 350cc. ohv Baughan complete (£57.10/-). Gate gear control, footrests, standard ratio, 700 x 80 on rear (9/-). Lamps and generator (£1.17.6d). Horn, insurance 3/- extra on £3.15/- (£3.18/-). I agree to take delivery of the above motor cycle when ready. Dennis Wheatley. No.27/219. (**DF3659**), 3/10/27.

(No.27) January 1927.
WE Hayward. Bideford, Bisley Road, Stroud, Glos. Delivery, when ready. Remarks: 1-250cc. ohv (special). Lightened, wide ratio gearbox, BTH lighting set, separate oil tank, mech lubrication, sports bars. 700 x 80 cover on back. No.28/220. (**DF4389**), 14/2/1927.

(No.28) November 1927.

G Iles. Churchfield Road, Stroud, Glos. Delivery, 14th January (1928). Remarks: 1 only 250cc, ohv. Standard ratio gearbox, gate control. 700 x 80, cover on rear, footrests, drip feed. B and B carburettor, deposit paid (£30). No.28/221.

(No.29) January 1928.

H Carter. Downfield, Stroud, Glos. Delivery, when ready. Remarks: 1 only 350cc, ohv, standard ratios, gate control, footrests, B and B, carburettor, carrier, engine No.CP479. Deposit paid (£16), (£11). (These remarks appear on the rear of the original.) Sold to M Angel, Chalford, 8th April, 1930. No.28/222 (**DF5413**), 4/6/27.

(No.30) 1928

Mr. T Gardiner. Address–Nr Chapel, Oakridge, Stroud, Glos. Delivery? Remarks: 1- 350cc side valve 'B.' Model. Valence mudguard, gear control on tank, lamp, horn. No.28/223 (**DF6786**), 25/1/29.

(No.31) 1929

WE Hayward. Delivery? Remarks: 1-500cc, ohv Blackburne with special wheel-drive. BTH dynamo lighting set. No.29/225. (**DF6788**), 25/1/29.

(No.32) June 1929.

Baughan Motors. Delivery? Remarks: used by Chris Stagg. 1-300cc. sv Model Blackburne camshaft. (These remarks appear on the rear of the original). Sold to Mr. Davis. Little London, Stroud, September,1930. No.29/226 (**DG2023**).

(No.33) June 19th, 1929/30.

Stroud MC and LCC. Delivery? Remarks: 1-350cc. Baughan special motor cycle football machine. 1 gall tank, short exhaust pipes, guards round engine. At cost special price. No.29/227.

(No.34) June 1929.

R Rogers. 15, Teme Street, Tenbury Wells, Worcs. Delivery. As soon as ready. Remarks: 1-350cc, ohv 2 port Sturmey Archer. Dry sump lubrication, lever control, 650 x 65 front, 700 x 80, rear, footrests high, standard ratio. No.30/228. (**DG1789**), See pages 338 to 340.

(No.35). March (June) 1930.

Baughan Motors. Delivery, as ready. Delivered May (demonstration). Remarks: 1-350cc. ohv 2 Port. Sturmey Archer dry sump. Gear tank control, BTH lighting set, Webb wheels, Druid enclosed forks, Amal carb. No.30/299 (**DF6783**), 25/1/29.

(No.36) 28th September 1930.

Mr. G Tye. C/O Miss James. Breams Eaves, Bream, Glos. Delivery, as ready, (Delivered 19th December 1930.) Sold by WE Hayward. Specification: Model. 350cc. ohv engine. Sturmey Archer, No.CPRO129. Gear. Sturmey Archer. No.LW170865. Control, long tank lever, forks, Druid, wheels, Webb, carb, Amal equipment. Special, hp DC.1635. 1-350cc. SA 2 port model (£56.10/-). Acetylene lamp set. No.31/230 (**DG1633**), 19/12/30.

(No.37) 22nd November.

CW Stagg. Aerodrome, Chalford, Glos. Deliver, January (delivered 28th February 1931). Sold by CS. Specifications: model 350cc. Sturmey Archer 2 port, engine. 348cc, dry sump. No.CPRO Gr box, 3 speed Sturmey S control, kick gear, positive stop, fork, Druid, wheels, wired 26 x 3.00. 26 x 3.50. Carb, Amal. Equipment, electric lighting BTH, clean handlebars, twist grip, chrome plate. No.31/231.

(No.38) 24th November 1930.

Mr. L Long. 4, Middle Hill, Stroud, Glos. Delivery, (delivered 18th April 1931). Sold by HPB. Specifications, model, 350cc, ohv engine. Sturmey Archer 166, gears, 3 speed, gate control, forks, Druid, wheels, Webb forks, Carb, Amal. Equipment, BTH lighting set, special gold line black tank, beaded covers, 26 x 3.00 (£42.10/-) less allowance (£22.10/-). (£20). No.31/232.

(No.39) 27th November 1930.

J Nurding. 8, Wallbridge, Stroud, Glos. Delivery, March (delivered 1st March, 1931). Sold by HD.* Specifications: Model, 250cc, sv engine. Sturmey dry sump, gear, 3 speed, control, gate, Druid forks, wheels Webb, carb, Amal. Equipment, special clean bars. No.31/233. *(Harry Daniels).

(No.40) 27th November 1930

P Wheatley. Horns Road, Stroud, Glos. Delivery, January. (delivered 23rd February 1931). Sold by HD. Specifications: model, 350cc, sv engine, Sturmey dry sump, gear, 3 speed, gate control, tank, forks Druid, wheels, Amal carb equipment, BTH lighting set, clean bars. 1-350cc. sv (£47.10/-). Lighting set (separate dynamo), (£5.10/-). No.31/234.

(No.41) Missing, or not completed.

(No.42) 6th March, 1931.

Lambert H. McGintey. Dominican Priory, South Woodchester, Stroud, Glos. Delivery (delivered 1st April 1931). Sold by, HD. Specifications: model, 300cc. sv Baughan AH3. engine, Sturmey Archer RSRO106, gears, 3 speed, 'A.' 11.9851, gate control, tank, Druid forks, Webb wheels. Carb, Amal flange, Equipment, chromium, clean bars, BTH lighting set, electric horn, special Olive Green, inlay* No.31/236. *(petrol tank).

(No.43) 17th March, 1931.

GH Pincott. Bussage, Stroud, Glos. Delivery? Sold by? Specifications: model, AH3. Engine, Sturmey Archer 108, gears, 3 speed, 'A.' 111 10078, gate control, tank, Druid forks, Webb wheels, carb, Equipment, BTH lighting set, chromium clean bars, carrier, Red inlay* panel tank. 1. Model AHB (£38.10/-), Lighting set, (£5.10/-), Horn. No.31/237. *(petrol tank).

(No.44) 20th March, 1931.

H Daniels. Delivery? Sold by, HD. Specifications: model, special football, engine, 348cc, ohv Sturmey, gears, 3 speed, control, kick, forks, Druid, wheels, carb, horizontal. Equipment, no inverted levers, lever mag, twist grip throttle, small saddle tank, double brake pedal, top chain guard, front short mudguard with stays. No.31/238.

(No.45) 23rd March, 1931.

Mr. AV Johnson. Culver House, Amberley, Stroud, Glos. Delivery? Sold by? Specifications: model, AH3 engine, 300 Sturmey Archer 107. Gears, 3 speed, control, twist grip, forks, Druid, wheels, 25 x 300, carb, Amal. Equipment, clean bars chromium, Red inlay* panel, Electric horn. No.31/239. *(petrol tank).

(No.46) 30th March, 1931.

P Baker. Washpool, Horsley, Nailsworth, Glos. Delivery, as ready (delivered May 1931). Sold by HD. Specifications: model, AH3 engine, Sturmey Archer 109, gears, 3 speed swivel, control, twist grip, forks Druid, wheels Webb 25 x 3.00, carb, Amal. Equipment, clean bars, Ivory inlay* panel. 1-300cc. AH3 (£38.10/-). No.31/240. This was registered by Chris Stagg on 27th Feb, 1931 as (**DG2023**), *(petrol tank).

(No.47) 21st November, 1932.

Mr. Wiltshire. 26, Sweetbriar Street, Gloucester. Delivery, as ready (delivered 21st January 1933). Sold by HPB. Specifications: model AH3 engine, 298

Sturmey Archer, gears, 3 speed, controls, tank, forks, Druid, wheels, 25 x 3.00. 26 x 3.25. Carb, Amal. Equipment, tank with Red inlay* panel, BTH lighting set. (£38.10/-) (£5.10/-) allowance S/H Raleigh (£9.10/-) Numbers (1/6d), Licence (8/3) (£34. 19. 9d). No.33/241. *(petrol tank).

(No.48) 1933.

GW Fisher. Rectory Cottage, Minchinhampton, Stroud, Glos. Delivery, as soon as ready. Sold by HPB. Specifications: model, 350cc, ohv Engine, Sturmey Archer, gears, 4 speed Sturmey, control, hand gear control, forks, Druid, wheels, British Hub, carb, Amal, twist grip. Equipment, lighting set, black and gold tank, Tyres 27 x 2.75 (front competition) 26 x 3.25 rear (Dunlop), plain front guard. No.33/242. (**DG6556**). 18/4/33.

(No.49) 1933.

EA Morris. Bower Road, Harrogate, Yorkshire. Delivery? sold by? Specifications: model, 500cc. Sidecar-wheel drive, engine, Rudge Python, TT replica, gears, 4 speed Sturmey Archer kick control. Control, twist grip, forks, Druid heavy, wheels, detachable, carb, Amal. Equipment, complete with sidecar shield under crankcase, competition pipes, ball rear connection, spare wheel, racing magneto. (£97.10/-). No.33/243. (The engine and accessories were fitted at Lower Street by Chris Stagg.) (**YG3433**).

(No.50) 12th January, 1934.

Sub Lt. J B St, L Tyrrell. RN Royal Naval Engineering Collect, Keyham, Devonport. Delivery, when ready. Sold by M and AGH.* Specifications: 250cc. ohv engine, 250 Rudge Python, gears, 4 speed kick control, control, straight pull levers and twist grip, forks, Druid, wheels, British Hub, carb, Amal. Equipment, rectangular tool box, Dunlop saddle, touring pipes, BTH lighting set (£42.10/-). No.34/244. *(the Heelas sisters).

(No.51) 1933/4.

EA Morris. 'Cotswold.' 44, St Hildas Road, Harrogate, Yorkshire. Delivery, sold by, HPB. Specifications: model, sidecar-wheel drive. Engine, 600cc, Blackburne special, (ex works twin port special piston and valves), HHA5354. Gears, 4 speed Burman K, control low standard BAB23793, control, kick gears, twist grip throttle, Druid forks, wheels, quick detachable, carb, Amal sprint racing. Equipment, TT magneto, extra large tank, 27 x 440 comp tyre, black and gold, 8 inch flanged brakes, motor cycle less engine = (£58.10/-), engine (£25), carb (£1.10/-), mag (£2.10/-), (£87.10/-), (£30), (£117.10/-). No.35/245. (See letter in appendix, page 348).

(No.52) 1933/4.

CW Stagg. Aerodrome, Chalford, Glos. Delivery? Sold by? Specifications: model, 350cc, ohv engine, Blackburne 2 port, gears, Burman 4 speed, 2 stud low standard, control, kick gear, twist grip, Druid forks, wheels, 27 x 2.75 front, 3.50 x 26 rear. Amal carb, Equipment, K, magneto, crankcase shield, black and gold, plain front guard. No.35/246. (**AAD286**), 18/10/34.

(No.53) 11th September, 1934.

AV Johnson. Culver House, Amberley, Stroud, Glos. Delivery? Sold by, HPB. Specifications: model, 350cc, Blackburne engine, Blackburne two port, gears, 4 speed Burman, control, foot control, twist grip, forks Druid, wheels, 25 x 3.50 rear, 27 x 2.75 front, racing Amal carb, Equipment, standard cover, competition pipes, upturned bars, lh brake, high saddle springs, black and gold, plain front guard. Motor cycle (£53.10/-), racing carb (10/-), Saddle springs (2/6d), (£53. 2. 6d). No.35/247. (Delivered as registration, (**AAD 752**), on 21/12/34.

(No.54). 11th January, 1935.

GW Fisher. Rectory Cottage, Minchinhampton, Stroud, Glos. Delivery, as ready, (Delivery 18th July, 1935). sold by? Specifications: model, 350cc, ohv trials engine, Blackburne 2 port, CWA3950. Gears, extra wide ratio, 4 speed, control, positive stop quick grip, forks Druid, wheels, 27 x 2.75 front, 26 x 3.50 rear, carb, needle type. Equipment, competition covers, BTH lighting set, black tank gold line, crankcase shield. No.35/248.

(No.55) 15th June, 1935.

JG Atkinson. Derbyshire Lane, Stratford, Manchester. Delivery, as ready, (Delivered 3rd August, 1933). Sold by, HPB. Specifications: model, 350cc trial model, engine, 348cc, Blackburne single port CW3956. Gears, 4 speed wide ratio, control, kick gear, clutch type levers, forks, Druid, wheels, interchangeable, Amal carb, TT needle type. Equipment. Electric lighting set, crankcase shield, silencer (baffled), enclosed chain, lifting handle, fork damper, 4 inch rear cover, 26 x 3.00, front, plug for h/lamp leads, Ivory inlay* tank. 350cc. Model lighting (£57.10/-), interchangeable wheels (£3), silencer (baffled), lifting handle, long levers, plug for leads (£1), (£62). No.35/249. (No.56) 21st, July 1935. *(petrol tank).

(No.56) 21st July, 1935.

AD Carn. Slad Road, Stroud, Glos. Delivery. As ready (Delivered 3rd August, 1935. Sold by HPB. Specifications: model, 250cc ohv engine, Blackburne dry sump, BM509. gears, 4 speed positive stop, control, twist grip (slow), Druid forks wheels, 26 x 3.25 Avon 'Gripster' covers. Amal TT needle type carb, Equipment. Electric lighting, BTH Miller lamps, alum chain guard, black tank less gold line, electric horn, crankcase shield, no carrier, motor cycle (£47.10/-). No.35/250.

(No.57) 27th July, 1935

KE Power. 30, Rye Croft Gloucester. Delivery. Sold by? Specifications: model, 350cc, engine, 348 Blackburne 2 port CWA3957. Gears, 4 speed positive stop control CPB10094. Control, twist grip, Druid forks, wheels 26 x 3.25 front, 26 x 3.50 rear, Comp tyres, Amal TT needle type carb. Equipment, alum chain guard, black 'Baughan.' Larger crankcase shield. No.35/251.

(No.58) 12th August, 1935.

Mr. A Butcher. 'IvanHoe.' Cainscross, Stroud, Glos. Delivery, when ready. Sold by? Specifications: model, 250cc engine, Blackburne 248cc ohv BM922. Gears, 4 speed wide ratio, control, twist grip, quick action, straight pull, Druid forks wheels, 27 x 2.75 front, 27 x 4.00 rear. Amal TT needle type carb. Equipment, BTH magneto, crankcase shield, chain guard, black and gold tank, lifting handle. No.35/252.

(No.59) 13th September, 1935.

Mr. A Wheatley. Chapel Street, Stroud, Glos. Delivery, as ready (cancelled), sold by? Specifications: model, 350cc ohv engine, Blackburne 2 port, gears, 4 speed standard ratio, control, hand control, foot control. Amal carb. Equipment, black and gold. Red inlay* panel, alum chain case, plated silencers, competition covers, lighting set, pillion rests and seat. No.36/253 (**BAD671**), 16/3/35. *(petrol tank).

(No.60) 18th September, 1935.

WH Hobson. 18, Brombil Street, Margan Road, Port Talbot, Glamorgan. Delivery (delivered 3rd March, 1936). Sold by? Specifications: model, 250cc ohv engine, Blackburne 250cc ohv BM933. Gears, 4 speed Burman, HP10231. Control, positive stop. Druid forks, wheels, 26 x 3.25 front, 26 x 3.60 rear, Amal carb. Equipment, pillion seat and rests, Red inlay* panel tank, electric horn, electric lighting set, motor cycle complete (£47.15/-), speedometer, (£2.10/-), pillion seat (15/-), footrests (4/6d), less 2.5%. No.36/254. *(petrol tank).

(No.61) 9th May, 1936.

A Phipps. Nelson Inn, Oakridge, Glos. Delivery, 1st July. (1936) Sold by HPB.

Specifications: model, 350cc. Engine, 350cc. 2 port Blackburne, gears, 4 speed standard ratio, control, foot, twist grip, Druid forks, wheels, 26 x 3.25 front, 26 x 3.50 rear. Amal carb. Equipment, black and gold tank, plated silencers, electric lighting, pillion rests and seat. No.36/253.

(No.62) 9th May, 1936.

C Stagg. Baughan Motors, Stroud, Glos. Delivery (delivered 29th May, 1936). Sold by? Specifications: model, 350cc ohv special engine, 348cc 2 cam, single port ex TT gears, 4 speed standard, control, foot, twist grip, Druid forks, wheels, 26 x 3.50 front, 27 x 2.75 rear. Carb, Amal racer. Equipment. No.36/255.

(No.63) 30th May, 1936.

R Watkins. 'IvanHoe.' Breams Eaves, Bream. Delivery, sold by, WEH. Specifications: model, 350cc ohv engine, 348cc, Blackburne special, gears, Burman 4 speed, control, Druid forks, wheels, British Hub, Amal carb. Equipment, Lucas lighting set, up-swept pipes. No.36/256.

(No.64) 30th May, 1936.

Mr. Cartwright. Delivery, 30th, June. (1936). Sold by? Specifications: model, 250cc engine, 248 Blackburne ohv, gears 4 speed, control, foot control, twist grip, Druid forks, wheels, standard Avon covers, 23 x 3.25. Amal touring carb. Equipment, BTH electric lighting, down-swept pipe, black and gold tank, carrier, pillion rests. No.36/257.

There were only twelve examples of Baughan motor cycles built with the distinctive coloured panels on the petrol tank.

Baughan Motor Cycles 1932 write-up including the sidecar-wheel drive.

The Baughan motor cycle, which is made by Baughan Motors, of Lower Street, Stroud, is a well known make in the West Country, where it has gained many successes in trials. A team of riders of these machines gained the premier award in the Stroud Team Trial recently. We are now able to give our readers details of the 1932 models. The passenger machines, it is particulary interesting to note, can be supplied with the sidecar-wheel drive. It is easy to see the trials experience in the design of these machines, particularly the ohv's which have a five and a half inch ground clearance and a low centre of gravity and saddle position which contribute to the exceedingly good steering qualities they possess, and in the provision which is made for wide adjustment of saddle, footrests and handlebars to suit individual riders. The general layout of the frames of all models is similar to that used last year, the chief alteration being a new under-tank fitting. This consists of two steel lugs, with flat sides which are brazed on the frame and through which are bolted two lengths of angled steel, having cross members welded to them. These last carry the tank, and the rear ends of the steel rails are shaped and drilled for the front saddle fixing. To the forward ends a steel plate is bolted, which serves as a steering stop and an anchor plate for the steering damper. The space between the rails provide a channel for the cables, and the dynamo cut-out is bolted to the side. All models have spring up rear and front stands with a positive stop. Tanks are normally finished in black and gold, but if desired can be supplied with red, ivory, or purple panels. (In later models there was provision for a green panel.) Four speed gearboxes are available on all models for £1.10/-. extra, and positive stop gear control adds £1 to the price. BTH dynamo lighting sets, with headlamp fitted with parking bulbs and dimming devices cost an extra £5.10/-. The range consists of seven machines–two 250s, sv and ohv, an 300 sv, two 350s and two 500s. All have Sturmey-Archer engines, but the 350 and 500 ohvs can have single port Blackburne engines if required for the same price or two-port Blackburnes for another £2.10/-.

Druid forks, with shock absorbers and steering dampers are used on all models. Three speed Sturmey-Archer gearboxes are standard. Transmission is by 1/2-inch by 305 inch. Reynold chains, the primary being fully enclosed, the rear guarded. On the 250s and 300 the tyres are 25in, by 3in. Avon cords, with 26in by 3.25in rear tyres optional; on the larger models 26in by 3.25in. tyres are standard and 26in by 3.5in. the optional size for the rear. The sidecar-wheel drive combination, which is a standard product, is the only machine of its kind on the market. The sidecar wheel is driven from the rear wheel of the motor cycle by a shaft having universal joints at each end. The drive is engaged by a dog clutch, and all wheels are easily detachable and interchangeable. One lever engages or disconnects the drive to the sidecar wheel. This drive can be supplied to any Baughan motor cycle of not less than 350cc at an extra charge of £30, which includes the sidecar chassis and connections, the wheel, tyre and mudguard, the driving mechanism and controls.

Baughan Models 1932.

AH.	250cc sv	£37 10/-
SV.	300cc sv	£38 10/-
MH.	250cc ohv	£42 10/-
SL.	300cc sv	£47 10/-
O.	350cc ohv	£52 10/-
SC.	500cc sv	£55 10/-
WH.	500cc ohv	£57 10/-

The WH model for swd was an extra £30.

Baughan Motors was the only manufacturer in the UK to offer sidecar wheel-drive as a stock item. Page 93 shows it illustrated in their sale catalogue.

Baughan Parts Inventory

1	Engine	1	Blackburne Bookham, Surrey.
2	Magneto	1	B.T.H.
3	Carburettor	1	AMAC.
4	Gearbox	1	Sturmey-Archer.
5	Saddle	1	Leatheries.
6	Fork	1	Drew and Co, Ltd.
7	Hub and Brakes (Front)	1	Webb.
8	Ditto (Rear)	1	Ditto.
9	Tyres 6.50 x 65	2	Avon's.
10	Head Lug	1	All Brompton.
11	Front Tank Lug	1	
12	Front Engine Lug	1	
13	Rear Tank Lug	1	
14	Rear Engine Lug	1	
15	Tank Supports	2	
16	Gearbox Support	1	
17	Rear Fork Ends	2	
18	Chain Adjustment Bolts	2	
19	Bottom Eyes	2	
20	Top Eyes	2	
21	Rear Stand Top Lugs	2	
22	Rear Stand Bottom Lugs	2	
23	Rear Stand Plugs	2	
24	Carrier Lugs	2	
25	Carrier Top Lugs	2	
26	Carrier Four Way Lugs	?	
27	Front Carrier Lugs	2	
28	Number Plate Clips	2	
29	Front Stafford Top Lugs	2	
30	Front Stand Top Lugs	2	

31	Bridge Piece	1	
32	Head Ball Races	3	
33	Crown Race	?	
34	Balls	?	
35	Head Lock Nut	1	
36	Front Engine Plates	2	
37	Rear Engine Plates	2	
38	Saddle Pillow Lug	1	
39	Missing	0	
40	Top Tube	1	
41	Tank Tube	1	All Tube Co, Ltd to No64.
42	Front Down Tube	1	
43	Seat Stay Tube	1	
44	Chain Stays	2	
45	Seat Stays	2	
46	Rear Stand Tubes	2	
47	Front Stand Tubes	2	
48	Rear Stand Cross Stay	1	
49	Front Stand Cross Stay	1	
50	Carrier Vertical Stays	2	
51	Carrier Bent Stays	2	
52	Carrier Top Frame	1	
53	Carrier Cross Pieces	2	
54	Carrier Fixing Studs Bottom	2	
55	Carrier Fixing Studs Front	2	
56	Stand Fixing Studs	2	
57	Bottom Eye Studs	2	
58	Saddle Bolts	3	
59	Front Stand Studs	2	
60	Front Engine Lug Bolt	1	
61	Rear Engine Lug Bolt	1	
62	Gearbox Bracket	1	
63	Saddle Pillar Down Tube	1	
64	Saddle Pillar Cross Tube	1	
65	Tank Fixing Studs	4	
66	Tank Buffers	4	
67	Magneto Platform	1	
68	Mag Adjusting Plate	1	
69	Missing	0	
70	Tank	1	

71	Tank Caps	2	
72	Oil Pump	1	Lloyd and Best.
73	Tap Priming	2	
74	Petrol Tap	1	
75	Tank Transfers	2	Transfer Co, Ltd.
76	Name Transfer	2	Ditto.
77	Tool Bag	1	
78	Tool Bag Clips	2	
79	Tool Bag Support	1	

The above has been compiled from Chris Stagg's check list he used when he started to build motor cycles at Lower Street in 1925.

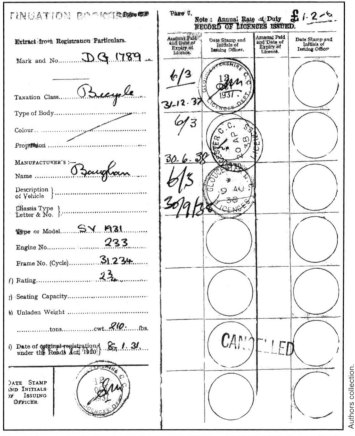

The last entry in the log book for the machine opposite before it was finally retired from road use.

Authors collection.

Is this the last example of a Baughan solo in existence? Fraser Partridge the present owner has restored a few items. The rear prop stand has been replaced and the original number plate has not yet been fitted to the front mudguard, otherwise pretty much as original. This Sturmey Archer 350cc sv was probably the last one fitted in a Baughan. Blackburne then became the norm.

As can be seen in the previous pages not every machine had its engine or frame number logged. This is No.34 (No.30/228), and the log book states 233 for the engine and 31234 for the frame. Although not recorded in the log book the gear box number is 164489. The entering of the machines built and recorded in the sales ledger was never very consistent, even the years do not always tally.

RESERVE COPY

PATENT SPECIFICATION

Application Date: March 1, 1933. No. 6237 / 32.

401,746

Complete Accepted: Nov. 23, 1933.

COMPLETE SPECIFICATION.

Improvements relating to Differential Devices.

I, HENRY PERCY BAUGHAN, a British Subject, of Lower Street, Stroud, in the County of Gloucester, do hereby declare the nature of this invention, and in what 5 manner the same is to be performed, to be particularly described and ascertained in and by the following statement :—

This invention relates to differential mechanism of the character in which a 10 member is adapted to be operatively connected to a pair of members by elements co-operating with cam surfaces provided on the said pair of members.

In connection with free wheel clutches 15 suggestions have been made previously to provide friction rollers between an inner cam member and an outer member, these rollers being urged towards their engaging positions by means of springs acting 20 on guiding blocks abutting against the rollers.

According to the present invention rollers or wedges arranged in pairs have the separate rollers of each pair urged in 25 opposite directions by a spring, the separate rollers or wedges of each pair co-operating with opposite ends of the cam surfaces, whilst a floating member is arranged between the various members 30 and is provided with projections which extend between the rollers or wedges of separate pairs.

The invention will now be described with reference to the accompanying draw-35 ings, in which :—

Fig. 1 shows a side view of one constructional form, one of the side members being removed, and

Fig. 2 is a section on the line 2—2 of 40 Fig. 1.

As shown in the drawings a driving member 37 is suitably secured to two side members 12, 13 and is provided with worm teeth 14 for engagement with a 45 driving worm, not shown. Between the members 12, 13 is mounted a floating member 40, which, as shown in Fig. 1 preferably extends between two driven members 38.

50 Two sets of roller pairs 42, 43 are provided between the driving member 37 and the two driven members 38. The driven members are keyed to two separate shafts

28, 29 for example the shafts of the rear wheels of a motor vehicle. The rollers 55 42, 43 co-operate with cam surfaces 39 formed upon the inner face of the member 37. The floating member 40 is provided with projections 41 which engage in the spaces between the roller pairs 42, 43. 60 One roller of each pair serves to lock in one direction and the other in the other direction, a spring 44 being interposed between each pair of rollers. These springs are supported by projections 45 65 provided on the floating member 40.

When the member 37 is driven by the engine in a clockwise direction Fig. 1 the two sets of roller pairs 42 are immediately locked between the cam surfaces 39 and 70 the driven members 38. The latter then turn with the driving member 37. Should one of the driven members 38 turn faster than the other, as, for example, at a bend, the rollers 42 associated with the 75 member are immediately disengaged from their corresponding cam surface and the rollers 43 are prevented from locking with the opposite ends of the cam surfaces by reason of the projections 41 on the 80 floating member. The projections 41 on the opposite side of the floating member 40, bear against the locked rollers 42 of the other driven member, thus preventing the floating member from turning. 85 Should, however, both driven members over-run then the rollers 43 engage with the opposite ends of the cam surfaces whereby they are locked so that the driven members drive the driving members 90 against the compression of the engine.

Whilst the floating member is preferably arranged to fit between the driven members it will be understood that it is not necessary to do so. 95

Having now particularly described and ascertained the nature of my said invention, and in what manner the same is to be performed, I declare that what I claim is :— 100

1. A differential mechanism including a member adapted to be operatively connected to a pair of members by elements co-operating with cam surfaces provided on the pair of members, characterised in 105 that rollers or wedges arranged in pairs

2   401,746

have the separate rollers of each pair urged in opposite directions by a spring, the separate rollers or wedges of each pair co-operating with opposite ends of the
5 cam surfaces, whilst a floating member is arranged between the various members and is provided with projections (41) which extend between rollers or wedges of separate pairs.
10 2. A differential mechanism con-

structed, arranged and adapted to operate as a whole substantially as described with reference to the accompanying drawings.

Dated the 1st day of March, 1933.
    For the Applicant:
        GEORGE HAM & Co.,
        Chartered Patent Agents,
93/94, Chancery Lane, London, W.C. 2.

Redhill: Printed for His Majesty's Stationery Office, by Love & Malcomson, Ltd.—1933.

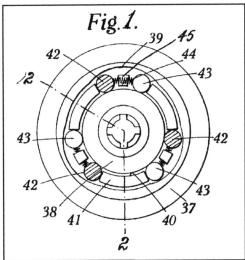

Fig. 1.

Harry Baughan submitted a number of drawings to the Patent Office he never had them officially creditied with an a approved patent. Here is another one that deals with a differential device. This one is dated 1933 which possibly was something that he submitted to the Army. The letter opposite does indicate that some form of advanced device was actually built and demonstrated.

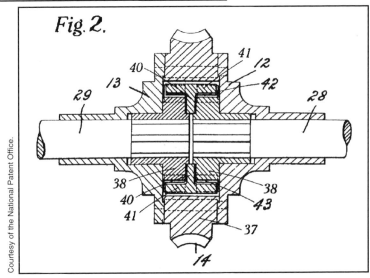

Fig. 2.

Headquarters,
R. A. O. C.
BOVINGTON CAMP,
Wareham, Dorset.
August 28th 1941

Ref:- BS/5/2/70.

Dear

Early in June, Colonel ADAMS 'phoned me to say that he had interviewed MAX YOUNG, Esq., and suggested that he should get in touch with me, so that I could see this invention, and pass an opinion before he went further into the matter.

I agreed to this, and this afternoon the above demonstrated the performance of a Vauxhall Car suitably fitted with Mr. BAUGHAN'S invention.

The enclosed is a copy of the description and sketch as fitted and tried out.   The invention itself was not seen, as this would have entailed the taking down of the back axle.

The car was driven both by Mr. YOUNG and myself over the tank tracks, and within limits, the performance was equal to that of the tanks.   Wheel spin appeared to be entirely eliminated, and it was demonstrated that the car would go where a moderately sane man would never attempt to take one.

The Inventor is prepared to supply a fitted back axle for demonstration, providing he has an axle case and half shafts put at his disposal.

I am of the opinion that if this is put into production, the ultimate costs would be less than those of the standard differentials; it is questionable, however, if Car Manufacturers would adopt it, as cars normally would not be expected to do cross-country work, but for Army use, after more exhaustive trials, it is thought the adoption would be universal.

My remarks do not apply to trench crossing in any way; wheels have obvious limits.

TEST.

In drive over very rough ground.
 "   "   through mud and water to the limit of clearance, i.e. petrol tank bottom.
Car driven up incline to maximum capability. of engine.

P.T.O.

- 2 -

All this on the actual track taken by the tanks.

Very good indeed, and wheel spin only experienced
when petrol tank was touching the ground; car however was driven
out in reverse with ease.

RECOMMENDATIONS.

That a 15 cwt. Morris Truck axle be converted, and
thoroughly tested against a standard vehicle, all tyres to be
the same.

Yours

Colonel C.M.Bostock, A.M.Inst. E.E.   A.M.I.Mech.E.
21, Bourne Avenue,
S A L I S B U R Y.
                                Repeated:-
                                Max Young Esq.,
                                H.P.Baughan Esq.,

The following hand written differential specification on the opposite page was a
product of Harry Baughan's very fertile mind. He was forever looking into the possibilities of designing a better differential drive. The opposite page is just one of
eight that exists. It is rather pointless in repoducing the remainder without reference
to the original drawings. This started with the original swd and then progressed to
the rear axles modified by the Baughan staff for the proving trials over the tank ranges at Bovington as indicated on the previous page. Was the following for the swd in
1928, or the Vauxhall/Morris? The one great drawback in trying to find anything at
Lansdown was the location of all the stored correspondence that HPB acquired over
the years. Everything was stored in tea chests right under the roof . . . which leaked
badly. Many valuable documents were lost, however, I did unearth most of Harry's
ISDT letters which ran into the thousands. I was fortunate to find what I did, Jan
Seymore had even more sucess, it still took a long while.

The invention will now be described with reference to the accompanying drawings, in which

Fig. 1. shows one constructional form which is a section on the line A-A. of Fig 2.

Fig 2. is a section on the line B-B. of Fig 1.

Fig 3. shows a modification, being a section on the line C-B of Fig 4

Fig. 4 is a section on the line D-D of Fig 3

Fig 5. shows a similar view to Fig 3 of a further modification.

Fig 6. shows a similar view to Fig 3 of a still further modification.

Fig 6 shows a similar view to Fig 3 of a still further modification.

Referring first to Fig 1 and 2. 11 is a driving member formed of two parts 12. 13 suitably secured together and provided with a worm wheel, bevel wheel, or the like to provide the means of drive. Between the parts 12. 13. is mounted a floating member 15, which, as shown in Fig 2 preferably extends between two toothed driven members 16. 17. Ratchet members 18, 19, 20, 21, 22, 23 and 24, 25, 26, 27, 28, 29, are mounted in pairs on pivots 31 carried by the floating member 15. The pivots 31 engage with slots 32 in parts 12 and 13 of the driving member and thus limit the relative movement between the floating member and the driving member.

1.

This is the first of eight pages that Harry Baughan outlined for a differential. Despite an extensive search of the Lansdown factory by Jan Seymore and the author, nothing has come to light. This detailed description must have had some form of drawing, even if in only a rough outline. The National Patent Office do not have any record of such a submission.

Bob Currie, when editor of *Classic Bike* was kind enough to place and appeal in the letters column for information on Ted Morris's swd Baughans on my behalf.

This letter below gives proof positive that Ted's last swd Baughan was destroyed, but the ex works 600cc Blackburne engine did survive. In some circles the thinking was that just one swd Baughan was bought by Morris and the engine was changed for various trials. This was much in the manner of the works Norton that Bill Mewis (both conventional and swd), built for Dennis Mansell; engines were changed on a regular basis if a trial warranted it.

J E (Jack) Smith,
61 Stainbeck Road,
Leeds,
West Yorkshire.
5th February 1985.

Dear Sirs,

With reference to A E (Ted) Morris's Baughan sidecar outfit, the following may shed a little more light on the subject for Mr. K Chandler. Feb issue.

I worked for the firm of Kitson's in Leeds for many years dismantling damaged motor cycles and reclaiming usable parts. Sometime in the 1938/39 period a sidecar outfit was brought to us which had been in a garage fire in Harrogate. I recognised it as Ted Morris's (works) Baughan outfit and this was confirmed by my employer.

The machine was completely burned out and the aluminium sidecar had melted with the heat. However, the obvious feature was the sidecar wheel drive transmission connected to the back wheel of the motor cycle with simple dog arrangement of an–in and out–gear. The frame, forks, wheels and sidecar chassis were all scrapped but the engine was salvaged. I particularly remember the polished flywheels and robust alloy con rod.

I note the outfit featured in the photograph has a Rudge engine and yet the engine I removed was a 600cc two port Blackburne. I suppose there is the possibility of two similar outfits but if only one existed the engine must have been changed and it would have been the same outfit, which I dismantled. The same Blackburne engine was later resold and fitted to a pre war KSS Velocette. (Burman gearbox).

Purely as a matter of interest when restarting the business after the war, we were looking for a sidecar float and eventually settled on an ex WD 633cc Norton which on inspection had an almost identical transmission to the sidecar wheel. This had been rendered inoperative by the army before sale on the grounds that it was not safe for road use.

Yours faithfully, Jack Smith.

Baughan Cyclecar and Motor Cycle production.

1920	2	Cyclecars	Pinner
1922	1	Cyclecar	Stroud
1923	1	Cyclecar	Stroud
1923	3	Motor Cycles	Stroud
1924	7	Dito	Dito
1925	4	Dito	Dito
1926	5	Dito	Dito
1927	5	Dito	Dito
1928	2	Dito	Dito
1929	4	Dito	Dito
1930	6	Dito	Dito
1931	5	Dito	Dito
1932	1	Dito	Dito
1933	2	Dito	Dito
1934	4	Dito	Dito
1935	6	Dito	Dito
1936	4	Dito	Dito

In total there were four cyclecars and fifty eight motor cycles in seventeen years. All the machines were built to order, there was never a production run, eveyone custom built.

Appendix

The Baughan family tree kindly compiled by Cliff Baughen in his research into all types of spelling of the name Baughan, and associates.

```
NAME    SAMUEL JOHN *BAUGHAN                      REF NO   1437
BORN    06121861   W BROMWICH        6B 603   BAP
MARR    25061887   READING           2C 658   TO 6097
DIED    25081938   STROUD            6A 455   BUR        SLAD,STROUD
FATHER  5769  MOTHER  6168  CHILDREN 2131 4277 1974


NAME    FLORENCE MARY *BAUGHAN                    REF NO   1812
BORN    00031875   W.BROMWICH        6B 815   BAP
MARR    00091903   WANTAGE           2C 669   TO 5364
DIED                                          BUR
FATHER  5769  MOTHER  6168  CHILDREN


NAME    JOHN KILMINSTER *BAUGHAN                  REF NO   1974
BORN    16031888   WYCOMBE           3A 657   BAP
MARR    25061914   W BROMWICH        6B 1817  TO 4484
MARR    00091956   HARROW            5F 1229  TO 5595
DIED    31031970   WATFORD           4B 914   BUR
FATHER  1437  MOTHER  6097  CHILDREN 2843


NAME    CHARLES EDWIN *BAUGHAN                    REF NO   2131
BORN    00031890   WYCOMBE           3A 693   BAP
MARR    00061935   ATCHAM            6A 1761  TO 4681
DIED    11021966   GLOUCESTER R      7B 633   BUR
FATHER  1437  MOTHER  6097  CHILDREN


NAME    HENRY PERCY *BAUGHAN                      REF NO   4277
BORN    12051895   NEWPORT,M         11A 241  BAP
DIED    13111968   STROUD            7B 593   BUR
FATHER  1437  MOTHER  6097  CHILDREN
```

Brough Superior COPY OF WORKS RECORD CARD

Supplied to: C.W.Smith, Darlington

Model: SS.80 Standard

Sidecar: Swallow

Engine No.: 16990

Frame No.: 125   Gearbox No.: 27279 (10.22.4P SA)

Petrol Tank No.: 791

Oil Tank No.:

Fork: Brampton No.2

Rear Wheel: Webb

Front Wheel:

Carb.: Mousetrap

Chains: Renolds

Magdyno:

Headlamp: Head & tail lamps

Horn: Electric   Oil Pump:

Speedo: Bonniksen with non-trip

Saddle: Terry

Sprockets: Engine: 16   Rear Wheel:

Clutch: Axle:

Front Tyre:

Rear Tyre:

Reg. No.:   Date Despached: 17 April 1924

Route: G.C.Rly. Passenger

Receipt
Advice Note   2997   Invoice No.: 3420

This was the machine that Ted Morris rode in the 1926 ISDT. This document was kindly unearthed by Mike Leatherdale, machine registrar for the marque. Courtesy: Mike Budd.

Yet another gem from the Lansdown factory. Graham Stagg while searching for the two-stroke engine that was built and susequently went 'missing' this engine was unearthed. While going through my tapes Chris makes due note of the two-stroke engine as being finished and run on the bench. The above engine he remembers was not complete but he never said who designed or cast the various components. As viewed it is unfinished, the cyclinder head lacks a sparking plug hole and was due to have a (single) overhead camshaft fitted driven by chain? The top three photos show the timing side with a narrow cover to be attached to the head to allow for a single camshaft. There are no internals but the bore is approximately 68mm. One distinct feature is the outside flywheel. Just who designed it and had the castings made remain a mystery. The engine is at present in the possession of Adrian Moss who kindly allowed me to take these photographs.

Telegrams : "AUTOCYCLE, PICCY, LONDON."
Telephone : WHITEHALL 4022-3.

AUTO-CYCLE UNION

Founded in 1903 as a Branch of the Royal Automobile Club

President :
The Rt. Hon. Lord Brabazon of Tara, P.C., M.C.

Secretary : S. T. HUGGETT

When Writing or Telephoning
Please Quote   **STH/LEC.**

83, PALL MALL, LONDON, S.W.I

31st July, 1953.

H. P. Baughan Esq,
"Lansdown",
Stroud,
Glos.

Dear Mr. Baughan,

<u>I. S. D. T. 1953.</u>

This morning I received a letter from Major H.R.
Watling enclosing one from Ralph Venables concerning the
imminent departure of John Giles to Egypt for foreign
service. I immediately telephoned Major Sconce who is
the Secretary of the Army Motor Cycling Association and
gave him all particulars. He told me that efforts had
been made by him in the past for secure the transfer of
Giles to the A.M.C.A. Section so that he could be safe-
guarded. Major Sconce felt that Giles, having now been
transferred to Borden, appeared to be rather ominous and
indicating his imminent departure overseas, but he promised
to do all within his power to secure his release for the
I.S.D.T., and also to let me know with what result.

Yours sincerely,

S. T. Huggett
S. T. Huggett
Secretary

Copy sent to:-   Mr. H.M. Palin
Major H.R. Watling
Mr. R. Venables.

P.S.   Since dictating the above I have heard that Giles
will not be on the overseas draft and will obtain
three weeks special leave to take part in the I.S.D.T.

The following letters give a clear indication of just how much Harry Baughan was
involved with the International Six Days Trial. As Chairman and C of C he did his
utmost for the riders that he required for this event. These two documents concerning John Giles are a very small amount that Harry Baughan had to contend with.
Ralph Venables MBE was equally in praise of HPB when influence was required
with officialdom. His cooperation with the Army Command certainly paved the way
concerning John Giles and Brian Martin . . . Harry Baughan always pushed the
manufactureres and the establishment *gently* to get what he wanted.

TELEPHONES
COVENTRY 60221
MERIDEN 331

MOTOR
CYCLES

TELEGRAMS
"TRUSTY" COVENTRY

MERIDEN WORKS
ALLESLEY
COVENTRY

TRIUMPH ENGINEERING
OUR REF.   COMPANY LIMITED   YOUR REF.

IGD/SH/1038.

31st. July, 1953.

Mr. H.P. Baughan,
The Auto-Cycle Union,
Lansdown,
STROUD, Glos.

Dear Mr. Baughan,

I do not know whether you have heard, but John
Giles has now been posted to the Bordon M.T. School
as a Motorcycle Instructor and will not therefore be
going abroad after all. This is splendid news of
course and we are grateful to you for your efforts in
this direction. He will now definitely be available
for the I.S.D.T. and I am sure will put up a very good
show.

The new machines are coming along nicely despite
the handicap of the factory being closed and I hope
to have them all ready before the end of next week.
This suggests that the tests might be held next Saturday and Sunday, 8th and 9th August, if this is agree-
able to you. I shall have to confirm this finally next
week, but would be glad to hear in the meantime if this
is a convenient suggestion for you. We do not particularly wish to extend the test over two days if this
can be avoided, but this of course is up to you and we
are quite prepared to fall in with your plans.

Kind regards,

Yours sincerely,

(I.O. Davies).